Who's Who in Russia Since 1900

D1111808

Martin McCauley is Senior Lecturer in Politics at the School of Slavonic and East European Studies, University of London. He has specialised in the politics and economics of Russia and Eastern Europe for over twenty-five years, and he acts as a consultant for investment in the former Soviet Union. He is the author of *Stalin and Stalinism*, *The Origins of the Cold War*, *The Khrushchev Era*, and is writing a biography of Mikhail Gorbachev.

WHO'S WHO SERIES

Other Who's Whos (available in USA from Oxford University Press):

Who's Who in the Old Testament
Joan Comay

Who's Who in the New Testament
Ronald Brownrigg

Who's Who in Classical Mythology
Michael Grant and John Hazel

Who's Who in Non-Classical Mythology
Egerton Sykes, new edition revised by Alan Kendall

Who's Who in Shakespeare
Peter Quennell and Hamish Johnson

Who's Who in World War Two
Edited by John Keegan

Who's Who in Jewish History
Joan Comay, new edition revised by Lavinia Cohn-Sherbok

Available from Routledge worldwide:

Who's Who in Military History
John Keegan and Andrew Wheatcroft

Who's Who in Nazi Germany
Robert S. Wistrich

Who's Who in World Politics
Alan Palmer

Who's Who in Christianity
Lavinia Cohn-Sherbok

Who's Who in Russia Since 1900

Martin McCauley

London and New York

HOUSTON PUBLIC LIBRARY

R01075 73588

First published 1997
by Routledge
11 New Fetter Lane, London EC4P 4EE

Simultaneously published in the USA and Canada
by Routledge
29 West 35th Street, New York, NY 10001

© 1997 Martin McCauley

Typeset in Sabon by
RefineCatch Limited, Bungay, Suffolk
Printed and bound in Great Britain by
TJ International Ltd, Padstow, Cornwall

All rights reserved. No part of this book may be printed or
reproduced or utilised in any form or by any electronic,
mechanical, or other means, now known or hereafter
invented, including photocopying and recording, or in any
information storage or retrieval system, without permission in
writing from the publishers.

British Library Cataloguing in Publication Data
A catalogue record for this book is available from the British Library

Library of Congress Cataloguing in Publication Data
McCauley, Martin.
Who's Who in Russia Since 1900 / Martin McCauley.
Includes bibliographical references and index.
1. Russia – Biography – Dictionaries.   2. Soviet Union – Biography – Dictionaries.   I. Title.
CT1203.M37   1997   96–42009
920.047 – dc20   CIP

ISBN   0–415–13897–3 (hbk)
ISBN   0–415–13898–1 (pbk)

Contents

Maps

Introduction

The October Revolution in 1917 gave birth to the Soviet Union. It took place in an underdeveloped country and this had a significant impact on the nature of the state which emerged. The majority of the population supported revolution in 1917 but what type of revolution was it to be? The Bolsheviks, who had launched the successful bid for power, were quite clear in their own minds. It was to be a socialist revolution. Lenin, their leader, was convinced that Karl Marx had arrived at a definitive analysis of world history and that, by following his writings, the Bolsheviks would succeed in building a new society in the Soviet Union. This would not only be true of the Soviet Union but the whole world would eventually become Marxist socialist. A major disadvantage of Marx's writings was that they declared the inevitability of socialism but did not provide a blueprint on how to get there. To Marx, capitalism would inevitably collapse and socialism take over. Hence Lenin and the Bolsheviks used Marx as an inspiration but had to find their own route to the promised land. Given the fact that imperial Russia was an autocratic state, only just beginning the process of industrialisation and the move to representative institutions and democracy, it was almost inevitable that the new Bolshevik state would borrow heavily from the old regime. Russia, an empire, was a strong, centralised state, or aspired to be one. There was considerable debate among the Bolsheviks about the direction of the new state: should it be weak or strong? In October 1917 Lenin proclaimed that a new state had come into being, one ruled by soviets, hence it was called Soviet Russia and, from 1922, the Soviet Union. In October 1917 the Bolsheviks set up their own government, the Council of People's Commissars (Sovnarkom) and the division of responsibilities mirrored very closely the last imperial government. There was a people's commissariat for internal affairs, for foreign affairs, for finance, and so on. To Lenin the key question was not administrative, it was who the official in the commissariat was. If he was a Bolshevik everything would be fine. Lenin chose to be head of the new government and remained so until his death in 1924. If the government was to exercise executive power, what was to be the role of the Communist Party (the name adopted for the Party in 1918)? Would it be consultative and restrict itself to providing ideological inspiration for the new government and state? There was certain to be tension between the government and the Party and how was conflict to be resolved? One of the striking features about the Soviet Union was that the relationship between the government and the Party was never defined. Which is more important? This problem was never resolved.

The experience of the Bolsheviks during their first four years in power shaped the Soviet Union. One of the first problems facing Lenin's government was how to end the war with Germany and its allies. This issue split the Bolsheviks, Lenin wanted peace at any price, Bukharin wanted revolutionary war and Trotsky proposed neither peace nor war. Lenin eventually had his way and the Treaty of Brest-Litovsk was signed in March 1918. However, it had to be ratified. In a free vote, there was not a majority in the Congress of Soviets, the parliament, for ratification so Lenin insisted that Bolshevik members did not vote according to their conscience but according to the decision of the Bolshevik Party to ratify the treaty. This was democratic centralism in action, and discipline held. The treaty was ratified. This underlined one of the problems of the rule of soviets; they would not necessarily do Lenin's bidding. Bolsheviks were often in the minority in the soviets. The onset of the Civil War in the summer of 1918 brought the problem of the relationship of the soviets and the Bolshevik Party to a head. The soviets were directly elected and enjoyed legitimacy. To the Bolsheviks their primary function was to implement central policy but the soviets wanted to rule their locality. The situation became so desperate that the Bolsheviks became more and more dictatorial in order to survive. The first Soviet government was all Bolshevik but in December 1917 Lenin bowed to pressure from within his own party to fashion a coalition socialist government but it did not survive the conflict over the signing of the Treaty of Brest-Litovsk. Hence from the spring of 1918 the Bolsheviks, a minority in the country, formed the government.

Lenin had not given much thought to the role of the Communist Party after October but the conflict over Brest-Litovsk and the onset of civil war drove the Bolsheviks in on themselves. Democracy within the Party was restricted because of the desperate struggle to survive, and democracy outside the Party, in the soviets, also suffered the same fate. All the leading Bolsheviks in the government were also members of the Party Central Committee (CC). The CC became too large for effective decision making and so a Politburo came into being in 1919, consisting of the top Bolsheviks, most of whom occupied key government posts. Gradually it emerged that the Politburo was more important than Sovnarkom. Given a choice, a minister would miss a Sovnarkom meeting but not a Politburo meeting. Lenin hastened this process by allowing ministers, outvoted in Sovnarkom, to appeal to the Politburo. By 1921, at the end of the Civil War, a pecking order had emerged: first, the Politburo, then Sovnarkom, then the soviets.

The Bolsheviks won the Civil War because they were ruthless in pursuing their objective – victory. However, Lenin came to the conclusion that the Bolsheviks would not stay in power if they continued with the policies that had won the Civil War. The most important problem was agriculture (about 80 per cent of the population lived in the countryside) and the peasants wanted relief from forced requisitioning. In March 1921, at the Xth Party Congress, Lenin proclaimed a retreat from socialism and the return of capitalism in the countryside; this was known as the New Economic Policy (NEP). How was he to convince delegates to vote for such a policy? Lenin managed to force through a resolution on Party unity which stated that decisions of higher Party bodies were binding on lower bodies. If a comrade opposed the decisions of the Party leadership he was guilty of factionalism and could be expelled from the Party. This also applied to members of the CC; if there was a two-thirds majority in favour of expulsion, the offending member could be expelled. This ban on factionalism was perceived by Lenin to be only temporary but it remained until the Gorbachev era. It had a formative influence on the Party because it prevented debate and democracy developing. It also stifled initiative and the introduction of new ideas. By definition they could only emerge from the top. This also meant that debates within the government on economic and social policy could be decided by the Politburo. Lenin, at the Xth Party Congress, introduced the doctrine of the infallibility of the Politburo. Inadvertently, he was shaping the power struggle which would take place after his demise. To dominate the country, one had to secure a majority in the Politburo. Since the CC elected the Politburo, the necessary stepping stone was a majority there. If one had a two-thirds majority in the CC, one could expel one's political opponents. Lenin had, without knowing it, put in place mechanisms that Stalin could skilfully use later, to the detriment of the Party and the country.

The Bolsheviks did not control the country before the onset of the Civil War but in 1921 they could expand into every part of the Soviet Union. Many officials were sent from the capital to rule in Moscow's name. They were called first Party secretaries and were responsible for everything in their region. Their main responsibility was to ensure that Party control in their territory was effective. In this they were aided by the political police, called Cheka in December 1917, and then under various names – the most well-known being the KGB – from 1922 onwards. The Cheka had proved itself during the Civil War as the ruthless defender of Party power. During NEP only the commanding heights of the economy (energy, communications, transport, heavy industry, and so on) were in state hands and light industry, trade and agriculture were in private hands. The mixed economy saw democracy develop in the country but the Bolshevik goal was always a socialist economy. The struggle to succeed Lenin began before he died in 1924 and went through various stages until Stalin became the principal leader by 1929.

One of Lenin's tenets in introducing NEP was that peasants could not be coerced into socialism. They had to join co-operatives voluntarily. The main reason for introducing NEP had been the fear that the peasants would cease feeding the cities. The decisive factor in ending NEP at the end of the 1920s was the victory of Stalin over his rivals in the fierce struggle to succeed Lenin. Since the Party leadership was not united during the 1920s, Sovnarkom played an important role and it was headed by one of Stalin's rivals. Stalin's power base was the Party apparatus and he had been made General Secretary in 1922. This ensured that there would be tension between the Party and government apparatuses during the 1920s. Should an aspiring young man or woman join the Party or state apparatus? It was not clear in the 1920s but it became clear later. When Stalin became leader it became likely that he would give preference to Party rather than to state institutions.

Stalin became head of government in 1941 and remained so until his death in 1953. His concept of government was to view it as the mechanism for implementing decisions taken by him and his associates. Who was to supervise the implementation of the plans? That function fell to the Party apparatus. Who supervised the Party apparatus and everyone else? The political police. Hence there were competing élites, all being juggled by Stalin to ensure that a coalition did not form which could topple him. Planning favoured the emergence of large enterprises and each one tried to become a monopoly. A ministry in Moscow was responsible for all the enterprises in its sector. A major problem for Stalin was to discover each plant's reserves and its true potential since it had a vested interest in concealing both in order to ensure a 'soft' plan. Among the tasks of the Party official was to collect such information and also to ensure the enterprise fulfilled its plan. If it did not, he and the enterprise would be punished. This system produced tension between the Party and the government apparatuses. Ministries enhanced their power during the Great Fatherland War (1941–5) when about a third of Soviet industry was moved from European Russia to the east. Local enterprises collaborated for their mutual benefit and Party officials had a vital role to play, ensuring that bottlenecks were eliminated. After the war ministries consolidated their position as the economy expanded and the Cold War got under way. The latter increased secrecy and made it easier for ministries and enterprises to conceal information.

The massive task of introducing a planned economy in a country undergoing rapid industrialisation and enforced collectivisation of agriculture could not have been achieved by democratic means. The population would not willingly have voted to undergo the exploitation of the 1930s. Stalinism saw the ruthless mobilisation of the population in the pursuit of one goal: to make the Soviet Union a modern state and a leading world power. Coercion was endemic and millions of lives were sacrificed. The system was effective in channelling human and physical resources towards certain goals. Heavy industry had priority and light industry was neglected. The successful official was someone who got things done, irrespective of the obstacles. Mutual suspicion reigned. Citizens were encouraged to denounce others. Party officials wished to become local Stalins, subservient to the master in the Kremlin, of course. If they reported success, they could prosper. These were known as the nomenklatura. There was the Party nomenklatura and the state nomenklatura and they were competitors. Stalin's system was effective but very wasteful. Since the decisions of the Party could not be criticised, conformism became the rule. If there was not an order to do something, initiative was not advisable. Stalinism was very hierarchical and as the economy became more complex the ability of Moscow to regulate it declined. Moscow attempted to ensure implementation of its plans by taking every decision and depriving localities of decision making. For instance, the hotel menu in Tbilisi, Georgia, was set in Moscow and could not be altered.

Stalin left a flawed legacy. However, under him the Soviet Union was modernised, defeated Germany and thus became the leading power in Europe in 1945, and by the 1970s was a superpower, in direct competition with the United States. One can speak of Stalin being absolute ruler from 1934 onwards. He acted like a Russian tsar and autocrat (ironic given that he was not Russian but Georgian) and centralised policy making. Stalinism is an amalgam of imperial Russian and Soviet political and economic cultures. Stalin did not achieve total control, never being able to take over the private sphere ('why will birth control never work in the Soviet Union? Because the means of production are in private hands!'), but he came nearer than any other Soviet ruler to achieving his goal. He was a brilliant and charismatic leader and inspired a whole generation. His concept of the state can be compared to a wheel, with the spokes being the efforts of the population to achieve the goals set by the master. He destroyed official intellectual life in the Soviet Union because he wanted to mobilise everyone to a single goal – make the Soviet Union great. The Communist Party withered under his leadership. After 1934 the Politburo did not meet regularly, nor did the CC. There was no Party Congress between 1939 and 1952. Stalin liked to use military metaphors. He talked of the leadership being the General Staff, Party cadres being the officers and the rest were the foot soldiers. His power structure was based on three institutions: the Party, the government and the political police. Policy making was concentrated in Stalin's inner circle and the dictator normally did not take counsel in large groups but in small functional groups. Ideology was simplified and to be learnt by rote. There was one correct view.

Khrushchev attempted to break the Stalinist mould but insisted that the Party retain the monopoly of power. He also rejected any market-oriented solutions to Soviet economic problems. Khrushchev was the last Marx-believing communist to rule the Soviet Union and he actually thought that communism (to each according to his needs, from each according to his abilities) could begin in 1980. After Stalin's death in 1953, Malenkov thought that the most important post was that of Prime Minister. Khrushchev's power base was the Party and eventually he defeated Malenkov and the other government-based opponents. His victory over the those who opposed his radical innovations, the Anti-Party Group, in 1957, enhanced the role of the Party by according it the dominant role in the economy. Khrushchev came to realise that Party officials were a brake on attempts to increase economic efficiency. Cadres were more concerned about increasing their privileges than increasing economic efficiency. He split the Party into industrial and non-industrial wings in 1962 and introduced restrictions on how long an official could occupy his office. However, the nomenklatura, the Party and state élites, eventually rebelled and deposed Khrushchev in 1964. The main reason why this was possible was because Khrushchev abjured the use of force to resolve problems. His removal demonstrated the influence of the nomenklatura and under Brezhnev it grew in self-confidence. Brezhnev prided himself that his expertise consisted of keeping cadres happy. This was fine as long as the Soviet economy was growing but was fatally flawed when things began to go wrong. Also Brezhnev's own health declined from the mid-1970s when he became increasingly dependent on sleeping drugs. The Brezhnev era was the golden period of the nomenklatura. There was stability of cadres; in other words, posts were usually for life and this led to the rise of the gerontocracy. By the early 1980s most Politburo members were pensioners, as was the majority of the government.

If Party officials had become very conservative and resented change, the government was in the same position. In a non-market environment, the state being the customer who ordered and who bought the product, no company went bankrupt. Each Party official sought to attract as much investment to his or her region as possible and the enterprises and government ministries also wanted more investment and subsidies. The most powerful regions were those associated with the military-industrial complex since they were immune to criticism, except from the Party leader himself. Leningrad oblast is an example of this. Gorbachev states in his memoirs that there were various policy areas which were no-go zones in the Politburo: defence, security, the military-industrial complex and foreign trade. The greater the secrecy the greater the opportunity for those involved to run their own domains. In these circumstances privileged ministries and enterprises paid no attention to the interests of others and were, literally, a law unto themselves.

When Gorbachev became General Secretary in 1985 he inherited a conservative Party, a conservative government and a nomenklatura which was not addressing the pressing economic and social problems of the moment. Kosygin had been frustrated by his inability to introduce significant economic reforms and the same problems surfaced under Gorbachev. So many institutions had to be consulted in order to introduce change that the whole process was cumbersome and lengthy. This style had developed under Brezhnev in order to ensure that decisions were implemented. Gorbachev introduced radical reforms and this disturbed the consensus at the top.

In order to comprehend the world in which Gorbachev operated, it is opportune to consider three institutions: the Party, the government and the soviets. According to the statutes of the Party the supreme policy-making body is the Congress, which convened every five years once the annual Congresses of the early post-revolutionary period came to an end. Congresses were normally meticulously planned with every speech checked and rechecked. It was like a play which unfolded before the audience who were also participants. Between Congresses, the Central Committee was the highest policy-making body and it was an assembly which Party leaders normally took seriously. However, whereas under Khrushchev it met quite often, under Brezhnev it convened twice or three times a year, and the same under Gorbachev, and this indicated that it was not the institution which ran the country on a month to month or day to day basis. That role fell to the CC Secretariat. Its apparatus consisted of departments, most of which paralleled, by design, government ministries. Each department had a head and secretaries of the CC supervised groups of departments covering his (rarely her) area of responsibility. Some CC secretaries were also members of the Politburo and this marked them out as powerful men and potential future Party leaders. The relationship between the CC secretary and a minister changed over time; after 1957 the CC secretary was normally superior to the minister. The top secretary was called the General Secretary, responsible for all the other secretaries, and indeed the Party. Stalin was General Secretary from 1922–34 but this post did not confer primacy in the Party and the state on him. He had to outmanoeuvre his competitors in order to become dictator. From 1934 to his death in 1953 he was referred to as a secretary of the Central Committee but this deceived no one. Stalin was boss. When Stalin died there was uncertainty about which institution was dominant, the Party or the government. Malenkov chose to be head of government but Khrushchev, given the title of First Secretary in 1953 (this was retained until 1966 when Brezhnev reverted to General Secretary), eventually proved the victor. After his defeat of the Anti-Party Group in 1957, so called because they opposed a greater role for the Party in the economy, the primary position in the state became the head of the Communist Party. This remained the case until Gorbachev was elected President of the USSR in 1990. The supreme policy-making body in the post-Stalin period was the Politburo. It consisted of the top élite in Party, government, security and armed forces. Until 1957 a majority of full members held government posts, after 1957 the majority was always made up of Party officials. In 1990 Gorbachev reformed the Politburo, with all those performing governmental functions leaving. The last Politburo consisted entirely of the Party élite. The Politburo was elected at each Congress and a comrade was, as a rule, first elected as a candidate member (he could attend, speak, but not vote) and then promoted to full membership. Gorbachev, in a hurry, advanced several supporters to full membership without going through the preliminary phase of candidate member. The Politburo was called the Presidium between 1952 and 1966.

There were twenty departments of the CC Secretariat in the autumn of 1988 before Gorbachev began pruning it back, in line with the decision to remove the Secretariat from involvement in the economy. He reduced the number to nine. There are several departments which appear often in this book, because of their significance in the management of the Party and state. The general department worked closest with the General Secretary, preparing the agenda for Politburo meetings and providing background papers. The organisational department was responsible for cadres. The administrative organs department supervised the Ministry of Civil Aviation, the Ministry of Defence, the KGB, the Ministry of Internal Affairs, the Ministry of Justice, the Procuracy, the Supreme Court and the civil defence apparatus.

The Communist Party of the Soviet Union was in theory a federal party, with each republic, except the Russian Federation until 1990, having its own Communist Party. In reality it was a highly centralised party with republican parties expected to go through Moscow in order to discuss policy with another Communist Party. This rigid centralism began to break down under Brezhnev and did not apply under Gorbachev. Gorbachev's goal was to promote a genuinely federal Communist Party, with each republican party autonomous and Moscow co-ordinating but not running affairs. The republican Communist Party was headed by a bureau (except in Ukraine where it was also called the Politburo), which was elected by a Central Committee at a Congress. There was also a Secretariat and CC secretaries. The top Party boss was the First Secretary. Meetings of the CC between Congresses were called plenums, as at the all-Union level. Republics were divided administratively into oblasts and krais, with the latter containing within its territory an autonomous oblast, in which lived a non-Slav nationality. Hence Stavropol krai included a non-Slav ethnic territory. Oblasts, krais and cities were divided into raions. The Party leader was the first secretary. In this book the first Party secretary in an oblast, krai, raion and city is referred to as the first secretary of the obkom, kraikom, raikom and gorkom. The backbone of the Party were the obkom and kraikom first secretaries. Most of them were elected to the CC, and the Party leader after 1953 had always occupied one of these posts. Gorbachev's decision to take the Party out of economic management in 1988 was a bitter blow to this élite, who previously had run their localities as their fiefdoms. Soviet politics was like Italian politics, personal relations taking precedence over law and the state.

The Komsomol (the Communist Party for youth) mirrored the Communist Party organisation and it was normal for officials to begin in the Komsomol, prove themselves and then be promoted to Party work. Patronage was very important in the Komsomol and Communist Party. Rising officials gathered around themselves reliable and effective men and a few women so that when they rose, their faithful retinue rose as well. Gorbachev's patrons were Kulakov and Andropov. When Gorbachev became General Secretary he brought a large number of officials from Stavropol krai to Moscow to work with him there.

State institutions consisted of the government, the executive, and elected agencies, the local soviets. The Constitution stated that the supreme power in the state rested with the USSR Supreme Soviet which elected the government and passed all the main legislation. In reality, the Party Politburo was the supreme policy-making body, the Prime Minister always being a member of it. Until the reforms of 1989, there was almost always only one candidate in elections to the soviets at all levels. The USSR Supreme Soviet met only twice a year, a week in all, and rubber stamped decisions taken elsewhere. Local soviets (all soviets below the level of the republic) were responsible for running local government but were subordinate to the Party organisation. If the Party secretary thought the soviets were not fulfilling their functions he could take decisions for them and order their implementation.

The USSR Council of Ministers was the Soviet government and each republic and autonomous republic had its own Council of Ministers. Some ministries were all-Union, in other words, responsible for the whole of the Soviet Union. All the key ministries were all-Union: the Ministry of Defence, the Ministry of Foreign Affairs, the Ministry for Light Machine Building (which produced atomic weapons for the military), and so on. Many ministries were Union-republican, in other words, there was a USSR ministry and a ministry in each republic, all subordinate to the Union ministry. The USSR Ministry for Agriculture was a case in point. Economic ministries were powerful as they and the enterprises subordinate to them attempted to become monopolies. It became very difficult to reform them as there was no market and all the high-technology ministries were connected with the military-industrial complex. They defeated Khrushchev's attempts to make them more accountable to the Party leadership, and under Kosygin (1964–80) there were no radical reforms. The overall plan was drafted by Gosplan, the State Planning Committee, which found it extremely difficult to promote innovation and risk taking. Throughout the Soviet period quantitative plan fulfilment was more important than qualitative. Under Brezhnev, the Party boss usually developed a close relationship with the KGB boss and also with enterprise directors. This led to increasing corruption under Brezhnev and republics such as Kazakhstan slipped out of the effective control of Moscow. Radical economic reform could not be carried through successfully if the government, industry and agriculture opposed it.

The most radical reforms of the Soviet political system since 1917 were implemented in 1989 and 1990. The essence of these was the transfer of power from the Party apparatus to the government and the soviets. The Party was no longer the manager of the country. Elected representatives became accountable, not only to those above them, but to those below them, the electors. Competitive elections were introduced, first and foremost to the USSR Congress of People's Deputies (it is true that 750 of the 2,250 places were reserved for social organisations such as the Party). This was a super-parliament. The Congress, in turn, elected from its members a USSR Supreme Soviet. Like the previous body, it was bicameral, Soviet of the Union and Soviet of Nationalities. It was expected to meet for about forty weeks a year. These institutions became genuine debating bodies and were parliaments in the western sense of the word.

Gorbachev came to the conclusion that an executive presidency was needed. The Soviet version, unique in Russian and Soviet history, was based on the French and American presidencies. The chairman of the Presidium of the USSR Supreme Soviet had been head of state and sometimes referred to as President. Now the word *Prezident* was introduced to the Constitution. Under the President were two new institutions, the Presidential Council and the Soviet (Council) of the Federation. They were both consultative. The President nominated his Council and the Soviet of the Republic brought together the top representatives of the fifteen republics. The latter was important in keeping the Union together and drafting the treaty for a Union of Sovereign States which would succeed the USSR. The USSR Security Council, dominated by the power ministries (internal affairs, defence and KGB), came into being. The Politburo began to meet less frequently and in July 1990 was completely remodelled, now only consisting of Party officials at the centre and the republican parties. The executive presidency was also accompanied by a radical shake-up of government. The USSR Council of Ministers was, according to the Constitution, subordinate to the USSR Supreme Soviet. Gorbachev wanted a government which was subordinate to the President. The result was a Cabinet of Ministers and a Prime Minister, a *Premer Ministr*. Gorbachev needed a body which could perform the function of manager of the state. It would be responsible for ensuring the implementation of reform. This was the USSR State Council but it was not very effective.

The republics elected their own parliaments in 1990 and only Russia chose to have the dual system of a Congress and a Supreme Soviet. All the others made do with a Supreme Soviet. One of the consequences of these elections was that the new parliaments could claim legitimacy and spoke for the people. In Russia this led to the election of Boris Yeltsin as President and in the Baltic republics their parliaments, led by Lithuania, made it clear that they wanted independence and therefore wished to leave the Soviet Union. This led to a system which can be called dual power, with the Soviet parliament passing legislation and it being annulled in some republican parliaments. More and more republics passed laws on sovereignty and defied Moscow. The key to the future of the Soviet Union was Russia, and Yeltsin's decision to go for independence destroyed Gorbachev's hope of a federal state to succeed the USSR. On reflection, had Gorbachev succeeded in fashioning a Union of Sovereign States (the Baltic states would never have joined), the former Soviet Union might have been better off today.

The attempted coup in August 1991 was timed to prevent the signing of the agreement establishing the Union of Sovereign States. It achieved the opposite of what it intended: the banning of the Communist Party, the emergence of President Yeltsin as a hero and, in consequence, the break up of the Soviet Union. Many republics rushed to escape from the USSR lest another coup succeed. Gorbachev's adoption of an executive presidency and a government subordinate to the President has stood the test of time and has functioned in Russia and other states since 1991.

The USSR was sometimes described as a Party–government state. The main features of the relationship between the Party and the government are shown below. The approximate equivalence of Party and governmental bodies is given at each territorial level.

Party	Government
Politburo (Presidium between 1952–66, Communist Party of the Soviet Union	Presidium of the USSR Council of Ministers
Central Committee (CC)	USSR Council of Ministers
CPSU Congress	Presidium of the USSR Supreme Soviet
No Party equivalent	USSR Supreme Soviet
Republican (e.g. Ukrainian) Party Secretariat	Republican Council of Ministers
Republican CC	Presidium of Republican Supreme Soviet
Republican Party Congress	Republican Supreme Soviet
Regional (krai, oblast) Party Committee	City, krai or oblast soviet
Regional Party Conference	No governmental equivalent
District (raion, etc.) Party bodies	Raion–village soviet
District Party Conference	
Primary Party Organisations (enterprises, collective farms, etc.)	No governmental equivalent
Rank and file Party members	Voters

NOTE ON RUSSIAN NAMES

Russian names consist of a first name, patronymic (father's name) and a surname. Hence Mikhail Sergeevich Gorbachev or Mikhail, the son of Sergei Gorbachev. A sister would have been called Anna Sergeevna (the daughter of Sergei) Gorbacheva. Gorbachev's wife was Raisa Maksimovna, Raisa, the daughter of Maksim, née Titorenko. (Titorenko is a Ukrainian name, hence does not end in the feminine 'a'.) Another Russian name is Rimashevsky (masculine) and Rimashevskaya (feminine). The latter denotes both the daughter and the wife.

Many Russian names end in 'ov' and 'ev'. This is the genitive plural. Gorbachev (pronounced Gorba-choff) has an 'ev' ending because it follows 'ch'. The stress is at the end, on the 'ev'. He would have been addressed formally as Mikhail Sergeevich, as the title gospodin (mister or lord) had been dropped in 1917. It is now again in use in Russia. He could also be addressed as Tovarishch (Comrade) Gorbachev.

Most Russian names have a diminutive. Sasha for Aleksandr, Volodya for Vladimir, Kolya for Nikolai, Seryozha for Sergei, Misha for Mikhail, Nadya for Nadezhda, Tanya for Tatyana, Raya for Raisa, and so on. Children, animals and close friends are addressed with the diminutive. There is also Ivan Ivanovich Ivanov: Ivan (John), the son of Ivan Johnson. Donald MacDonald, Donald, the son of Donald, would be Donald Donaldovich Donaldov in Russian.

Ukrainian names sometimes end in 'a' – for example, Kuchma – but this is both masculine and feminine. As above, Titorenko is masculine and feminine. Some names end in 'o' – for example, Chernenko. This would be Chernenkov in Russian. There are also names ending in 'enko', 'chenko', 'lenko', denoting the diminutive – for example, Kirilenko, little Kiril or Cyril; Mikhailichenko, little Mikhail or little Michael. A common Armenian surname ending is 'yan' – for example, Mikoyan (the stress is always at the end). Common Georgian surname endings are 'vili', 'adze', 'elli' – for example, Dzhugashvili (or Djugashvili); Shevardnadze; Tseretelli; Chekhidze. Muslim surnames adopt the Russian ending 'ov' or 'ev' – for example, Aliev, Kunaev, Rakhmanov, Nazarbaev.

NOTE

In this book the Russian endings 'ii', 'yi' have been rendered 'y' – for example, Malinovsky, Podgorny. The phonetic 'y' has been omitted – for example, Erin, not Yerin, Efimov, not Yefimov. The exception is Yeltsin as this is now the accepted English spelling. Evtushenko is retained even though he is often known in English as Yevtushenko. The soft sign in Russian has been omitted throughout.

Chronology

Where there are two dates, the first date is according to the Julian calendar and the second (in brackets) is the Gregorian calendar. There is a difference of thirteen days in the twentieth century. Soviet Russia moved to the Gregorian calendar on 1 February 1918.

1917	*25 October (7 November)*: The IInd Congress of Soviets of Workers' and Soldiers' Deputies opens and declares that power has passed from the provisional government to the soviets *26–7 October (8–9 November)*: At an all-night sitting the Congress confirms a new government, the Sovnarkom or Council of People's Commissars, consisting entirely of Bolsheviks and chaired by Vladimir Lenin.
1918	*3 March*: Treaty of Brest-Litovsk between Germany, Austria-Hungary, Bulgaria and Turkey and the RSFSR is signed. Russia loses 26 per cent of its population, 27 per cent of its arable land, 73 per cent of its steel industry and 75 per cent of its coal industry. *June*: Civil War between Reds (Bolsheviks) and Whites (anti-Bolsheviks) begins. *13 November*: The Soviet government annuls the Treaty of Brest-Litovsk and sends the Red Army into the German occupied areas.
1921	*8–16 March*: The Xth Congress of the Communist Party (Bolsheviks) bans factionalism in the Party and introduces the New Economic Policy (NEP).
1922	*30 December*: The Ist All-Union Congress of Soviets votes for the formation of the Union of Soviet Socialist Republics.
1924	*21 January*: Lenin dies at Gorky, near Moscow.
1928	*1 October*: The first Five Year Plan begins (ends on 31 December 1932).
1929	*16 January*: Stalin's proposal that Trotsky be deported from the Soviet Union is adopted by the Politburo.
1931	*2 March*: Mikhail Gorbachev born at Privolnoe, Stavropol krai, North Caucasus.
1936	*5 December*: A new Soviet Constitution is adopted which establishes the USSR Supreme Soviet, consisting of two houses, the Soviet of the Union and the Soviet of Nationalities.
1939	*23 August*: Molotov and von Ribbentrop sign in Moscow the Soviet–German Non-Aggression Treaty, including a secret protocol on their spheres of influence in Europe (also called the Stalin–Hitler Pact).

1941	*22 June*: German and allied forces invade the Soviet Union.
1942	*August*: The Wehrmacht overruns and occupies Stavropol krai. It withdraws in January–February 1943.
1943	*31 January*: Field Marshal Paulus surrenders at Stalingrad.
1945	*30 April*: Red Army soldiers hoist the Red Flag over the Reichstag in Berlin. *2 May*: German troops surrender to the Red Army in Berlin. *9 May*: German commanders sign the unconditional surrender of German forces in Berlin Karlshorst, thus ending the Second World War in Europe.
1953	*5 March*: Stalin dies after suffering a stroke on 1 March. *6 March*: Georgy Malenkov becomes Prime Minister and head of the Party. *14 March*: Malenkov leaves the Party Secretariat and thus ceases to be head of the Party. The main beneficiary is Khrushchev. *26 June*: Lavrenty Beria is arrested (and executed in December). *13 September*: Khrushchev is elected First Secretary of the CPSU.
1954	*2 March*: Khrushchev launches his Virgin and Idle Lands programme which envisages the rapid expansion of the sown area in north Kazakhstan, west Siberia, the Urals, the Volga and the north Caucasus.
1955	*8 February*: Malenkov resigns as Prime Minister and is succeeded by Nikolai Bulganin, a Khrushchev nominee.
1956	*14–25 February*: At the XXth Party Congress Khrushchev delivers his Secret Speech, attacks Stalin's personality cult and demands a return to Leninist principles.
1957	*19 June*: The Party Presidium votes to dismiss Khrushchev as Party leader but he argues successfully that only the Central Committee can do this. On 4 July, he eventually defeats his opponents (known as the Anti-Party Group) and thereby becomes undisputed leader of the Soviet Union.
1961	*12 April*: Yury Gagarin becomes the first man in space and circles the earth in his spacecraft, Vostok-1. *14 October*: A CC plenum adopts a new Party programme and statute replacing those of 1919. The new programme defines the Party as a Party of the whole people. *17–31 October*: At the XXIInd Party Congress Khrushchev proposes a twenty-year plan which was to usher in a communist society. As part of this, over the years 1961–70, the Soviet Union was to surpass the US in per head production and by 1980 the Soviet Union would be close to introducing distribution according to need. Gorbachev attends as a delegate.
1962	*22 October*: President John F. Kennedy announces to the American people that the US is aware that there are Soviet missiles on Cuba and imposes a naval blockade. Eventually Khrushchev backs down, removes the missiles but gains the concession from Kennedy that the US will not attempt to invade Cuba.
1964	*14 October*: Khrushchev is dismissed as First Party Secretary by a Central Committee plenum which elects Leonid Brezhnev as his successor. Aleksei Kosygin becomes Prime Minister. It is also agreed that in future the same

person cannot occupy simultaneously the posts of Party leader and Prime Minister.

1965   *9 December*: Anastas Mikoyan resigns as chairman of the Presidium of the USSR Supreme Soviet (President) and is succeeded by Nikolai Podgorny.

1968   *21 August*: Soviet and other Warsaw Pact states' troops invade Czechoslovakia bringing to an end the era of 'socialism with a human face'.

1970   *Spring*: Gorbachev appointed first Party secretary, Stavropol kraikom.

1975   *1 August*: The Helsinki Final Act is signed by Leonid Brezhnev thus bringing the third session of the Conference on Security and Co-operation in Europe to a successful end.
        9 October: The Nobel Peace Prize is awarded to Academician Andrei Sakharov.

1977   *4 June*: A new draft Constitution is published for discussion.
        16 June: Nikolai Podgorny resigns as chairman of the Presidium of the USSR Supreme Soviet and is succeeded by Leonid Brezhnev.
        30 September: Discussion of the new Constitution is concluded and the amended text is approved by the Central Committee plenum on 3 October.

1978   *27 November*: Gorbachev appointed Central Committee secretary for agriculture, succeeding Kulakov.

1979   *26 December*: Soviet troops move into Afghanistan.

1980   *21 October*: Gorbachev is elected a full member of the Politburo.

1982   *10 November*: Leonid Brezhnev dies and is succeeded as General Secretary of the Communist Party by Yury Andropov who also becomes President. When Andropov is ill, Gorbachev often chairs Politburo meetings.

1984   *9 February*: Yury Andropov dies and is succeeded by Konstantin Chernenko on 13 February. The latter later also becomes President.

1985   *10 March*: Konstantin Chernenko dies.
        11 March: Mikhail Gorbachev is elected General Secretary of the Communist Party.
        8 April: Gorbachev announces suspension of deployment of SS-20 missiles in Europe.
        23 April: The Central Committee plenum adopts a mild reform, proposed by Gorbachev. Viktor Chebrikov, Nikolai Ryzhkov and Egor Ligachev are elected full members of the Politburo.
        15 May: Gorbachev visits Leningrad, is warmly received and makes a vigorous speech advocating change.
        1 July: Central Committee plenum removes Grigory Romanov from Politburo. Boris Yeltsin is appointed a CC secretary.
        2 July: USSR Supreme Soviet elects Andrei Gromyko chairman of its Presidium (making him President). Eduard Shevardnadze takes over from Gromyko as Minister of Foreign Affairs.
        27 September: Nikolai Ryzhkov takes over from Nikolai Tikhonov as chairman of the USSR Council of Ministers (Prime Minister).

2–6 *October*: Gorbachev visits France, his first official visit abroad as Soviet leader.

18–21 *November*: Presidents Gorbachev and Reagan meet in Geneva, have a fireside chat and agree to further meetings.

24 *December*: Boris Yeltsin succeeds Viktor Grishin as first secretary of Moscow gorkom.

1986 25 *February–6 March*: XXVIIth Party Congress in Moscow. Gorbachev calls for radical economic reform.

26 *April*: Explosion at the Chernobyl nuclear reactor. Two dead are reported but it is stated that there is no additional danger of radiation.

14 *May*: Gorbachev speaks for the first time to the nation on the Chernobyl disaster but gives few details.

30 *September*: A Central Committee resolution criticises the slow pace of perestroika and names some ministries.

10 *October*: Gorbachev flies to Reykjavik for a two-day summit with Reagan. The two Presidents almost reach agreement on extensive cuts in offensive arms.

16 *December*: Gorbachev phones Academician Andrei Sakharov in Gorky (now Nizhny Novgorod), inviting him and his wife, Elena Bonner, to return to Moscow after six years of involuntary exile.

1987 26 *January*: A much postponed Central Committee plenum convenes and Gorbachev proposes multi-candidate elections, the promotion of non-party persons to senior government posts and the expansion of co-operatives.

6 *May*: About six hundred members of Pamyat, a new Russian nationalist organisation, demonstrate in Moscow and are then received by Boris Yeltsin.

28 *May*: Mathias Rust, a young West German, lands a single-engine plane near Red Square.

30 *May*: Wholesale military personnel changes are announced in the wake of Rust's penetration of Soviet airspace. Dmitry Yazov becomes Minister of Defence.

25 *June*: At a Central Committee plenum Gorbachev criticises the head of Gosplan and other top economic officials.

28–30 *June*: At a USSR Supreme Soviet session, Nikolai Ryzhkov describes the central (from Moscow) management of Soviet enterprises as 'obsolete'. A law on state enterprises was passed that afforded enterprises autonomy over their budgets and was to come into force in January 1988.

1 *November*: Gorbachev's book *Perestroika* is published in Moscow.

11 *November*: Boris Yeltsin is sharply criticised by Gorbachev and many Moscow party officials and is succeeded as first secretary, Moscow gorkom, by Lev Zaikov.

December: Gorbachev visits London and Washington and meets Margaret Thatcher and Ronald Reagan. In Washington he signs a treaty banning medium-range nuclear missiles. His first visit to America is a personal triumph.

1988 27 *February–4 March*: Further violence in Nagorno-Karabakh where Armenians are demonstrating for the transfer of the region from Azerbaijan to Armenia. Armenians and others are murdered in Sumgait, Azerbaijan. Tass states that thirty-one people were killed.

13 March: *Sovetskaya Rossiya* publishes Nina Andreeva's letter attacking reformers.

14 April: Accords ending the Afghan War are signed. The United States and the Soviet Union are to guarantee the accords and not interfere in the internal affairs of Afghanistan and Pakistan.

29 May–2 June: President Reagan visits Moscow for his fourth summit with Gorbachev.

28 June: XIXth Party Conference opens in Moscow and Gorbachev proposes a presidential system for the Soviet Union, a new parliament to be called the USSR Congress of People's Deputies and an increase in the power of local soviets at the expense of the Communist Party.

30 September: At a Central Committee plenum many members retire and Gromyko leaves the Politburo. The following day Gorbachev replaces Gromyko as chairman of the Presidium of the USSR Supreme Soviet.

7 December: At the United Nations in New York, Gorbachev announces a reduction of 500,000 in Soviet military personnel within two years.

1989   *15 February*: The last Soviet troops leave Afghanistan.

26 March: Elections are held to the USSR Congress of People's Deputies. Many Party candidates lose and the pro-independence parties win in the Baltic states. Boris Yeltsin wins in Moscow.

18 May: Estonia and Lithuania declare their sovereignty. Latvia follows on 29 July.

25 May: The USSR Congress of People's Deputies opens in Moscow and is televised live. Gorbachev is elected chairman and on 26 May the members of the USSR Supreme Soviet are elected from among the Congress's members.

July: Coal miners in the Kuzbass, Siberia, go on strike, followed by those in the Donbass, Ukraine.

29 July: The Inter-Regional Group is formed in the USSR Congress of People's Deputies to promote reform. Among the leaders chosen by these 250-odd deputies are Boris Yeltsin, Gavriil Popov and Andrei Sakharov.

7 October: Gorbachev, in East Berlin, tells the crowds that 'life punished those who fall behind' and this further undermines the authority of Erich Honecker, the GDR leader. He is replaced by Egon Krenz on 18 October.

9 November: The Berlin Wall comes down.

2–4 December: Gorbachev and Bush meet in Malta and discuss recent developments in eastern Europe and arms control.

14 December: Andrei Sakharov dies.

20 December: The Communist Party of Lithuania declares itself independent of the Communist Party of the Soviet Union in Moscow.

1990   *10 January*: Gorbachev travels to Lithuania to discuss the republic's desire to break away from the Soviet Union. However, Lithuanians demonstrate for independence.

19–20 January: Clashes in Baku between Soviet forces and the local population leave many dead.

5 February: At a Central Committee plenum Gorbachev proposes the Party abandon its leading role, accept a multi-party system and adopt 'humane, democratic socialism'. These proposals are accepted on 7 February after a stormy debate.

February-March: Local elections are held throughout the Soviet Union with pro-independence candidates winning in the Baltic states while in Moscow and Leningrad the official Party candidates are rejected.

6 March: The USSR Congress of People's Deputies amends article six of the Soviet Constitution, thus ending the Party's monopoly of power.

11 March: Lithuania declares independence and elects Vytautas Landsbergis President.

15 March: Gorbachev is elected Soviet President by the USSR Congress of People's Deputies.

24–6 March: Gorbachev chooses his fifteen-person Presidential Council.

29 May: Boris Yeltsin is elected chairman (or President) of the Presidium of the RSFSR Supreme Soviet.

30 May: Gorbachev travels to Washington for his second summit with Bush.

8 June: The Russian parliament declares its laws take precedence over Soviet laws.

19 June: The founding Congress of the Russian Communist Party convenes in Moscow.

22 June: Ivan Polozkov, a conservative, is elected leader of the Russian Communist Party.

2 July: The XXVIIIth Party Congress opens in Moscow. Gorbachev is re-elected leader. The new Politburo contains only Party officials and will have no role in governing the country.

16 July: Ukraine declares its sovereignty.

20 July: The 500-day programme of the Russian Republic is published. It envisages moving to a market economy in 500 days.

23–4 August: Armenia, Turkmenistan and Tajikistan declare their sovereignty.

9 September: Gorbachev and Bush meet for a one-day summit in Helsinki to discuss the crisis in Kuwait.

24 September: The USSR Supreme Soviet grants Gorbachev special powers to rule by decree during the transition to a market economy but cannot agree on an economic programme.

3 October: Germany is reunited.

15 October: Gorbachev is awarded the 1990 Nobel Peace Prize.

17 November: The USSR Supreme Soviet accepts Gorbachev's proposal to set up a new Soviet government, consisting of representatives from all fifteen republics, to be called the Soviet (Council) of the Federation.

23 November: The draft treaty of a new union is published, to be called the Union of Sovereign Soviet Republics.

2 December: Vadim Bakatin is removed as USSR Minister of Internal Affairs and succeeded by Boris Pugo.

20 December: Eduard Shevardnadze, Minister of Foreign Affairs, resigns and warns of the threat of dictatorship.

26 December: Gorbachev chooses Gennady Yanaev as the new Vice-President of the Soviet Union but he is rejected on the first ballot by the Congress and accepted on the second.

1991   *11–13 January*: Soviet black berets (Omon forces under the Ministry of the

Interior) fire at the main printing press in Vilnius, Lithuania, and on 13 January attack and take over the TV station there.

17 March: Referendums on the future of the USSR, on the creation of a presidency (in the RSFSR) and a directly elected mayor (in Moscow).

23 April: In Novo-Ogarevo President Gorbachev and the heads of state of nine republics sign a joint statement on speeding up a new Union agreement.

12 June: Boris Yeltsin elected President of the RSFSR in Russia's first democratic elections. He receives 57.3 per cent of the vote in a turnout of 74 per cent. Zhirinovsky polls 8 per cent. Gavriil Popov elected mayor of Moscow with 65.3 per cent of the vote.

17–21 June: USSR Cabinet of Ministers attempts to restrict the power of President Gorbachev.

10 July: Boris Yeltsin sworn in as President of the RSFSR and receives the blessing of the Russian Orthodox Church.

18–21 August: Attempted coup against President Gorbachev by the Emergency Committee.

20 August–22 September: Estonia, Latvia, Ukraine, Belorussia (Belarus), Moldavia (Moldova), Georgia, Azerbaijan, Kirgizia (Kyrgyzstan), Uzbekistan, Tajikistan and Armenia declare independence; only the Baltic states are recognised internationally (Lithuania had declared independence on 11 March 1990).

23 August–5 September: President Yeltsin orders the Communist Party of the Soviet Union to suspend its activities on the territory of the Russian Federation. The Central Committee building at Staraya Ploshchad is sealed (22 August). The Russian national flag flies from the Kremlin, alongside the Soviet flag. Gorbachev resigns (24 August) as General Secretary of the CPSU and advises the Central Committee to dissolve.

18 October: Treaty on an economic community signed by President Gorbachev and representatives of eight republics: Azerbaijan, Georgia, Moldavia (Moldova) and Ukraine decline to sign.

28 October: Russian Congress of People's Deputies elects Ruslan Khasbulatov its chairman and speaker of the Russian Supreme Soviet.

6 November: President Yeltsin bans the activities of the CPSU and the Russian Communist Party on the territory of the Russian Federation.

9–10 November: IInd Congress of Democratic Russia (DemRossiya).

1 December: In a referendum, Ukrainian voters confirm Ukrainian independence.

8 December: In Belovezh Forest, near Minsk, the Presidents and Prime Ministers of Russia, Ukraine and Belarus declare the USSR dissolved and found a Commonwealth of Independent States.

17 December: Yeltsin and Gorbachev agree that by 1 January 1992 the Soviet Union will no longer exist.

25 December: USSR President Gorbachev resigns.

27 December: President Yeltsin takes over President Gorbachev's office in the Kremlin.

31 December: the Soviet Union ceases to exist.

1992   *2 January*: Yegor Gaidar launches his price liberalisation policy, also known as shock therapy.

13–31 March: President Yeltsin and representatives of all territorial and national regions of the Russian Federation, except Tatarstan and the Chechen-Ingushetia, sign the Federal Treaty on the delimitation of power between the centre and the regions.

7 May: President Yeltsin signs a decree establishing the armed forces of the Russian Federation with himself as commander-in-chief.

6 July: Russian Constitutional Court begins the case against the CPSU.

30 November: The Constitutional Court ends proceedings against the CPSU without any verdict.

14 December: President Yeltsin is forced by the Congress of People's Deputies to drop Gaidar as Prime Minister. He chooses Viktor Chernomyrdin as the new Prime Minister.

1993 *20 March*: On television, President Yeltsin announces the introduction of a 'special regime' and a referendum on 25 April.

24 March: Yeltsin's decree of 20 March is published but 'special regime' has been removed.

26–9 March: Motion to impeach President Yeltsin at the IXth Congress of People's Deputies just fails.

25 April: In a nation-wide referendum voters express their confidence in the President and his economic policy.

12 July: Constitutional Assembly, called by Yeltsin, adopts text of draft Constitution.

21 September: President Yeltsin signs a decree dissolving parliament and the election of a State Duma on 11–12 December. Parliament deposes the President and appoints Rutskoi to replace him, also new Ministers of Defence and Security.

3–4 October: Conflict between forces supporting parliament and President Yeltsin results in bloodshed with Yeltsin's forces bombarding the White House.

15 October: President Yeltsin signs a decree for a referendum on the draft Constitution on 12 December: Georgian President Eduard Shevardnadze signs a decree on Georgian entry to the CIS which now consists of all ex-Soviet republics except Moldova and the Baltic states.

12 December: Elections to the State Duma, and the draft Constitution is confirmed.

A

Abakumov, Viktor Semenovich (1894–1954), one of the most brutal henchmen of STALIN and BERIA, who as head of Smersh, 1942–6, was ruthless in eliminating Stalin's perceived foes. Apparently he gave the order in 1944 to kidnap Raoul Wallenberg, the Swedish diplomat who had saved thousands of Hungarian Jews by issuing them with Swedish passports. Rumour has it that Abakumov personally shot Wallenberg during interrogation in his Lubyanka office. Abakumov was USSR Minister of State Security, 1946–51, and, as such, in charge of fabricating the Leningrad Affair after the death of Andrei ZHDANOV in August 1948. The Affair cost many their lives and thousands others their posts. While in Berlin in April 1946 to arrest some Soviet officers, Abakumov clashed with Marshal ZHUKOV, commander of Soviet forces. This led to Zhukov being recalled to Moscow and accused of conspiratorial activities. Stalin had became suspicious of Beria and ordered Abakumov to fabricate a conspiracy against several of Beria's Mingrelian (one of the nationalities in Georgia) associates. He claimed later that Stalin had told him to 'go after the big Mingrelian [Beria]'. Just as all this was moving into place Stalin had Abakumov arrested in June 1951. Abakumov's bitter rival, Merkulov, had written a letter to Stalin denouncing Abakumov. The latter's deputy, M. D. Ryumin, informed Stalin that Abakumov had known for some time about a Jewish bourgeois nationalist plot, involving American spies, but had for some reason kept it secret. Abakumov had allegedly also murdered a prisoner, a Kremlin doc-

tor, who had important information. Stalin appointed Semen IGNATEV to succeed Abakumov in 1951. Abakumov sent many letters to Beria about being tortured and begging for help to get out of prison. Abakumov was not taken in by the Doctors' Plot, launched in January 1953, according to which a group of doctors (mainly Jewish) had as their aim the shortening of the life of leading Soviet officials. He was arrested on Stalin's orders but released after the master's death by Beria who brought him back into state security work. The fall of Beria signalled Abakumov's demise. He was put on trial in Leningrad for his role in the Leningrad Affair and he was executed in December 1954.

Abalkin, Leonid Ivanovich (*b.* 1930), One of the leading economic reformers during perestroika and supporter of GORBACHEV until he lost patience in November 1990. He graduated from the prestigious Moscow Plekhanov Economics Institute, 1952, and taught at the institute from 1971 to 1977, becoming a professor. He then moved to the Academy of Social Sciences where he rose to become head of the department of political economy in 1985. He became director of the Institute of the National Economy, USSR Academy of Sciences, 1986, and was elected an academician (member of the USSR Academy of Sciences), 1987. He was a deputy chair of the USSR Council of Ministers, 1989–91. He was elected a deputy to the USSR Congress of People's Deputies, 1989, and then became the first chair of the State Commission on Economic Reform when it was set up, June 1989. This meant that he had to give up his mandate as a deputy. He found working with Nikolai Ryzhkov, the USSR Prime Minister, frustrating, as RYZHKOV was not as enamoured of market solutions as Abalkin.

Abashidze, Irakly Vissarionovich (1909–92), a leading Georgian poet and literary figure who mixed politics and culture. He was born in Mingrelia, Georgia, and graduated from Tbilisi University. He attended the 1st Congress of the USSR Union of Writers, 1934, when socialist realism was laid down as the cultural orthodoxy. He was sent to labour camp (Gulag) immediately afterwards but wrote a highly flattering poem in honour of Lavrenty BERIA (another Mingrelian). Abashidze was released and became editor of several literary journals. He became a member of the Communist Party, 1939, and secretary of the Union of Georgian Writers (subordinate to the USSR Union of Writers). He became chair of the Georgian organisation in 1953 and remained until 1967. In 1958 he played his part in attacking Boris PASTERNAK for his novel *Doctor Zhivago* and the award of the Nobel Prize for Literature to him. He also joined in attacks on the United States and Britain when the US intervened in Lebanon, 1958. He was a leading member of the Georgian Academy of Sciences, becoming its vice-president, 1960. He was also a deputy of the USSR Supreme Soviet. He cultivated relations with KHRUSHCHEV and BREZHNEV, flattering them when the occasion arose. Under perestroika he revised his biographical entry in the Soviet Georgian Encyclopedia to excise his former good understanding with Beria. For ever an establishment figure, he supported Zviad GAMSAKHURDIA, a fellow Mingrelian, when he came to power after Georgian independence, 1991. Gamsakhurdia's dictatorial behaviour quickly produced many enemies and Abashidze consequently went over to the op-

position. The Military Council which removed Gamsakhurdia by force afforded Abashidze a state funeral.

Abdrashitov, Vadim Yusupovich (*b.* 1945), a leading film director who rose to prominence under glasnost. He developed his skills as a pupil of Romm and had a fruitful partnership with Aleksandr Mindadze which produced many films, including *The Parade of the Planets,* 1984. A constant theme in his work was the reality of everyday Soviet life and *The Train Has Stopped,* 1982, was daring in its portrayal of small-time corruption. He gained an international reputation with *Plumbum, or a Dangerous Game,* 1986, which portrays the malaise of society, especially its pessimism, towards the end of the communist era.

Abdulatipov, Ramazan Gadzhimuradovich (*b.* 1946), an Avar, he became a leading specialist on nationality issues under GORBACHEV. He was born in Dagestan into a large family and graduated from the history faculty, Dagestan State University, Makhachkala, and worked in the agitation and propaganda department of the Party apparatus in Dagestan, 1974–5. In 1975 he became a postgraduate student in the faculty of philosophy, Leningrad State University, and successfully presented his candidate dissertation on personality and ethnic relations in a developed socialist state (PhD). He returned to a pedagogical institute, Makhachkala, and later headed a sociological laboratory in Murmansk. In 1985 he successfully presented his doctoral dissertation on ethnic relations in a developed socialist society (DLitt). In 1978 he became head of faculty, Murmansk Higher Marine Engineering Technical College, and in 1987 he returned again to Makhachkala to head the department of philosophy, Dagestan Pedagogical Institute. In 1988 he was invited to Moscow to head a section of the department for inter-ethnic relations,

Central Committee Secretariat and remained there until June 1990. He was elected to the RSFSR Congress of People's deputies and the RSFSR Supreme Soviet, 1990, and was elected speaker, Soviet of Nationalities, RSFSR Supreme Soviet, June 1990. He was a member of the Communist Party, 1973–91. Abdulatipov, mainly due to his Dagestani background, was a leading advocate of reconciliation between nationalities in the Soviet Union. He quickly came to distrust Boris YELTSIN and became an ally of Ruslan KHASBULATOV when the latter succeeded Yeltsin as speaker of parliament. He belonged to the centre right bloc which attempted to impeach President Yeltsin, March 1993.

Abel, Rudolf Ivanovich (Fischer, William) (1903–71), a successful Soviet spy who was exchanged for Francis Gary Powers, the US U-2 pilot shot down over Sverdlovsk in May 1960. Abel was born into the family of a German communist who moved to the Soviet Union after the Nazis came to power. He spent part of his childhood in England. He was a GRU (military intelligence) agent in Germany during the Second World War. In 1947 he entered Canada on a German passport and moved to the US, using a forged Canadian passport. The Communist Party of the USA provided him with the birth certificate of a dead child. He set up a business in Brooklyn where he displayed his multi-faceted talents. He was an excellent musician, radio engineer and linguist. He operated a large network of Soviet agents throughout the US under the name of Emil Robert Goldfus. He was recalled to Moscow, and then sent to Finland where he married a Finn. He reentered the US with her in 1952. His cover was blown by another GRU agent and he was arrested and sentenced to thirty years, 1957. He was exchanged for Francis Gary Powers in 1962 in East Berlin. On his return to Moscow he took up residence in the Lubyanka and headed the Anglo-American desk. Louise Bernikow: *Abel,* New York, 1970.

Abramov, Fedor Aleksandrovich (1920–83), a Russian writer who championed the rural community against the depradations of the planned economy. He was born in Arkhangelsk oblast and was an officer in Smersh (death to spies) during the Great Fatherland War. He graduated from the faculty of philology, Kirov Leningrad State University, 1948. He taught at the university and became a professor of literature. He participated in the campaign during the Zhdanovshchina against cosmopolitanism (mainly anti-Semitic). He first came to the notice of a wider public in 1954 in an article attacking the over-optimistic representation of rural life in Soviet novels. He knew of the drudgery and poverty of many rural areas, especially in the north, at first hand. He devoted a trilogy of novels to rural life in Arkhangelsk oblast (*The Pryaslins,* 1974) which depicts the stark reality of the effects of collectivisation on the rural community and the land. He praised the stoicism of the peasant and as such was a precursor of the rural school of writers, the *derevenshchiki.*

Abuladze, Tengiz Evgenevich (*b.* 1924), a Georgian film producer who became an overnight sensation in 1987 when his film, *Repentance,* about the dreadful times under STALIN, hit the box office. It had been completed in 1984 but with Konstantin CHERNENKO in the Kremlin it was wiser to conceal its existence until the first shoots of glasnost appeared. It became an immediate success and provided a great stimulus to glasnost, especially in the film world. Abuladze studied in State Film School, Moscow, under Yutkevich and Romm. His first feature film (with Revaz Chkheidze), *Magdan's Donkey,* 1955, won a prize at the Cannes Film Festival, 1956. He concentrated on the realities of everyday life and as such was skating on thin ice with the Soviet cultural establishment. He became very popular in the Soviet Union and became an internationally acclaimed director with *Repentance*.

Adamishin, Anatoly Leonidovich (*b.* 1934), a senior Russian diplomat who was born in Kiev and graduated from the Lomonosov Moscow State University, 1957. He was a member of the Communist Party, 1965–91. He worked in the USSR Ministry of Foreign Affairs (MID), 1957–9; then in the USSR embassy in Rome as attaché, third and second secretary, 1959–65. There he struck up relationships with leading Italian communists and their families. Then he returned to MID, as second and first secretary, counsellor and consultant to the First European department, 1965–71. He was a senior counsellor in MID, 1973–8. Then he headed the First European department, 1978–86. He was promoted to deputy USSR Foreign Minister, May 1986, and remained in that post until 1990. He became first deputy Russian Foreign Minister, 1992–4. He then replaced Leonid ZAMYATIN as Russian ambassador to the Court of St James, London.

Adamov, Arkady Grigorevich (1920–91), the Soviet Agatha Christie who was hugely popular for his detective stories in the Soviet Union. His first book, *Delo Pestrykh* (The Motley Case) was published in 1956 in *Yunost*. It was an instant hit and revealed the almost insatiable appetite for thrillers in the USSR. He wrote over thirty books, almost all of which were turned into films.

Adzhubei, Aleksei Ivanovich (*b.* 1924), KHRUSHCHEV's son-in-law whose family connections led to a glittering career as a journalist. He became known as the king of the Soviet press. He was born in Samarkand, Uzbekistan, the son of a Ukrainian peasant who later became a well-known singer, working on occasions

with Fedor CHALIAPIN. His mother was a dressmaker and among her clients was NINA, the wife of Lavrenty BERIA. Adzhubei moved to Moscow with his mother, 1932. He graduated from Lomonosov Moscow State University in journalism, 1952. By this time he and Rada KHRUSHCHEVA had already married and Adzhubei became a top Soviet journalist, becoming editor-in-chief of *Komsomoloskaya Pravda,* and *Izvestiya.* He accompanied his father-in-law on many of his western jaunts, including the hugely successful visit to the United States, 1959. During the summer of 1964 Adzhubei unwittingly helped the opposition to oust Khrushchev. His father-in-law wanted to introduce the five-day week, something that would have been very popular at a time when Khrushchev's star was in the descendant. Adzhubei, at the instigation of some of the conspirators, persuaded him otherwise without realising that they had an ulterior motive. One of the accusations levelled against Khrushchev in October 1964 was that he had turned Adzhubei into a shadow foreign minister and had attempted to meddle in diplomatic matters at the highest level, confusing the Soviet ambassadors. On one occasion in Bonn, Adzhubei had made a slighting reference to Walter Ulbricht, the East German leader. The latter had personally complained to Moscow and it had taken some effort to smooth his ruffled feathers. Adzhubei's visits to Prague and Bonn led to a rumour that he was preparing the way for another Khrushchev initiative on Germany. He fell like a stone with Khrushchev in October 1964 and his official career was over.

Adzhubei, Rada Nikitichna (née **Khrushcheva**) (*b.* 1929), the daughter of Nikita and Nina KHRUSHCHEV. She was born in Kiev where her father was a Party official. She graduated from Lomonosov Moscow State University, 1952, in journalism and biology. She and ALEKSEI

ADZHUBEI had already married as students. She worked as an editor of journals such as *Nauka i Zhizn,* from 1956 onwards. Her husband became the journalist of the moment while her father was in power, rising eventually to become editor-in-chief of *Izvestiya.* She continued her career after her father's removal and in 1990 she was deputy editor-in-chief of *Nauka i Zhizn.* Their son, Aleksei Alekseevich, born in 1954, is a biophysicist and in 1990 began working for the Imperial Cancer Research Fund, London.

Afanasev, Viktor Grigorevich (*b.* 1922), a leading Soviet journalist who was removed as editor-in-chief of *Pravda* for not being sufficiently enthusiastic about perestroika. He was born in Aktanysh in present-day Tatarstan and is Russian. He served in the Red Army, joined the Communist Party, 1943, and graduated from the Chita Pedagogical Institute, 1950. He was Professor of Marxism–Leninism at the institute, 1954–9, then Professor of Scientific Communism at the Academy of Social Sciences of the Central Committee of the Communist Party, 1960–8. He then moved into journalism, working on *Voprosy Filosofii* and *Pravda,* 1968–74, ending up as first deputy editor-in-chief of the latter. He was promoted to the position of editor-in-chief of *Kommunist,* the Party's theoretical journal, 1974. He moved back as editor-in-chief of *Pravda* in 1976 and remained there until 1989 when he was sacked and replaced by Ivan Frolov. Afanasev was also chair of the USSR Union of Journalists, 1976–90. He was elected a member of the Central Committee of the Communist Party, 1976, and remained there until 1990. He was elected a member of the USSR Academy of Sciences, 1981, and this afforded him the much sought after title of academician. Such a career reveals an orthodox, conservative communist turn of mind but, in line with the BREZHNEV times, he did support

modest reform in the economy and society. Under GORBACHEV he found himself out of temper with the times and he was ill-suited to be an iconoclastic editor when radical solutions were needed.

Afanasev, Yury Nikolaevich (*b.* 1934), one of the most prominent reformers during the GORBACHEV era who eventually became frustrated with the Soviet leader's lack of consistency. He was born into a Russian worker's family in Ulyanovsk (Simbirsk). He graduated from Lomonosov Moscow State University, 1957, in history, worked in the Komsomol in Krasnoyarsk, Siberia, and joined the Communist Party, 1961. He became a specialist in French history in 1968 (the year of momentous changes in de Gaulle's France), specialising in the French Revolution, at the Academy of Social Sciences of the Central Committee of the Communist Party, undertaking research in France. He became editor of the history section of the Party journal, *Kommunist,* 1980. He moved back to academic life to become rector of the Moscow State Archive Institute, 1986, and he immediately used his access to Soviet archives to begin unearthing information about the past. As such he was an enthusiastic supporter of glasnost. STALIN and Stalinism quickly became targets (he claimed that Stalin had destroyed history in the USSR) and as he delved further he became more and more radical, not fearing to criticise the founding father, LENIN. He went into politics in March 1989 when he was elected to the USSR Congress of People's Deputies, representing Noginsk, near Moscow. As a radical Communist, Afanasev became one of the leaders of the Inter-Regional Group in the parliament. As an effective and energetic speaker, he addressed many demonstrations and gained respect and support from a wide spectrum of opinion. Conflict was bound to accompany such a high-profile figure who was impatient with anything but radical and speedy reform. Inevitably he became disillusioned with Gorbachev who had the unenviable task of balancing various power interests in the leadership. One of his accusations against the Soviet leader was that he was trying simultaneously to be leader of perestroika and the nomenklatura. Afanasev resigned from the Communist Party, April 1990, the first prominent person to do so. He was active in the Memorial Society, whose main task was to make known the repressions of the Stalin era and to erect a memorial to its victims. During his time at the Archive Institute, Father Aleksandr Men, the charismatic Orthodox priest, began giving lectures in theology, the first biblical teaching since the early 1930s. Afanasev was a prolific author and among his publications is a two-volume history of the Soviet Union, 1991, which reveals an impressive knowledge of western writing on the Soviet Union. He became rector of the Russian Humanitarian University, May 1991.

Afinogenov, Aleksandr Nikolaevich (1904–41), a playwright who was born in Ryazan guberniya, joined the Communist Party, 1922, and published his first play in 1924. During the 1920s he was associated with the proletarian culture movement (Proletkult) and directed plays. He became a member of the Russian Association of Proletarian Writers (RAPP) when it was formed in 1928. These writers were dedicated to producing a truly proletarian literature, imbued with communist ideology. He became a leading theorist of the movement but wrote plays depicting characters living in an epoch of permanent fear. *Fear*, 1931, and *The Lie* made him well known. He married an American. He came under criticism, 1936, and was expelled from the Party and the USSR Union of Writers, 1937, but was readmitted to both after recanting, 1938. He carried on writing and was killed during a German air raid on Moscow while waiting to be sent

to the US as a representative of the Soviet Information Bureau (Sovinformburo).

Agadzhanova-Shutko, Nina Ferdinandovna (1889–1974), a leading scriptwriter whose earlier career was in intelligence. She was an active worker for the Bolshevik Party, 1911–16, being arrested several times. She participated in the Civil War as a member of the Cheka. She was posted to the Soviet embassy in Czechoslovakia, 1921–2, and the Soviet embassy in Latvia, 1934–8, gathering intelligence in both countries. She temporarily retired from intelligence, 1924, and devoted herself to writing film scripts: *1905 God*, (*The Year 1905*), became the basis of Sergei EISENSTEIN's *The Battleship Potemkin*, 1926. She co-scripted with Lev Kuleshov the film, *Dva Buldi Dva* (*The Two Buldis*), 1930, and also co-scripted with V. Pudovkin, *Dezertir* (*The Deserter*), 1933. She taught at the All-Union State Institute of Cinematography (VGIK), 1945–52.

Aganbegyan, Abel Gazevich (*b.* 1932), one of the key Soviet economists during the early phase of GORBACHEV's perestroika. An Armenian, he was born in Tbilisi, Georgia. He graduated from the State Institute of Economics, Moscow, 1954, and joined the Communist Party, 1956. He was engaged in the USSR State Committee on Labour and Wages, 1955–61. When KHRUSHCHEV supported the concept of moving many scientists out of Moscow to the USSR Academy of Sciences, Novosibirsk, Siberia, Aganbegyan was among the first to go. He was head of the laboratory of the Institute of Economics and Organisation of Industrial Production, Siberian Section, USSR Academy of Sciences, 1961, and was the institute's director, 1967–85. He also edited the institute's journal, *EKO*, which quickly established itself as one of the leading economics journals and the most interesting. One of the reforms floated was to remove subsidies from everything except education, health, care for the elderly and book publishing. Gorbachev had been introduced to some radical-thinking specialists, including Tatyana ZASLAVSKAYA, in the early 1980s, and Aganbegyan in due course attended Gorbachev's discussion group. Aganbegyan was not as radical (pro-market) a reformer as others and his star, which had been brightest in the early years of perestroika, waned with him being overtaken by YAVLINSKY, SHATALIN and others. Aganbegyan chaired many influential committees, such as the committee on productive forces, 1985–91. He was academic secretary of the USSR Academy of Sciences, 1987–9. He was also director of the Academy of National Economy. Abel Aganbegyan: *Moving the Mountain. Inside the Perestroika Revolution*, London 1987.

Agursky, Mikhail Samuilovich (1933–91), a leading writer on the Soviet Union after he emigrated to Israel, 1975. He was born in Moscow, the son of a founding member of the Communist Party of the USA. He graduated as a mechanical engineer and became a candidate of technical science (PhD (Eng)). He became a leading human rights activist from the early 1970s. After emigration, he studied in Paris and obtained another doctorate from the Ecole des Hautes Etudes. He revisited the Soviet Union during the 1980s and became well known internationally as a commentator on the Soviet Union. He died of a heart attack in Moscow a few days after the failed coup in August 1991.

Airikyan, Paruir Arshavirovich (b. 1949), an Armenian nationalist leader who became involved in the independence movement in the 1960s. He became a leading member of the National United Party of Armenia, was arrested in 1969 and sentenced to four years' imprisonment. He was released in March 1973 but rearrested, February 1974, and sentenced to seven years in prison and three years' exile. In 1988 he was a leading light in demonstrations demanding the transfer of Nagorno-Karabakh from Azerbaijan to Armenia. He was accused of inciting national unrest, March 1988, was expelled from Armenia to Ethiopia, July 1988, and had his Soviet citizenship cancelled. He moved to France and thence back to Armenia. He was later elected a deputy to the Armenian Supreme Soviet.

Aitmatov, Chingiz Torekulovich (also **Aytmatov**) (b. 1928), a Kirgiz (Kyrgyz) who writes in his own language and Russian, he acquired an international reputation by the late GORBACHEV era. He first published in 1952, became first secretary of the Union of Kirgiz Writers, 1964, and was elected to the Kirgiz Academy of Sciences, 1974. He achieved Soviet and international prominence through his story, *Dzamilia*, 1958, which chronicles the struggle of a Kirgiz woman to choose her husband herself rather than follow tradition and have him presented to her. His collection of short stories, *Povesti gor i stepei*, 1962 (*Tales of the Mountains and Steppes*, 1969), introduces local myths and values. He was elected a deputy to the USSR Supreme Soviet, 1966. The following year he was elected to the executive board of the USSR Union of Writers and was awarded the Soviet state prize for literature, 1968. Aitmatov was a member of the editorial board of *Novy Mir*, and was editor-in-chief of *Inostrannaya Literatura* (*Foreign Literature*), 1988–90. He was elected to the USSR Congress of People's Deputies, 1989, and its USSR Supreme Soviet. Gorbachev made him a member of his Presidential Council, March 1990, and he was Soviet ambassador to Luxembourg, 1990–1. His literary themes are love, friendship, the emancipation of Kirgiz youth and spiritual quest. Like most writers on traditional values, there is an anti-urban and anti-technological streak in his work.

Akaev, Askar Akaevich (*b.* 1944), the most enthusiastic supporter of perestroika among the Muslim republics of the Soviet Union, he was elected the first President of Kirgizia (Kyrgyzstan). He was born into a Kirgiz (Kyrgyz) family in Keminsky raion, Kirgizia, and graduated from the Institute of Precision Engineering and Optics, Leningrad, specialising in the use of computers in engineering. There he successfully presented his candidate dissertation (PhD (Eng)) and his doctoral dissertation at the Moscow Institute of Physics and Engineering (DSc (Eng)), 1980. He then joined the staff of Frunze (Bishkek) Polytechnic Institute, founding a chair of computer technology. In 1986 he was elected a member of the Central Committee, Communist Party of Kirgizia. In March 1989 he was elected president of the Kirgiz Academy of Sciences and was also elected to the USSR Congress of People's Deputies and the USSR Supreme Soviet, 1989. He joined the Communist Party, 1981, and joined the Central Committee at the XXVIIIth Party Congress, July 1990. In October 1990 he was elected the first President of Kirgizia and in October 1991 he was elected the first President of the Republic of Kyrgyzstan. In February 1992 he also became Prime Minister of his country. He enjoys a good reputation abroad as a champion of the market and democracy.

Akhmadulina, Bella Akhatovna (*b.* 1937), a leading poetess and literary personality, her star rose under glasnost. She was born in Moscow of Italian–Tatar background. She graduated from the Gorky Institute of Literature and quickly became a member of the group which flowered under KHRUSHCHEV in the early 1960s, including EVTUSHENKO and VOZNESENSKY. She married Evtushenko, after their divorce, Yury Nagibin, and after their divorce, Boris Messerer. She was awarded the state prize for poetry, 1989. Her poems are personal, lyrical and often speak of friendship. She travelled widely but never quite achieved the same impact as Evtushenko and Voznesensky.

Akhmatova, Anna Andreevna (1889–1966) a great poet of Soviet literature, she survived vilification by ZHDANOV in 1946 to blossom in the post-STALIN era. She was born near Odessa but moved to Tsarskoe Selo (Pushkin) in 1890 and went to school there. She moved to Kiev in 1907 and married Nikolai GUMILEV, 1910. She began publishing poetry, 1912, and soon became a leading figure of the Silver Age of Russian poetry. A member of the Acmeists (Gumilev's group) for a time she branched away and developed her own lyrical style. She declined to emigrate after the October Revolution and her bitter and tragic experiences (her husband was shot and her son, Lev Gumilev spent many years in the Gulag) found expression in her poetry. She managed to escape from Leningrad before the German siege became effective, 1941. She lived in Tashkent, Uzbekistan, until 1944 when she returned to Leningrad after the siege was lifted. Mikhail ZOSHCHENKO and she were the main targets of Zhdanov's vituperations against foreign influences on Soviet culture, August 1946. Referring to Akhmatova, he commented, 'It would be difficult to say if she is a nun or a whore; better perhaps to say she is a little of both, her lusts and her prayers intertwine.' Spiritual values were unwelcome, materialism was the order of the day. Her expulsion from the USSR Union of Writers meant that her work could not be published in the Soviet Union. She continued to write: her *Poem without a Hero,* 1940–62, published outside the USSR in 1962, portrays life in St Petersburg on the eve of war and revolution. Her tribute to the victims of Stalin's repressions is *Requiem,* 1935–40 (published outside the Soviet Union, 1963, and in the Soviet Union, 1987). She published several volumes of verse after Stalin's death and earned enormous respect and prestige in the Soviet Union. Among her foreign honours is an honorary doctorate from the University of Oxford, 1965.

Akhromeev, Marshal Sergei Fedorovich (1923–91), he ended his brilliant military career by hanging himself in his Kremlin office after the failed coup against GOR-BACHEV in August 1991. A Russian, he joined the Red Army, 1940, the Communist Party, 1943, and he graduated from the Military Academy of Tank Troops, 1952, and the Military Academy of the General Staff, 1967. He rose to become a commander of a tank battalion on the 4th Ukrainian Front by 1945. From 1946 to 1964 he progressed from chief of staff of a regiment to commander of a division. After 1967 he was qualified for senior posts and in 1972–4 he was chief of staff, Far Eastern military district; then deputy Chief of the General Staff, 1972–9; first deputy Chief of Staff, 1979–84. He was elected a candidate member of the Central Committee of the Communist Party, 1981, and a full member, 1983. In the same year he was promoted Marshal of the Soviet Union. There was a vigorous debate about military doctrine in the early 1980s and Marshal Nikolai OGARKOV, Chief of the General Staff, argued strongly in favour of expanding conventional (non-nuclear) forces. Akhromeev had been careful not to commit himself and was rewarded by being chosen to replace the at times abrasive Ogarkov, September 1984. His position qualified him for the post of deputy USSR Minister of Defence, 1984. He accompanied Gorbachev to various summits but was regarded as more conservative than the Soviet leader. His view of the US remained adversarial and when Gorbachev announced unilateral defence cuts at the United Nations, December 1988, Akhromeev resigned as Chief of the General Staff. However, he remained an adviser to Gorbachev and addressed the US Congress, July 1989.

Held in high regard by western specialists, Akhromeev, however, could not move with the political times. He became one of the ringleaders of the attempted August coup against Gorbachev and became one of the few top conspirators to commit suicide.

Aksenov, Vasily Petrovich (b. 1932), the son of Evgeniya GINZBURG, he became a leading novelist in the Soviet Union. He was born in Kazan, Tatarstan, where his father was chair of the soviet. His parents were put in the Gulag when he was four years old. His grandmother brought him up and he was reunited with his mother when he was sixteen and together they lived in Magadan, Siberia, in exile. He graduated from the Leningrad Medical Institute, 1956, and worked as a doctor in the north, 1956–60, in Leningrad and Moscow afterwards. His first novel, *Kollegi*, (*Colleagues*), 1960, became an instant bestseller. His second novel, *Zvezdny Bilet* (*Ticket to the Stars*), 1961, confirmed his reputation. His books record the slang of youth culture (eventually to cause a rift with the establishment which saw it as bad language), pop culture, sport and the concerns of the younger generation. Elders are treated with little respect but his novels end with youth dedicating itself to the goals of communism. He attempted to promote the emergence of a group of youth writers by bringing out an almanac, *Metropol*, 1979, to which the authorities took great exception. This led to a final break with the establishment and he emigrated to the US, 1980. He has continued to publish and teach at American universities. He revisited the Soviet Union, 1989, and his work was republished there from 1990.

Aksyuchits, Viktor Vladimirovich (b. 1949), he used the opportunities under glasnost to promote Christian values and became active in politics in the Democratic Russia movement in the Russian

Federation. He was born in Belorussia and is a Belorussian. His father was a stevedore in the port of Riga, Latvia, and Aksyuchits attended the marine technical college there, 1965–9. He served in the Soviet Navy in the Baltic, 1969–73, and joined the Communist Party, 1971. He moved to Moscow to study in the faculty of philosophy, Moscow State University, and graduated, 1978. In 1979 he was arrested by the KGB for reading and distributing religious and political literature. During the search of his flat, the KGB found a library of samizdat (material illegally printed in the Soviet Union and abroad). He was expelled from the Communist Party and his postgraduate course and obliged to make ends meet by taking well-paid work in many parts of the country until 1986. During these years he wrote theological, religio-philosophical and other works which were published in the Russian émigré press. In 1987 Aksyuchits and Gleb Anishchenko began publishing the illegal Christian religio-philosophical and literary journal, *Vybor* (*Choice*). From 1988–91 he was a 'hidden member' (he was permitted to conceal his membership) of the People's Labour Union (NTS), an anti-communist but mainly émigré organisation whose headquarters were in Frankfurt-am-Main, Germany. In 1988 he joined the board of Perspektiva, a scientific-technical co-operative, an ostensibly commercial organisation whose main purpose was to further the activities of various informal political movements which were then springing up in the Soviet Union. Aksyuchits was a skilled businessman and made a fortune. During the 1990 elections to the RSFSR Supreme Soviet he stood as a member of the Democratic Russia movement and was elected by a Moscow constituency. Aksyuchits was the driving force behind the founding congress of the Russian Christian Democratic Movement, April 1990. In parliament, he and Mikhail ASTAFEV founded the Russian Union

deputies' group, December 1990. This was the term used by Aleksandr SOLZHENITSYN to describe the proposed state of the eastern Slavs. Aksyuchits sided with those who advocated the retention of the Union after the collapse of communism and opposed those in the Democratic Russia movement who supported independence for their republics. He supported the struggle of the South Ossetians to leave Georgia and unite with Russia and those in Moldavia who wanted autonomy or even to leave Moldavia. During the attempted coup in August 1991 Aksyuchits was one of the most active defenders of the Russian White House. However, he soon fell out with President Boris Yeltsin afterwards.

Alekhin, Aleksandr Aleksandrovich (1892–1946), one of the greatest chess players of all time, he reached the heights after emigrating from Soviet Russia. He was born into a noble family in Moscow and graduated from the school of law in St Petersburg. He emigrated in 1920 and settled in France, becoming a French citizen, and known as Alekhine. He graduated in law from the Sorbonne. He was world champion from 1927 to his death in 1946 (except in 1936). His untimely death prevented the eagerly awaited contest between him and Mikhail BOTVINNIK, the new Soviet master. Instead a competition was arranged which involved five top players and Botvinnik won it comprehensively. Alekhin was a brilliant innovator and advanced chess during his lifetime.

Aleksandrov, Aleksandr Danilovich (*b.* 1912), a brilliant Soviet mathematician and the founder of the Soviet school of geometry. He was attracted to the theory of relativity and the philosophy of science. He graduated from Leningrad State University, 1933, and then taught at the university until 1964. He carried out research at the Leningrad branch of the Institute of Mathematics,

USSR Academy of Sciences. His work on geometry won him a state prize, 1942, and election as corresponding member of the USSR Academy of Sciences, 1946. He became a member (academician), 1964. The 1948 Party decree which outlawed, among other things, genetics was a blow and led to many areas of science coming under attack but mathematics escaped almost unscathed. His continued support for the theory of relativity was brave at a time when Einstein was vilified. Aleksandrov was rector of Leningrad State University, 1952–64. He did much to overcome the Stalinist legacy in science and was a resolute opponent of Trofim LYSENKO. He was one of the scientists who pushed for the acceptance of genetics but this was impossible under KHRUSHCHEV, given his blind faith in Lysenko. Genetics was rehabilitated under BREZHNEV, in 1966. Aleksandrov moved to Akademgorodok (Science City), Novosibirsk, where he joined the Institute of Mathematics, Siberian branch, USSR Academy of Sciences, and continued his work on geometry, the theory of relativity and other scientific pursuits.

Aleksandrov, Anatoly Petrovich (b. 1903), one of the most brilliant nuclear scientists in the Soviet Union and one of the fathers of the Soviet atomic bomb. He was born near Kiev and graduated from Kiev University, 1930. He worked on the bomb and on other civilian and military projects from 1946, becoming director of the Kurchatov Institute of Nuclear Energy, 1960. He joined the Communist Party, 1960, and was elected a member of the Party's Central Committee, 1966. Among his many honours were five Lenin prizes and the Kurchatov, 1968, Lomonosov, 1979, and Vavilov, 1978, gold medals. He was also president of the USSR Academy of Sciences. He retired in 1986.

Aleksandrov, Boris Aleksandrovich (b. 1905), he became very well known in the west as conductor of the Red Army Choir and Dance Ensemble which toured the world before the Soviet invasion of Czechoslovakia, 1968, soured relations between the Soviet Union and the non-communist world. When the choir visited London it could be guaranteed to fill the Royal Albert Hall. His father was the composer, Aleksandr Vasilevich Aleksandrov, who founded the choir, 1928, and composed the music for the Soviet national anthem. Boris Aleksandrovich took over the choir after the death of his father, 1946, conducting it in the same style. Besides conducting he composed several operettas.

Alekseev, Mikhail Nikolaevich (b. 1918), a leading Russian novelist and editor who was born in Monastyrskoe, Saratov oblast. His peasant parents died in the famine of 1932–3. He joined the Red Army, 1938, and the Communist Party, 1942. He graduated from the Higher Literary Courses, USSR Union of Writers, 1957. During the war he kept a diary which later was woven into his novels. His first novel, *Soldaty (Soldiers)*, 1951–3, reveals first-hand experience of war and portrays soldiers with humanity and frankness. He was appointed editor-in-chief of the literary journal, *Moskva*, 1968. He can be classified as a member of the *derevenshchiki* (village prose) writers who laud Russian peasant, rural and traditional values. Under GORBACHEV he was critical of the trends in glasnost and in a meeting with Gorbachev complained about the media treatment of Soviet history, lamenting the attacks on the Soviet Union's past. Despite his conservative views, *Moskva* published some radical material, including Nabokov's *The Defence,* and a biography of BULGAKOV.

Aleksi II (Aleksi Mikhailovich Ridiger), Patriarch (b. 1929), the head of the Russian Orthodox Church, Aleksi was born in Tallinn, Estonia, and his family is of Baltic German origin. He was brought up bilingually in Russian and Estonian. His parents were devout and the two pilgrimages he made as a child to the Valaam Monastery on Lake Ladoga had a lasting impact on his spiritual development. The annexation by the Soviet Union of Estonia, 1940, was a disaster for the family. STALIN's policy was to deport all independent-minded Estonians to Siberia and elsewhere. The invasion of the German Wehrmacht, 1941, halted this process but it recommenced when the Red Army reoccupied the republic, 1944–5. He applied to the Leningrad Theological Seminary, 1947, and despite being considered too young, began to study and graduated, 1949, completing the four-year course in two years. He then returned to Tallinn and pastoral work. For the next forty years he experienced the radical changes in Estonia, the growing importance of the Russian language and traditions. Culturally he belonged to the Russian minority whereas most believers in Estonia were Lutheran. He is not on record as having opposed the atheist state. Under KHRUSHCHEV there was harsh repression of the Orthodox and other Churches and about 13,000 out of 20,000 Orthodox Churches throughout the Soviet Union were closed. It was during these trying times that the Soviet authorities gave permission for the Russian Orthodox Church to join the World Council of Churches, at its New Delhi meeting, 1961. Aleksi became Bishop of Tallinn in the same year. This meant that the KGB had discovered no antagonism to the Soviet state or any commitment to Estonian nationalism in him. Proposed by the Orthodox Church, he became a member of the central committee, World Council of Churches. He was elected Archbishop, 1964, and Metropolitan, 1968, and he became a member of the Holy Synod, the governing body of the Church. In 1986 he became Metropolitan of Leningrad and number two

in the Orthodox Church but retained responsibility for Estonia as the only bishop who spoke Estonian. In Geneva, he was elected president of the Conference of European Churches, World Council of Churches, 1972, and chair, 1987, a post he still holds. The GORBACHEV era brought profound changes and in 1988 Gorbachev, in the Kremlin, promised the clerics a new deal if they supported perestroika and glasnost, talking of a common cause between religion and Marxism–Leninism. This was a strange concept but Gorbachev had been baptised as a child and his mother was an Orthodox believer. Patriarch Pimen died in May 1990. For the first time since the October Revolution, the Church was able to choose its own head without the state dictating to it. Aleksi was quickly elected and he took the name of Pimen's predecessor, becoming Aleksi II. He has his detractors who are critical of his compliant attitude towards the communist and post-communist state. He is a man of compromise and consensus, not of bold and original initiatives. Boris YELTSIN, immediately after his election as President of Russia in June 1991, began elevating the Orthodox Church as a pillar of Russian culture and nationhood. The patriarch blessed the Russian President at his inauguration and, as tradition requires, reminded him to think of the difficulties which the people face. During the attempted coup of August 1991 the Patriarch stated that the church 'would not and could not bless illegal, violent or bloody acts'. He added, 'I beg all of you, dear people, to do your utmost to put out the flame of civil war. Stop!' This was a neat compromise as it appealed to everyone without taking sides. However, President Yeltsin looked to the Church for moral support during those critical days and it did play a leading role during the burial of the three young men killed during the attempted coup. One of them was given a Jewish burial. The animosity between the Orthodox and Roman

Catholic Churches surfaced at Lambeth Palace, November 1991, when Aleksi, as chair of the Conference of European Churches, attacked Catholics for their 'illegal' missionary activity in Siberia. The Roman Catholic Church has been experiencing a renaissance in many regions of Russia and Roman Catholic bishops have been appointed to new Russian sees.

Aliev, Haydar Ali Rza Ogly (*b.* 1923), the President of the Republic of Azerbaijan, who has made the transition from Communist to nationalist politician effortlessly. An Azeri, he was born in Nakhichevan, he joined the NKVD there, 1941, and did not serve in the Red Army. He became a member of the Communist Party, 1945, and graduated from the Azerbaijan State University, Baku, as an extra-mural student, 1957. He became deputy head of the KGB in Azerbaijan, 1964, and was head of the KGB there, 1967–9. An abrasive anti-corruption campaign led to him taking over as first secretary of the Communist Party of Azerbaijan, 1969, and he remained until 1982, the year that BREZHNEV died. When his patron, ANDROPOV, succeeded Brezhnev, he brought Aliev to Moscow as first deputy USSR Prime Minister and made him a full member of the Politburo of the Party (he had been elected a candidate member of the Politburo at the XXVth Party Congress, 1976). After five years, in 1987, GORBACHEV encouraged him to retire from the Central Committee, and Politburo, for 'health reasons'. He was clearly not a member of Gorbachev's inner circle and not well suited for radical politics at the centre. He re-entered politics when he vigorously condemned the actions of the Soviet Army in Baku in January 1990, which had resulted in several hundred fatalities. He then moved from Moscow to Baku and eventually to Nakhichevan in late 1990. He was elected a deputy of both the Supreme Soviet of Azerbaijan and the Nakhichevan autonomous republic during the autumn of 1990. In June 1993, after the democratically elected President ELCHIBEY had fled in the face of an armed revolt, Aliev returned to Baku and was elected speaker of the Milli Meijlis, the parliament, and hence acting President. Later he was elected President with an overwhelming majority.

Aliger, Margarita Iosefovna (née **Makarova**) (*b.* 1915), a very successful patriotic poet, who made her name under STALIN but declined in popularity afterwards. She was born in Odessa and graduated from the Moscow Chemical School and then from the Gorky Institute of Literature, 1937. She published during the 1930s and her collection, *God Rozhdeniya* (*Year of Birth*) glorified the first Five Year Plan. She achieved fame in 1942 with her poem 'Zoya' which lauded a young schoolgirl, aged seventeen, who volunteered to become a partisan, was captured by the Germans and hanged. She also joined the Communist Party the same year. She was married to Aleksandr FADEEV, the establishment author and general secretary of the USSR Union of Writers, 1946–55. After KHRUSHCHEV's Secret Speech at the XXth Party Congress, 1956, Fadeev feared that his murky activities since the 1930s (he had denounced many colleagues and they had been dispatched to the Gulag) would be investigated and as a consequence committed suicide. Aliger, in the first flush of the Khrushchevian thaw, contributed to the independent publication *Literaturnaya Moskva,* 1956, but retracted her views the following year.

Alikhanov, Abram Isaakovich (1904–70), brilliant Soviet nuclear physicist, the brother of Artemy Isaakovich ALIKHANYAN. He was born in Kars and graduated from the Leningrad Polytechnic Institute, 1931. He was employed at the Physical-Technical Institute, 1928, and later director of the power engineering laboratories of the institute. He collaborated with his brother in X-ray, cosmic ray and nuclear research. He was responsible for the construction of the first heavy-water reactor in the Soviet Union, 1949. He was director of the Institute of Theoretical and Experimental Physics, USSR Academy of Sciences. He was elected academician of the USSR Academy of Sciences, and the Armenian Academy of Sciences and was awarded the Stalin Prize in 1941, 1948 and 1953.

Alikhanyan, Artemy Isaakovich (1908–78), brilliant Soviet physicist who worked with his brother, Abram ALIKHANOV. An Armenian, he was born in Tbilisi, Georgia, and graduated from the Leningrad State University, 1931. He collaborated with his brother in nuclear physics and cosmic ray research. He played a leading role in establishing a cosmic ray station on Mount Aragats, Armenia, 1945. He was director of the Erevan Institute of Physics, Armenian Academy of Sciences, 1943–78. He was an academician of the Armenia Academy of Sciences and was awarded the Stalin Prize, 1941, and the Lenin Prize, 1970.

Alksnis, Viktor Imantovich (b. 1950), he became notorious during the GOR-BACHEV era for his attacks on glasnost which he regarded as a licence to attack the Communist Party, the Soviet Union, and everything which had been achieved by the October Revolution. He was born in Kemerovo oblast and his Latvian father, Imants Alksnis, was a dedicated Communist. Alksnis graduated from the Alksnis (named after his grandfather Ekabs) Higher Aeronautical Technical College, Riga, Latvia, and became a radio electronics engineer in a unit in the Moscow military district, later in a unit in the Baltic military district. In 1988 he became senior engineer inspector of the combat training department of the Baltic district air force. He became well known, together with other military men such as

General Albert MAKASHOV, as an eloquent defender of pre-perestroika Party discipline. Mikhail Gorbachev was one of their particular targets. Although a Latvian he spoke as an assimilated Russian and urged Russians and others in the Baltic republics to organise and resist the rising tide of nationalism. Alksnis was passionately opposed to the break up of the Soviet Union and the granting of independence to the Baltic republics. He had many platforms from which to articulate his hard-line views: he was a USSR people's deputy, a member of the Soyuz parliamentary faction (composed of conservative Communists) and a member of the Latvian Supreme Soviet. He was also a delegate to Communist Party Congresses. He acquired the sobriquet the 'black colonel' (linked to his clandestine activities and his contacts with OMON, the special forces of the USSR Ministry of the Interior who wore black berets). He supported the Emergency Committee during the attempted coup in August 1991 and cut a fine figure, especially in the TV studio. So linked was he in the public mind with the conservatives, that an American TV journalist returning to Moscow from the US towards the end of the attempted coup, on seeing Alksnis dressed in his best uniform in the TV studio, took it for granted that the coup had succeeded. After the attempted coup he was a hunted man and resigned his commission but he was not attractive to the Russian nationalists or to Latvians.

Allilueva, Nadezhda Sergeevna (1902–32), STALIN'S wife who eventually committed suicide because she could not cope with the harsh political reality of the time. She was the daughter of Sergei Alliluev, a Bolshevik, and a Georgian mother. She met and eventually married Stalin at the age of seventeen as his second wife. She worked for the Party in Moscow but became a student at the Industrial Academy, Moscow, which aimed to train Communists for leading positions in the new industrialising Soviet Union. It was there that KHRUSHCHEV met her when he went up to the Academy in 1929. He was astonished to discover that the attractive, modest woman who travelled to lectures by tram was the wife of the General Secretary of the Party. She presumably talked about him to Stalin and Khrushchev became a visitor to their home in Moscow. She was the mother of Vasily Stalin and Svetlana ALLILUEVA. Nadezhda took an instant dislike to BERIA and protested strongly, as early as 1929, against inviting him so frequently to their home. However, it was all to no avail as Beria was of great use to Stalin politically. Nadezhda's intense aversion to Beria may have derived from her instinct that he was a bad influence on her husband. Her death came as a great shock to Stalin, who never remarried. Her suicide may have been brought on by Stalin's cruelty to her or her anguish at the human cost of collectivisation and industrialisation or a mixture of both. Stalin made a great show of sorrow at her funeral.

Allilueva, Svetlana Iosefovna (also Stalina) (*b.* 1926), the daughter of STALIN and his second wife, Nadezhda Sergeevna ALLILUEVA, Svetlana has led a peripatetic existence since her defection to the west in March 1967. She had a privileged upbringing in Moscow but she lost her mother to suicide in 1932. She was her father's favourite but she found it difficult to come to terms with the world she inhabited. Her second husband, Bradegh Singh, was an Indian communist and, surprisingly, the authorities permitted her to accompany his ashes back to his native India. Her defection caused a sensation inside and outside the Soviet Union and she vented her ire on the Soviet Union and its establishment in many television and newspaper interviews. She settled in Princeton, New Jersey, and produced three interesting books,

Twenty Letters to a Friend (1967), *Svetlana, the Story of Stalin's Daughter* (1967) and *Only One Year* (1969). She provided a vivid account of domestic life in the Stalin household and the Kremlin court. She vented her spleen on BERIA whom she accused of poisoning her father's mind. She could never forgive him for laughing when her father lay dying. She fell in love with Louis Fischer, a senior specialist on Soviet affairs, but he died in 1970 and she descended into despair. In 1970 she married William Peters, an American architect (died 1991). Their daughter, Olga, was born in 1971. The couple separated in 1972 and Svetlana moved to Cambridge, England, in 1982, to permit her daughter to attend a Quaker boarding school. In August 1984 she returned to the Soviet Union with Olga, who spoke no Russian, and predictably caused a sensation. Her Soviet citizenship was immediately restored. The authorities preferred her to live in Gori, Georgia, her father's birthplace, but her Georgian relatives found her difficult. She was always in conflict with the Soviet authorities and under GORBACHEV she was allowed to return to the US in November 1986. She also lived in England and struck up a warm friendship with Malcolm Muggeridge, the English journalist. This led to some memorable interviews. She declined to see academics whom she regarded as being only interested in her father, not in her.

Almarik, Andrei Alekseevich (1938–80), a very influential historian, writer and dissident who was at odds with Soviet society most of his life. He was born in Moscow and his father was an historian. He wrote plays and essays and they circulated in samizdat, 1953–65; he was expelled from Moscow State University, 1963. He was arrested and sent into Siberian exile, 1965, for parasitism (meaning that the authorities judged that he did not hold down a full-time job), for two and a half years, by a state which was uneasy at his historical probing into the Soviet past. His experiences formed the background for his *Involuntary Journey to Siberia, 1970.* His best-known work, *Will the Soviet Union Survive until 1984?* (a play on Orwell's famous satire of socialism, *1984*), was published in the west, 1969, and it led to his arrest, 1970. Almarik was sentenced to three years in the Gulag and a further three years' exile. At the time it was inconceivable that the Soviet Union could collapse – Almarik was only out by seven years – but the questions he raised were vigorously debated among dissidents in the 1970s. International protests led to his release, 1976, and he then emigrated and lived in Paris. He was killed in a car crash in Spain on his way to the Madrid International Conference on Human Rights, a major topic of which was the Soviet record on human rights.

Altmann, Natan Isaevich (1889–1970), a leading Soviet painter who emigrated and then returned to the USSR in 1935 to continue working. He was born in Vinnitsa and studied art at the Odessa art school, 1901–7. He lived and worked in Paris, 1910–11, then returned to Vinnitsa and then St Petersburg. He gained quite a reputation for his Cubist paintings, especially his portrait of Anna AKHMATOVA, 1914. He was an enthusiastic supporter of the October Revolution (most Jewish artists were because it promised a new dawn for them) and was very active in the reorganisation of Russian culture. The immediate post-revolutionary years were the most creative during the Soviet era, partly because LENIN had no fixed ideas about art, permitting artists to experiment providing they supported socialism. Altmann was a modernist, who besides painting produced sculptures and illustrations. He worked with MEYERHOLD and contributed to official art, such as the May Day celebrations, and so on. The coming to an end of NEP restricted innovatory art and he moved

back to Paris, 1929, but returned to Leningrad, 1935, and managed to survive the harsh STALIN times, being subjected from time to time to severe criticism as his past work did not fit the canon of socialist realism. He lived in the second capital until his death.

Ambartsumov, Evgeny Arshakovich (*b.* 1929), a prominent politician and journalist who acquired a reputation in the west of being an astute political analyst. He was born in Moscow, the son of an Armenian engineer and Russian mother. He graduated from the Moscow State Institute of International Affairs, USSR Ministry of Foreign Affairs, 1951, and successfully presented his candidate dissertation in history (PhD). He was for many years head of department, Institute of Economics of the World Socialist System, USSR Academy of Sciences. He lived for some years in Prague when working for the *World Marxist Review* and this appears to have deepened his criticisms of the Soviet system. As a Communist, he advocated reform under BREZHNEV and in 1984 *Kommunist,* the Party's theoretical journal, attacked his views. A very widely read academic, he published widely and among his books was one on LENIN and the origins of socialism in Russia, 1978, and *NEP, A Modern View,* 1988, at a time when NEP was proving of great interest to those around GORBACHEV. He wrote for many of the pro-reform journals during glasnost and was a political commentator on *Moskovskie Novosti.* He was elected to the RSFSR Congress of People's Deputies in March 1990 and during the election campaign signed the platform of the Democratic Russia 90 electoral bloc. He was elected at the Ist Congress to the Council of the Republic, RSFSR Supreme Soviet, and then as chair of the Supreme Soviet committee on foreign affairs and foreign economic relations. In foreign policy he was critical of Foreign Minister Andrei KOZYREV'S pro-western orientation, preferring general emphasis on Asia (the Eurasian view).

Ambartsumyan, Viktor Amazaspovich (*b.* 1908), an outstanding Soviet astronomer and astrophysicist, who enjoyed an international reputation. An Armenian, he was born in Tbilisi, Georgia, graduated from Leningrad State University, 1928, and continued teaching there until 1944. He then moved to Erevan University, Armenia, and was the founder and director of the Byurakan Observatory, 1946. He was elected a corresponding member of the USSR Academy of Sciences, and eventually became president of the Armenian Academy of Sciences. His international reputation led to election as vice-president of the International Union of Astronomers, 1948–55. He was its president, 1961–4. He published many important articles on astronomy and astrophysics, and among his many awards was the Stalin Prize, 1950. He was appointed editor-in-chief of *Astrofizika,* 1965.

Andreev, Andrei Andreevich (1895–1971), a successful Stalinist politician who occupied several influential posts. A Russian, he was born near Smolensk. During the First World War he worked in an arms plant in Petrograd and was an active Bolshevik, playing an important role in the metalworkers' union. After the October Revolution he was prominent in trade union affairs as secretary of the All-Union Central Council of Trades Union, 1920–2. Hence he played his part in subjugating trade unions to the Bolshevik Party. He then became leader of the Railwayworkers' Trade Union, 1922–7. He was a secretary of the Central Committee of the Party, 1924–5. Andreev was USSR People's Commissar for Transport, 1931–5. He was a candidate member of the Politburo, 1926–30, and was then made chair of the Party's Central

Control Commission (supervising members). In 1932 he was elected a full member of the Politburo and remained as such until the XIXth Party Congress, 1952. He was chair of the USSR Supreme Soviet, 1938–45, and USSR People's Commissar for Agriculture, 1943–6.

Andreeva, Mariya Fedorovna (1868–1953), a prominent actress who was also much admired as a lover. She was born in St Petersburg and took to the stage in 1894. She joined the Bolshevik Party, 1904, and during the 1905 revolution her name appeared on the masthead as the publisher of the pro-Bolshevik newspaper, *Novaya Zhizn.* She married a prominent official, Zhelyabuzhsky, but soon left him to live with Maksim GORKY. The couple went to the US, 1906, and their liaison caused a scandal there. She was acquainted with LENIN and eventually returned to Russia, 1913. After the October Revolution she was prominent in various official cultural organisations. When Gorky moved abroad in late 1921 (the official reason was for health reasons) she accompanied him and returned to STALIN's Russia with him, 1931. She was reputed to be the lover of some NKVD officials.

Andreeva, Nina Aleksandrovna (*b.* 1938), she became notorious overnight in March 1988 after the publication of an article savaging perestroika and glasnost. She was born into a Russian family in Leningrad and her father was killed at the front during the Great Fatherland War. She joined the Communist Party, 1966, and became a lecturer in chemistry, Leningrad Technology Institute, in 1973. Her article, 'I cannot forego my principles', appeared in *Sovetskaya Rossiya,* and contained anti-Semitic overtones. She had submitted the original letter some time before but it was reworked (it contained information to which an ordinary Party member would not have had access) and published when Mikhail GORBACHEV was out of the country. Many observers regarded Egor LIGACHEV as her patron but he always denied any connection with the publication. A blistering reply was published only after Gorbachev's return. In May 1989 she was elected chair of the political executive committee of the society Unity: For Leninism and Communist Ideals. She was active in the founding of the All-Union Communist Party of the Bolsheviks. At the founding Congress in November 1991 she was elected General Secretary of the Central Committee, which consisted of fifteen comrades, with the Party claiming 35,000 members. She was hostile towards the Russian government's domestic and foreign policies and greatly admires Fidel Castro.

Andropov, Yury Vladimirovich (1914–84), a transitional figure between the conservatism of BREZHNEV and the radicalism of GORBACHEV. He was born near Stavropol, the son of a railway worker. He began work in 1930 as a telegraph worker, film projectionist and seaman on the Volga. He gained entry to the Rybinsk technical school for water transport, 1932, and soon after graduating became a full-time Komsomol official, 1936. He headed the Komsomol in Yaroslavl and, in 1940, moved to Petrozavodsk, Karelia, to take over the Young Communist League there. The incumbent first Party secretary was Otto KUUSINEN, a Finnish Communist and Comintern official whose task was to win over Finland for STALIN. Kuusinen proved one of several valuable patrons for Andropov. Andropov, always a voracious reader, was also a part-time student at the University of Petrozavodsk and the Higher Party School. He became a member of the Communist Party, 1939. He appears to have become involved with the security forces at this time and during the war he was involved with supervising the partisans in Karelia. He was elected

second secretary, Petrozavodsk city Party committee, 1944, and second secretary, Central Committee, Communist Party of Karelia, 1947–51. Andropov moved into the diplomatic service (communist-controlled countries were the responsibility of the Communist Party) in 1953 and was Soviet ambassador to Hungary 1954–7. As such he was the senior communist official in Hungary and played a ruthless role in suppressing the Hungarian Revolution, 1956. He permitted or conspired with the authorities to arrest Imre Nagy, the Prime Minister, after he had been guaranteed safe passage on leaving the Yugoslav embassy, where he had sought asylum. Nagy was executed two years later. János Kádár, Andropov's protégé, was installed as Party leader, in due course becoming a reform-minded Hungarian leader. KHRUSHCHEV had been impressed by Andropov's handling of the difficult Hungarian dilemma and he made him head of a new department of the Party Central Committee, the department for relations with communist and workers' parties of socialist countries, 1957. This body was the successor to the Cominform which had been abolished as a result of Khrushchev's desire to improve relations with Yugoslavia's Tito. The Cominform had drummed Tito out of the Soviet camp in 1948. Andropov was now in charge of Moscow's relations with ruling communist parties and aspiring parties world-wide. His Party promotion came in due course: he was elected a member of the Central Committee, 1961, and a secretary of the Central Committee, 1962–7. Andropov was astute enough to attract advisers who provided him with some unorthodox views. Those who worked with Andropov included Fedor BURLATSKY and Georgy ARBATOV. Many observers were surprised when, in 1967, Andropov left the Party apparatus to take over the KGB. This move may have been initiated by Mikhail SUSLOV, guardian of the Party's ideological orthodoxy, who was more conservative than Andropov, as a device to prevent Andropov making a serious challenge if and when Brezhnev departed the scene. There was general agreement that the head of the KGB could not become Party leader. It is significant that when Suslov died in 1982, Andropov immediately gave up his KGB job and returned to the Central Committee secretariat. To compensate for his departure from the Secretariat in 1967, Andropov was made a candidate member of the Politburo and became a full member in 1973. Andropov transformed the KGB into a formidable agency for the surveillance of Soviet citizens and the suppression of dissent and opposition by imprisonment, depriving activists of their jobs and thereby making them liable to prosecution for parasitism, incarceration in psychiatric hospitals, voluntary and involuntary emigration. Andropov was astute enough to move Academician Andrei SAKHAROV to Gorky (Nizhny Novgorod), a closed city (he did not risk imprisoning him as this would have led to a boycott of the Soviet Union by leading western scientists). The abuses of psychiatry for political ends in the Soviet Union led to a campaign to remove the USSR from the world psychiatric body. Moscow resigned rather than face the ignominy of expulsion. Andropov also stressed discipline but found it difficult to cope with the rising tide of corruption in the Soviet Union, especially since a major source of it was the Brezhnev family and court. The KGB committed terrorist acts abroad under Andropov (the murder of the Bulgarian Markov in London and the attempted assassination of Pope John Paul II). Andropov made a distinction between those whom he judged to be 'within system' reformers and those whom he regarded as 'system destroyers'. He encouraged many of the former but repressed the latter. Brezhnev's choice as his successor was Konstantin CHERNENKO but Andropov took over as Party leader. His health was

already failing and his last contact with foreigners was in August 1983 but his press officer kept on insisting that he was suffering only from a cold. Some cold! – he was on a dialysis machine. There were some terrible jokes at his expense. 'Contact Comrade Andropov, he is the most switched on man in Moscow!' 'Comrade Andropov can light up any discussion!' He initiated various reforms, aimed mainly at improving the existing system and instilling more discipline, including an anti-alcohol campaign. His foreign policy moves did not bear fruit. On Germany, he mistakenly believed that the deployment of Pershing and Cruise missiles could be halted by the anti-nuclear lobby in Germany. Another embarrassment was the shooting down of Korean Airlines 007 en route to Seoul with the loss of 269 lives, in September 1983. Marshal OGARKOV's performance at the news conference sent shivers down many spines and heightened tension at a time when Andropov was mortally ill. Andropov did promote such reform-minded politicians as Nikolai RYZHKOV and Egor LIGACHEV whom he brought to Moscow and placed in the Central Committee secretariat. He also divined Mikhail Gorbachev as a talented politician, becoming one of his patrons, and would have liked Gorbachev to take over from him, but the conservative Chernenko got the top post instead. Andropov was respected in the Soviet Union as a strong leader, intelligent, not personally corrupt and a man of considerable culture. Abroad he had few friends or admirers. Zhores Medvedev: *Andropov*, Oxford, 1983; Jonathan Steele and E. Abraham, *Andropov in Power*, Oxford, 1983.

Anokhin, Petr Kuzmich (1898–1974), a brilliant Russian physiologist with a world reputation who was born in Tsaritsyn (Volgograd) and graduated from the Leningrad Medical Institute, 1926. He collaborated with such famous scientists as Bekhterev and PAVLOV during the 1920s. He was director of the Institute of Physiology of the USSR Academy of Medical Sciences, 1946–50. He was particularly interested in the brain and cybernetics and published many important scientific papers.

Antonov, General Aleksei Innokentevich (1896–1962), one of the top generals of the Red Army during the Great Fatherland War (1941–5), Antonov went on to become Chief of the General Staff of the Red Army and Chief of Staff of the Warsaw Pact forces. He was born in Grodno and his father was an officer. He fought in the First World War and joined the Red Army in 1919 as a staff officer. He graduated from the Frunze Military Academy in 1931 and the Academy of the General Staff in 1937. He was one of those officers who emerged into the limelight after STALIN'S slaughter of the top military in 1937–8. He became Chief of Staff on the South and North Caucasian and Transcaucasian Fronts in rapid succession after the German invasion of June 1941. VASILEVSKY picked him as his representative in Moscow but he did not get on with Stalin and he was posted to the Voronezh Front. His ability led to his appointment as deputy Chief of Staff and Chief of the Operations Department. He participated in the planning of the Kursk, Belorussian and Berlin offensives. At the conferences of Moscow, Yalta and Potsdam, 1944–5, he was the chief Soviet military representative. He became Soviet Chief of Staff in February 1945 but, like many other high-ranking officers, was demoted after the war. He was appointed Chief of Staff of the Warsaw Pact forces in 1955. He is buried in Red Square.

Antonov, Oleg Konstantinovich (1906–84), one of the most brilliant aircraft designers, after whom many aircraft were named. A Russian, he was born in Troitskoe, Moscow guberniya, and graduated from the Leningrad Polytechnic Institute, 1930. He worked in design bureaux (these bureaux competed with one another for state contracts), in a factory producing gliders and in the government, 1930–62. In 1938 he joined the A. Yakovlev Aviation design bureau, became deputy chief designer, 1943, and chief designer, 1946. The Antonov (Ant)-10, Ant-22 and Ant-24 aircraft carry his name. Other aircraft were named after YAKOVLEV (Yak). He became a member of the Communist Party, 1945, and a doctor of technical sciences (DSc), 1960. He moved to the USSR Ministry of Aviation in the late 1940s as senior designer and remained until 1962. He published many books and articles on powered aircraft and gliders.

Antonov-Ovseenko, Anton Vladimirovich (*b.* 1920), the son of the Old Bolshevik V. A. ANTONOV-OVSEENKO, who disappeared during the purges. His mother then committed suicide. Antonov-Ovseenko was arrested for the first time in 1937 but was almost immediately released. He was rearrested in 1941 and spent the war years in prison camps in Turkmenistan and elsewhere. He was released after the war and permitted to live in Moscow but was again held in 1948 and sent to the Vorkuta and Pechora camps in the frozen north of the country. He was released in the wake of KHRUSHCHEV's Secret Speech at the XXth Party Congress, 1956, and rehabilitated, 1957. In 1967 he joined Old Bolsheviks who had survived STALIN's camps to protest against the possible rehabilitation of Stalin under BREZHNEV. He was continually under KGB surveillance and harassed, arrested and released from time to time. He published interesting historical material on his father's life and the 1930s and his output increased under glasnost. Anton Antonov-Ovseenko: *Portrait of the Tyrant*, New York, 1983.

Antonov-Ovseenko, Vladimir Aleksandrovich (1883–1939), one of the many Old Bolsheviks (Party members before 1917), he was born in Chernigov, Ukraine, and intended to follow his father as an officer but was expelled from the military engineering school at Nikolaevsk for refusing to take the oath of allegiance. In 1902 he moved to St Petersburg, was attracted by the Social Democrats (RSDRP), took up his military training again and in 1904 was jailed for ten days for possessing revolutionary literature. Posted to an infantry corps in Warsaw (then part of Russia) he set up a RSDRP military committee which in the 1905 revolution gave him scope for his revolutionary activities. In and out of prison, he led a charmed existence, avoided the death penalty and floated in and out of Moscow. In 1908 he organised workers' co-operatives and became an editor of a Social Democrat newspaper but decided in 1910 to quit Moscow for good, mainly to stay out of prison. He lived and worked in Paris from 1910 to the February Revolution of 1917, mainly as an editor. He soon joined the Bolsheviks where he put his journalistic and military expertise to good use. He was one of the organisers of the seizure of the Winter Palace and the arrest of the provisional government on 25 October 1917. He was appointed one of the three Commissars for Military and Naval Affairs, and commander-in-chief of the Petrograd military district. He was a successful commander during the Civil War and fought in many theatres. He sided with TROTSKY during his brushes with STALIN. He led the suppression of the peasant revolt in Tambov in 1921. In late 1922 he was made head of the Political Administration of the Red Army (responsible for propaganda) but the rise of Stalin and his men brought his military responsibilities to an end. When Trotsky resigned as War Commissar in 1925 Antonov-Ovseenko was posted to Czechoslovakia, then Lithuania and then Poland, 1925–30, as Soviet ambassador. He came over to Stalin in 1928. During the Spanish Civil War he was Consul General in Barcelona, 1936–7. He returned to the Soviet Union, was arrested in 1938, and became a victim of the purges in 1939. He was rehabilitated under KHRUSHCHEV.

Arakishvili, Dmitry Ignatevich (né Arakchiev) (1873–1953), one of the founding fathers of modern Georgian music who made many contributions to ethnomusicology. He was born in Vladikavkaz (now North Ossetia, Russia) and graduated from the School of Music and Drama, Moscow Philharmonic Society, 1901. He studied composition under Aleksandr Ilinsky and Aleksandr Grechaninov, and conducting under V. Kes. In addition he graduated from the Moscow Archaeological Institute, 1917. He was one of the founders of the Moscow People's Conservatory and offered free musical classes in Arbatsky Square, 1906. He was editor-in-chief of *Muzika i Zhizn* (*Music and Life*), 1908–12. One of his major interests was Georgian folk music and he moved to Georgia in 1918 and founded a conservatory which was merged with the Tbilisi Conservatory, 1923. He taught and composed, and was director of the Conservatory, 1926–9. He composed one of the first Georgian national operas, *The Story of Shota Rustaveli*, which was premiered in Tbilisi, 1919, and is still popular. He was elected a member of the Georgian Academy of Sciences, 1950.

Ararktsyan, Babken (b. 1944), one of the founders of the Armenian national movement in the wake of the events in Nagorno-Karabakh. He graduated in mathematics from Moscow State University, 1968. He participated in demonstrations supporting the transfer of Nagorno-Karabakh from Azerbaijan to Armenia, 1988. He was arrested in Moscow but released, May 1989. He, Levon Ter Petrosyan and others were the leading lights in the revival of the Armenian national movement and in May 1990 the movement won the Supreme Soviet elections in Armenia. Ararktsyan was elected a deputy and then deputy speaker of parliament. When Levon Ter Petrosyan was elected President of Armenia, Ararktsyan succeeded him as speaker of parliament, December 1991.

Arbatov, Georgy Arkadevich (*b.* 1923), one of the most influential academics and journalists in the Soviet Union, and the leading specialist on the US, especially in the GORBACHEV era. He is of mixed Russian and Jewish background and was born in Kherson, Ukraine. He served in the Red Army during the Great Fatherland War, joined the Communist Party, 1943, and graduated from the Institute of International Relations, Moscow, 1949. His subsequent career was in journalism and in institutes concerned with advising on policy making. He was editor of *Voprosy Filosofii* (*Questions of Philosophy*), *Novoe Vremya* (*New Times*), and *Kommunist* (the Party's theoretical journal), 1949–60. Then he moved to Prague to be a columnist on *Problemy Mira i Sotsializma* (*World Marxist Review*) and in 1962 he returned to Moscow to become a section head at the Institute of World Economy and International Relations (IMEMO), USSR Academy of Sciences. In 1964 he transferred to the apparatus of the Party Central Committee to become an adviser on foreign policy to Yury ANDROPOV who at that time was in charge of the Central Committee department for relations with communist and workers' parties of socialist countries. In 1967 he became the founding director of the Institute for the Study of the USA (renamed the Institute for the Study of the USA and Canada, 1974). As such he became one of the most influential voices on policy towards the United States and trained a generation of specialists on North America. Lacking the natural charm of a

Gorbachev, Arbatov articulated the official Soviet line on foreign policy on his visits to the US and was respected but not loved. He was elected a candidate member of the Party Central Committee, 1976, and a full member, 1981. He also became an academician of the USSR Academy of Sciences. His institute blossomed under Gorbachev and was a major centre of the New Political Thinking but it gradually lost its commanding position on policy towards the US. Gorbachev's gifts in foreign policy presentation lessened his reliance on any one adviser and Arbatov's glory days were almost over. Arbatov was elected to the USSR Congress of People's Deputies, 1989. He continued to advise President YELTSIN after 1991.

Aristov, Averky Borisovich (1903–73), a Party official who became a diplomat towards the end of his career. He joined the Communist Party in 1921 and became a Party official in Siberia and Urals oblasts, 1943–52. He was elected a full member of the Central Committee at the XIXth Party Congress, 1952. He was also chosen as a Central Committee secretary and a member of the Politburo at the Congress but lost these positions immediately after STALIN's death. However, he was again a secretary of the Party Central Committee, 1955–60, and a member of the Politburo, 1957–61. Then he became USSR Ambassador to Poland (ambassadors in socialist countries were almost always Party officials) and was ambassador to Austria, 1971–3. He left the Central Committee in 1971.

Arkhipov, Ivan Vasilevich (*b.* 1907), a Soviet official who was a specialist on China. He joined the Communist Party in 1928, and graduated from the Moscow Machine Tools Institute. He worked in various metallurgical enterprises until 1938 when he switched to being a full-time Party official as first secretary of the Krivoi Rog city Party committee,

Ukraine. He was transferred to Moscow in 1939 and worked in the Central Committee Secretariat, concerned with heavy industry. He became deputy people's Commissar for Non-Ferrous Metallurgy, 1943, until 1957. Arkhipov was chief Soviet adviser to the Chinese during their first Five Year Plan during the 1950s. On his return to Moscow he became deputy chair of the state committee on foreign economic relations, USSR Council of Ministers, 1958–9. He was first deputy chair of the USSR Council of Ministers, 1959–74, then deputy chair until 1974–1980, when he again became first deputy chair. Arkhipov was a member of the Party Central Committee, 1976–89. Under GORBACHEV he visited China again, becoming the most senior Soviet government official to visit Beijing since the early 1970s, and signed a Soviet–Chinese trade agreement covering the years 1986–90.

Armand, Inessa Theodorovna (née Steffen) (1874–1920), born in Paris on 26 April 1874 but soon orphaned, she was brought up by an aunt who was a governess with the Armand family at Pushkino. She married one of the sons and had four children; later she married one of her first husband's brothers and had another son. She was involved in running a school for peasant children and in 1899 joined the Moscow Society for the Improvement of Women, which saw her develop her concern for feminist issues. She wanted to run Sunday schools for poor women and publish a newspaper but the authorities opposed this. She joined the RSDRP in 1903 and worked for the Party in Moscow and Pushkino. She took part in the 1905 revolution, was arrested for the third time in 1907 and exiled to the north of Arkhangelsk for two years but escaped. She made her way to Paris, via a year at the University of Brussels, met LENIN and remained the love of his life until her death. She reciprocated: 'I love you greatly. Even now I could cope with-

out the kisses; just to see you and talk with you would be a great joy – and this could bring pain to no one.' (Recent research has failed to discover whether the relationship was merely platonic.) So understanding was Nadezhda Konstantinovna, Lenin's wife, that she offered to move out to allow Inessa to move in. Inessa devoted herself to the Bolshevik cause, translated Lenin's writings into French, acted as liaison with the French Socialist Party and helped finance the Party school established by Lenin at Longjumeau in 1911. In July 1912, at Lenin's bidding, she returned to St Petersburg to help reanimate the Party's committee there. She was arrested in September, sentenced to six months in prison, and then left Russia in August 1913. She moved to Switzerland in 1914 and organised various conferences against the war. She attended the international socialist conferences at Zimmerwald and Kienthal. The famous resolution calling for an end to the war without 'annexations and contributions' (reparations) was adopted at Zimmerwald and endorsed by many future leaders of the provisional government. She supported Lenin's call for the defeat of imperial Russia but it did not carry the day. She was one of the nineteen revolutionaries who returned to Petrograd in April 1917 on the sealed train (so called because the carriage doors were sealed). She did not play an important role during the October Revolution but then supported the (anti-Lenin) Left Communists against the Brest-Litovsk Treaty. She was elected to various soviets, including the All-Russian Central Executive Committee (VTsIK) and was chairwoman of Moscow region sovnarkhoz (council of the national economy). She became the first director of Zhenotdel (women's section of the Central Committee of the Party) and fought for female equality in the Party and in the economy. She organised the first Conference of International Women Communists in Moscow in 1920. It met at the same time as the Second Congress of the Comintern. She contracted cholera while on holiday in the Caucasus and died. During her burial outside the Kremlin wall, Lenin was emotionally overcome. Famous as the lover of Lenin outside Russia, Inessa's work for women's equality quickly faded away at home. Ralph Carter Elwood: *Inessa Armand: Revolutionary and Feminist,* Cambridge, 1992; Dmitry Volkogonov, *Lenin: Life and Legacy,* London, 1994.

Arseny (Zhadanovsky), Bishop of Serpukhov (1874–1935), a leading Russian Orthodox bishop who was martyred for his faith. He was born in Kharkov and graduated from the Moscow Theological Academy, 1903. He was elected Bishop of Serpukhov, 1914, and opposed the Bolshevik regime's efforts to impose its authority on the Church. He was not as outspoken as some other clerics but was nevertheless arrested, 1929, imprisoned and shot, 30 June 1935 in Medgora labour camp.

Arutyunyan, Aleksandr Grigorevich (*b.* 1920), a prominent Armenian composer and soloist who was born in Erevan and graduated from the Erevan Conservatory, 1941. He later studied at the House of Armenian Culture, Moscow, and became director of the Armenian Philharmonic Orchestra, 1954. He joined the Communist Party in 1952. Arutyunyan taught composition at the Erevan Conservatory from 1964, becoming a professor, 1971. His music is closely associated with Armenian folk melodies and he often performed as a soloist.

Arutyunyan, Suren Gurgenovich (*b.* 1939), the last but one first Party secretary in Armenia, Arutyunyan was engulfed in a nationalist tide. An Armenian, he was a Komsomol official in Armenia and then in Moscow, later moving into the Party Secretariat in Moscow, 1970–86. He then returned to Erevan to become first

deputy chair of the Armenian Council of Ministers. In May 1988 he was chosen by GORBACHEV to take over the Communist Party of Armenia after the tumultuous events involving Nagorno-Karabakh had begun. Some Armenians believed falsely that Gorbachev was willing to transfer the region from Azerbaijan to Armenia and Arutyunyan's task was to dampen the fires of Armenian nationalism. Nagorno-Karabakh was too emotive an issue and eventually Arutyunyan resigned in April 1990.

Ashkenazy, Vladimir (*b.* 1937), a pianist with a world-wide reputation who is also known as a conductor. He was born in Gorky (Nizhny Novgorod) and attended the Central Music School, Moscow, making his debut in 1954. He was awarded second prize in the Chopin Competition, Warsaw, 1955. His teacher at the Moscow Conservatory was Lev OBORIN. He secured first place and the gold medal in the Queen Elizabeth International Competition, Brussels, 1956. Ashkenazy toured the United States and Canada, 1957. In the Tchaikovsky Competition in Moscow, 1962, he was awarded joint first prize (with John Ogden). After making his début in London, he announced that he, his Icelandic wife and child, had decided to stay in the west but they soon returned to the Soviet Union, before leaving again in 1968. Ashkenazy moved to Iceland and was appointed conductor of the Iceland Symphony Orchestra, 1969. Other orchestras he has conducted include the Royal Liverpool Philharmonic Orchestra and the New Philharmonic Orchestra. He moved to Lucerne, Switzerland, and became well known for his recordings of Mozart. In 1981 he became the principal guest conductor of the Philharmonia Orchestra, London, and in 1983 he took up the baton to conduct the Cleveland Orchestra. He toured the Soviet Union, 1990, and was very warmly received. He has conceded that he cooperated with the KGB as a student.

Astafev, Mikhail Georgevich (*b.* 1946), a leading democrat during the latter stages of perestroika, he became leader of the Party of Constitutional Democrats (Kadets). He was born into a Russian family in Moscow and never joined the Communist Party. He graduated in physics from Moscow State University and then worked in the Institute of Physical Chemistry, USSR Academy of Sciences. In February 1989, during the election campaign to the USSR Congress of People's Deputies, he joined the Moscow popular front and became one of the leaders of its non-socialist democratic faction. In August 1989 he was elected deputy chair of the council of the Moscow popular front and in January 1990 he was one of the founders of the electoral bloc, Democratic Russia 90. He was elected to the RSFSR Congress of People's Deputies, March 1990. During the autumn of 1989 he had joined the Union of Constitutional Democrats and in May 1990 he was present at the founding congresses of the Party of Constitutional Democrats, headed by Viktor Zolotarev, and the Democratic Party of Russia, led by Nikolai TRAVKIN. During the summer of 1990 he took part in various attempts to unite the various liberal parties but without success. In August 1990 he joined the Small Constitutional Democratic Party of Popular-Freedom and was elected chair of their central committee. During the summer of 1990 he was elected to the organisational committee of the Democratic Russia (DemRossiya) movement and in December 1990 became a member of its co-ordinating committee. He left Dem-Rossiya in the autumn of 1991 over policy issues and this underlined the weakness of the democrats, their inability to settle their differences and unite.

Astafev, Viktor Petrovich (*b.* 1924), one of the leading *derevenshchiki* (village prose) writers who laud the virtues of the Russian peasant and rural values. A Russian, he was born near Krasnoyarsk, Siberia, and grew up in an orphanage. He fought in the Great Fatherland War in the Red Army. He graduated from the higher literary courses, Institute of Literature, Moscow. He began publishing in the 1950s and emerged in the 1960s as a leading exponent of village prose, weaving in dialect and folk tales. Common to the school are the depredations caused by the advance of modern technology and urban culture. He is no admirer of urban culture and in the *Grustny Dektektiv* (*Sad Detective*), 1986, he portrays urban life with all its soullessness, violence, nihilism, loneliness and drunkenness. He was elected to the USSR Congress of People's Deputies, 1989, and a member of the Soviet of Nationalities' commission on culture, language and historical heritage.

Avksentev, Nikolai Dmitrievich (1878–1943), a powerful orator and one of the few politicians of the Party of Social Revolutionaries (SRs) who could move an audience. He was born in Penza into a lawyer's family and was expelled from Moscow University in 1899 for leading a political strike. He then moved to Germany to study and formed a group which later established the SR Party in Russia. He returned to Russia in 1905 and became a member of the St Petersburg Soviet of Workers' Deputies (TROTSKY was also a member) until he was arrested and exiled. He was elected to the Central Committee of the SR Party in 1907 and edited its newspaper in Paris. He strongly opposed the use of terror for political ends. He became an active supporter of Fedor KERENSKY in the latter's activities in the Fourth Duma (1912–17) and this paved the way for their active collaboration in 1917. During the First World War Avksentev was a patriot and supported the war effort. After returning to Russia after the February Revolution he became an influential member of the Petrograd Soviet, a member of its executive committee and chair of the All-Russian Soviet of Peasants' Deputies. He became Minister of the Interior in the second coalition government (25 July–27 August 1917). As chair of the Pre-Parliament he attempted to wean the Petrograd garrison away from supporting the Bolshevik seizure of power – a hopeless task. He actively opposed the Reds after the October Revolution and organised resistance in the Volga region and Siberia. He was head of the Ufa Directorate before it was taken over and abolished by supporters of Admiral KOLCHAK in November 1918. He then moved to Paris and was co-editor of an émigré journal. An active anti-Bolshevik, he moved to the United States but died in New York shortly after his arrival.

Axelrod, Pavel Borisovich (1850–1928), born in Chernigov into a Jewish family, Axelrod began as a populist (narodnik) and later became one of the founders of Russian Marxism. While at Kiev University he organised the first socialist circle and participated in the 'going to the people' movement in 1875. In exile in Switzerland, he came under the spell of Georgy PLEKHANOV and together with Plekhanov, Lev DEICH and Vera Zasulich founded the Liberation of Labour Group, the precursor of the RSDRP. A fluent writer, he published many pamphlets during the 1890s, developing Plekhanov's views on social democracy, the party of the proletariat, during the 'first' Russian revolution which would usher in the bourgeois stage of Russian development. He was a co-founder and editor of *Iskra,* the RSDRP newspaper. Axelrod supported MARTOV in his dispute with LENIN at the Second Congress of the Party in 1903. When the Party split into Bolsheviks and Mensheviks he sided with the latter who preferred an open party rather than Lenin's insistence on a professional revolutionary party. He feuded with Lenin and argued in favour of a workers' congress in 1905–7, the liquidation of the underground groups and the evolution of a parliamentary social democratic party and trade unionism in the years before 1914. He was a Menshevik representative at the international peace conferences at Zimmerwald, Kienthal and Stockholm (1917). He tried in vain to promote the unity of the various strands of Menshevism and after his return to Russia in May 1917, as a member of the Menshevik Organisational Committee, he carried on with his appeals but few were listening. He was clearly not the decisive politician needed in the maelstrom of 1917. He was elected to the executive committee of the Petrograd Soviet. A strong opponent of the October Revolution which he viewed as a 'crime', he moved abroad and attempted to mobilise support for socialist intervention against the Bolsheviks. A leading Menshevik, he continued to his dying day to oppose the 'autocratic' tendencies of Bolshevism and preached the message of a humane, democratic socialism, or in modern parlance, socialism with a human face. Abraham Ascher: *Pavel Axelrod and the Development of Menshevism,* Cambridge, Mass., 1972.

B

Babel, Isaak Emmanuilovich (1894–1940), a Jewish writer who identified completely with the revolution. He was born in Odessa and spoke Yiddish until he was sixteen years old. He graduated from the Nikolaev Commercial School, Ukraine, 1915, and began writing. His life changed in 1916 when he met Maksim GORKY who became his hero. His first work was published by Gorky. The latter advised him to experience life by living among the people and he thereafter led a peripatetic existence. He enlisted in the Romanian Army, joined the Cheka, flirted with the Whites but then linked up with Semen BUDENNY's first Red Cavalry Army during the Russian–Polish War. Later he was a journalist in St Petersburg and Tbilisi, Georgia. His experiences in the Red Army were the basis for short stories which first appeared in MAYAKOVSKY's *Lef* (*Left Front*) and later in his novel *Konnaya Armiya* (*Red Cavalry*), 1926. Budenny took exception to the realistic portrayal of the Russian Cossack soldiers. Babel learnt many foreign languages and was widely read. He wrote striking stories about Jewish life in Odessa and also about Jewish criminals there, such as *Odesskie Rasskazy* (*Odessa Tales*), 1931. His writings were very popular in the 1920s and 1930s and he is regarded as a masterly short-story writer. He was arrested in May 1939 and accused of spying for France. He was shot on 27 January 1940. He was posthumously rehabilitated after the XXth Party Congress and his works were reissued in the Soviet Union in 1957.

Baburin Sergei Nikolaevich (*b.* 1959), a Russian politician who gradually moved to the right and is one of the leaders of the national patriotic movement. He was born in Semipalatinsk, Kazakhstan, and graduated from the faculty of law, Omsk State University, specialising in the history of the state and law, 1981. While a student at the university he wrote a letter to BREZHNEV pointing out the need to rehabilitate BUKHARIN, ZINOVIEV and Sokolnikov. After graduating, he served in the Red Army in Afghanistan, 1981–3, and was with the front-line troops for a year as a member of the main political department. He studied for his candidate dissertation in law (LLM) at Leningrad State University, 1983–6, and successfully presented his dissertation on the political and legal theories of George Forster. He returned to Omsk State University and in 1988 became head of the faculty of law there. In 1988 he wrote a letter to *Sovetskaya Rossiya* condemning the letter by Nina ANDREEVA and condemned the campaign against the playwright Mikhail Shatrov. He was elected to the RSFSR Congress of People's Deputies in 1990 and also to the RSFSR Supreme Soviet. He was chair of the sub-committee on legislation, RSFSR Supreme Soviet. He stood against Ruslan KHASBULATOV for the post of speaker of the RSFSR Supreme Soviet on October 1991 but was defeated. He was elected leader of the Rossiya faction in parliment and became chair of the board of the Russian People's Union. In October 1992 he was elected co-chair of the Front for National Salvation. He was a member of the CPSU from 1981 to 1991. He became a vigorous critic of President YELTSIN in the RSFSR Congress of People's Deputies and developed a reputation as a rising politician. He was elected to the first Russian Duma in December 1993 and to the second Russian Duma in December 1995 and became a deputy speaker in the latter. He is married with three sons and is one of the best dressed and groomed politicians in Russia. Some would call him a dandy.

Bagirov, Mir Dzhafar Abassovich (1895–1956), an Azeri and a close associate of Lavrenty BERIA who fell with him. Bagirov became active in revolutionary affairs in Azerbaijan in 1915, joined the Bolshevik Party in Baku, 1917, and participated in the Civil War as a political officer in the Red Army. He joined the Cheka and distinguished himself by his brutality against civilians in Azerbaijan. In 1920 he began forging a close friendship with Lavrenty Beria which was to last until Beria fell in 1953. Both had successful Bolshevik careers under STALIN, a feat which required ruthlessness and great political cunning, but they never turned against one another, except after Beria's arrest when Bagirov 'grassed' on Beria in a vain attempt to save his own skin. It may have been due to his close ties with Beria but Bagirov became deputy chair of the Azerbaijani Cheka in 1921, becoming chair in due course. He then became first secretary of the Communist Party of Azerbaijan, 1933–53. Beria was the master of Transcaucasia during the 1930s and Bagirov was his faithful number two. A curious episode involving Bagirov was the sudden illness of Sergo ORDZHONIKIDZE in November 1934, shortly before Sergei KIROV was murdered in Leningrad. Ordzhonikidze had travelled to Baku with Beria and they all dined at Bagirov's home and afterwards Ordzhonikidze began to suffer internal bleeding. The doctors could find no explanation and it is possible that a substance was added to Ordzhonikidze's food. The latter was a close ally of Kirov and was ordered by Stalin to stay put and follow the advice of the doctors. Stalin clearly did not want Ordzhonikidze accompanying him to Leningrad to investigate Kirov's murder. Bagirov was the only prominent Azerbaijani Party official in 1938 to escape being purged and presumably this was due to his protector, Beria. The latter initiated his own personality cult, being careful of course to give precedence to Stalin. Bagirov followed suit and then copied Beria when the latter published a book about the revolutionary struggle in the region. Bagirov read the book aloud in Baku in December 1939, as a contribution to Stalin's sixtieth birthday celebrations. Here Beria and Bagirov parted company. Stalin called Beria to Moscow but Bagirov remained in Baku. In 1950 Stalin instructed the USSR Minister of State Control, Lev Mekhlis, to send a commission of inquiry to Azerbaijan to investigate allegations that Bagirov was running the state as his personal fiefdom. Bagirov turned to Beria for support and they managed to involve some of the commission members in a scandal which brought the investigation to an end. In March 1953, in the first distribution of power after Stalin's death, Bagirov became a candidate member of the Party Politburo. He also gave up his Party post and switched to chair of the Council of Ministers of Azerbaijan. After Beria was arrested in June 1953 Bagirov was left without his protector. In July 1953 he was dismissed from the Central Committee of the Communist Party of Azerbaijan, being accused of a 'shameful style of leadership' and 'crude, dictatorial administration'. He was sent off to an oil-drilling enterprise outside Baku as deputy head. He was probably arrested a year later and his open trial in Baku did not take place until April 1956. He was accused of treason, terrorism and participation in a counter-revolutionary organisation, found guilty and executed, together with three others, in May 1956. KHRUSHCHEV used the trial against Bagirov for political gain. As part of the verdict against Bagirov, the judge read out a long list of the victims of repression during the Stalin era. The Party leader was preparing the ground for accusations against those close to Stalin. At the XXIInd Party Congress, 1961, he accused MALENKOV, MOLOTOV and KAGANOVICH (at a time when they were politically spent forces), of having protected Bagirov. Amy Knight: *Beria, Stalin's First Lieutenant,* Princeton, NJ, 1993.

Bagramyan, Marshal Ivan Khristoforovich (1897–1982), one of the successful Soviet commanders during the Great Fatherland War (1941–5), he was born in Azerbaijan into an Armenian worker's family. He joined the Red Army in 1920 and participated in the Civil War. He graduated from the Frunze Military Academy in 1934 and from the Academy of the General Staff in 1938. His promotion was hastened by STALIN's purge of the top military in 1937–8. He was Chief of Staff to TIMOSHENKO but was given command of an army in July 1942. He fought on the Western Front and at Kursk, in July 1943. In November 1943 he was made General and became commander of the First Baltic Front. During the Belorussian campaign his armies killed 20,000 Germans and captured 10,000. His armies then moved into Latvia and in January 1945 were ordered to take Königsberg. Stubborn German resistance held up the Red Army until April 1945 and the blame for the delay was placed at Bagramyan's door. After the war he became commander of the Baltic military district. He was appointed deputy Minister of Defence in 1954, later chief inspector of the Ministry of Defence and commander of the Rear Army. He was elected a member of the Central Committee at the XXIInd Party Congress in 1961.

Baibakov, Nikolai Konstantinovich (b. 1911), the chief planner in the Soviet Union until GORBACHEV arrived on the scene and revealed the perilous state of the Soviet economy. He was born in Sabunchi, Azerbaijan, and graduated from the Azerbaijan Petroleum Institute, 1932. He was head of an oil company, 1932–7. He then worked in Kuibyshev oblast and headed the Eastern Oil Drilling Extraction Board, 1937–40. He joined the Communist Party, 1939, was a member of the Party Central Committee, 1952–61, and 1966–89. Baibakov was deputy USSR People's Commissar, 1944–8 (deputy Minister from 1946), then USSR Minister for the Petroleum Industry, 1948–55. In 1955 he was appointed as head of Gosplan, responsible for the planning of the Soviet economy. It could be argued that the oil industry was not the ideal preparation for such a task since technology and processing were relatively straightforward. He remained until 1957 when he became first deputy chair, RSFSR Council of Ministers. When councils of the national economy (sovnarkhozy) were instituted by KHRUSHCHEV in an attempt to decentralise economic decision making and increase efficiency, Baibakov moved to the north Caucasus to head sovnarkhozy there, 1958–63. He then returned to Moscow to co-ordinate the chemical and petroleum industries, 1963–4, then to chair the state committee on the petroleum industry, 1964–5. He again returned to head Gosplan, and had the rank of a deputy chair of the USSR Council of Ministers, until November 1985, when he was sacked. Baibakov must bear some of the blame for the decline of the Soviet economy during the late 1970s and early 1980s. However, his expertise was in economic management, not in politics, but he should have done more to highlight the growing weaknesses of the Soviet economy. Of course, various cosmetic reforms were initiated but to little avail. Baibakov could argue that with KOSYGIN as Prime Minister, his orders came from him.

Bakatin, Vadim Viktorovich (*b.* 1937), after the attempted coup of August 1991, he was appointed head of the USSR KGB with a brief to break it up. A Russian, he was born in Kiselevsk, Siberia, and graduated from the Novosibirsk Engineering and Construction Institute, 1960, and from the Academy of Social Sciences of the Party Central Committee, 1985. He worked as a construction engineer in Kemerovo, 1960–73. He then moved into full-time Party work when he was elected second secretary, Kemerovo city Party committee (gorkom). In 1975 he became head of department, and in 1977 secretary of the Kemerovo oblast Party committee (obkom). In 1983 he moved to the Party Central Committee Secretariat in Moscow as an inspector. In 1985 he became first secretary of Kirov (now Vyatka) obkom and in 1987 he was appointed first secretary of Kemerovo obkom. He was a member of the Party Central Committee, 1986–91. In 1988 GORBACHEV brought him back to Moscow as USSR Minister of Internal Affairs, a very sensitive post at a time of rising ethnic tension. In March 1990, at the IIIrd USSR Congress of People's Deputies, he was nominated for the post of USSR President by the Soyuz group of parliamentary deputies, but withdrew and left the field to Mikhail Gorbachev. Also in March 1990 he was appointed to the USSR Presidential Council. In June 1990 he was nominated for the post of first secretary of the Russian Communist Party, but again withdrew. In December 1990 he was dismissed as USSR Minister of Internal Affairs in line with the swing to the right by President Gorbachev. He was not regarded by conservatives as willing to use sufficient force to maintain the continued dominance of the Communist Party. He was succeeded by Boris PUGO, one of the leaders of the attempted coup of August 1991. In February 1991 Bakatin was made a member of the USSR security council. He stood against Boris YELTSIN in the RSFSR presidential election in June 1991 and suffered the humiliation of coming bottom of the poll of six candidates, with 3.4 per cent of the votes. On 23 August 1991 he was made chair of the USSR KGB, renamed the Inter-republican Security Service, following the arrest of the KGB chief, Vladimir KRYUCHKOV, and the suicide of Boris Pugo. Bakatin's task was to liquidate the KGB and divide it up into three independent branches: law and order, intelligence, and counter-intelligence. He was interviewed on television from his office in the Lubyanka and debated with Vladimir BUKOVSKY, a well-known former dissident who had direct experience of KGB prisons and camps. Bakatin stated that he was not in favour of granting public access to KGB files but that the greater part of them should be transferred to national archives, something which has yet to happen.

Bakh, Aleksei Nikolaevich (1857–1946), a prominent populist in the late 1870s and early 1880s who returned to Russia after the October Revolution and became a renowned chemist. He emigrated to France in 1885, then moved to Geneva, 1894, and built up an international reputation in medical and agricultural chemistry for his research on catalysis and photosynthesis. A Bolshevik sympathiser, he moved back to Russia, 1917, and founded the Central Chemical Laboratory (the Karpov Physical Chemistry Institute from 1922), and remained there until his death. He undertook important research during the 1920s and advanced the use of chemicals in the food industry. He joined the Communist Party, 1927, and was made a member of the Soviet Central Executive Committee (VTsIK), 1927. He was elected to the USSR Academy of Sciences, 1929, and president of the All-Union Chemistry Society, 1932. He founded the Biochemistry Institute,

USSR Academy of Sciences, 1935, and also edited a biochemistry journal. As such he can be regarded as the father of Soviet biochemistry. He was elected a people's deputy, USSR Supreme Soviet, 1937, and became director of the department of chemical sciences, USSR Academy of Sciences, 1939. He was awarded a state prize, 1941. Bakh was elected a member of the Party Central Committee, 1945.

Bakhtin, Mikhail Mikhailovich (1895–1975), an influential writer on the theory of the novel and language. He was born in Orel and graduated from the University of Petrograd, 1918, and then formed discussion circles to debate neo-Kantian philosophy and other problems of existence. During the 1920s he published several books and articles on Freud, Marx, the philosophy of language, and Dostoevsky, under pseudonyms. He was arrested in 1929 and suspected of belonging to a religious group but was released and moved to northern Kazakhstan and Mordovia, where he joined the university in Saransk, and remained there until 1972, when he moved to Moscow. A major interest was the theory of the novel and he published books on, among others, Rabelais. A common theme running through his work was the collective nature of human existence and the need for human interaction.

Baklanov, Oleg Dmitrievich (*b.* 1932), a member of the Emergency Committee which staged the attempted coup of August 1991. A Ukrainian, he was born in Kharkov, Ukraine, and began work in 1950 in a Kharkov enterprise as a fitter, rising to be deputy chief engineer. He graduated from the All-Union Extramural Institute of Energy, 1958. In 1969 he successfully presented his candidate dissertation in technical sciences (PhD). From 1963 to 1976 he was chief engineer, director of an enterprise and general director of a production association. Then he moved into the USSR Ministry of General Machine Building, the ministry responsible for the production of nuclear weapons, as deputy Minister, then in 1981 he became first deputy Minister, and in 1983 Minister. He joined the Communist Party in 1953, and was elected a member of the Central Committee, 1986. In 1988 he was appointed a secretary of the Party Central Committee, responsible for the military–industrial complex. In March 1989 he was nominated by the Communist Party as one of its deputies to the USSR Congress of People's Deputies, and elected. Among his many awards are the Order of Lenin, two Orders of the Red Banner of Labour, and Hero of Socialist Labour. He received the Lenin Prize in 1982. It was not surprising that Baklanov became involved in the abortive coup as he was the most senior Party official concerned with the military economy. He was arrested, imprisoned but later released and amnestied.

Balanchine, George (né **Balanchivadze, Georgy Melitonovich**) (1904–83), one of the most famous and influential choreographers in the history of ballet. He was born in St Petersburg and his father was the Georgian composer Meliton BAL-ANCHIVADZE. He studied at the Imperial School of Ballet at the Mariinsky (later Kirov) Theatrical School, Petrograd, 1914–21. Besides dancing he also studied music at the Petrograd Conservatory, 1921–4. He went on tour with the Soviet State Dancers in 1924 but the following year decided to stay, and he worked as a choreographer with Diaghilev's Ballets Russes until the latter's death in 1929. He staged ten ballets for Diaghilev and during this time he developed his neo-classical style. He was invited by Lincoln Kirstein to organise the School of American Ballet and the American Ballet company, 1933, and thus began his famous sojourn in the United States. Besides classical ballet he choreographed for Broadway shows and the cinema, becoming a hit with the *Slaughter on Tenth Avenue* ballet in *On Your Toes* (1936). Balanchine became the co-founder and artistic director of the New York City Ballet when it was established in 1948. He fashioned over 150 ballets for the company, most notably *The Nutcracker* and *Don Quixote*. So influential has he been that almost every ballet company in the world has staged one of his ballet interpretations. Balanchine toured the Soviet Union with the New York City Ballet, 1962 and 1972, where he was received with great enthusiasm.

Balanchivadze, Andrei Melitonovich (*b.* 1906), a foremost Georgian composer who was born in St Petersburg, the son of Meliton BALANCHIVADZE, the composer, and brother of George BALANCHINE, the famous choreographer. He graduated from the Tbilisi Conservatory, 1927, and the Leningrad Conservatory, 1931. He then returned to Georgia where he became the musical director of several theatres, 1931–4. He joined the Tbilisi Conservatory, 1935, becoming a professor in 1942, and was artistic director of the Georgian State Symphony Orchestra, 1941–8. He became an influential force in musical politics as chair, 1953, and first secretary, 1955–61 and 1968–72, of the Union of Composers of the Georgian Soviet Socialist Republic. He composed the first Georgian ballet, the *Heart of the Mountains,* 1936, and the first Soviet Georgian symphony of distinction.

Balanchivadze, Meliton Antonovich (1862–1937), a noted Georgian composer whose two sons, George BALANCHINE and Andrei BALANCHIVADZE had famous careers. He was trained at the Tbilisi Seminary and began an operatic career in 1880. He had a special interest in Georgian folk songs, collecting them and training folk choirs. He entered the St

Petersburg Conservatory in 1889. One of his teachers was Rimsky-Korsakov. He toured Russia giving concerts of Georgian folk music, 1895–1917. Balanchivadze was one of the founders of Georgian classical music and he composed the first Georgian opera, *Daredzhan Tsbieri,* 1897.

Baltin, Admiral Eduard Dmitrievich (*b.* 1936), a leading Soviet naval officer who often came into conflict with democrats and environmentalists under GORBACHEV. A Russian, he was born in Smolensk. He graduated from the Kirov Caspian Higher Naval Technical School, mine torpedo department, 1958, the Naval Academy, 1975, and the Military Academy of the General Staff, 1980. He specialised in naval operational tactics. He was a member of the Communist Party, 1959–91. He began his career on surface ships in the Black Sea but soon volunteered for service in the submarine formation of the Black Sea Fleet. He graduated to command of a submarine. He was one of the initial Soviet commanders to engage in long sea voyages and among the first to take Soviet ships into the Mediterranean. He was appointed senior assistant commander of a nuclear submarine, Northern Fleet, 1969, and assumed command of a nuclear submarine in 1971. In 1983 he became commander of a nuclear submarine flotilla in the Pacific Fleet, and in 1987, first deputy commander-in-chief, Pacific Fleet. He found it difficult to come to terms with the new political thinking of the Gorbachev era and was often in conflict with civilian groups. In 1990 the media publicised the tussle between him and democratic organisations and the greens over his siting of a base to make use of obsolete nuclear submarines near a town in Maritime krai. In 1990 he moved to Moscow as head of the naval department of operational art, Military Academy of the General Staff. Politically he expressed conservative views and advocated a strong Soviet state. After the collapse of the attempted coup Baltin, like most conformist Soviet generals and admirals, renounced communist ideology and the retention of the Soviet Union, and voiced his support for the new Russian authorities. Among his many awards is an Order of Lenin. He was appointed commander-in-chief of the Russian Black Sea Fleet, January 1993, and was dismissed in January 1996 as a gesture by Russia to improve relations with Ukraine.

Bandera, Stepan Andreevich (1909–59), a noted Ukrainian nationalist who fought against both Poland and the USSR. He was born in west Ukraine which at the time was part of the Austro-Hungarian empire. In his teens he joined Ukrainian nationalist youth groups in Galicia against Polish rule. He was a student at Lvov (Poland) technical college and became the chair of the OUN (Organisation of Ukrainian Nationalists), 1933. He helped stage the assassination of the Polish Minister of the Interior in Warsaw, June 1934. He was sentenced to death but this was commuted to life imprisonment which ended when Poland collapsed in 1939. Immediately after the Germans attacked the Soviet Union, in June 1941, some Bandera supporters proclaimed Ukrainian independence in Lvov. The Germans moved quickly against them and Bandera was transported to Berlin and later put in Sachenhausen concentration camp. Two of his brothers died in Auschwitz. In 1944 the Germans released Bandera and other Ukrainian nationalists to fight against the Red Army. While living in Munich under a pseudonym, he commanded the Ukrainian partisans fighting against Soviet occupation of west Ukraine. The Soviet side sustained considerable losses, especially before 1953, but armed troops still guarded railway tunnels against attack as late as 1957. He was assassinated by a poisoned bullet on the personal in-

structions of Aleksandr SHELEPIN, then head of the KGB. The agent who murdered him defected to West Germany, 1961, and provided details of the case.

Barannikov, Viktor Pavlovich (*b.* 1940), an important ally of President Boris YELTSIN during the attempted coup of August 1991. A Russian, he was born in the Maritime krai and began working in 1957 as a turner in Tatarstan. After national service he joined the police. He graduated from the Sverdlovsk (Ekaterinburg) department, Moscow Higher School USSR Ministry of Internal Affairs (MVD), 1969. He was a district police officer working in the criminal investigation department and serving in high-profile areas, such as Chelyabinsk-65, then a closed city engaged in nuclear research and development, Kalinin (Tver), 1973–83, and then in Moscow. In 1985 Barannikov was head of the main department to combat the theft of socialist property in the central apparatus of the USSR MVD. When Yeltsin was first Party secretary in Moscow he encouraged Barannikov to move against corruption and the mafia in the capital. After Yeltsin was dismissed as Moscow Party boss, in October 1987, Barannikov's career in the capital was in jeopardy and in 1988 he was posted to Azerbaijan as first deputy Minister of the Interior. It is unclear when Yeltsin and Barannikov struck up an acquaintance but it may go back to Yeltsin's days as Party boss in Sverdlovsk (Ekaterinburg). After Yeltsin had been appointed speaker of the Russian Supreme Soviet, in June 1991, he lost no time in recalling Barannikov from Azerbaijan and appointing him Russian Minister of Internal Affairs. Barannikov sided unequivocally with Yeltsin and his claims for Russian sovereignty. One claim was that Russian laws took precedence over Soviet laws. This led to conflict between Barannikov and the USSR MVD, to whom he was nominally subordinate. During the attempted coup of August

1991 Barannikov was one of the organisers of the defences of the White House and ensured the arrival of MVD units. He personally participated in the arrest of some of the members of the Emergency Committee. On 23 August 1991 he was appointed USSR Minister of Internal Affairs (succeeding Boris PUGO who had committed suicide) and the following month he was promoted colonel general. Barannikov became responsible for restructuring the MVD and he immediately ended all Party and political activities in the ministry. When the amalgamated Ministry of State Security and Internal Affairs was set up in October 1991, President Yeltsin appointed Barannikov the first minister. This revealed Yeltsin's complete trust in Barannikov. However, the unification of the ministries caused a public uproar since to many it was reminiscent of STALIN's People's Commissariat of Internal Affairs (NKVD). The Constitutional Court ruled against the new ministry and as a result it was split again into two ministries. Barannikov became Russian Minister of State Security. One of the tasks of the new ministry was to examine the distribution of flats and dachas among generals. As a result about twenty top officials in the Ministry of State Security were dismissed and lost their abodes.

Barchuk, Vasily Vasilevich (*b.* 1941), a financial bureaucrat who rose to become Russian Minister of Finance after the collapse of the Soviet Union. A Russian, he was born in Komsomolsk-on-Amur, Siberia, and from 1958 worked in the financial inspectorate there and was also an extra-mural student of the All-Union Institute of Finance and Economics, Moscow, graduating in 1966. He continued to work in the financial inspectorate and then he moved to the USSR Ministry of Finance, 1972. He graduated from the Academy of the National Economy of the USSR Council of Ministers, 1984, and he was appointed

deputy head, and then head of the budgetary administration of the USSR Ministry of Finance. In April 1991, Barchuk became deputy Russian Minister of Finance, and later first deputy Russian Minister of Economics and Finance, under Egor GAIDAR as minister. In December 1992 he was appointed Russian Minister of Finance.

Barmin, Aleksandr Grigorevich (1899–1987), one of the most important Soviet defectors during the 1930s. He gained promotion in the Red Army to colonel general, specialising in intelligence. He was first secretary of the Soviet legation in Athens in 1935 and this was a cover for his activities as a GRU (military intelligence) officer. He defected in Paris in 1937, denounced STALIN and called for protection for other Soviet diplomats. He escaped from France, 1940, and reached the United States where he enlisted as a private in the US Army. He married President Roosevelt's granddaughter, Edith. He worked as a journalist for Voice of America and the onset of the Cold War in 1947 increased his profile. In 1951 he denounced the head of the Russian section as a Soviet spy, assuming the post himself in 1953. Unlike many other top-level Soviet defectors Barmin eluded the assassin's bullet and died of natural causes in the United States.

Baryshnikov, Mikhail (*b.* 1948), one of the outstanding ballet dancers of his generation, he defected to the west in 1974 and enjoyed a glittering career. He was born in Riga, Latvia, and his father, a colonel in the Soviet Army, found it difficult to come to terms with his son's choice of career. His mother committed suicide when he was very young. He began ballet lessons in Riga and then transferred to the Leningrad Ballet School, 1964. He joined the Kirov Ballet in 1967 and quickly established himself as a highly talented soloist, dancing a wide repertoire. He defected while on tour with the Kirov in Canada and moved to the United States, joining the New York City Ballet under the famous George BALANCHINE who, however, was not in good health and near the end of his artistic career. He left in 1978 and returned to the American Ballet Theater, 1979, as artistic director, and as such staged many classic ballets. Besides the theatre he has performed in films and on television.

Basov, Nikolai Gennadevich (*b.* 1922), a leading world authority on lasers and a Nobel Prize laureate, he was born in Voronezh and graduated from Moscow Engineering and Physics Institute, 1950. He joined the Institute of Physics, USSR Academy of Sciences, 1950. He taught at the Moscow Engineering and Physics Institute and became a professor, 1963. His major field of research is lasers and he has made fundamental contributions to the subject, becoming a world authority. He was awarded the Nobel Prize for Physics, 1964. He became chair of the Znanie (Knowledge) Society, whose task was to disseminate scientific knowledge. He edited a book on quantum physics, *Kvantovaya Fizika,* and was awarded the A. Volta Gold Medal, 1977.

Bazarov, Vladimir Aleksandrovich (né Rudnev) (1874–1939), a leading Russian Marxist theorist and economist who contributed much to the revolution but fell victim to Stalinism. He was born in Tula into a doctor's family and studied at Moscow University. He was arrested in 1896 and was exiled to Tula and then Kaluga. In both places he encountered Aleksandr BOGDANOV and I. I. SKVORTSOV-STEPANOV, who became leading Marxist philosophers, and they exerted a powerful intellectual influence on him. After exile he moved to Berlin in 1901 and sought to bring the various social democratic groups together. He returned to Moscow almost immediately and was elected to the Moscow commit-

tee of the RSDRP but was arrested and exiled to Siberia. In 1904 he joined Bogdanov and LENIN in the Bolshevik faction of the RSDRP. He worked for the Bolsheviks in St Petersburg during the 1905 revolution. Lenin presented the Bolshevik approach to philosophy in *Materialism and Empiriocriticism* and the Bolshevik leader condemned Bogdanov's and Bazarov's views as un-Marxist. In 1917 he wrote for GORKY's newspaper *Novaya Zhizn* and after the October Revolution advocated a coalition socialist government. In 1922 he became one of the many non-Bolsheviks to join Gosplan, the state planning committee. He was arrested, along with many other non-Bolshevik specialists in 1930 and during the Menshevik Trial of March 1931 he was accused, together with Vladimir GROMAN, of heading a counter-revolutionary organisation within Gosplan since 1923. The logic behind this extraordinary accusation was that Bazarov was not in favour of the teleological approach to planning (fantastic growth rates) favoured by STALIN and his supporters. Bazarov was jailed and then exiled to Saratov. In 1935 he moved to Gagry, Georgia, to be with his son but after the latter's death he returned to Moscow and died of natural causes on 16 September 1939. Astonishingly he had cheated the Stalinist 'meat-grinder'. Naum Jasny, *Soviet Economists of the Twenties,* Cambridge, 1972; Alexander Erlich: *The Soviet Industrialization Debate,* Cambridge, MA, 1960.

Belov, Vasily Ivanovich (*b.* 1932), a leading representative of the *derevenshchiki* (village prose) writers. A Russian, he was born in Vologda oblast and graduated from the Gorky Institute of Literature, Moscow, 1964. He was secretary of the RSFSR Union of Writers.

Bely, Andrei (né Bugaev, Boris Nikolaevich) (1880–1934), one of the most influential figures in twentieth-century

Russian literature. He was born in Moscow and his father was a well-known mathematician. He followed him and graduated in mathematics from Moscow University, 1903. While a student he was already writing and publishing poetry and he became famous as a symbolist poet. He and Aleksandr BLOK were close friends and both drew inspiration from the philosopher, Vladimir Solovev. Bely ranged widely and covered the arts and the sciences, as well as a trace of mysticism which was common at the time. He was impressed by Rudolf Steiner and went to Switzerland to work with him but fell out with him. He returned to Russia, 1916, emigrated soon after the October Revolution, but returned, 1923. He then devoted himself mainly to prose and attempted to put a Marxist gloss on his writings. In the post-STALIN era his talents were again recognised and his influence grew.

Belyakov, Oleg Sergeevich (*b.* 1933), a leading Party official concerned with the defence industry under GORBACHEV, he graduated from a military academy and joined the Communist Party, 1955. He also worked in the Leningrad Party organisation at a time when Grigory ROMANOV was Party leader there. In 1972 Belyakov moved into the Secretariat of the Party Central Committee, Moscow, and from 1983–5 was one of the assistants of Romanov at a time when he was Central Committee secretary for the defence industry. Belyakov was an adviser on national security. In 1985 he became the head of the department of the defence industry of the Party Central Committee and remained there until August 1991. He was also a member of the Party Central Committee until August 1991. He was elected a deputy for the Mari autonomous republic to the USSR Congress of People's Deputies, 1989.

Belyakov, Rotislav Appololovich (*b.* 1919), a leading Soviet aircraft designer who graduated from the Ordzhonikidze Aviation Institute, Moscow, 1941. He then began working in a design bureau (the bureaux competed with one another for defence contracts), Institute of the Aviation Industry, USSR Ministry of Defence, beginning as an aeronautical engineer, later becoming deputy chief, and chief designer. He joined the Communist Party, 1944, and was awarded the Stalin Prize, 1952. In 1971 he moved to the Mikoyan Design Bureau as chief designer and became responsible for the development of MiGs and other aircraft. He was awarded the Lenin Prize, 1972, and became a doctor of technical sciences (DSc), 1973, a corresponding member of the USSR Academy of Sciences, 1974, and an academician, 1982.

Beregovoi, Georgy Timofeevich (*b.* 1921), one of the first Soviet cosmonauts, he was born in Poltava oblast and joined the Red Army, 1938. During the Great Fatherland War he was a pilot, becoming a test pilot in 1948. As such he was selected as a cosmonaut in 1964, and went into orbit in October 1968. In 1972 he became head of the Cosmonauts' Training Centre. He was promoted lieutenant general in 1977.

Beria, Lavrenty Pavlovich (1899–1953), a gangster in politics, Beria served STALIN well but lost out in the succession struggle. Like MOLOTOV he wore a pince-nez. He was born near Sukhumi, Georgia, into a Mingrelian family. He studied in Baku and became involved in social democrat activities. He joined the Bolsheviks in March 1917. He was active in Azerbaijan and Georgia after 1917 and joined the secret police in 1921. He had contacts with British forces at this time and this was used against him at his trial in 1953. He occupied senior posts in the NKVD in Azerbaijan and Georgia, 1921–31, and then became first secretary of the Party in Georgia. He supervised the brutal collectivisation of agriculture in

Transcaucasia. Stalin brought him to Moscow in 1934 for security work and he was elected a member of the Central Committee at the XVIIth Party Congress. He replaced EZHOV in 1938 as People's Commissar for Internal Affairs and replaced him as candidate member of the Politburo in 1939. In 1941 he was made deputy chair of Sovnarkom. When war broke out Beria became a member of the State Committee for Defence (GKO) and in 1944 he became its deputy chair. He was promoted Marshal of the Soviet Union in July 1945, the highest rank below that of Generalissimo, which Stalin had claimed for himself. There was no love lost between Beria and the military and a special target was Marshal ZHUKOV. Beria was fashioning a case against Zhukov in the summer of 1945 and kept the Soviet commander in Berlin in the dark about certain discoveries: for instance, that Hitler's body had been found and that autopsies were being carried out to establish identity and cause of death. Beria was elected a full member of the Politburo in 1946, and a member of the Presidium (formerly the Politburo) and Secretariat in 1952 at the XIXth Party Congress. He was also deputy chair of the USSR Council of Ministers. At the end of Stalin's life his position was under threat and he was pleased when Stalin died in March 1953, earning the undying hatred of Stalin's daughter, SVETLANA. Beria played a key role in developing the gulag (forced labour camps) system and the Sovietisation of eastern Europe after 1945. He was universally feared but was always obsequious to Stalin in company. He was highly intelligent, a master of intrigue and as deadly as a viper. He had a huge sexual appetite, having his agents pick girls off the streets if he fancied them. After Stalin's death, he fatally underestimated KHRUSHCHEV's abilities, writing him off as a moon-faced idiot. Khrushchev conspired with MALENKOV against him and had him arrested (by Zhukov and other officers: this

was sweet revenge for Zhukov), accusing him of attempting a coup (quite untrue) and smuggling him out of the Kremlin without his guards realising it. At his trial he was accused of, among other things, being a British agent and conspiring to undermine nationality relations in the Soviet Union. He had sought support from non-Russians by proposing that non-Russian areas should be run by natives. On Germany, he was willing to contemplate a united, neutral Germany, and he was accused of being willing to sacrifice East Germany to imperialism. He was a coward at his trial and begged on his knees for his life to be spared but provided Khrushchev with much ammunition to use against his political opponents later. Had Beria taken power he might have brought about the unification of Germany (arguably a better option for Moscow than a divided Germany and an accelerated arms race). He was one of the monsters around Stalin and history will judge him harshly. He was denied an opportunity to redeem himself after Stalin's death. Amy Knight, *Beria Stalin's First Lieutenant,* Princeton, NJ, 1993.

Beria, Nina Teimuazovna (1907–91), the loyal wife of Lavrenty BERIA, STALIN's blood-stained secret police chief. She was a scientist, born in Georgia and the niece of Noi Zhordania, Minister of Foreign Affairs in the Georgian Menshevik government (until the 1921 armed take-over by the Bolsheviks). She and Beria had one son, Sergo, who is a specialist in anti-aircraft defence technology. They were both arrested and imprisoned after her husband's fall. She refused to give testimony against Lavrenty Beria and the interrogators left her alone. However, they eventually laid charges against her. One was that she had used state transport to move some soil from the Black Earth region of Russia to Moscow to study at the Agricultural Academy. Another was that she had employed foreign labour. She had brought a Georgian tailor with her from Tbilisi to Moscow to make her clothes. She and Sergo were released after a year and exiled to Sverdlovsk (Ekaterinburg). Later they were informed they could live anywhere except Moscow. Sergo moved to Kiev while his wife remained in Moscow with the children. Nina returned to her native Mingrelia, Georgia, but was soon told by the authorities that she could not reside there. She then moved near Sergo in Kiev. She had tolerated her husband's many extra-marital affairs and surfaced during the GORBACHEV era, revealing that she still stood by her man and providing incisive views on MOLOTOV and other Soviet leaders. According to his wife, Beria had a practical mind and understood that it would be impossible for another Georgian to succeed Stalin. He therefore looked around for someone he could use and consequently approached MALENKOV. She died sad, bitter and very homesick for her native land. In her last interview, she lamented the roles played by Beria, Stalin and other political actors in the Soviet Union. 'They at least believed that they were fighting for some goal . . . And what came of it? Not one of them did their own nation and motherland any good and the second nation [the USSR] did not recognise their work. These men were left without a country.'

Berzarin, Nikolai Erastovich (1904–45), the first Soviet commander to lead his troops into Berlin in April 1945, he was made commandant of the city but was killed riding a motorcycle before he could have any impact. He was born into a working-class family in St Petersburg and joined the Red Army in 1918, participating in the Civil War. He commanded the 32nd Infantry Division during the battle against the Japanese at Lake Khassan, 1938. He became known as a Soviet front commander (5th Shock Army), on various fronts, for example, at Jassy and Berlin. His task in Berlin was to take control of the city and secure anything of value (in-

cluding archives) for Moscow before the British and US forces entered the German capital in July 1945. Marshal Georgy ZHUKOV took over from Berzarin.

Bessmertnykh, Aleksandr Aleksandrovich (*b.* 1933), a brilliant career diplomat who lacked the political judgement to support President GORBACHEV during the attempted coup of August 1991. A Russian, he was born in Altai krai and graduated from the Moscow State Institute of International Relations, USSR Ministry of Foreign Affairs (MID). He was seconded from MID to the UN secretariat, 1960–6, became the second, then the first secretary of the Secretariat, MID, 1966–70. Bessmertnykh was then posted to the Soviet embassy in Washington as first secretary, then minister counsellor, 1970–83. On his return to Moscow he became head of the United States department, MID, 1983–6. As a specialist on the United States he made rapid headway after Eduard SHEVARDNADZE had become USSR Minister of Foreign Affairs, in the summer of 1985. Bessmertnykh was appointed deputy USSR Minister of Foreign Affairs in 1986, and his main task was to implement the new political thinking of Gorbachev, especially as it affected the United States. He was first deputy USSR Minister of Foreign Affairs, 1988–90. He then returned to Washington as Soviet ambassador, 1990, and after the resignation of Shevardnadze in December 1990, Bessmertnykh was appointed his successor in January 1991. He prevaricated during the events of August 1991 and failed to signal his support of Gorbachev until it was certain he would return from Foros. He was immediately invited to retire. In March 1991 he was elected president of the foreign policy association. He was a member of the Communist Party, 1963–91, and a member of the Party Central Committee, 1990–1.

Biryukova, Aleksandra Pavlovna (*b.* 1929),

the most prominent woman politician during the GORBACHEV era, she became the first woman since Ekaterina FURTSEVA to be elected to the Politburo. A Russian, she was born in Voronezh oblast and graduated from the Moscow Textile Institute, 1952, and then worked in a textile factory in Moscow. She joined the Communist Party in 1956. She moved from direct production experience in the cotton industry in 1968 into trade union affairs when she was appointed secretary and Presidium member of the All-Union Central Council of Trade Unions, advancing to become deputy chair in 1985. She was elected a member of the Party Central Committee in 1976. She was plucked from domestic and international obscurity at the XXVIIth Party Congress, 1986, by Gorbachev, who was looking for women who could spearhead what became known as perestroika. She was the first woman to be elected to the Party Secretariat for over twenty years and became responsible for light industry and consumer goods production. She was also a deputy to the USSR Supreme Soviet and the RSFSR Supreme Soviet. The Herculean task of turning round one of the least efficient sectors of the Soviet economy was beyond her (and was beyond the skills of any politician). However, in October 1988 she was elected a candidate member of the Politburo, and shortly afterwards she was appointed deputy USSR Prime Minister and chair of its bureau of social development. Such was the decline of the Soviet economy that it was decided that the best way to improve the provision of consumer goods to the Soviet population was to import them from the west. She came to London to buy goods, paying due attention to the needs of Soviet women. She gave a revealing interview to a national newspaper in which she disclosed her own personal anguish at a family loss. She resigned from all her positions in September 1990 and was judged to have made little impact in her policy areas.

Biryuzov, Marshal Sergei Semenovich (1904–64), a leading military officer who rose to be Chief of the General Staff. He was born near Ryazan and joined the Red Army, 1922, graduating from the Frunze military academy in 1937. After commanding the 48th army on the Voronezh front, 1942, he became chief of staff of the 2nd Guards Army on the Stalingrad Front, 1942–3. He then became chief of staff of various armies during the liberation of Ukraine and Crimea from the Germans and Romanians, and then during the occupation of Bulgaria and Romania, 1943–4. Biryuzov was deputy head of the Allied Control Commission in Bulgaria for two periods between 1944 and 1947. In common with many high-ranking Red Army officers with excellent war records, STALIN transferred him away from Europe to assume command of the Far East military district, 1947–53. He and Marshal MALINOVSKY had to cope with the outbreak of the Korean War, 1950, and it appeared at one time that Soviet forces might intervene on North Korea's behalf. After the Korean War ended, Biryuzov was commander-in-chief of Soviet forces in Hungary, 1953–4. He became a specialist in anti-aircraft defence forces and was commander-in-chief of these forces, 1955–62. He was promoted Marshal. KHRUSHCHEV then chose him as commander-in-chief of the strategic rocket forces, 1962–3. He was then promoted Chief of the General Staff and first deputy USSR Minister of Defence, March 1963, but he was killed near Belgrade in an aircrash the following year and is buried in the Kremlin wall. His rapid promotion under Khrushchev points to the fact that he was a professional soldier who was willing to obey politicians. This type of officer was particularly attractive to Khrushchev after the latter's experiences with the ambitious Marshal ZHUKOV. Biryuzov was awarded many decorations, among which were five Orders of Lenin.

Bitov, Oleg Georgevich (*b.* 1932), he became notorious as a Soviet defector but he then returned to Moscow to write vitriolic copy about life in the west. He was a journalist and among the editors of *Literaturnaya Gazeta* before defecting at the Venice Film Festival, 1983. He asked for and was granted political asylum in Britain and made a name for himself in interviews and articles which were very critical of the Soviet Union. However, he only stayed about a year and then resurfaced in Moscow claiming that he had been kidnapped in Italy and tortured by British intelligence. He resumed his activities on *Literaturnaya Gazeta* and, predictably, penned articles which excoriated capitalism and the western way of life. The whole episode may have been planned by the KGB to discourage Soviet citizens from defecting but it had little effect as the flow of defectors continued, underlining the malaise of the Soviet system at the end of the BREZHNEV era.

Blake, George (né Behar, Georgy Ivanovich) (*b.* 1922), a colourful Soviet agent who did much harm to the efforts of British intelligence to counter communism. He can be put in the same category as Burgess, Maclean and Philby. Blake was born in Rotterdam; his father, an Egyptian Jew, was a naturalised British citizen, and his mother was Dutch. He linked up with the communist resistance in the Netherlands but managed to escape to Britain in 1943. He immediately changed his name to Blake and enlisted in the Royal Navy as an ordinary seaman, quickly being commissioned as an officer. He worked for naval intelligence in Hamburg, with a brief to move around the Soviet Zone of Occupation to recruit Soviet personnel. According to a KGB officer in the GORBACHEV era, Blake became of use to Moscow in 1947. He was brought back to London and sent to the University of Cambridge to learn Russian. He and other Britons were captured by the North Koreans at the beginning of the Korean War and when Blake returned to England in 1953 he was treated as a hero. Marriage followed to the daughter of a Foreign Office Russian linguist. In April 1955 he was posted to West Berlin and quickly informed the Soviets of the various tunnels which gave the west access to the Berlin telephone lines which served East Berlin. His next posting was Beirut but his luck ran out and his cover was blown. He was recalled to London, arrested, tried *in camera*, and sentenced to forty-two years' imprisonment. Again his ingenuity surfaced and with the collusion of an Irish prisoner he escaped from Wormwood Scrubs Prison, London, and made his way back to Moscow, via East Berlin. He was once more the conquering hero and he was provided with all the accoutrements of a successful KGB officer, including a Russian wife. There were rumours that he would be extradited to Britain after the collapse of the Soviet Union and he thought Wormwood Scrubs would be a more congenial environment than North Korea, probably the only country which would have welcomed him.

Blok, Aleksandr Aleksandrovich (1880–1921), a leading symbolist poet and dramatist and the tragic conscience of immediate post-revolutionary Russia. He was born in St Petersburg and graduated from the university there in philology, 1906. His milieu was that of the Russian intelligentsia: he was the son-in-law of Mandeleev, the world-famous chemist. His early poetry is suffused with the vision of a beautiful lady, reminiscent of Vladimir Solovev's philosophy. Like many members of the intelligentsia he saw the coming revolution as inevitable, something which would cleanse Russia from the dark forces, and therefore reacted positively to the October Revolution. In many works he explored the yawning gulf between the intelligentsia and the narod, the people, again a popular theme of the time. He was a shy, retiring person, whose outlook on life was in reality pessimistic. He was influenced by the radical thinker, Ivanov-Razumnik, the inspiration behind the scythian movement in Russia. Blok produced his poem 'The Twelve', 1918, which is the major literary celebration of the October Revolution and likens the twelve red guards to the apostles, including a vision of Christ. The poem was attacked from all sides. He also published *The Scythians* in 1918. He soon found the communist view of culture too restrictive and his early death was seen as symbolising the end of the blossoming of Russian culture.

Blokhin, Oleg Vladimirovich (*b.* 1952), one of the most talented Soviet footballers of his generation, he was a free-scoring striker who won the Golden Boot as Europe's highest-scoring player in 1975. A Ukrainian, he achieved fame with Dinamo Kiev, whom he joined in 1962 and was a member of the team when it achieved its greatest successes, between 1969 and 1987. He played 432 times for Dinamo and scored 211 goals in the Soviet championship, an astounding strike rate. He was a member of the Dinamo team which won the USSR championship in 1974, 1975, 1977, 1980, 1981, 1985 and 1986, and gained five winners' medals as a member of their USSR Cup team. He was top scorer in the Soviet league five times. A regular member of the Soviet national team he holds the record for most games played, 112, and number of goals scored, 42. He was a member of the Soviet team during the 1982 and 1986 World Cups. He holds a coaching diploma from the Kiev Institute of Physical Culture and he graduated in law from Kiev State University, 1983. When the Soviet authorities relaxed their ban on Soviet players playing abroad, permitting those at the end of their careers to move, Blokhin signed for Vorwärts Steier, Austria in 1987 and stayed until 1988. In 1989 he moved to Aris

Limassol, Cyprus, until 1990, and then was appointed trainer (manager) of Olympiacos Athens, Greece.

Blyukher, Marshal Vasily Konstantinovich (1890–1938), a leading Red Army commander in the Far East who fell victim to the bloodletting in the military in the late 1930s. He was born in Yaroslavl guberniya, worked as a metalworker and was soon involved in revolutionary activity. He was conscripted into the Imperial Army during the First World War and was wounded, 1915. After the October Revolution he participated in the Bolshevik take-over of Chelyabinsk, where he became head of the local soviet. He had an illustrious career during the Civil War, especially along the Volga and in the Urals, defeating Admiral KOLCHAK, and later General WRANGEL, in the south. He was then posted to the Far East Republic and became Minister of Military Affairs, 1921–2, until the Whites and Japanese had been expelled and the region finally became part of Soviet Russia. He became senior military adviser to the Chinese revolutionary forces, 1924–7. In 1929 he became commander of the Far Eastern Red Army and commanded Soviet forces in the conflict with the Chinese nationalist (Kuomintang) forces, 1929. He led the attempt by the Soviet Union to colonise militarily the Manchurian frontier by establishing the Kolkhoz Corps (this was reminiscent of the military colonies in Russia, founded by Arakhcheev, under Nicholas I in the 1830s). Blyukher was commander in the Soviet Far East during a very sensitive time, given the desire of Japan to penetrate into China and Siberia. His troops scored a notable victory over the Japanese at Lake Khasan, July 1938. (A further Soviet victory at Khalkin Gol led to the Japanese abandoning their push westwards into the USSR.) Blyukher's victory had been very skilful and his forces had out-thought and outfought the Japanese. However, at the pinnacle of his military glory, Blyukher was arrested along with several other members of the Far East military. Despite the fact that he had been a member of the military tribunal which had sentenced Marshal TUKHACHEVSKY and seven other top commanders to death for treason, Blyukher could not avoid the 'meat grinder'. He died from beatings he received but was rehabilitated under KHRUSHCHEV.

Blyumkin, Yakov Grigorevich (1898–1929), the left socialist revolutionary who assassinated Count von Mirbach, the German ambassador, in Moscow, on 6 July 1918, in protest against the terms of the Brest-Litovsk Treaty. The goal was to provoke German military intervention against Russia but Berlin desisted. The assassination served as a signal for the Left SR revolt against the Bolsheviks in Moscow, one aspect of which was the attempted assassination of LENIN by Fanya Kaplan in August 1918. During the revolt the left SRs captured DZERZHINSKY, the head of the Cheka, but only hurt his feelings. He was ruthless in organising the crushing of the revolt, with Latvian Chekists playing an important role. Like some other Left SRs, he was recruited by the Cheka, and was involved in Ukraine against German forces there (Ukraine was a German protectorate according to the Brest-Litovsk Treaty). Blyumkin worked in intelligence in the People's Commissariat for War, under Trotsky, and later in the Cheka and military intelligence (GRU). He was a GRU agent in Georgia, Mongolia and Palestine. He sympathised with TROTSKY and as GRU chief in Turkey when he met Trotsky in Istanbul he agreed to act as courier and delivered a letter from Trotsky to his followers in the Soviet Union. On his return, he was arrested, tried and executed for treason.

Bobrov, Vsevolod Mikhailovich (1922–79), an outstanding sportsman, who achieved the unique distinction of captaining the Soviet teams in football (1952) and ice hockey (1956) at the Olympic Games. A Russian, he was born in Tambov oblast and became an honoured master of sport in 1948. He graduated from the N. Zhukovsky Air Force Academy, 1956, and from the Military Institute of Physical Culture, 1956. He joined the Communist Party in 1952. He was a member of the Soviet ice hockey teams that won the world championship in 1954 and 1956, and were also European champions. He gained many USSR champions' medals between 1945 and 1956.

Bogdanov, Aleksandr Aleksandrovich (né Malinovsky) (1873–1928), one of the many Marxists who collaborated with LENIN but later fell out with him. He was one of the co-founders, with Lenin, of the Bolshevik faction of the RSDRP. Born in Sokolka, Grodno region, into a village schoolmaster's family, he graduated in medicine from the University of Kharkov in 1899. Like many Marxists he began his political career as a populist (narodnik). He was arrested and exiled in 1901. He sided with Lenin when the RSDRP split in 1903 and was a member of the Bolshevik Central Committee, 1905–7. He was the organiser of the Capri Party School (financed by Maksim GORKY) and similar courses at Bologna. However, Lenin came to perceive him as a philosophical rival and demolished him in his *Materialism and Empiriocriticism* in 1908. The following year he managed to have Bogdanov removed from the Party and Bogdanov and others established the Vpered (Forward) group; but Bogdanov left in 1911. He continued to write prolifically and devoted considerable attention to the problem of raising the cultural level of the workers. The Proletkult (proletarian culture) movement was a direct descendant of his ideas. He favoured democratic socialism and the convention of the Constituent Assembly and opposed Lenin's appeal of 'all power to the soviets' in 1917. He had little faith in the concept of a world socialist revolution. He opposed war communism (he was one of the first to use the term) as the subjugation of the economy to military ends. He favoured a democratic socialist state, dedicated much energy to the Proletkult until he was removed in 1921 and became a member of the Communist Academy in 1918. He was greatly interested in certain medical developments, especially in haematology and gerontology. He experimented on rejuvenating the body by blood transfusion: his last experiment was on himself but it proved fatal. Bogdanov was a polymath and a product of the extraordinarily creative intellectual climate in Russia in the first two decades of the twentieth century. Zenovia Socher: *Revolution and Culture: The Lenin–Bogdanov Controversy*, Ithaca, 1988.

Bogolyubov, Nikolai Nikolaevich (1900–92), a world-famous mathematician who made major contributions to various fields of the discipline. A Russian, he was born in Nizhny Novgorod and graduated from Kiev University where his teachers included Dmitry Grave, a specialist in algebra, and N. Krylov. He was on the teaching staff of the university, 1936–41 and 1945–9. He became a professor of mathematics at Moscow State University, 1950. He became an academician of the USSR Academy of Sciences, 1953. Among the fields into which he researched and made fundamental contributions were function theory, differential equations and the theory of stability.

Bogomolov, Oleg Timofeevich (*b*. 1927), a leading pro-reform economist during the GORBACHEV era, a Russian, he was born in Moscow and graduated from the Moscow Institute of Foreign Trade, 1949. He joined the USSR Ministry of Foreign Trade and then the Council for Mutual Economic Assistance (CMEA or Comecon), 1954–6. He joined the staff

of Gosplan and then the Secretariat of the Party Central Committee where he was one of the assistants recruited by ANDROPOV who was head of the department of relations with communist and workers' parties of socialist countries. In 1969 he was appointed director of the Institute of Economics of the World Socialist Systems, USSR Academy of Sciences, and as such was in a position to influence the economic research agenda and the advice offered to the Party leaders. He paid particular attention to the inefficiencies of the Soviet system and possible reforms to improve efficiency. This was a thankless task during the late BREZHNEV era but Bogomolov and other reform-minded economists were able to sow the seed which bore fruit under Gorbachev. Bogomolov advised against the Soviet invasion of Afghanistan, 1979. This was not surprising, given that at the time the Soviet economy was going into terminal decline. He came into his element under Gorbachev and advanced radical pro-market reforms. He was elected to the USSR Congress of People's Deputies in 1989. In 1990 he became director of the Institute for International Politics and Economic Research, USSR Academy of Sciences. He was also a member of the USSR Academy of Sciences and, when it was established, of the Russian Academy of Sciences. Bogomolov joined the YELTSIN economic management team in December 1991.

Boldin, Valery Ivanovich (*b*. 1935), one of the plotters during the attempted coup against GORBACHEV in August 1991, a Russian, he graduated from the Timiryazev Agricultural Academy, Moscow, 1961. He was an official in the apparatus of the Party Central Committee, 1961–5. Boldin joined *Pravda* and became head of its agricultural section, 1969. He was also a student at the Academy of Social Sciences of the Party Central Committee and graduated, 1969, having successfully presented his dissertation in economics (PhD (Econ)). In 1981 he moved into the Secretariat of the Party Central Committee, and began his association with Mikhail Gorbachev who was, at the time, Central Committee secretary for agriculture. Boldin was a personal assistant of Gorbachev, 1985–7, then became head of the general department of the Central Committee, a key appointment which involves close liaison with the General Secretary, including drafting the agenda for Politburo meetings and supplying the necessary background papers. Boldin was elected a candidate member of the Central Committee, 1986, and a full member, 1988. In March 1990 Boldin was appointed one of the members of Gorbachev's Presidential Council, and was the top official in the President's office. He was a leading member of the Emergency Committee which attempted to take power during the abortive coup of August 1991. Boldin was arrested after the coup collapsed but was released from prison in December 1991, for health reasons. One of the first actions of the Duma, elected in December 1993, was to declare an amnesty for all plotters involved in the events of August 1991 and October 1993. His memoirs are very entertaining and revealing as he casts a caustic eye over the Gorbachev era. Valery Boldin: *Ten Years that Shook the World: The Gorbachev Era as Witnessed by his Chief of Staff,* London, 1994.

Bonch-Bruevich, Vladimir Dmitrievich (1873–1955), a leading Bolshevik publisher and expert on Russian religious sects, he was born in Moscow on 11 July 1873 into a land surveyor's family. He was expelled from the Land Survey Institute and exiled in 1889. When he returned to Moscow in 1893 he joined Marxist circles and encountered LENIN. He moved to the University of Zürich to study and soon joined the Emancipation of Labour group. In 1899 he went with the Dukhobors to Canada. He sided with

the Bolsheviks in 1903 and continued his literature work. During the 1905 revolution he founded many newspapers and became director of the Bolsheviks' publishing house. He was involved with *Pravda* when it was set up in 1912 and was arrested several times (*Pravda* had many members on its editorial board as it was assumed that some of them were bound to be in jail). After February 1917 he was a member of the editorial board of *Izvestiya* (originally the newspaper of the Petrograd Soviet). After the July Days Lenin hid in Bonch-Bruevich's dacha in Finland. He participated in the October Revolution and was a member of the Military Revolutionary Committee. He was the first chair of the Petrograd Cheka. When the Council of People's Commissars (Sovnarkom) was set up, he became its secretary. He organised the transfer of the government from Petrograd to Moscow in February 1918 and Lenin called on him to carry out many special assignments. A great admirer of Lev Tolstoy, he edited his collected works between 1925 and 1939. His wife played a prominent role in developing health care and his brother was the first ex-Tsarist military commander to come over to the Reds. He was director of the Museum of the History of Religion and Atheism in Leningrad, 1945–55.

Bonner, Elena Georgievna (*b.* 1923), a famous Soviet dissident and the wife of Academician Andrei SAKHAROV, scientist, human rights activist and Nobel Prize laureate. She was the daughter of an Armenian Communist and her Jewish grandmother had been a revolutionary. She worked as a nurse during the Great Fatherland War, losing much of her sight in an accident. She qualified as a doctor and practised medicine, 1953–83. She was a member of the Communist Party, 1965–72. In 1970 her whole lifestyle changed when she became a human rights activist, and married Sakharov. The Helsinki Final Act, signed by Leonid

BREZHNEV in 1975, included obligations to respect human rights, and activists in the Soviet Union began to set up Helsinki monitoring groups. Bonner was a leading figure in the establishment of the Moscow group, 1976. In 1980 ANDROPOV decided that the best way to deal with Andrei Sakharov was to exile him to Gorky (Nizhny Novgorod), a closed city because of its defence plants, where he would be cut off from contact with other dissidents and the world's media. Bonner regularly visited her husband and brought back news of him. In 1984 she was sentenced to five years' exile but was released along with her husband in 1986, under GORBACHEV. *Alone Together,* London, 1986.

Borodin, Mikhail Markovich (né **Gruzenberg**) (1884–1951), an active Bolshevik, Borodin propagated communism in China but later fell foul of STALIN. He joined the RSDRP, siding with the Bolsheviks, 1903, and lived in Bern, Switzerland, 1904–5. He moved to Riga, then part of the Russian empire, and was active as a social democrat. He then emigrated to Britain, moving on to the United States, where he was a member of the Socialist Party of America, 1907–18. While there he helped the Cheka to screen Russians returning to their homeland from the United States. Borodin became the first Soviet consul in Mexico, 1919, and then worked in the Comintern, 1919–23. While in Scotland in 1922 he was arrested in Glasgow and spent six months in jail before being expelled. Sun Yat Sen, the Kuomintang leader, invited him to become an adviser to the nationalist Chinese organisation and while there, 1923–7, he worked for the communist cause. He was appointed editor of the English language, *Moscow News,* 1932, and was later deputy director of the TASS (telegraphic agency of the Soviet Union) news agency. Borodin was a very high-profile journalist dealing with the outside world and his many duties included that of being editor-in-chief of *Sovinformburo,* 1941–9. In 1949 *Moscow News* was shut down and Borodin's star was in decline. He was arrested and executed.

Borovoi, Konstantin Natanovich (b. 1948), one of the most spectacularly successful businessmen to emerge under perestroika. He was born in Moscow and graduated from the Moscow Institute of Railway Transport and Mathematics and Mechanics, Moscow State University, and later successfully presented his candidate dissertation in technical sciences (PhD). Afterwards he taught mathematics in various Moscow higher educational establishments. In 1987 he switched to business and became the president and the chief manager of the Moscow Commodity and Raw Materials Exchange. As such he was involved in many large deals and became synonymous with the new freewheeling private sector of the Soviet economy. From September–December 1991 Borovoi was a member of the council on entrepreneurship of USSR President GORBACHEV. In December 1991 he became economic adviser to the chair of the All-Union State Radio and Television Company (Gosteleradio). In 1992 he was elected president of the Congress of Exchanges. In March 1992 he was appointed a member of the council on entrepreneurship of Russian President YELTSIN and, in May 1992, he established his own political party, the Party of Economic Freedom.

Borzov, Valery Filipovich (b. 1949), the first Soviet athlete to win the 100 metres in the Olympic Games and the greatest Soviet sprinter of all time. A Ukrainian, he was born in Lvov oblast and graduated from the Kiev Institute of Physical Culture, 1971. He was made an honoured master of sport in 1970. Borzov won the gold medal in the 100 metres and the 200 metres at the 1972 Olympics and also a silver medal in the 4×100 metre relay. In the 1976 Olympics he won bronze medals in the 100 metres and in the 4×100 metre relay. He won many European sprint titles, 1970–5. He and his wife, the gymnast, Lyudmila TURISHCHEVA, acted as coaches in Kiev from 1979.

Botvinnik, Mikhail Moiseevich (1911– 95), one of the greatest chess players of his generation, Botvinnik, a grand- master, combined chess with a scientific career. He trained as an electrical engin- eer and his work on electric power sta- tions in the Urals during the Great Fatherland War was rewarded with the Order of the Badge of Honour. STALIN encouraged his combining technical work for the state alongside his prowess at chess which won respect for the Soviet Union abroad. In 1955 he moved to the Research Institute for Electrical Energy as a senior research scientist. Botvinnik, like his great adversary Emanuel Lasker, was a dedicated, disciplined player, who revealed great perseverance, especially when attempting to reclaim his titles. Botvinnik won the world title three times and was Soviet champion seven times be- tween 1931 and 1962. When defeated, he would study carefully the psychological weaknesses and playing technique of his conqueror. In 1946 the eagerly awaited contest between him and Aleksandr ALEKHIN had to be cancelled due to the untimely death of the world champion. Instead a tournament of five rounds, in- volving Botvinnik, Vasily SMYSLOV, Samuel Rashevsky, Paul Keres and Max Euwe, was held and Botvinnik won with four rounds to go. He remained world champion for the next fifteen years, with two short breaks when he was defeated by Smyslov and Mikhail Tal. In 1957 he lost his world title to Smyslov but re- gained it the following year; in 1961 he was comprehensively beaten by Tal but again turned the tables the following year. In 1963 he lost the world champion-

ship for the third time, to the Armenian grandmaster Tigran PETROSYAN. Botvinnik's great days were over but he continued to win prizes, including first prize at the Hastings Tournament in 1966. He retired from competition in 1970 and devoted himself to writing computer chess programs. He was mar- ried with one daughter.

Bovin, Aleksandr Evgenevich (*b.* 1930), a highly respected and influential Soviet journalist who specialised in foreign af- fairs but was also authoritative as a TV presenter of news programmes. A Rus- sian, he was born in Leningrad, but spent much of his youth in the Soviet Far East and graduated in law from the University of Rostov-on-Don, 1953. He worked for a time as a judge in Krasnodar krai, 1953–6, but then moved to Moscow State University where he successfully pre- sented his dissertation on Marxist phil- osophy (PhD). He then worked for the Party's theoretical journal *Kommunist,* 1959–63, in the philosophy section. Fedor BURLATSKY then recruited him as one of the advisers to ANDROPOV, who was head of the department of ruling communist and workers' parties, Party Central Committee Secretariat, eventu- ally becoming head of this group. This position afforded him the opportunity to make outstanding contacts. Bovin re- mained there until 1972 when he moved to *Izvestiya* and developed into a skilful and penetrating political columnist. He also developed a TV career as a presenter and commentator. His star rose under Andropov when the latter became leader of the Communist Party but dipped, pre- dictably, under CHERNENKO. Glasnost was ideal for him, and he availed himself of the privilege of criticising Soviet for- eign policy (siding, of course, with the new political thinking). This was sen- sational in the staid world of Soviet jour- nalism. He was a member of the Party and a member of the Central Revision Commission, 1981–6. In 1989 he was voted most popular commentator. In November 1991 he was appointed Russian Ambassador to Israel. Bovin was awarded the Order of Lenin, the USSR State Prize and the V. V. Vorovsky Prize.

Brazauskas, Algirdas-Mikolas Kazevich (*b.* 1932), the first former communist leader to be elected democratically the president of a successor state of the Soviet Union. A Lithuanian, he was born in Roniskis, in the independent Republic of Lithuania, graduated from the Kaunas Technical University in civil engineering, 1956, and successfully presented his candidate dissertation in economics (PhD (Econ)), 1974. He joined the Communist Party of Lithuania in 1959. He was first deputy chair of the Lithuanian Gosplan, 1966–77, and then moved into the Communist Party of Lithuania apparatus as a secretary, remaining there until 1989. In that year he was elected first secretary of the Central Committee, Communist Party of Lithuania, and was also chair of the Supreme Soviet of the Lithuanian Soviet Socialist Republic (this made him, in effect, president of the country). Brazauskas and other leading Communists decided to swim with the nationalist tide in Lithuania and in December they declared that the Communist Party of Lithuania be renamed the Lithuanian Democratic Labour Party (LDLP) and become independent of the Communist Party of the Soviet Union. This was a blow directed at President GORBACHEV and meant that Brazauskas and other reform-minded Communists intended to support the bid for independence advocated by non-communist Lithuanians. Those Communists who preferred to remain loyal to Moscow, and to oppose the goal of independence for Lithuania, set up their own party, the Communist Party of Lithuania. Brazauskas was deputy Prime Minister of Lithuania, 1990–1. President Vytautas Landsbergis and the Sajudis nationalist movement perceived no threat from Brazauskas and the former Com-

munists, so virulent was nationalism in the new Lithuania. However, poor economic management by President Landsbergis led to an astonishing reversal in the first democratic elections after independence, in September 1992. The LDLP turned out to be the leading party in the elections with almost 45 per cent of the vote and during the second round of voting in November 1992 the party swept the board and became the largest party in parliament. Brazauskas became the leading political figure in the republic and it was no surprise when he was elected President, winning over 60 per cent of the vote. The astonishing revival of the ex-Communists in Lithuania was followed later in other ex-communist states, such as Hungary and Poland.

Brezhnev, Leonid Ilich (1906–82), paradoxically, Brezhnev was leader of the Soviet Union at the apogee of its powers and influence but presided over its precipitate decline. A Russian, he was born in Kamenskoe (later Dneprodzerzhinsk), began his working life as a land surveyor and then worked in agriculture and industry in the Urals and Belorussia before returning to Ukraine to begin his long association with the Dneprodzerzhinsk iron and steel enterprise. He already had political ambitions and became a member of the Communist Party, 1931, and studied part time at the Dneprodzerzhinsk Metallurgical Institute, graduating in 1935, and was also active in its trade union. His political career took off in 1937 when he was elected deputy chair of the city soviet but he moved into the Party apparatus in 1938. Brezhnev was ideally suited to benefit from the end of Stalinist purges which had left many appealing positions to be filled. In February 1939 he became a secretary of the Dneprodzerzhinsk oblast Party committee (obkom) and at the outbreak of war he became a political officer in the Red Army and saw action on several fronts, including Crimea. When he was at the zenith of his power laudatory accounts of his wartime activities were published but most observers regard these as exaggerations and part of the Brezhnev personality cult. However, they did underline his vanity. Brezhnev participated in the Sovietisation of western Ukraine (ex-Polish territory) and left the army in 1946 as a major general. Both before and during the war Brezhnev cultivated relations with Nikita KHRUSHCHEV (Party boss in Ukraine, 1938–49, except for a spell in 1947 when KAGANOVICH took over) and the future successor of STALIN liked the energetic Brezhnev. The latter was given more and more senior posts, eventually becoming first secretary, Dnepropetrovsk oblast, Communist Party of Ukraine, and also membership of its Central Committee. In 1950 Brezhnev became first secretary, Communist Party of Moldavia (now Moldova), part of which had been outside the Soviet Union until 1940. The future Soviet leader was already building up his 'tail', subordinates who could be relied upon to do a good job and be loyal. In Moldavia there were two who later assumed prominence: Nikolai SHCHELOKOV, a future USSR Minister of Internal Affairs, and Konstantin CHERNENKO, then head of the Party department of propaganda and agitation. In 1952 Brezhnev broke through to the inner Party élite when he was elected, at the XIXth Party Congress, a secretary of the Central Committee and to the new and expanded Politburo which took over from the old Politburo. Many observers believe that Stalin was preparing a purge of the old élite at the time. Brezhnev was too new to the Moscow scene to be influential during the struggle to succeed Stalin but Khrushchev chose him, in 1954, as his man in the virgin lands and made him second secretary of the Communist Party of Kazakhstan. A year later he took over as Party boss there. His brief was simple: make the new lands

bloom. Brezhnev was fortunate that he was recalled to Moscow in 1956 because every other year in the new lands turned out to be disappointing. Had he stayed longer in Kazakhstan, his political career would have suffered. At the XXth Party Congress he was elected a secretary of the Central Committee and a candidate member of the Politburo. Brezhnev had the prescience to side with Khrushchev during the struggle with the Anti-Party Group (so called because they opposed the Party assuming a high-profile role in the economy), June 1957, and Brezhnev became a full Politburo member. In 1960, Khrushchev, desiring to expand Brezhnev's horizons, made him President of the Soviet Union, but Brezhnev saw this as a demotion. It was also the time when Khrushchev's star began to descend and Brezhnev became one of the plotters against the incumbent First Secretary. A stroke of luck for Brezhnev was the brain haemorrhage which Frol KOZLOV, regarded by Khrushchev as his likely successor, suffered in June 1963 and from which he was never to recover. Brezhnev came back into the Secretariat as secretary for Party organs, or, in other words, he became responsible for cadres policy. Khrushchev's son, SERGEI, sensed there was something wrong in the summer of 1964, and even warned his father about an attempted coup against him, when Brezhnev, a brilliant mimic, poked fun at the Soviet leader. Brezhnev, never a bold or daring man, would not have risked doing so unless very certain that Khrushchev's days were numbered. In October 1964 Brezhnev became First Secretary (renamed General Secretary in 1966) of the Party, with Aleksei KOSYGIN taking over as USSR Prime Minister, and Nikolai PODGORNY becoming Soviet President. Just as after Stalin's death there was a collective leadership but Brezhnev wanted to become boss. His opportunity came in 1968 when the Prague Spring developed to such an extent that it appeared that the Communist

Party of Czechoslovakia might lose power. In August 1968 the Soviet Union and several of its allies intervened and began the process of 'normalisation'. Brezhnev, as Party leader, took prime position during the conflict because Czechoslovakia was a socialist country and therefore under the supervision of the Soviet Communist Party. Kosygin, who had launched some useful reforms, was pushed aside as economic orthodoxy became the order of the day. He lacked the political guts to fight for primacy. By 1969, one can regard Brezhnev as top dog. Soviet intervention gave rise to the Brezhnev Doctrine: the right of Moscow to intervene in any socialist country where it deemed communist power was under threat. In the early 1970s, Brezhnev took the lead in articulating Soviet foreign policy and made many visits abroad, including going to Washington in June 1973 and receiving two US Presidents, Nixon and Ford, in Moscow and Vladivostok. Various agreements were reached and the Americans accepted, for the first time, the concept of nuclear parity between the two superpowers. In Europe, Brezhnev searched for increased security and signed the Helsinki Final Act, 1975, which accepted that the post-1945 frontiers could only be changed by negotiation. In order to sign, the Soviet Union had to make concessions on human rights and the distribution of information. These concessions were to cause Brezhnev and his KGB chief, ANDROPOV, much heartache. Although Brezhnev was only Party leader, he acted as head of state, and it came as no surprise that he became President of the Soviet Union in 1977. He offered Podgorny the position of Vice-President but the latter was not amused and the two old cronies fell out. Brezhnev once remarked that his strength was in cadres policy: finding the right men and a few women for important posts. He was not a man of bold initiatives and innovative thinking – one of the reasons why his comrades had chosen

him to follow the quixotic Khrushchev – and left the running of the economy to Kosygin. He rarely met a problem head on, preferring to wait his chance to deal with the person who was criticising him. Brezhnev, in the mid-1970s, was at the pinnacle of success and arguably the Soviet Union had never been as strong internationally. It was the era of détente and Marxist–Leninist regimes were spreading throughout Africa like wildfire. Then it began to go downhill. He appears to have become dependent on drugs in the mid-1970s, once remarking that the more he took the better he slept. The Soviet Union also went into physical decline. His last summit was in Vienna in 1979 when an agreement on the limiting of strategic arms was signed but because of the Soviet intervention in Afghanistan, December 1979, was never ratified. This disastrous policy came at a time when Soviet economic growth probably stopped and shortages multiplied. The tragedy for the Soviet Union was that at a crucial point in its decline, it was being run by a man who could only function part of the time. Kosygin died in 1980 and was followed by the almost as old Nikolai TIKHONOV as Prime Minister. The Politburo had become an old man's club. Politically, Moscow gradually lost control over the republics and regions with the local élites running things in their own interest. Corruption began to be dysfunctional and to make the country very difficult to govern. All this at a time when the Soviet military enjoyed an unprecedented influence in security and foreign affairs and some in the top military regarded a pre-emptive US nuclear strike as likely. Brezhnev became the butt for many cruel jokes. He comes into his Kremlin office one day and his embarrassed secretary says, 'Leonid Ilich, one of your shoes is blue and the other red.' Brezhnev beams, 'And I have another pair just like these at home!' Brezhnev instructs a clever assistant to write him a ten-minute speech. The next day Brezhnev is livid and abuses the unfortunate scribe. 'I told you to prepare me a ten-minute speech and it took me twenty minutes to read it. You idiot!' The assistant, in an embarrassed tone rejoins: 'But Comrade Brezhnev, I gave you two copies!' Brezhnev, had he lived, would have handed over the reins to Chernenko, but Yury Andropov picked up the poisoned chalice. John Dornberg: *Brezhnev,* London, 1974.

Brezhneva, Galina Leonidovna (1929–94), the colourful daughter of Leonid BREZHNEV who had a passion for younger men and who caused her father many a heartache. She studied at the Dnepropetrovsk Pedagogical Institute and Kishenev State University, Moldavia. She was greatly attracted to the circus and the men associated with it. She married, first, a circus strongman and acrobat, in Kishenev, 1951. In 1959 she decided she needed a change and later married an illusionist, fifteen years her junior. Her father had the marriage annulled. He had a major say in the choice of her next husband, Yury CHURBANOV, who was later to become first deputy USSR Minister of the Interior. Just before their wedding Churbanov had had a wife and two children. With her father in the Kremlin, she was almost untouchable and had many affairs with circus artists. One of them, nicknamed Boris the Gypsy, was involved in diamond smuggling and black market dealings. Boris was prosecuted but Galina went scot-free. With her father's death, she lost her protector. Her husband, Yury Churbanov, implicated in many financial scandals, was sentenced to twelve years' imprisonment. She spent her declining years, surrounded by drink and nostalgia, in a large flat in central Moscow. Galina was the butt of many cruel jokes but, in reality, was a tragic figure, unrestrained by any code of moral or political behaviour.

Brodsky, Iosef Aleksandrovich (Joseph) (1940–96), a great Russian poet of memory and exile, Brodsky wrote in Russian and English. He was born in Leningrad, the only child of well-read Jewish parents. He had a great affection for the city and eulogised in many poems. Bored with school, he left at fifteen and got a job in an armaments factory. He also worked in a mortuary. Four of his poems appeared in Leningrad anthologies, 1966 and 1967. Anna AKHMATOVA, the great poet, recognised his talent and arranged for him to meet NADEZHDA, the widow of Osip MANDELSTAM. One of his themes was the past glory of Leningrad, another the self-defeating savagery of the Soviet state. In 1964 he was sentenced to five years in a prison camp in the north of the country and it changed his life. There he came across the poetry of W. H. Auden, in translation, and was deeply impressed by Auden's poem about W. B. Yeats, written in 1939, commanding the poet to transform poetry into a moral force. When Brodsky was deported from the Soviet Union, in June 1972, to Israel, via Vienna, he made at once for Auden's summer home outside Vienna. Auden managed to secure Brodsky a post: poet in residence at the University of Michigan. His first book of poems, *Selected Poems,* was published by Penguin in England in 1973. He prospered in the United States but his parents were never allowed to visit him. In 'In a Room and a Half ' (the family had lived in a room and a half in Leningrad), he describes the anguish of hearing of his mother's death while being far away. In 1980, in *A Part of Speech,* poems written in English appear for the first time. His book of essays, *Less than One: Selected Essays,* 1986, reveal his love for Leningrad, its glorious past and the abominations of the communist present. He became the first Russian writer to be awarded the Nobel Prize for Literature, 1987, since PASTERNAK. His acceptance speech was devoted to the moral purpose of literature. It was not enough to read books, for LENIN, Hitler and STALIN had all read many books. Imaginative literature took as its subject 'human diversity and perversity. . . What these men had in common was that their hit-list was longer than their reading list.' After his Nobel Prize he began again to be published in the Soviet Union. Brodsky was US Poet Laureate in 1991. His last book, in 1992, was about Venice, which, in exile, became a substitute St Petersburg for him.

Brumel, Valery Nikolaevich (b. 1942), the greatest Soviet high jumper of all time, he was born near Chita, and became an honoured master of sports (track and field), 1961. Brumel joined the Communist Party, 1964, and graduated from the Moscow Institute of Physical Culture, 1967. He first came to prominence in 1960 at the Rome Olympics when he won the silver medal but jumped the same height as the winner. Brumel broke the world high jump record six times between 1961 and 1963, and was Olympic champion, 1964. During this period he was voted premier world athlete three times and was awarded many prestigious trophies, including the Golden Caravel. Disaster struck in 1965 when he suffered multiple fractures of his right leg in a motorbike accident. Thereafter he devoted himself to writing on athletics and sport.

Bubka, Sergei (b. 1964), the Soviet Union's and world's greatest pole vaulter of all time, he made a practice of beating his own world record. A Ukrainian, he was born in Donetsk, Ukraine. He and his older brother, Vasily, began pole vaulting when Sergei was ten. He became the first athlete to clear 6 metres, in Paris, in July 1985. He was world champion in 1983, 1987, 1991 and 1993 and Olympic champion, 1988, 1992. He was one of the first Soviet athletes to become rich by competing internationally, made his home in Berlin and said that he needed the money for his family. He was virtually unbeatable in European and world championships and other special international events. He developed a very distinctive high grip style and loping run-in.

Bubnov, Andrei Sergeevich (1883–1938), an active participant in the October Revolution, he was a Left Communist, supporter of TROTSKY and then of STALIN. He was born in Ivanovo-Voznesensk, the son of a textile director, but joined the RSDRP, siding with the Bolsheviks, 1903. He was in and out of prison in the years before 1917, including four years' incarceration because of his activities as a Bolshevik organiser. In August 1917 he was elected to the Party Central Committee and was Commissar for All Railway Stations in Petrograd during the Bolshevik seizure of power. He was a member of the Military Revolutionary Committee (the general staff of the revolution) and was active during the Civil War, especially in Ukraine. He was a Left Communist during the immediate post-revolutionary period (the most prominent Left Communist was Nikolai BUKHARIN), opposed the signing of the Brest-Litovsk treaty, 1918, sided with Trotsky, was part of the Democratic Centrist opposition (favouring less decision making at the centre) at the Xth Party Congress, 1921, and was a co-signatory of the Declaration of the 46, with Trotsky, 1923. He took part in the suppression of the Kronstadt rebellion, 1921. He changed sides and associated himself with Stalin, being head of the political administration of the Red Army, 1924–9. He conducted a purge of the military commissars, weeding out those associated with Trotsky. From 1925 he was in the Secretariat of the Party Central Committee. He was RSFSR People's Commissar for Education, 1929–37, responsible for the radical school reforms of the 1930s, and was also a member of the Party Central Committee. He was one of the many Old

Bolsheviks (those who had joined the Party before 1917) who fell victim to the purges, He was arrested in 1937, tried and sentenced to death, being shot on 1 August 1938. He was rehabilitated under KHRUSHCHEV.

Budenny, Marshal Semen Mikhailovich (1883–1973), he became one of STALIN's favourite military men but mechanised warfare at the beginning of the Great Fatherland War totally bewildered him. He was born in Rostov guberniya and joined the Imperial Army in 1903, fighting in a Cossack regiment (he was not a Cossack) in the war against Japan, 1904–5. He had a distinguished First World War, winning four decorations for valour as an NCO. He joined the Bolsheviks in 1918 and became famous as the commander of the First Cavalry Army during the Civil War with VOROSHILOV as his political commissar. He had little formal education, but was a skilled horseman and sporting a huge handlebar moustache he became a folk legend. He was inspector of the Cavalry of the Red Army, 1924–37. He sided unequivocally with Stalin during the mass slaughter of the top military, 1937–8. His failure, as commander of the Red Army in Ukraine and Bessarabia, to cope with modern warfare would have cost lesser men their lives but after being dismissed on 13 September 1941 Stalin shunted him off into administrative tasks at headquarters. He never returned to active command but remained as commander-in-chief of various Caucasian fronts until January 1943 when he was appointed commander of the Red Army Cavalry. He was a member of the Central Committee of the Party, 1939–52. As he aged he became a symbol of the heroic era of Soviet life.

Bukharin, Nikolai Ivanovich (1888–1938), in LENIN's phrase, the 'darling of the Party', Bukharin was a sophisticated, urban intellectual who became a leading economic theorist but proved no match for STALIN. Born in Moscow, both his parents were schoolteachers, and he quickly developed a taste for literature and bird and butterfly collection. He joined the Bolsheviks in 1906 and studied economics at Moscow University, 1907–10. He soon made a name for himself as a Bolshevik leader and was arrested in 1909. Imprisoned and then exiled to Arkhangelsk region in June 1911, he managed to escape in August 1911 and remained abroad until the February Revolution. In 1913 in Vienna, at Lenin's behest, he helped Stalin (who knew no German) when the latter was writing *Marxism and the National Question*. Bukharin was often absent-minded and once when carrying on a conversation while making soup, poured sugar instead of salt into it. He stayed in Switzerland, Norway and Sweden, before moving to New York in November 1916 and there becoming an editor, alongside TROTSKY, of *Novy Mir*. During his exile he wrote many of his most influential works, including one on finance capital which was heavily influenced by German Marxist thinking. He differed with Lenin on various issues, including the national question. Bukharin adopted the orthodox Marxist position that national self-determination was erroneous and potentially dangerous. He returned to Moscow via Japan and Siberia in May 1917 and immediately reasserted his influence among the city's Bolsheviks. He adopted a far left Bolshevik position and this led to close collaboration with Lenin. After the October Revolution he formulated Bolshevik economic policy and advocated the immediate nationalisation of industry and the building of a socialist economy. This did not please Lenin and Bukharin became a prominent Left Communist, opposing a peace treaty with Germany and instead advocating revolutionary war. However, he remained a leading member of the Bolshevik Central Committee. Bukharin came round to Lenin's views by the end of 1918 and he was as ruthless as the latter in persecuting perceived opponents of the regime. He was elected a member of the Politburo in 1924 and chair of the Communist International (Comintern) the following year. After Lenin's death in 1924, the strongest apparent contender for the succession was Trotsky. Bukharin entered into a tactical alliance with Stalin to vitiate the brilliant, far left firebrand. Bukharin was one of the first, if not the first, to use the expression 'socialism in one country'. This implied putting the interests of Soviet Russia ahead of world revolution. It also involved moderation at home in order to consolidate Bolshevik power. So which path was the Soviet Union to take to achieve socialism? Bukharin, taking his cue from Lenin's last writings about the peasantry, viewed it as a long road. Since 90 per cent of the population were rural dwellers, agriculture would dictate the pace. Hence the genetic or organic approach was advisable. With Trotsky ridiculing the concept of socialism in one country and advocating radical economic policies and world revolution, Bukharin and Stalin had to bide their time. Bukharin had moved far from his early extreme radicalism. As agriculture prospered, demand for industrial goods would fuel an expansion of output and the state would accumulate more taxes. The left pointed out that Soviet industry was in a sorry state and unlikely to respond to increasing demand. The question was stark: would industrialisation be achieved with the peasants as beneficiaries or at the expense of the rural sector? Whereas the left, in the works of PREOBRAZHENSKY and others, articulated their economic programme, Bukharin omitted to provide a powerful, theoretical apologia for the right-wing view. The question was settled politically with Stalin the victor. He then adopted, in the Five Year Plans, a more extreme version of the left's policy. Bukharin appears to have been appalled by the prospect of forced industrialisa-

tion and the concomitant authoritarian state which would automatically emerge. The nightmare of forced collectivisation was something he did not envisage. In the GORBACHEV era there was considerable interest in Bukharin's views and the possibility that they represented an alternative course to Stalin's policies. Were they of value for the 1980s? We shall never know. Such was Bukharin's lack of political perception that he believed himself to be the chief beneficiary of Trotsky's defeat. Bukharin was ruthless towards the Party's opponents immediately after the revolution, but this cutting edge left him when he needed to deploy it in the intra-Party conflicts. The triumvirate of Bukharin, RYKOV and TOMSKY, the union of the humane and all that was best in Bolshevik socialism, was no match for the killer instincts of a Stalin. Bukharin was hugely popular within the Party and this was something Stalin could not tolerate. The Politburo dumped him on 17 November 1929, and he was reduced to recanting several times in order to stay in political life. He even functioned as editor of *Izvestiya* from 1934 to 1936. Many believe that he penned the 1936 Soviet Constitution (the most democratic in the world, in Stalin's words, and it was – at least on paper). In 1936, he was entrusted with the task of attempting to acquire archives in western Europe and met many Russian émigrés. He spoke frankly of his disgust and resignation about Stalin's revolution but determined to return to Moscow where he was aware he was facing imminent death. He was implicated in the ZINOVIEV and KAMENEV show trials in 1936 and was arrested on 27 February 1937. He was the principal target of the last great show trial in March 1938. In a whole litany of accusations, it was claimed that he had plotted to kill Lenin during the Brest-Litovsk negotiations in early 1918. After being promised that his and his young wife's lives would be spared by Stalin and VOROSHILOV, Bukharin confessed to the most extraordinary and ludicrous (when one reads them today) crimes. He told his wife (who lived into the 1990s) that he had ruined her life. He, Rykov and others were sentenced to be shot on 13 March 1938 and *Pravda* confirmed his death two days later. It was usual for prisoners to be executed immediately after their sentence by a bullet in the back of the head but it would appear that Bukharin was given a further two days' grace. His widow described him as a 'sensitive, emotional man', in *Ogonek* in late 1987. His farewell letter, addressed to a Future Generation of Soviet Leaders, was published in *Moskovskie Novosti* (*Moscow News*) on 3 December 1987 and described his 'helplessness in the face of a murderous machine seeking his physical destruction'. He was rehabilitated by the USSR Supreme Soviet, together with nine others, on 4 February 1988. Nikolai Bukharin: *Imperialism and the World Economy*, New York, 1929; (with E. Preobrazhensky): *The ABC of Communism*, Harmondsworth, 1969; Stephen F. Cohen: *Bukharin and the Bolshevik Revolution: A Political Biography, 1888–1938*, New York, 1973; R. V. Daniels: *The Conscience of the Revolution: Communist Opposition in Soviet Russia*, Cambridge, Mass., 1960; George Katkov: *The Trial of Bukharin*, New York, 1969.

Bukovsky, Vladimir Konstantinovich (*b.* 1942), a well-known human rights activist and writer who acquired an international reputation in exile. The son of a Communist Party official, he became involved in the human rights movement while reading biology at Moscow State University. He was first arrested in 1963 for photocopying Milovan Djilas's book, *The New Class* (a reference to the communist nomenklatura), was held in a psychiatric hospital in Leningrad, 1963–5, and classified as criminally insane and a schizophrenic (both diagnoses were false). He was arrested again at the end of 1965 in Moscow for

organising a protest meeting in defence of the sentenced writers SINYAVSKY and DANIEL. Again he was placed in a psychiatric hospital, 1965–6. He was arrested again in Moscow for organising a protest meeting in support of Galanskov and in January 1967 was sentenced to three years in a labour camp. In January 1971 he forwarded documents he had collected on the political misuse of psychiatry in the Soviet Union to the World Congress of Psychiatrists, meeting in Mexico, for their comments. Arrested in March 1971, Bukovsky was sentenced to seven years' imprisonment and five years' exile but, in December 1976, was exchanged for the Chilean communist leader, Louis Corvalan. Bukovsky was then deported to Great Britain where he wrote on his experiences, *To Build a Castle*, 1978, and resumed his science studies at the University of Cambridge. He was elected President of the Resistance International, 1983. He was a chain smoker and found it impossible to give interviews without smoking.

Bulgakov, Mikhail Afanasevich (1891–1940), one of the great Soviet writers, his satire, *Master i Margarita* (*Master and Margarita*), was hugely influential and ensures him everlasting fame. He was born in Kiev, where his father was a professor of comparative religion, and he graduated in medicine from Kiev University (his experiences provided material for his *A Country Doctor's Notebook*). He intended to emigrate during the Civil War but typhus prevented him doing so and he moved to Moscow in 1921 and began his literary career. He is reminiscent of Gogol in his biting satire of everyday Soviet life. His breakthrough came with his novel, *Belaya Gvardiya* (*White Guard*), which became the stage play, *Dni Turbinykh* (*Days of the Turbins*), which managed to portray sympathetically a monarchist family in Kiev during the Civil War and impressed STALIN by presenting the revolution as an irresistible force. He followed this with another play about the defeat of the Whites but in 1929 his plays were banned. This embittered him at a time when he was writing *Master i Margarita,* 1928–40, which had to be composed in secrecy. His plays in the early 1930s deal with the subject of the artist and the political dictator. Bulgakov's last play, *Batum,* 1939, is a facile attempt to praise the young Stalin and was clearly written in an attempt to alleviate his own and his family's plight at a time when his plays were banned (the ban on his plays had been renewed in 1936). *Master i Margarita* is fascinating: is the master Stalin? Margarita is based on his third wife, the love of his life. It is a satire of life in Moscow during the 1920s when the devil pays a visit and the confrontation of Christ and Pontius Pilate is deftly woven in. Bulgakov died of an hereditary disease.

Bulganin, Marshal Nikolai Aleksandrovich (1895–1975), a political marshal who occupied many high-ranking posts, always concerned with defence and security. When he and KHRUSHCHEV visited Britain in 1956 (they were known as B and K), he cut a fine figure with his grey goatee beard, in sharp contrast to the barrel-shaped, ill-dressed Khrushchev. He joined the Bolsheviks in 1917 and was in the Cheka, 1918–22. He was in the Supreme Council of the National Economy, 1922–7. He was mayor of Moscow (chair of the city soviet), 1931–7, and worked closely with Khrushchev when he was Party boss in the capital. Together they oversaw the building of the Moscow Metro and other feats of engineering and architecture. Bulganin was deputy chair of Sovnarkom, 1938–41. As a political commissar, his task at the beginning of the Great Fatherland War was to ensure the military obeyed STALIN and implemented his orders. He was made deputy Commissar for the Armed Forces, 1944, and Minister for the Armed

Forces, 1947–9. He became deputy chair (Prime Minister) of the USSR Council of Ministers, 1949. After Stalin's death, Khrushchev moved quickly to recruit him against BERIA; he was Minister of Defence, 1953–5, and when MALENKOV was obliged to resign as Prime Minister in 1955, Bulganin was chosen to succeed him. He had previously been first deputy Prime Minister and Minister of Defence. He participated in discussions which improved relations between the USSR and the west and also in the summit meeting at Geneva in 1955. When he accompanied Khrushchev to Britain, Khrushchev answered questions addressed to his Prime Minister. There was never any doubt about who took precedence. Bulganin blotted his copybook in July 1957 when he sided with the Anti-Party Group against Khrushchev. According to the memoirs of the Yugoslav ambassador, Micunovic, he persuaded Khrushchev not to sack Bulganin at the time, along with all the others, because of the poor image this would create in the outside world. He pointed out to Khrushchev that this would make him look like Stalin mark II. Khrushchev bided his time and took over as Prime Minister himself in 1958. Bulganin was a member of the CPSU Politburo, 1948–58. He also lost his rank as a Marshal of the Soviet Union in 1958 – he had been promoted in 1947. He went to work in the USSR State Bank (in those days the State Bank had little economic influence) and in the Stavropol sovnarkhoz (economic council). He retired in 1960 and lived near Moscow.

Bunich, Pavel Grigorevich (*b.* 1929), a strong voice during perestroika in favour of privatisation, a Russian, he was born in Moscow and graduated from the faculty of economics, Moscow State University, 1952, and successfully presented there his candidate dissertation in economics, 1955. He was a member of the Communist Party, 1956–91, and was a member of the Central Committee,

1990–1. After university Bunich joined the Research Institute of Finance, USSR Ministry of Finance, eventually becoming deputy director. In 1961, at the G. V. Plekhanov Institute of the National Economy, Moscow, he successfully presented his doctoral dissertation on basic funds in socialist industry (DSc(Econ)). In 1971 he was elected a member of the presidium of the Far East Scientific Centre, USSR Academy of Sciences, in 1975 he became a professor at Moscow State University, and in 1976 head of the S. Ordzhonikidze Institute of Management, Moscow. He was elected to the USSR Congress of People's Deputies, as a nominee of the USSR Academy of Sciences, 1989, and was a member of the USSR Supreme Soviet committee on economic reform. In 1990 he became pro-rector for scientific work of the Academy of the National Economy, USSR Council of Ministers, and was also elected president of the USSR Union of Lease Holders and Entrepreneurs. In 1991 he became rector of the Academy of the National Economy. He was a corresponding member of the USSR Academy of Sciences. He has published many books, among which are *The Economic Mechanism of Developed Socialism*, 1982, and *The Problem of Stabilising the Market Economy in the USSR*, 1991. On 19 August 1991, as rector of the Academy of the National Economy, he ordered the implementation of the decrees of RSFSR President YELTSIN and he became a member of the Russian Presidential Council, 1992. Bunich advocated a much more rapid move to the market than USSR Prime Ministers Nikolai RYZHKOV and Valentin Pavlov. He was particularly keen on privatisation and the introduction of private property.

Bunin, Ivan Alekseevich (1870–1953), the first Russian writer to receive the Nobel Prize for Literature, but he was in exile at the time. A Russian, he was born in Voronezh and worked as a journalist after leaving school. He was awarded the Pushkin Prize, 1901. He travelled widely in Europe and was acknowledged as a master of Russian prose. He returned to Russia but emigrated from Odessa, 1920, after it became clear that the communist regime, which he resolutely rejected, would take over. He lived in the south of France and was a Nobel Prize laureate for literature, 1933. His view of the world was morose and he was not published in the Soviet Union during his lifetime. However, he was later recognised as one of the greatest of Russian writers and published in large editions in the Soviet Union.

Burbulis, Gennady Eduardovich (*b.* 1945), an influential democratic politician in the late GORBACHEV and the early YELTSIN eras. He was born in Pervouralsk, Sverdlovsk oblast. His grandfather had migrated to the Urals from Lithuania in 1915 but Burbulis's father did not speak Lithuanian and his mother was Russian. Rumours circulated that his grandfather had not been Lithuanian but Latvian and had been one of the Latvian sharpshooters who had saved LENIN's bacon in the early days of the revolution. Burbulis worked as an electrical mechanic in Pervouralsk and Sverdlovsk (Ekaterinburg), 1962–4, served in the Army Rocket Forces and then studied at Urals State University. He taught at Sverdlovsk Polytechnic Institute, 1974–83, and successfully presented his candidate dissertation (PhD), 1978, and his doctoral dissertation (DLitt), 1981, on an aspect of Marxism–Leninism. He became head of faculty, then deputy director of the Institute for Raising the Qualifications of the Specialists of the USSR Ministry of Non-Ferrous Metallurgy, 1983–9. He came into contact with Boris Yeltsin when he was first secretary, Sverdlovsk obkom. In May 1987 a political club, Tribune for Discussion, was set up on the initiative of the Sverdlovsk gorkom. Burbulis quickly became the leading light and in September 1988 he became one of the organisers of the Sverdlovsk Association of Public Organisations and in September 1988 of the Sverdlovsk branch of the Memorial Society. Burbulis was elected as one of the deputies for Sverdlovsk to the USSR Congress of People's Deputies, 1989, and he joined the Inter-Regional group of deputies in the Congress. Close collaboration between Burbulis and Yeltsin began in the summer of 1989. In January 1990, for a few months, he was a member of the Democratic Platform of the CPSU. He was prominent at the founding of the Democratic Party of Russia, led by Nikolai TRAVKIN, and was elected a deputy chair but quickly left the party, the main reason possibly being the inability of the democrats to unite and form a powerful party. He was regarded by many as the most influential adviser around Yeltsin and he ran the campaign to elect Yeltsin President of the Russian Federation, June 1991. He played an important role during the attempted coup of August 1991. He was head of the State Council of the Russian President, July–November 1991, and was made a state secretary. He fell out with Ruslan KHAS-BULATOV, speaker of parliament, and Vice-President Aleksandr RUTSKOI, in what was a naked power struggle. After he was made deputy Prime Minister of the Russian Federation in December 1991, Burbulis saw to it that Russian television stated that the stress on his name is on the first syllable, not the second syllable as most Russians pronounced it. This was but one example of his vanity. He was one of the strongest advocates of Russia breaking with the Soviet Union and he regarded the hoisting of the Russian flag over the Kremlin on 25 December 1991 as an historic day. In April 1992 Yeltsin was forced by the Russian Congress of People's Deputies to make concessions and one of these was to sack Burbulis as deputy Prime Minister. There was certainly no love lost

between the Congress and Burbulis. His influence declined rapidly after Yeltsin's mishandling of the Congress of People's Deputies in December 1992, with Burbulis being blamed for the confrontational pose adopted by the Russian President.

Burlatsky, Fedor Mikhailovich (*b.* 1927), a reform-minded Communist, close to KHRUSHCHEV, and quite prominent during the GORBACHEV era, he was born in Kiev (his father was Russian and his mother Ukrainian), graduated in law. from the Tashkent Institute of Law, and then successfully presented his candidate dissertation in law at Moscow State University (LLM). He later successfully presented his doctoral dissertation in philosophy at Moscow (LLD). In 1951 he began working in the presidium of the USSR Academy of Sciences and, in 1953–60, on the Party theoretical journal, *Kommunist*. Then he became one of the consultants to Yury ANDROPOV, being head of the group for a time, when the latter was Central Committee secretary for relations with communist and workers' parties. Burlatsky also became a speech writer for Khrushchev and travelled abroad with him. He joined *Pravda* but was obliged to leave after co-authoring an article criticising censorship of the theatre in 1967. Burlatsky then returned to academic life and in 1972 was head of a section at the Institute of Law, then became head of the department of philosophy, Institute of Social Sciences, which was part of the international department, Party Central Committee, 1975–89. He wrote prolifically, travelled widely and advocated the evolution of political science as a separate discipline in the Soviet Union (politics came under law in Soviet universities). In 1983 he became a political observer on *Literaturnaya Gazeta* and in March 1990 the staff elected him editor-in-chief. He was elected to the USSR Congress of People's Deputies, 1989, also the USSR Supreme Soviet. In 1989 Gorbachev included him as a member of the Constitutional Council, entrusted with the task of drafting a new USSR Constitution (it never emerged). He was actively concerned with human rights and was chair of the public commission on humanitarian problems and human rights, an official Soviet state body, 1987–91. After the failed coup of August 1991 he was obliged to resign as editor-in-chief of *Literaturnaya Gazeta*.

Bychkov, Aleksei Mikhailovich (*b.* 1928),

an engineer by training, he became the leading Baptist in the Soviet Union. He actively helped train pastors for the ministry and church workers and was elected vice-president of the executive of the All-Union Council of Evangelical Christians–Baptists. He became general secretary, 1971, and hence in the forefront of the battle with the state authorities to expand Christian work. Many new churches were established, greatly needed after the depredations of the KHRUSHCHEV era.

C

Chabukiani, Vakhtang Mikhailovich
(*b.* 1910), a brilliant Georgian ballet
dancer, choreographer and teacher who
was also highly regarded abroad. He was
born in Tbilisi and graduated from the
Mariya Perini Ballet Studio, Tbilisi,
1924, continuing his studies at the Leningrad Choreographic School, 1926–9. He
made his début at the Kirov Theatre,
Leningrad, 1929, and remained there
until 1941, becoming leading dancer.
Acknowledged as an outstanding dancer,
he developed new techniques, and danced
in a host of classical and modern ballets.
He returned to Tbilisi in 1941 to the
Paliashvili Theatre of Opera and Ballet
and was chief dancer and choreographer
there until 1973. He played an outstanding role in developing ballet in Georgia
and in the training of two generations of
dancers. Chabukiani was also director of
the Tbilisi Choreographic School after
1973. He was director of ballet at the
Rustaveli Theatre School, Tbilisi, 1965–
70. He also worked on several films and
staged ballets throughout the world. He
was awarded the Lenin Prize, 1957.

**Chagall, Marc (né Segal, Mark Zakha-
rovich)** (1887–1985), a highly talented
artist, he was born into a Jewish family
near Vitebsk and in 1907 he moved to St
Petersburg in search of work. Chagall enrolled in an art college and in 1910 he
made for Paris and lived in an artists'
commune with, among others, the still
unknown Modigliani. Cubism was then
in vogue. Returning to Russia in 1914 he
supported the October Revolution and in
1918 he became director of the Vitebsk
Popular Arts Institute. He worked with
the State Jewish Theatre, Moscow,
1920–1, and was then made People's
Commissar for the Fine Arts in Vitebsk
but soon fell out with the Soviet authorities. He emigrated in 1922 to Berlin and
the following year to Paris. Chagall's art
was a mixture of various styles but it retained a distinctive blend of Russian and
Jewish themes. He was invited to the
United States, 1941, by the Museum
of Modern Art, New York, but returned
to Paris, 1948, and was based there for
the rest of his life. Besides painting
he excelled at designing stained-glass
windows. This work can be admired,
particularly, in Jerusalem and Chiches-
ter, England. An exhibition of his work,
arranged by his widow, was a great
success in Moscow in 1987.

Chaliapin, Fedor Ivanovich (Shalyapin)
(1873–1938), one of the most famous
basses of all time, Chaliapin was born
near Kazan and made his operatic début
in Moscow, 1896. He sang at La Scala,
Milan, 1901, and in the United States,
1908 and co-operated with Diaghilev in
Paris, 1908–9. He appeared in London in
1913 and was a hit there as everywhere
else. His Boris, in *Ivan the Terrible,* was
probably the definitive version as, besides
being a singer of genius, he could act. He
emigrated from Soviet Russia, 1921, and
worked in the United States, 1922–5.
Afterwards he moved to Paris but his
health began to decline. After Chaliapin
had died in Paris and been buried near
by, the Soviet authorities approached his
family many times requesting permission
to move his remains from France to the
Soviet Union. This was always rejected

until finally, in 1984, permission was granted and he was reburied at Novodeviche Cemetery, Moscow, with great ceremony.

Chayanov, Aleksandr Vasilevich (1888–1939), a great agrarian economist who was born in Moscow and graduated from the Moscow Institute of Agriculture, 1910, remaining there to become a professor, 1918. Chayanov also studied archaeology and art and became well known for his science-fiction novels. He published his first book, *Ocherki po Teorii Trudevogo Khozyaistva* (*Essays on the Theory of the Working Enterprise*), 1912–13. After 1920 he was director of the Research Institute for Agricultural Economics, Moscow, which became known as the Chayanov Institute. Chayanov's work on the optimum size of farms, first published in 1922, became a standard work on the subject and gained him an international reputation. His research favoured the large farm but he did not believe that this applied to the peasant family farm, which operated according to other criteria than profit. Despite this, Chayanov was known as a representative of the working-peasant philosophy (individual production by the peasants, co-operative sales and purchases). He and some of his collaborators fell foul of ZINOVIEV who launched a vitriolic attack on them, 1927, and they were accused of running an anti-Soviet working-peasant Party (it only existed in the mind of the prosecutor). Chayanov buckled under the pressure and published an article, 'From Class Peasant Co-operative to the Socialist Reconstruction of Agriculture', in February 1929, and followed this up with others on a similar theme. He wrote that the future organisation of agriculture should be viewed as consisting of single socialist economies embracing whole districts. He attempted to outdo the Bolsheviks in their thinking about the massive factory farms. He wrote two articles advocating that if

tractors, combine harvesters and lorries were available, the size of a purely grain farm was almost limitless. It is uncertain whether the Communists were influenced by this thinking but when the huge grain factories were tried out, they failed miserably within two to three years. He even asked the Communists why, as a small but united army, they were driving the peasants into kolkhozes by military force. This wild rhetoric did not save Chayanov's skin. He was arrested during the brutal collectivisation campaign, 1930, and sentenced to death, 1937, being executed two years later. His pre-1929 work came into vogue again in the GORBACHEV era as the Soviet leader searched for ways of making socialist agriculture more efficient. However, his work was no longer relevant since the risk-taking peasant with a love of the land had become extinct by the 1980s. Naum Jasny: *Soviet Economists of the Twenties*, Cambridge, 1972.

Chazov, Evgeny Ivanovich (*b.* 1929), the leading cardiologist in the Soviet Union during the 1970s and 1980s, he was personal physician to BREZHNEV, ANDROPOV and CHERNENKO. He graduated from the Kiev Medical Institute, 1953, was a Doctor of Medicine Sciences (MD), 1963, and a professor, 1965. He was a member of the Communist Party, 1962–91, and a corresponding member of the USSR Academy of Medical Sciences. He joined the staff of the Institute of Cardiology, Moscow, 1958, and became head of the department of intensive care there, 1967. The following year he was appointed deputy USSR Minister of Health. In 1976 he became director of the All-Union Cardiology Scientific Research Centre, 1976. He was elected a candidate member of the Party Central Committee, 1981, and became a full member, 1982–90. Chazov raised his political profile when he took over as chair of the committee of Soviet Physicians for the Prevention of Nuclear War,

1981 (remaining until 1987), and together with the American cardiologist Lown, set up the organisation International Physicians for the Prevention of Nuclear War. In 1985 the Nobel Peace Prize was awarded to them jointly for their work. By the 1980s Soviet health care was deteriorating fast and GORBACHEV, in an effort to improve the situation, appointed Chazov USSR Minister of Health in February 1987. Given the declining budget allocations to the health sector, Chazov had an unenviable task and was eventually relieved of his duties in April 1990.

Chebrikov, Viktor Mikhailovich (*b.* 1923), one of the Politburo conservatives who supported the election of Mikhail GORBACHEV as General Secretary of the Communist Party, March 1985, but who came to rue the decision as Gorbachev became too radical for comfort. A Russian, he served in the Red Army during the Great Fatherland War and joined the Communist Party, 1944. On leaving the army, 1946, he enrolled in the Dnepropetrovsk Metallurgical Institute, graduating in 1950. He began his Party career in 1951 and was second, then first secretary, Dnepropetrovsk city committee (gorkom), Communist Party of Ukraine, 1961–7. Then he moved into the KGB, as head of cadres, under Yury ANDROPOV, who had become chair of the KGB, also in 1967. In 1968 Chebrikov became deputy chair of the KGB and in 1982 first deputy chair. When Andropov became General Secretary of the Communist Party, November 1982, one of his first moves was to appoint Chebrikov head of the KGB, December 1982. This reveals that Chebrikov had developed closer ties to Andropov than to BREZHNEV. Chebrikov was promoted army general, November 1983. He had been elected a candidate member of the Party Central Committee, 1971, becoming a full member in 1981. In 1983 he was promoted to candidate member of the Politburo, a position which was fitting for the chair

of the KGB. Chebrikov was among those who preferred Gorbachev as General Secretary, March 1985, and was immediately rewarded with full membership of the Politburo, April 1985. It soon became apparent that Chebrikov was a supporter of moderate reform and as Gorbachev became more radical, especially in June 1988, at the XIXth Party Conference, they parted company. In October 1988 Gorbachev managed to move Chebrikov to the new post of head of the commission on legal policy, making him also a secretary of the Party Central Committee. In September 1989 he lost both posts and retired on pension. Chebrikov was head of the KGB at a time when many officers were looking to the future and feathering their own financial nests. However, the chair appeared to have been incapable of stemming the rising tide of corruption in the organisation. Gorbachev appointed Vladimir KRYUCHKOV as Chebrikov's successor and was later to regret the decision.

Chelomei, Vladimir Nikolaevich (1914–84), one of the designers of the Sputnik and other space vehicles, he graduated from the Kiev Aviation Institute, 1937, and joined the Central Aviation Engine Design Institute, 1941. He joined the Communist Party, 1941. Specialising in missile design, Chelomei made original contributions, for example, the Proton launcher, used in the space programme from 1965 onwards, and also contributed to the development of Soviet ICBMs. He became a professor at Moscow Technical University, 1952, being elected to the USSR Academy of Sciences, 1962. He received many awards, including four state prizes and was a Hero of Socialist Labour in 1959 and 1963.

Chernavin, Admiral Vladimir Nikolaevich (*b.* 1928), an advocate of a permanent Soviet naval presence in the oceans of the world, Chernavin, a Russian, was born in Nikolaev, Ukraine, joining the navy in 1947. He graduated from the M. V. Frunze Higher Naval Technical School, 1951, the Leningrad Naval Academy, 1965, and the Military Academy of the General Staff, 1969. During his higher technical training, he specialised in naval operations and tactics. He was a member of the Communist Party, 1949–August 1991. Chernavin was a submariner and became the youngest senior aide to a commander of submarines of the Northern Fleet, 1954. In 1956 he was appointed commander of a nuclear submarine under construction. He was commander of a flotilla of submarines, 1973–4, then he was appointed chief of staff and first deputy commander, Northern Fleet. In 1981 he moved to Moscow as Chief of the General Staff and first deputy commander-in-chief of the navy. Chernavin was skilful at developing good personal relations with the then commander-in-chief of the navy, Admiral Sergei Gorshkov, who, in turn, was close to Leonid BREZHNEV, General Secretary of the Communist Party. Chernavin was elected a candidate member of the Party Central Committee, 1981, and a member, 1986–90. He supported those who advocated the emergence of a powerful ocean-going fleet, and the construction of submarines armed with rockets and torpedoes, aircraft carriers, and surface ships, capable of matching the naval power of the US and NATO. When Gorshkov stepped aside in 1985, Chernavin became commander-in-chief of the navy and deputy USSR Minister of Defence. In 1989 he was elected to the USSR Congress of People's Deputies and supported those who advocated the retention of Communist Party power and a strong Soviet Union. He publicly opposed democrats and their aspirations. During the attempted coup of August 1991 he was on leave but Admiral Panin, head of the political administration of the navy, published a message of support for the Emergency Committee. Presum-

ably he had informed Chernavin of his intentions. The navy was quiescent during these events but some officers and ratings who supported the Russian leadership were severely punished. When it became clear that the attempted coup was going to fail, Chernavin worked closely with Boris YELTSIN to raise the blockade of Mikhail GORBACHEV's dacha at Foros, Crimea. In February 1992 he was appointed commander of the navy and deputy commander-in-chief, unified forces of the Commonwealth of Independent States. Among his many awards are two Orders of Lenin.

Chernenko, Konstantin Ustinovich (1911–85), he contradicted the rule that losers never made a political comeback in the Soviet Union. He failed in his attempt to acquire the top prize after BREZHNEV's death, being edged out by ANDROPOV, but managed to push GORBACHEV aside in 1984, when Andropov favoured Gorbachev as his successor. If the American political dream was to move from log cabin to the White House, Chernenko actually did move from an izba (cottage) to the Kremlin. Some have unkindly intimated that the reason why he did get to the top was because he carried Brezhnev's briefcase, in other words, his patron made him. He was born into a peasant family in Krasnoyarsk krai, and joined the Communist Party in 1930. He saw service in the border guards, 1930–3, then became a Party official, concentrating on propaganda and agitation. He was promoted secretary of the Krasnoyarsk Party krai committee (kraikom), 1941, and then secretary of the Penza Party oblast committee (obkom), 1945–8. He was transferred to Moldavia to become secretary for propaganda and agitation there at a time when the republic was being fully integrated into the Soviet Union. More significantly he established contact with Leonid Brezhnev, who was first secretary of the Party in the republic. Chernenko was brought to Moscow by Brezhnev when the latter moved there in 1956 and when Brezhnev became chair of the Presidium of the USSR Supreme Soviet (President), 1960, he recruited Chernenko to be his *chef de cabinet*. When Brezhnev became head of the Communist Party, 1964, he moved quickly to place Chernenko in the responsible position as head of the general department of the Party Central Committee, which worked closely with the leader. Other promotions followed: he was elected a candidate member of the Central Committee, 1966, and a full member, 1971. He accompanied Brezhnev to Helsinki in 1975 and the following year he was made a secretary of the Central Committee, a candidate member of the Politburo, 1977, and a full member of the Politburo, 1978. Brezhnev by this time was only able to function part of the time and this afforded Chernenko the opportunity to profile himself as the General Secretary's successor. Had he not died suddenly in November 1982 (partly as a consequence of standing in the bitter cold on the Lenin Mausoleum on the anniversary of the October Revolution, 7 November), he would probably have handed over to Chernenko. As it was Chernenko was no match for the astute Andropov. However, Andropov soon fell ill and Chernenko and Gorbachev played more important roles. Despite Andropov favouring Gorbachev, Chernenko got the nod from the ageing Politburo, mindful of the fact that the 'young' man, Gorbachev, might sweep them all away. Personal ambition came before national duty. At the burial of Andropov, Chernenko cut a poor figure. He attempted to salute the dead leader and failed to get his arm above his shoulder. When it came to his oration, he could hardly get the words out; he was clearly suffering from emphysema. The Chernenko reign was an interregnum and marked the end of the Brezhnev era. When he died, after thirteen months in office, the baton then passed to Mikhail Gorbachev, but he was to admit ruefully later that he was quite unaware that the Soviet system was then in deep crisis. Chernenko had passed the baton to him at a time when the race was already lost.

Chernomyrdin, Viktor Stepanovich (*b.* 1938), an industrialist who became a successful Prime Minister of Russia after the collapse of the Soviet Union. A Russian, he was born in Orenburg oblast and began work in 1957 as a fitter and mechanic at the Orsk oil refinery, Orenburg oblast. After serving in the Red Army he returned to the refinery but began to study at the Kuibyshev Polytechnic Institute, Kuibyshev, 1962, graduating 1966. Again he returned to the Orsk refinery. In 1967 he moved into Party work in the Orsk city committee (gorkom), beginning as an instructor, becoming deputy head, then head, of the industry and transport department. In 1972 he graduated from the All-Union Extra-mural Polytechnic Institute as an engineer–economist. In 1973 he was appointed deputy chief engineer of the Orenburg gas refinery, then becoming director until 1978. The Party Central Committee apparatus called him to Moscow in 1978 and he became an instructor in the department of heavy industry. During this time he established contact with Boris YELTSIN and Arkady VOLSKY. In 1982 he became deputy USSR Minister of the Gas Industry. The following year, still remaining a deputy minister, he was appointed head of the All-Union Industrial Association for the Extraction of Gas in Tyumen oblast, west Siberia. Chernomyrdin was USSR Minister of the Gas Industry, 1985–9. During this time he clashed with Egor GAIDAR, who was at the time on the editorial staff of *Kommunist*, the Party's theoretical journal. Gaidar fiercely attacked plans to construct five multi-billion-ruble gas projects and the initiative did not go ahead in Tyumen oblast. In 1989 the ministry became the State Gas Concern (Gazprom), with Chernomyrdin as chair of the board. It had a monopoly on gas production and sales and provided about one-third of the Soviet Union's hard currency export earnings. Chernomyrdin was opposed to the break-up of the gas monopoly, by privatisation or other means. He favoured huge vertically integrated concerns, controlling everything from raw material inputs to banking. He was a USSR people's deputy, 1981–9, and in 1990 was defeated by General Dmitry VOLKOGONOV in elections to the RSFSR Congress of People's Deputies. Chernomyrdin is a candidate of technical sciences (PhD (Eng)) and an academician of the Academy of Engineering. In 1992 when the Minister for Fuel and Energy, Lopukhin, wanted to break up the oil and gas industry, Chernomyrdin organised an industrial lobby and eventually wore down President Yeltsin. Chernomyrdin became deputy Russian Prime Minister, responsible for fuel and energy, in June 1992. He was appointed Russian Prime Minister, December 1992, replacing the acting Prime Minister, Egor Gaidar.

Chernov, Viktor Mikhailovich (1873–1952), one of the founders, theoretician and leader of the Party of Social Revolutionaries (SRs), he was born in Novouzensk, Samara region, on 2 December 1873. He quickly became involved in populism and studied law at Moscow University, becoming head of the students' union. Imprisoned and exiled, he eventually moved to the University of Bern to study, among other things, philosophy. When the SR Party was set up in Russia, Chernov was invited to edit its journal, *Revolyutsionnaya Rossiya*. This afforded him the opportunity almost single-handedly to develop SR thought, a programme and tactics. Unlike many others, he was not impressed by PLEKHANOV and crossed swords with him. Chernov did not convert to Marxism and remained al-

ways an agrarian socialist. There were many similarities between SR ideology and Marxism – both, for instance, opposed private property, the hiring of labour and favoured the socialisation of land. However, Chernov argued that the relations of distribution were more important than the relations of production. For him, workers and peasants had the same interests and the main conflict in Russia was between autocracy and the people. To the Marxists, industrial socialists, it was class conflict. The SRs joined the Socialist International in 1904. He made little impact during the 1905 revolution and afterwards did little to provide direction to the party and evolve tactics to counter the rise of the social democrats. He was the quintessential provisional government politician, decent, weak, full of rhetoric, following events rather than shaping them and devoid of hard policy solutions. He was Minister of Agriculture in the first and second coalition governments (5 May-27 August 1917). The SRs triumphed in the elections to the Constituent Assembly and he presided during the only session the Bolsheviks permitted, on 5 January 1918. By then the SRs had split into those who opposed the October Revolution, the Right SRs, and those who supported the Bolsheviks, the Left SRs. Needless to say, Chernov was on the right. He was ineffective in organising opposition to the Reds during the Civil War and moved abroad in 1920. He presided over the rapid disintegration of the largest political party in Russia and presented LENIN with hardly a problem. After emigration he continued his agrarian sociological writings, exploring the reasons why the SRs failed, and died in New York. He failed to make his mark in the land of the proletariat and died in the land of capital. His agrarian socialism died with him. Oliver H. Radkey: *The Agrarian Foes of Bolshevism, Promise and Default of the Russian Socialist Revolutionaries. February to October 1917*, New York, 1958.

Chernyaev, Anatoly Sergeevich (*b.* 1921), the man who always seemed to be at GORBACHEV's elbow at international meetings, Chernyaev gained a reputation as an astute and flexible politician who promoted the new political thinking in the international arena. He served in the Red Army during the Great Fatherland War, joining the Communist Party, 1942. After graduating from Moscow State University in history he worked before joining the Communist Party apparatus after STALIN's death, soon specialising in foreign affairs, in the international department of the Central Committee. He worked on the *World Marxist Review*, in Prague, 1958–61, and this afforded him a wider spectrum of experience than in Moscow. Chernyaev then returned to Moscow to the international department and was deputy head, 1970–86, when Mikhail Gorbachev approached him and offered him the post of adviser on foreign affairs. According to his memoirs, at first he was reluctant to go. However, his balanced judgement, wide knowledge, extensive range of contacts inside and outside the Party apparatus, and loyalty suited Gorbachev. He remained with Gorbachev until the latter resigned as USSR President on 25 December 1991. His memoirs, a graphic account of the five momentous years he spent with Gorbachev, have been translated into German, but not English. Anatoli Tschernajew: *Die letzten Jahre einer Weltmacht Der Kreml von innen*, Stuttgart, 1993.

Chernyakhovsky, General Ivan Danilovich (1906–45), most famous Jewish general in the Red Army, he was the youngest high commander in the military. He joined the Red Army in 1924 and the Communist Party in 1928. He graduated from the Mechanisation Academy of the Red Army in 1936. His rapid career advance owed much to Marshal ZHUKOV's recognition of his talents. As commander-in-chief of the 60th army he recaptured Voronezh in January 1943

and then retook Kursk. He was made commander of the 3rd Belorussian Front and his troops attacked the Wehrmacht near Vitebsk. His troops penetrated Latvia and took Vilnius (July 1944) and then Kaunas. He continued the offensive against Königsberg but was killed by a shell near Mehlsack in February 1945. The East Prussian town of Insterburg (in Kaliningrad oblast) was renamed Chernyakhovsk in his honour. He was made a Hero of the Soviet Union on two occasions. He is buried in Vilnius.

Chicherin, Georgy Vasilevich (1872–1936), the diplomat who afforded the Bolsheviks some respectability, Chicherin was of noble birth, well educated, spoke all the main European languages except English, and was a wizard at presenting the communist case. With him in full flow, who could believe that the Soviets were the major threat to world civilisation? He was secretary of the central foreign bureau of the RSDRP from 1907 to 1914 but remained a Menshevik. He was a leader of the Mensheviks in Berlin for a time. He was put in Brixton Prison in August 1917 for his opposition to the war, and treated as a Bolshevik agent. He was exchanged for Sir George Buchanan, the former British ambassador. On his return to Russia in January 1918 he was appointed deputy Commissar for Foreign Affairs (under TROTSKY). LENIN regarded him as extremely hard working, conscientious but quite lacking in leadership qualities – an excellent choice as successor to Trotsky who quickly departed since he did not wish to sign the Treaty of Brest-Litovsk. He, following Lenin's instructions, played a formative role in establishing the Commissariat of Foreign Affairs (Narkomindel), becoming its head in May 1918 and remaining until ill health forced him to retire in July 1930. He made a good impression at the Genoa Conference (Lenin had initially intended to attend in person but was advised this was not a good idea for security reasons) and advocated rapprochement with Germany. This bore fruit in the Treaty of Rapallo (April 1922). Chicherin was playing the balance of power game, trying to offset the impact of France and Britain, seeing the latter as the main opponent. When the Civil War ended in 1920 the Bolsheviks gradually established relations with all contiguous states and abandoned the concept of a fluid frontier – any new Soviet republic could join. Chicherin articulated the view that diplomacy represented state interests, the Comintern, international communist interests, and the Red Army the security of the state. These three entities acted independently of one another. Chicherin was signalling the end of Soviet Russia as a revolutionary state. Its diplomacy had become traditional and Soviet Russia was a normal state. Of course, the Communist Party could never abandon its revolutionary pedigree and the need to promote Marxism–Leninism abroad. However, given the fact that the Soviet Union was a weak state, it was politic to act with caution and not overtly to support uprisings abroad. Chicherin's star began to descend after the Treaty of Locarno (1925) which saw a German–French rapprochement. The rising star was Maksim LITVINOV who effectively took over in 1928. In retirement Chicherin devoted himself to writing a book on Mozart and playing his piano music. The book was published in Moscow in 1973. (Chicherin belonged to an era when there was more culture in the Commissariat of Foreign Affairs. It requires quite a feat of imagination to see either MOLOTOV or GROMYKO playing a Mozart étude almost as well as Schnabel.).

Chkalov, Valery Pavlovich (1904–38), a record-breaking pilot during the 1930s, Chkalov joined the Red Army, 1919, and graduated from an airforce school. He qualified as a fighter pilot, 1924, and as a test pilot, 1930. He achieved several world long-distance records, including Moscow–Kamchatka, 1936, Moscow–North Pole–Vancouver, 1937, but, almost inevitably, he died in an air crash. This was the heroic period of Soviet achievements and he was fêted by Stalin and the Soviet population. Chkalov symbolised the brave new world of science and technology which was being forged during the first Five Year Plans. It appeared that there was no barrier that a Bolshevik could not overcome. When he died, his home town, Orenburg, was renamed Chkalov in his honour. It reverted to Orenburg in 1957.

Chornovil, Viacheslav Maksymovych (b. 1937), a leading Ukrainian nationalist under the Soviets who has made a political career in independent Ukraine. A Ukrainian, he was born in Cherkassy oblast, central Ukraine, where both parents were village teachers. He graduated from the faculty of journalism, Kiev State University, 1960, and subsequently worked in radio, TV and newspapers. His application to proceed to a candidate degree in Ukrainian literature, 1963, was blocked because he was already associated with the dissident cultural intelligentsia. Many of his friends were arrested, 1965–6, and he wrote up the trials, published in English as *The Chornovil Papers*. This earned him his first spell in prison, 1967–70. On his release he moved to Lviv (Lvov) and edited the leading samizdat journal of the period, *The Ukrainian Herald*, which concentrated on human rights. In January 1972 he was arrested and later sentenced to six years in prison followed by exile in Yakutia, where he was again arrested and received another five years for attempting to establish contact with the Ukrainian Helsinki Group, in Ukraine. He only returned to Lviv in 1985. His open letter to Mikhail GORBACHEV, 1987, marked the rebirth of open dissent in Ukraine. However, he soon fell out with other nationalists. In March 1990 he was elected a people's deputy to the Ukrainian Supreme Soviet, for a Lviv constituency, and also as a local deputy. He did not play an important role in local Lviv politics as those opposed to Chornovil dominated but he moved to take over the oblast soviet. He was a charismatic speaker and effective populist politician, carrying weight in the Ukrainian Supreme Soviet. On 1 September 1991, Rukh (the nationalist organisation) nominated Chornovil as its official candidate in the forthcoming presidential elections. Some of Rukh's leading members campaigned, nevertheless, for Levko Lukianenko. On 1 December 1991 Chornovil came a respectable second to Leonid KRAVCHUK, polling over 23 per cent of the vote. He was elected leader of Rukh in December 1992.

Chubais, Anatoly Borisovich (*b.* 1955), the father of Russian privatisation, he was born into a Russian military family in Borisov, Belorussia (Belarus), and graduated from the Leningrad Engineering Economics Institute, 1977, then joined the staff and successfully presented his candidate dissertation in economics (PhD (Econ)), 1983. In 1984, he and other graduates of the institute began analysing the economic policy of various Soviet periods, foreign experience and contemporary problems. They found out that another group in Moscow, led by Egor GAIDAR, was engaged on somewhat similar work and began collaborating with them. Chubais was one of the leaders of the democratic movement in Leningrad, 1985, and he was one of the organisers of the Leningrad Perestroika Club, 1987. His elder brother, Igor, was a leading light of the Moscow Perestroika Club and more radical than Anatoly. As a member of the CPSU, Anatoly was regarded as too loyal to Mikhail GORBACHEV. Chubais consistently refused nomination as a deputy to the Leningrad city council or any other political organisation, stating that he had no wish

to pursue a political career. However, in 1990, Chubais was elected deputy chair and then first deputy chair, Leningrad city soviet executive committee, supported by the democratic majority in the soviet. His nickname at the time was Len-gor-Abalkin, Leningrad's Abalkin. In 1991 he became the senior economic adviser to Anatoly SOBCHAK, the mayor of Leningrad (St Petersburg). In November 1991 Gaidar appointed Chubais head of the state committee for the administration of the state property of the Russian Federation (Goskomimushchestvo), which was to develop a programme for the privatisation of state property. This programme eventually became very successful but at the cost of much insider dealing.

Chuikov, Marshal Vasily Ivanovich (1900–82), he became famous at the Battle of Stalingrad and afterwards occupied many high posts. He joined the Red Army in 1918 and participated in crushing the Left SR uprising in Moscow in August 1918. He joined the Bolshevik Party in 1919 and fought in the Civil War as a regimental commander against Admiral KOLCHAK and other White commanders. He was a Soviet military adviser to Chiang Kai-shek, 1926–37. He participated in the occupation of Eastern Poland in 1939 and the war against Finland, 1939–40. He was USSR Minister of War, 1940–2. He was then appointed commander of the 62nd Army at Stalingrad. His army was the mainstay of the defence of the city. It was honoured by being renamed the 8th Guards Army and he remained its commander until the end of the war, taking part in the battle for Berlin. He was deputy commander, then in 1949 commander of the Soviet occupation forces in (East) Germany. As such he played a role in suppressing the Berlin uprising of June 1953 (the uprising had spent itself before Soviet troops moved in). He was then appointed commander of the Kiev military district. He became commander-in-chief of land forces and deputy USSR Minister of Defence in 1960. He was elected a candidate member of the Central Committee of the Communist Party in 1952 and a member of the Central Committee in 1961. He was commander-in-chief of the USSR civil defence forces, 1961–72. He was awarded eight Orders of Lenin. His memoirs of the Battle of Stalingrad, *The Beginning of the Road,* provide a graphic and incisive account of that epic battle, one of the turning points of the Second World War.

Chukovskaya, Lidiya Korneevna (*b.* 1907), a respected writer whose work could only be published fully under glasnost. The daughter of Kornei CHU-KOVSKY, the novelist, she was born in Helsinki (then part of Russia), and grew up among the literati. Her novels, *Opustely Dom* (*Sofiya Petrovna*) (*The Deserted House*), 1939–40, and *Zapiski ob Anne Akhmatovoi* (*Memoirs of Anna Akhmatova*), established her reputation. *The Deserted House* is a story about Leningrad life and reality under Stalinism. She was a close friend of Anna AKHMATOVA. She had the courage to criticise Mikhail SHOLOKHOV openly for his attacks on SINYAVSKY and DANIEL, 1966. Chukovskaya was expelled from the USSR Union of Writers in 1974.

Chukovsky, Kornei Ivanovich (né Korneichukov, Nikolai Vasilevich) (1882–1969), a famous writer of children's stories, literary critic, historian and translator, born in St Petersburg but grew up in Odessa with his mother, a Ukrainian peasant. He began writing in Odessa and was a correspondent in London, 1903–4, becoming a successful journalist before 1914. He put his knowledge of English to good use, translating, among other authors, Walt Whitman. He was interested in the art of translation and published a work on it, together with GUMILEV, 1919. Chuko-

vsky started writing for children; the first publication was *The Crocodile,* 1917, and he developed into the most successful of all Russian writers in this genre. His books are full of humour, word play, metaphors, puns, and made-up words. These stories were often the source and inspiration for radio, television and film scripts. Chukovsky was particularly interested in Nekrasov and his researches led to an edition of his complete works, 1927. Chukovsky's own complete works, in six volumes, were published in Moscow, 1965–9. His daughter, Lidiya CHUKOVSKAYA, is also a noted literary figure. Chukovsky received an honorary doctorate in literature (DLitt) from the University of Oxford, 1962.

Churbanov, Yury Mikhailovich (*b.* 1936), his career really took off after Leonid BREZHNEV chose him as his daughter GALINA's third husband. He graduated from Moscow State University, 1964, having already joined the Communist Party. Before becoming a student he had begun his career in the Young Communist League (Komsomol), 1957–70. In 1971 he became deputy head of the militia, USSR Ministry of Internal Affairs (MVD). He had joined the KGB as a young man and, in 1971, he received his first overtly security police post, becoming deputy head of the militia administration of security police forces (troops under the command of the MVD), until 1975. He was deputy USSR Minister of Internal Affairs, 1977–80, when he was promoted first deputy chair of the KGB. Brezhnev assigned Churbanov to look after his daughter Galina, with a brief to keep her out of trouble, especially with men who may have been attracted to her more for her position than her charms. He then married her, leaving his wife and two children. He was elected a member of the Party Central Auditing Committee, 1976 (this organisation was often the stepping stone to membership of the Central Committee). In 1981 he became a candidate member of the Central Committee. Churbanov became enmeshed in many shady financial deals and was known as a bribe taker; if one was not offered, he requested one, naming the appropriate sum. He was not arrested until 1986, probably because trying him in public would have caused acute embarrassment to many members of the nomenklatura, and in 1988 he was sentenced to twelve years' imprisonment for bribery and corruption.

D

Dan, Fedor Ivanovich (né Gurvich) (1871–1947), a leading Menshevik, Dan was born in St Petersburg and graduated in medicine. He was attracted to Marxism and joined the St Petersburg Union for the Struggle for the Emancipation of the Working Class in October 1895. However, a year later, he was arrested and exiled to Orlov for three years. He moved to Germany in 1901, headed the Berlin Group and helped to organise the IInd Congress of the RSDRP in 1903. When the Party split, Dan joined the Mensheviks and remained thereafter one of the most resolute opponents of Bolshevism in the social democratic Party. He returned to Russia during the 1905 revolution and came close to TROTSKY's views on permanent revolution. He was active as an editor of Menshevik publications and in 1908 became co-editor with Yuly MARTOV of *Golos Sotsial Demokrata* (*Social Democratic Voice*) in Paris (Dan's wife was Martov's sister). He returned to St Petersburg in 1913. On the outbreak of war Dan was arrested, exiled and sent to Irkutsk in 1915 as a military surgeon. There he encountered Irakli TSERETELI. They supported Russia's right to defend itself (revolutionary defensism). He returned to Petrograd in March 1917, was elected deputy chair of the Central Executive Committee (VTsIK) of the soviets, edited *Izvestiya*, supported Tsereteli when he became Minister for Posts and Telegraph in the first coalition government (5 May–2 July 1917), accepting that Mensheviks had to come to the support of the 'bourgeois' government to stave off right-wing reaction. He was a target for virulent Bolshevik abuse. After the October Revolution he and Martov were the leading Menshevik-Internationalists. Dan also worked as a doctor. He was arrested in 1921, expelled abroad in 1922 and stripped of his citizenship in 1923. After Martov's death he became one of the leaders of the Mensheviks in exile. He moved to the left and came to support STALIN's Five Year Plans and collectivisation. To him, the Soviet Union was the main barrier to fascism. He left France in March 1940 for New York. He finally parted from Menshevism in 1943 and penned the *Origins of Bolshevism*, a paean of praise to Stalin and his men. He saw Bolshevism as the legitimate heir of Russian social democracy, chosen by history to carry out the noble task. Dan's later years were tragic – his espousal of Bolshevism negated his active political life and denied his struggle for humane socialism and he died in the New World instead of in Stalin's 'beautiful, new world'. Fedor Dan: *The Origins of Bolshevism*, New York, 1964; Boris Sapir (ed.): *Theodore Dan, Letters (1899–1946)*, Amsterdam, 1985.

Daniel, Yuly Markovich (pseudonym Arzhak, Nikolai) (1925–88), co-defendant with Andrei SINYAVSKY in a famous trial which marked the end of the 'thaw' in Soviet literature. He was the son of the Jewish writer, Mark Daniel and was in the Red Army during the Great Fatherland War. He graduated from the Moscow Oblast Teachers' Institute and became a schoolteacher and translator of poetry. He published satirical short stories in the west, under the pseudonym of Nikolai Arzhak, during the 1950s and 1960s (the best known is *Moscow Speaks,* 1962, which describes Moscow during a 'day of unpublished murders'), but was arrested, along with Sinyavsky, in 1965. The trial was reported world wide as it was the first time since the Stalin era that writers were sentenced on the basis of literary texts. Daniel was accused of anti-Soviet propaganda and slandering Soviet life. He was sentenced to five years in a labour camp, February 1966. After serving his sentence he was not allowed to return to Moscow and settled in Kaluga. He later returned to Moscow where he died.

Dankevich, Konstantin Fedorovich (1905–84), a versatile composer of operas, musical comedies and choral works, whose work was condemned by the authorities, 1951. He was born in Odessa and graduated from the Odessa School of Musical Drama, 1929, staying on as a teacher. He joined the Odessa Institute of Musical Drama, 1935 (professor from 1948) and was director of the Odessa Conservatory, 1944–51. When his opera, *Bohdan Khmelurtsky,* was performed it ran foul of the authorities. He survived this vote of no confidence and, after STALIN'S death in 1953, he was appointed a professor at the Kiev Conservatory.

Davidovich, Bella Mikhailovna (*b.* 1928), a talented pianist who was one of the many artists to abandon the Soviet Union. She was born in Baku and at the Moscow Conservatory her teachers included Konstantin Igumnov and Yakov Flier. Davidovich was awarded first prize at the International Chopin Competition, Warsaw, 1949. After postgraduate studies at the Moscow Conservatory, she was appointed to the staff, 1962. She became an honoured artist of the RSFSR, 1972, but in 1977 she decided to leave the Soviet Union, together with her son, Vitaly Sitkovsky, a violinist, for Israel.

She gave concerts throughout the world and was especially well received in the United States.

Davitashvili, Evgeniya Yuvashevna (*b.* 1940), she became the most famous magician in the Soviet Union, acquiring the Georgian sobriquet, Dzhuna, magician. She was born in Krasnodar krai, of Assyrian background, and soon discovered that she had healing hands, treating all manner of complaints, especially back pains. She was invited to come to Moscow, set up a private clinic and was given a diploma as a nurse and masseuse. Her skills were acknowledged by the USSR Academy of Medical Sciences and she became the political and artistic establishment's magician. She is reputed to have healed Leonid BREZHNEV, Boris PONOMAREV and Yury ANDROPOV (but not during his fatal illness). Even the USSR Minister of Health, Boris Petrovsky, asked her to look at his back. The Soviet press had some fun with her, calling her the female RASPUTIN. Lurid stories circulated about her lifestyle, bohemian of course, and she was certainly a ruble millionairess. Her career was extraordinary in a country which officially based itself on dialectical materialism. Leonid Brezhnev, especially, given his desire for immortality, was especially susceptible to her charms and claims.

Deborin, Abram Moiseevich (1881–1963), one of the high priests of Soviet philosophy under STALIN, Deborin was born in Lithuania and joined the RSDRP soon after it was established. He sided with LENIN during the split, 1903, but changed sides, 1908, and became a Menshevik. In 1917 he reverted to the Bolshevik camp and joined the Communist Party, 1928. He was editor of the Marxist–Leninist philosophy journal, *Pod Znamenem Marksizma* (*Under the Banner of Marxism*), 1926–30. As a former Menshevik he was lumped together with other Mensheviks, March 1931, who were among the first to be involved in a show trial and accused of running a counter-revolutionary organisation. While others were sentenced to prison, Deborin managed to escape the net. His career took off later and he was the quintessential orthodox Bolshevik Marxist philosopher. Among the controversies he was involved in was the struggle over genetics in the Soviet Union. This discipline was officially outlawed in 1948, as a bourgeois deviation.

Deich, Lev Grigorevich (1855–1941), one of the founders of Marxism in Russia, Deich like many others was a Jew and began his political life as a populist. He first became politically active when he participated in the 'To the People' movement. He was first arrested in 1875 but soon escaped. When the populists in the Land and Liberty group split over the tactical use of terror for political ends in 1879, Deich sided with Georgy PLE-KHANOV who opposed terror and joined his Black Repartition group. The group moved to Switzerland and in 1883 converted to Marxism and called themselves the Emancipation of Labour Group. Deich was arrested in Germany on group business in 1884, extradited to Russia and served thirteen years' forced labour in Siberia for the attempted murder of a tsarist agent. He eventually escaped from Russia and helped LENIN and the other editors of *Iskra,* the RSDRP newspaper. He played a role in organising the IInd Congress of the RSDRP in Brussels and London (1903). When the Party split, Deich abandoned Lenin and sided with the Mensheviks. After returning to Russia in 1905 he was soon arrested but again managed to escape, reaching London where he participated in the Vth Congress of the RSDRP. He moved to New York in 1911 and supported the Menshevik position when war broke out. This was known as 'revolutionary defensism', that Russia should defend itself

against Germany. He moved with Plekhanov to Petrograd after the February Revolution and supported KERENSKY's call to continue the war until victory was secured. He lived the rest of his life under the Bolsheviks, published his memoirs and edited some volumes on the Liberation of Labour Group.

Demichev, Petr Nilovich (*b.* 1918), a chemist by training, he was USSR Minister of Culture during the latter part of the BREZHNEV era, a period of cultural conservatism and decline. He was born in Kaluga oblast and graduated from the Mendeleev Institute of Chemical Technology, Moscow, 1944, and the Party Central Committee's Higher Party School, 1953. Demichev began in the Komsomol organisation, 1937, joined the Communist Party, 1938, and served in the Red Army, 1939–44. In 1945 he joined the Moscow city Party organisation (gorkom) and was a secretary of the Moscow oblast Party organisation (obkom), 1956–8, then first secretary, 1959–60, then first secretary of Moscow gorkom, 1960–2, and a member of the Party bureau for the RSFSR, 1959–61. Demichev then became a secretary of the Central Committee, responsible for ideology, and was elected a candidate member of the Politburo, 1964. When he became USSR Minister of Culture, November 1974, he gave up his secretaryship of the Central Committee. This was a difficult time for the creative intelligentsia and, with Yury ANDROPOV at the KGB, the regime was severe on its critics. Demichev was embarrassed by the number of leading Soviet cultural figures who either defected or left the Soviet Union, one of the most famous deportations being Aleksandr SOLZHENITSYN. The gulf between the official and unofficial cultures in the Soviet Union widened during this period and when Demichev retired as USSR Minister of Culture in 1986 glasnost began to undo everything he had defended.

Denikin, Anton Ivanovich (1872–1947), an infantry officer, Denikin graduated from the General Staff Academy and participated in the Russo-Japanese War. He did well during the First World War and his war record together with his modest social origins ensured rapid promotion after February 1917. In August 1917 he became commander-in-chief of the South West Army Group. He sided with General KORNILOV in his abortive push against Petrograd, was imprisoned and escaped after October 1917. He then joined the Volunteer Army in south-east Russia, under Generals Kornilov and ALEKSEEV. When Kornilov was killed by a shell in April 1918, Denikin assumed command and after Alekseev's death in October 1918, Denikin was in sole charge. He developed into the most important White commander during the Civil War with the Reds and was often victorious in the north Caucasus. However, the Bolsheviks could not be defeated by the Whites holding on to southern Russia and the weakness of other White commanders proved fatal. Denikin was a Russian nationalist, with a professional soldier's distrust of civilians, and evinced little sympathy for the nationalities, a glaring weakness in the north Caucasus. He issued a political manifesto in July 1919 but it was too late. He, like the other White commanders, had not grasped early enough that the Civil War was not only a military campaign but a political conflict. The Reds had realised this from the beginning and won over many waverers in the countryside. His defeated troops retreated to Crimea where he handed command over to WRANGEL. Discipline broke down and there was a disgraceful scramble to escape to France. Once there Denikin became a member of the disillusioned White community and published several volumes of memoirs.

Dimitrov, Georgy (1882–1949), a Bulgarian, he became famous at the Reichstag Fire trial, 1933, when he and a Dutch communist were accused of arson. He made stirring speeches from the dock and accused Göering and Goebbels, who were witnesses for the prosecution, of being the real instigators of the crime. Dimitrov was acquitted but his co-defendant was executed. (It later transpired that neither the communists nor the Nazis were responsible for the fire.) He was one of the founders of the Communist Party of Bulgaria, 1919, attempted to seize power in Bulgaria, failed, was sentenced to death and eventually granted political asylum by Yugoslavia. Life in a Nazi prison was easy and, on release, he travelled to Moscow. He became a Soviet citizen and was elected to the USSR Supreme Soviet. Dimitrov was always loyal to STALIN and the Soviet dictator made him general secretary of the Comintern. He was as ruthless as his master in eliminating foreign communists in Moscow suspected of (imaginary) crimes. The Comintern was dissolved in 1943 to allay the suspicions of the western allies about the Red Army exporting revolution. Dimitrov entered Bulgaria on the coattails of the Red Army, 1944, and set about imposing a Stalinist state, with great dedication and ruthlessness. In 1948, Stalin suspected President Tito of Yugoslavia and Dimitrov of planning to establish a Balkan federation outside his control (totally untrue). Dimitrov was recalled to Moscow for health reasons and it was typical of him that he immediately obeyed. He died in Moscow.

Dobrynin, Anatoly Fedorovich (*b.* 1919), a long-serving Soviet ambassador in Washington who enjoyed the respect of several US Presidents. He was born near Moscow and graduated from the Moscow Aviation Institute, 1942, and the Higher Diplomatic School, USSR Ministry of Foreign Affairs. Dobrynin joined the diplomatic service, 1946, and became assistant deputy USSR Minister of

Foreign Affairs, 1949–52. He began his long association with the United States in 1952 when he was sent to the Soviet embassy in Washington. He returned to Moscow in 1955 as assistant deputy USSR Minister of Foreign affairs and in 1957 he moved to the United Nations in New York, and worked in its secretariat until 1960. On his return to the Soviet Union he became head of the American department, USSR Ministry of Foreign Affairs. He was appointed Soviet Ambassador to Washington, 1962, just before the Cuban Missile Crisis occurred. Dobrynin was in a difficult position as it transpired that the Americans knew more about the Soviet deployment of missiles on Cuba than the Soviet ambassador. He remained in Washington until 1986 when Mikhail GORBACHEV recalled him to become a secretary of the Party Central Committee and head of the international department of the Party Secretariat. This, on first glance, was a surprising appointment, since Dobrynin had always been a professional diplomat and had little expertise in the inner workings of the Party apparatus. It would appear that Gorbachev was concerned about ensuring that his new political thinking – including the de-ideologisation of foreign policy – was implemented in the Party apparatus, in parallel with the work of Eduard SHEVARDNADZE, the new USSR Minister of Foreign Affairs. Dobrynin was elected a candidate member of the Party Central Committee, 1966, and a full member, 1971. Like many others, he was invited to retire from the Central Committee in October 1988. He then drew his pension.

Dolgikh, Vladimir Ivanovich (*b.* 1924), a leading politician who never made it to the top, finding his way blocked by GORBACHEV. he was born in Krasnoyarsk krai, served in the Red Army during the Great Fatherland War, joining the Communist Party in 1942. Dolgikh graduated from the Irkutsk Mining–Metallurgical Institute, 1949, and then worked as an engineer in Krasnoyarsk krai, and was director of the Zavenyagin Metallurgical Combine, Norilsk, 1962–9. He was recruited into the Party apparatus as first secretary of the Krasnoyarsk krai committee (kraikom), was elected to the Party Central Committee, 1971, and was brought to Moscow, 1972, and made a secretary of the Central Committee, responsible for heavy industry and energy (until 1983). It was not until May 1982 that he was promoted to candidate membership of the Politburo. This implied that his performance was solid but he did preside over industry at a time when it was in decline. He was not promoted to full membership of the Politburo. Had this happened, together with his secretaryship of the Central Committee, he would have been in a strong position to challenge for the top prize, the post of General Secretary of the Party. Perhaps he was too young to ingratiate himself with the old men of the Politburo. Dolgikh was a technocrat but he revealed little passion for the market solutions which were circulating in the Gorbachev era. He was pushed out in late 1988 and the department of heavy industry and energy he had run until 1983 was dissolved.

Drach, Ivan Fedorovych (*b.* 1936), a leading Ukrainian nationalist politician who was born near Kiev and graduated from Kiev State University. He joined the Communist Party of Ukraine, 1959, and during the 1960s he was one of the leading figures in the new generation of Ukrainian poets and writers, promoting a Ukrainian cultural renaissance. Most of Drach's best writing was published in the 1960s before the cultural climate became more oppressive. He was first secretary of the Writers' Union of Ukraine and, in 1991, was appointed head of the cultural society, Ukraina. After the abortive attempt to establish Rukh (Ukrainian Popular Front), under the leadership of the Ukrainian Helsinki Union and other informal groups, during the summer of 1988, leadership passed to the Union of Writers in the winter of 1988–9. Drach played a leading role in forming the new organisation and was elected leader at Rukh's first congress, September 1989, a position he retained at the second congress, October 1990. In March 1990 Drach was elected a people's deputy in Lviv (Lvov) oblast to the Ukrainian Supreme Soviet and resigned from the Communist Party. He was close to Leonid KRAVCHUK and supported him during his election as President of Ukraine in December 1991. He hoped to place Rukh firmly behind Kravchuk but this never materialised as Drach had little interest in day to day politics and political organisation.

Dudintsev, Vladimir Dmitrievich (*b.* 1918), he became famous in 1956 when his novel, *Ne Khlebom Edinom* (*Not by Bread Alone*), was published in *Novy Mir*. It charts an inventor's eight-year struggle to have his more efficient machine replace the existing one, made by someone enjoying the favour of the authorities. Dudintsev was born near Kharkov, Ukraine, and graduated in law from Moscow State University, 1940, and served in the Red Army during the Great Fatherland War. The impact of this novel, attacking Soviet bureaucracy, and as its title suggests, questioning the Party's overriding concern with material progress, is on a par with Aleksandr SOLZHENITSYN's *One Day in the Life of Ivan Denisovich*. Dudintsev's anti-hero, the bureaucrat Drozdov, became a symbol of the self-seeking, complacent official. Under GORBACHEV, Dudintsev's novel, *Belye Odezhdy* (*White Coats*), about the campaign against genetics, targeting especially LYSENKO, was published in 1987, although written two decades before.

Dzasokhov, Aleksandr Sergeevich (*b.*

1934), a leading Soviet official concerned with the Third World, a Russian, he was born in Vladikavkaz, North Ossetia, and graduated from the North Caucasian Mining–Metallurgical Institute and from the extra-mural department, Academy of Social Sciences, Party Central Committee, with a PhD in history. After the institute he began a career in the Komsomol in North Ossetia, then in Moscow, and in 1963–4 he led a group of young Soviet specialists in Cuba. In 1965 he was appointed responsible secretary, in 1966 deputy, then first deputy chair of the committee of USSR youth organisations. He was then responsible secretary, deputy, then first deputy chair of the Soviet committee for solidarity with the countries of Asia and Africa, 1967–86. He was Soviet Ambassador to Syria, 1986–8, then returned to work in North Ossetia as first Party secretary, 1988–90. He was elected to the USSR Congress of People's Deputies, 1989, and in the USSR Supreme Soviet, he was chair of the committee on international affairs, 1990–1. He was a member of the Communist Party, 1957–91, a member of the Central Committee, July 1990–August 1991, a secretary of the Central Committee and member of the Politburo, July 1990–August 1991, and chair of the permanent ideology commission of the Central Committee, April–August 1991. Dzasokhov received many awards from foreign countries.

Dzerzhinsky, Feliks Edmundovich (1877–1926), many sobriquets were applied to Dzerzhinsky by the Bolsheviks: Iron Feliks, the Shield of the Revolution, and so on. They illustrate his steel-like qualities, his single-minded dedication, his ruthlessness in protecting the revolution against its enemies. He was the first head of the political police, first called the Cheka, then OGPU and eventually the KGB. There was always tension between the Bolshevik Party and the political police but the relationship between

Dzerzhinsky and LENIN was an exception to this. Dzerzhinsky came from a Polish landed family and like many Bolsheviks of 'bourgeois' origin, made up for it by zealously destroying the bourgeoisie and intelligentsia after October 1917. He joined the Lithuanian Social Democratic Party in 1895 and soon became a full-time revolutionary. He was arrested in 1897 but escaped from Siberian exile in 1899 and made for Warsaw. He founded the Social Democratic Party of the Kingdom of Poland and Lithuania, the precursor of the Polish Communist Party, in 1900. He first encountered Lenin at the IVth Congress of the RSDRP in Stockholm in 1906 and was elected to its Central Committee. Repeatedly arrested and imprisoned, he was incarcerated altogether for about eleven years before the February Revolution liberated him from a Moscow jail. He immediately sided with Lenin and was prominent in the October seizure of power. Thereupon he concentrated on the internal security of the new regime and was appointed the first head of the Cheka in December 1917. Lenin trusted him explicitly so he was given *carte blanche* to make Russia safe for Bolsheviks. Dzerzhinsky answered White Terror with Red Terror, beginning in the countryside and then spreading to the cities, after the attempted assassination of Lenin by Fanya Kaplan. He became People's Commissar for Internal Affairs (NKVD) in March 1919 and hence could integrate the functions of the militia and the political police. Organisationally talented, dynamic, almost tireless, consumed by work, Dzerzhinsky was always in demand when new tasks appeared. He became chair of the committee for universal labour conscription, and the commission for improving the lot of children. He commanded the rear of the south-west front during the Soviet–Polish War and had the Bolsheviks not lost Dzerzhinsky almost certainly would have taken over as Polish Bolshevik leader.

Polish nationalism was resolutely opposed. Dzerzhinsky had become an assimilated Great Russian. He was the natural candidate for the post of People's Commissar for Transport in April 1921 and was given the task of rehabilitating Soviet Russia's devastated transport system. When the Cheka was transformed into the State Political Administration (GPU) in 1922, and placed in the NKVD, he remained head of both. In 1923 the GPU became the Unified State Political Administration (OGPU) and was formally subordinated to Sovnarkom but in reality to the Communist Party. Dzerzhinsky continued as OGPU head. These frequent changes revealed the difficulty the Party faced in shaping and controlling the fearful weapon it had created. Dzerzhinsky's Great Russian chauvinism surfaced to Lenin's dismay during the 1922–3 Georgian affair. The conflict was over whether Tbilisi would be directly subordinate to Moscow, as an autonomous republic of the RSFSR, or indirectly, as a sovereign Soviet republic. Had Lenin lived he would have sided with the Georgians against Dzerzhinsky and STALIN – the arch centralisers. Dzerzhinsky became chair of VSNKh but continued as head of OGPU. When once made aware by an aide that everyone feared him, he appeared surprised and rejoined that no one who was not guilty need fear him. He was never Stalin's man and when he died suddenly of a heat attack in July 1926 the way was open for Stalin to attempt to take control of OGPU. George Leggett: *The Cheka: Lenin's Political Police,* Oxford, 1981.

Dzhemilev, Reshat (*b.* 1931), a leading campaigner for the return of the Crimean Tatars to their homeland, he was deported, along with all other Crimean Tatars, 1944, for allegedly collaborating with the Germans during the Great Fatherland War (this accusation was dropped under KHRUSHCHEV). The movement began in 1956 after Khrushchev's Secret Speech at the XXth Party Congress had demolished STALIN's reputation. Whereas many other deported nationalities from the north Caucasus were permitted to return, the Crimean Tatars and the Germans were not. The main reason for this was that the homes of the Crimean Tatars had been taken over by Russian and Ukrainian settlers and the Soviet authorities would not consider expelling them. Dzhemilev was a member of the Tatar delegation which met Yury ANDROPOV, 1967, to state their case. Dzhemilev became a thorn in the flesh of the Soviet authorities and was sentenced three times to spells of imprisonment in labour camps. The Soviet government would also not grant him a visa to seek medical treatment in the United States. He was a member of the Tatar delegation which met Andrei GROMYKO, Soviet President in 1987. He claimed that there were over 1 million persons of Crimean Tatar origin in the Soviet Union and that 125,000 of the 250,000 who were deported died en route to the east. Crimean Tatars were very active in business in Central Asia. Under communism they were never granted permission to return to their homeland. In the late 1980s Dzhemilev returned to Crimea and became a leader of his people there and gradually after 1991 Tatars began to return but received little official help. Perhaps if the Crimean Tatars en masse had attempted to return, the Soviet authorities could not have prevented them. At present they are confined mostly to the infertile north of the republic. A. W. Fisher: *The Crimean Tatars,* Stanford, Calif., 1978.

Dzhugashvili, Yakov Iosifovich (1904–43), the elder son of STALIN by his first marriage to Ekaterina Svanidze, a Georgian woman. His mother died in 1907 and he grew up in Georgia and Moscow in the privileged environment of the Soviet Party élite. When the Germans invaded in June 1941, he volunteered to go to the front, having received military training, but was soon taken prisoner by the Germans near Smolensk. After Field Marshal Paulus had been captured by the Red Army after the defeat of Stalingrad, the German High Command offered Dzhugashvili in exchange for Paulus. Stalin's curt reply was: 'There are no Soviet prisoners of war, only traitors.' Dzhugashvili became very depressed in Sachsenhausen concentration camp and deliberately threw himself on to the barbed-wire fence surrounding the camp. Every prisoner was aware that the SS guards had orders to shoot if this occurred. A British fellow prisoner confirmed that Dzhugashvili had deliberately sought death. The Allies did not inform Stalin about the way his son had died, judging that it might upset him.

E

Eikhe, Robert Ivanovich (1897–1940), KHRUSHCHEV, in his Secret Speech at the XXth Party Congress in October 1956, cited the fate of Eikhe as typical of the crimes of the STALIN era. Eikhe joined the Bolshevik Party in 1915. He was elected a candidate member of the Politburo in February 1935. As first secretary of the Siberian kraikom (krai Party committee), he had vigorously purged his region of Trotskyites and Bukharinites in the late 1930s. He was appointed People's Commissar for Agriculture, 1937. He was arrested on 29 April 1938 on evidence provided by the NKVD, which had forced former Trotskyites and Bukharinites in West Siberia to testify that Eikhe had been a member of their organisation. He was forced under torture to sign a confession but when this was forwarded to Stalin on 1 October 1939 Eikhe categorically denied his guilt and asked for a re-examination of his case. He sent Stalin another memorandum on 27 October 1939, pulling the case against him apart. He states that he made the confession under torture and that one of the policemen had made use of the fact that his broken ribs had not healed to break him. On 2 February 1940 Eikhe appeared in court and again refuted his confession, stating that he would die 'believing in the truth of Party policy'. He was shot on 4 February 1940.

Eisenstein, Sergei Mikhailovich (1898–1948), the most famous film director, producer and theorist of the Soviet cinema, he was born in Riga and trained as a civil engineer. In 1918 he volunteered for the Red Army and was assigned to a theatrical group where he was director, stage designer and actor in his first production. After army service he studied Japanese at the General Staff Academy. He became director for Proletkult (proletarian culture movement) and worked with Vsevolod MEYERHOLD. In 1925 he began working on his first film, *The Strike*. The same year he made *The Year 1905*, later renamed *The Battleship Potemkin*, which received its premiere at the Bolshoi Theatre, December 1925. He then went to Berlin to study the latest film techniques and he became a household name in Germany, the Soviet Union and elsewhere. *The Battleship Potemkin* was even more popular in Germany than in the Soviet Union. In 1926 Goskino commissioned him to make a film about collectivisation, *The General Line,* and in 1927 he shot *October* in Leningrad as a celebration of the tenth anniversary of the revolution. *The General Line* was completed in 1929 but by then the attitude towards collectivisation had changed – previously it had been voluntary. This required re-editing of the film and it appeared under a new title, *The Old and the New.* This prompted him to go abroad with his assistants, Grigory Aleksandrov and Eduard Tisse, to experience the new medium, the sound film. After visiting several countries, he signed a contract to make a picture for Paramount in Hollywood, 1930. He met Charlie Chaplin and Walt Disney but Paramount were not happy with his proposals and cancelled the contract. Eisenstein then went to Mexico but returned to Moscow in 1932. He even thought of filming *Das Kapital* by Karl Marx. In July 1935 he began shooting *Bezhin Meadow* but it was halted in 1937. Towards the end of 1938, he completed *Aleksandr Nevsky,* which turned out to be his most popular film. Besides filming he was a professor at the All-Union State Institute of the Cinema, Moscow. He began making *Ivan the Terrible* in October 1942 and the first part received its première in January 1945 and was an immediate hit. Eisenstein and his associates received the Stalin Prize for it. The second part, which revealed the similarities between Ivan and STALIN, was withdrawn in 1946 and not screened until 1958, well after the dictator's death. Eisenstein's health suffered and he died of a heart attack and is buried in Novodevichy Cemetery. As a brilliant innovator, Eisenstein suffered attacks from all quarters and many of his projects were left unfinished. Sergei Eisenstein: *Immortal Memories, An Autobiography,* London, 1983.

Elchibey Abdulfaz Gadirgulu Ogly (né Aliev), (*b.* 1938), the first democratic President of the Republic of Azerbaijan, he was however deposed in June 1993, being succeeded by Geidar ALIEV, the former Party boss of the republic. He was born into an Azeri family and graduated in Arab philology from Azerbaijan State University, Baku, and then worked as a translator in Egypt. In 1965 he became a postgraduate student at the university and successfully presented his candidate dissertation in history (PhD), 1969. He then taught in the oriental faculty of the university but was arrested in 1975 for 'slandering the Soviet state', banned from teaching and imprisoned for two years. In 1989 he was elected chair at the founding congress of the Popular Front of Azerbaijan, being reelected in July 1991. He succeeded President Ayaz MUTALIBOV in 1992 but was in turn removed in 1993. A major reason for this was the continuing defeat of Azeri forces in the war against Armenia over Nagorno-Karabakh.

Epishev, Aleksei Alekseevich (1908–85), the Party's watchdog in the armed forces for over two decades, he worked in the fishing industry before joining the Communist Party, 1929, and the Red Army the following year. As a political officer, he proved adept at presenting the Party to the military and ensuring Party control at a time when there were relatively few Communists in the armed forces. He became secretary of the Kharkov oblast Party committee (obkom), 1940–3, and was a secretary of the Central Committee, Communist Party of Ukraine, 1946–50. A major task during this period was to reimpose communist authority in Ukraine and introduce it in west Ukraine. In 1950 he became first secretary of the Odessa obkom, in 1951–3 he was deputy USSR Minister of Internal Affairs (Security) and would appear to have been a KHRUSHCHEV protégé. He later stated that he felt that someone did not want him in the post; that someone was probably BERIA. The latter dismissed Epishev in 1953 and he returned to his Odessa post. Shortly afterwards he went into the diplomatic service and was ambassador to Romania and Yugoslavia, 1955–62. In May 1962 Khrushchev chose him to head the political administration of the Soviet armed forces, a sensitive post given the trouble that Khrushchev had had with Marshal ZHUKOV, for instance. Epishev was elected to the Party Central Committee in 1964. He was loyal to Khrushchev but also to BREZHNEV, ANDROPOV and CHERNENKO, only giving way under GORBACHEV.

Eremenko, Marshal Andrei Ivanovich (1892–1970), one of the most successful Red Army front-line commanders during the Great Fatherland War. He joined the Communist Party and the Red Army, 1918, and fought in the Civil War as commander of a cavalry regiment. He graduated from the Frunze Military Academy, 1935. STALIN recalled him from the Soviet Far East after the German invasion, appointing him commander of the Bryansk Front, August 1941. He was severely wounded during the retreat from Bryansk in October 1941 and was out of action for a year. He was made commander of the Southeast Front, August 1942, and took part in encircling the Germans and their allied forces at Stalingrad. Stalin diverted him from mopping up Paulus's 6th German Army (the task was handed to ROKOSSOVSKY) and Eremenko was sent after von Manstein's forces. He participated in the advance on Smolensk and was then made commander of the Independent (Black Sea) Maritime Front, the task of which was to liberate Crimea from German and Romanian troops. Eremenko and TOLBUKHIN began their offensive in April 1944 and the enemy surrendered in May 1944. Eremenko was then transferred to command of the 2nd Baltic Front, liberated Dvinsk and afterwards participated in the offensive against Riga, Latvia. He was then moved to command the Carpathian Front until 1946. He retired from the Red Army in 1958.

Erenburg, Ilya Grigorevich (Ehrenburg) (1891–1967), a highly cultured writer who became an apologist for Stalin. Erenburg was born into a Jewish family in Kiev and was arrested, 1908, for revolutionary activity. He moved to Paris, 1908, and wrote for Russian newspapers during the First World War. He returned to Russia, July 1917, but condemned the Bolshevik seizure of power in verse, 1918, sided with the Whites during the Civil War and emigrated again, spring 1921, to Paris. He knew all the radical artists of the period, including Picasso, and Erenburg published his first novel in Berlin, 1922, and played a leading role in the flowering of Russian émigré literature. He floated between Soviet Russia and the west during the 1920s but was taken by

STALIN and the first Five Year Plan (1928–33), and his novel, *The Second Day,* is a celebration of it. He became prominent as a Soviet spokesman on anti-fascism and he was an *Izvestiya* correspondent during the Spanish Civil War, 1936–9. He witnessed the fall of Paris to the Germans in 1940 personally and this is recorded in his novel, *The Fall of Paris,* 1941. He visited the front several times and thought up the slogan 'Ubei nemtsa' (Kill every German). Erenburg was involved in preparing *Chernaya Kniga,* an account of German crimes against the Jewish population on Soviet soil and though Stalin stopped its publication it was published later in Israel. He regarded himself very lucky to have survived late Stalinist anti-Semitism and once remarked that he had drawn a lucky lottery ticket (KHRUSHCHEV put his survival at the court of Stalin down to the same luck). His remarkable political skill in sensing the mood of the moment was illustrated when his novel, *Ottepel (The Thaw),* was published in 1956 and gave its name to a whole period of Soviet literature. The novel advocates a less xenophobic view of the world. His memoirs, *People, Years, Life,* opened up a European cultural world to the Soviet reader which had been closed for over three decades. Erenburg's collected works came to nine volumes. He was also an art collector and amassed a valuable gallery, including several Picassos.

Erin, Viktor Fedorovich (*b.* 1944), born on 17 January 1944 in Kazan, Tatarstan, into a Russian family and a member of the CPSU until July 1991, he has spent all his working life in the militia (police). He began his career as a militiaman in the Ministry of Internal Affairs in Kazan in 1964. In 1967 he moved to the criminal investigation department of the Ministry of Internal Affairs, Tatar ASSR, and was involved in the investigation of very serious crimes. In 1973 he graduated from the higher school of the militia, USSR

Ministry of Internal Affairs. During 1980–1 he served in Afghanistan and hence belongs to the ranks of the Afgantsy. Afterwards he was promoted to Moscow and from 1983 to 1988 headed a department of the main administration, USSR Ministry of Internal Affairs. Having proved himself in Moscow, he was appointed first deputy Minister of Internal Affairs of Armenia in 1988 and remained there until 1990. He then returned to the capital and became deputy head of the criminal militia (with the rank of general-major) and from 28 February 1991 first deputy Minister of Internal Affairs of the RSFSR. The man who chose him as his deputy was General Viktor BARANNIKOV. He had garnered wide experience in dealing with serious and organised crime and this would stand him in good stead in post-communist Russia where he was confronted with the rising power of the mafia. Erin played a key role in the suppression of the attempted coup in August 1991 and was personally involved in the arrest of Boris PUGO, USSR Minister of Internal Affairs, Valentin Pavlov, USSR Prime Minister, and V. Ivanenko, chair of the RSFSR KGB. Pugo and Pavlov were key members of the conspiracy to remove President Mikhail GORBACHEV and replace him with his deputy, Gennady YANAEV. In early September 1991 Erin became first deputy Minister of Internal Affairs of the USSR. (At that time the USSR and RSFSR Minister of Internal Affairs was Viktor Barannikov, as President YELTSIN was gradually subordinating USSR institutions to himself.) During the autumn of 1991 Erin was involved in a head-on conflict with General A. Gurev, head of the administration for combating organised crime in the USSR Ministry of Internal Affairs. Erin won and Gurev was pushed out of the USSR Ministry of Internal Affairs. His career was given another boost in December 1991 when he was appointed first deputy of Viktor Barannikov in the newly formed Ministry of Security and Internal Affairs of the Russian Federation. He was a very active supporter of the unification of the Ministries of Security and Internal Affairs and played a leading role in drafting the decree which President Yeltsin signed. Erin favoured strong measures to combat rising crime. However, the decree met widespread hostility from democrats who regarded it as a throwback to Stalinist times. Ominously, the last person in charge of the unified ministry had been Lavrenty BERIA. There were fears that too much power was being concentrated in one ministry in the volatile, post-communist period. The matter was referred to the Constitutional Court and it ruled in January 1992 that the joint ministry was unconstitutional, a blow against the President. However, this did not prevent Erin from being appointed, on 15 January 1992, Russian Minister of Internal Affairs by presidential decree with the rank of general-colonel of internal forces. He was a career officer who quickly changed direction in 1991 and strongly supported the view, held by the President, that the CPSU and its organizations should be excluded from the law-enforcing agencies. He was one of the first in the leadership to abandon the CPSU in mid-1991. He has earned a reputation as a highly skilled professional and specialises in dealing with organised crime. Erin's appointment as minister did not meet with support from many middle- and lower-ranking officers who were loyal to the outgoing minister A. Dunaev. Erin met this challenge by choosing a team of skilled professionals who had long experience in the agencies of the USSR and RSFSR Ministries of Internal Affairs. He enjoys the reputation among his superiors of being a total professional, without any trace of ideological bias. However, this, at times, can lead to pedantry and the implementation of orders irrespective of the cost. He has been awarded the Order of the Red Star and medals for investigating very serious crimes. The fact that he has remained in office during the whole post-communist period testifies to his skill, both professional and political, but the growth in the mafia has undermined confidence in him and his officers. Many of them are rumoured to take bribes, but his name has never been associated with corruption. He lives in Moscow.

Ershov, Ivan (b. 1922), the deputy Chief of Staff of the Supreme Commander of the Warsaw Pact forces, August 1968, who had personal command of troops which suppressed the Prague Spring. A dedicated Communist, he was outraged when his daughter, Tatyana, married her Jewish mathematics teacher and wanted to join him in emigration in Israel. Tatyana then went on hunger strike and her father relented after thirty-three days. The arrival of glasnost led him to a reappraisal of the events of 1968 and he travelled to Prague in early 1990 to apologise personally to Alexander Dubcek for his role in the 1968 Warsaw Pact invasion.

Esenin, Sergei Aleksandrovich (1895–1925), a very popular poet with an unconventional lifestyle whose suicide sparked off many others, bringing to an end the romantic revolutionary period. A Russian, he was born in Ryazan oblast into a peasant family. He began writing poetry very early and by the time he was eighteen his poems had been published in the leading St Petersburg journals. An ardent revolutionary, he never joined the Bolshevik Party because he regarded it as not sufficiently leftist. As a blond with blue eyes, he was all the rage and everything he did and said was outré. He married, as his second wife, the American dancer Isadora Duncan, many years his senior, and they toured Europe and the United States. The marriage did not last, not least because they did not have a common language and he was addicted to drink. He abandoned her and returned to Moscow, marrying again in 1925. Distraught, he hanged himself in a hotel in Leningrad, writing a farewell poem in his own blood. Esenin's death caught the mood of cultural and youth despair at the time and there was a wave of suicides in sympathy. He was never accepted by the Soviet literary establishment and his poems are peopled by anarchists and others resisting authority. Some of his poems were turned into songs and became immensely popular.

Evtushenko, Evgeny Aleksandrovich (b. 1933), he became the voice of youth during the post-1956 thaw period and had a dazzling career as an open-air poet. He was born in Zima, Siberia, and moved with his mother to Moscow, 1944. He graduated from the Gorky Literary Institute, 1954. Together with VOZNESENSKY and AKHMADULINA he starred at many sessions in football stadia. Evtushenko personified the anti-STALIN cultural mood of the time and his Babi Yar (about the Nazi murder of Ukrainian Jews), 1961, and Nasledie Stalina (Stalin's Legacy), 1962, where he asked for the guards at Stalin's grave to be doubled lest the old dictator and his times be resurrected, were published in the central media and caused a sensation. In 1963 he published his autobiography in France without first obtaining clearance. He had his wings clipped and was not permitted to travel abroad for a time. Internationally, he was also very popular but was guarded in his comments about Soviet life. He influenced a whole generation of perestroika politicians. For a time, his wife was Bella Akhmadulina, a very successful poetess of the same generation. He was appointed to the presidium of the USSR Union of Writers, 1967, and was influential during the glasnost period in the organisation. In 1993 he published a novel about the failed August 1991 coup, Don't Die before Your Death.

Ezhov, Nikolai Ivanovich (1895–1939), the 'bloody dwarf' and 'iron people's commissar', Ezhov, gave his name to the bloodiest period of the purges, the *Ezhovshchina*. He joined the Bolsheviks in April 1917 and the Red Army in 1918 as a political commissar and participated in the Civil War. He was elected to the Central Committee of the Party, 1934. He succeeded YAGODA as People's Commissar for Internal Affairs in September 1936, after the latter's fall from grace. STALIN believed that the NKVD was 'four years behind' in applying mass repression and consequently there was a need to 'catch up'. Ezhov is reported to have spent his first six months in office liquidating about 3,000 of Yagoda's men. In October 1937 Ezhov became a candidate member of the Politburo. He was dismissed as People's Commissar in December 1938, being replaced by BERIA. Ezhov was then appointed People's Commissar for Water Transport. The previously powerful head of the police attended meetings of his new commissariat but never said anything. He spent the time making paper aeroplanes and birds, tossing them into the air and then crawling under the table to retrieve them. The security police finally arrived for him, in the middle of a commissariat meeting, in March 1939. He is reported to have stood up, thrown his gun on to the table and stated, 'I have been waiting for this for a long time.' He was taken away and never seen again. Stalin had decided he needed a scapegoat for the excesses of the purges which were coming to an end in 1939. Ezhov was addicted to drugs and was rumoured to have shot Yagoda personally. Before 1937, there was a general rule that there should be some semblance of sanity about the confessions of prisoners and some indication of their guilt. In 1937 this did not matter any more. Also until 1937 most NKVD officers believed they were helping the state to build a better society. Most of these men were then liquidated and killing became just another job.

F

Fadeev, Aleksandr Aleksandrovich (1901–56), an establishment author under STALIN who became a feared literary bureaucrat but ended his life with his own hand, fearing retribution for the crimes of the past. A Russian, he was born near Moscow, moved to Vladivostok, 1912, joined the Communist Party, 1918, and fought in the Civil War. He returned to Moscow, 1926, and became the leader of the proletarian literary movement, RAPP. He became famous after publishing *The Rout,* 1927, which was regarded as a brilliant example of the new school of socialist realism and deals relatively frankly with Red partisans in the Russian Far East. He never completed his second major novel, *The Last of the Udegs,* 1929–40, about a Siberian tribe for whom political and economic progress is viewed as the solution to all their ills. He made a career in the USSR Union of Writers and headed the organisation, 1946–54, during the terrible years of the Zhdanovshchina. His novel, *The Young Guard,* about Komsomol resistance to the Germans in the Donbass, was published in 1945 but had to be revised in order to emphasise the leading role of the Party in the partisan movement. KHRUSHCHEV's denunciation of Stalin at the XXth Party Congress, February 1956, plunged him into a fit of despair and he hanged himself, a tragic end to a tragic career.

Falin, Valentin Mikhailovich (*b.* 1926), one of the leading Soviet specialists on Germany, he was born in Leningrad and worked in a Moscow factory, 1942–5. He graduated from the Moscow Institute of International Relations, 1950, and joined the Communist Party, 1953. He worked in the USSR Ministry of Foreign Affairs, 1952–71, in a variety of areas, but acquiring expertise in German affairs, and he was head of the third European department (German and Austrian affairs), 1968–71. Then he was appointed Soviet Ambassador to West Germany, staying in Bonn until 1978. Hence he was head of the Soviet mission at an important stage in Soviet–German relations, contributing to the improved climate. On his recall to Moscow he moved into the Party Central Committee apparatus as deputy head of the international department, leaving in 1983 to take up a senior editorial post with *Izvestiya.* Falin became head of APN (Novosti) in 1986. In tune with the new political thinking of GORBACHEV, he succeeded Anatoly DOBRYNIN as head of the international department, October 1988. Falin became a candidate member of the Central Committee, 1986, and a full member, April 1989. He was also elected to the USSR Congress of People's Deputies, March 1989, and its inner body, the USSR Supreme Soviet. Falin spoke almost faultless German, and was liked for his fairness and attention to detail. The attempted coup in August 1991 was a disaster for him and he was upset at the way he was treated, regarding himself as a professional official and not as an intriguer. Falin was not allowed to clear his drawers in the Central Committee building and this made it more difficult for him when it came to writing his memoirs. They have appeared in German translation and reveal an almost detached, stoical view of life.

Fedin, Konstantin Aleksandrovich
(1892–1977), a writer, playwright and literary bureaucrat who began as a radical and ended as a conformist. He was born in Saratov, the son of a merchant, and was studying in Germany when war broke out and he was interned there. He returned to Soviet Russia after Germany had been defeated and worked in the provincial press, joined the Red Army, and the Communist Party, for a time. He moved to Petrograd in 1921 to join the literary circle, the Serapion Brothers. His best-known work, *Goroda i Gody* (*Cities and Years*), 1924, is about war and revolution in Germany and Russia and is one of the first novels to deal with the role of the intelligentsia in these events. Fedin visited Berlin regularly during the 1920s and his second novel, *The Brothers*, 1928, is about a musician who swims against the revolutionary tide and is left stranded. During the 1930s Fedin is representative of socialist realism and his writing contrasts the rise of the Soviet Union with the decline of the west (an age-old Russian theme). In 1940 he published another novel about a healthy Soviet Union and a diseased Europe. In a trilogy, begun during the 1940s, Fedin presents a socialist realist hero at three important stages of his life but distorts history to conform to the Soviet norms of the time. He was elected to the USSR Academy of Sciences in 1958. Fedin was appointed first secretary of the USSR Union of Workers, 1959, and then was chair of the board of the union, 1971–7. He is now regarded as a typical establishment figure of the years of stagnation, the BREZHNEV years.

Fedorchuk, Vitaly Vasilevich (*b.* 1918), a tough Ukrainian KGB officer who failed to make the grade when he was promoted to head the USSR organisation. He worked on various local newspapers in Ukraine, 1934–6, then studied at a military school, 1936–9. He joined the Communist Party, 1940, and was an

officer in Smersh, 1943–7, then in the GRU (military intelligence), until 1970. Fedorchuk was appointed chair of the KGB in Ukraine, 1970, and remained there until 1982. During this period he dealt heavy-handedly with Ukrainian nationalists, placing many of them in the camps. BREZHNEV chose Fedorchuk to succeed Yury ANDROPOV as chair of the USSR KGB when Andropov left the organisation to become a secretary of the Central Committee and plot his rise to power as General Secretary of the Party, May 1982. When Andropov took over from Brezhnev, Fedorchuk was shunted sideways to the less important post of USSR Minister of Internal Affairs, December 1982, being replaced by Viktor CHEBRIKOV. Fedorchuk was a candidate member of the Politburo of the Communist Party of Ukraine, 1973–6, and a full member, 1976–82. He retired from office in 1986.

Fedorov, Boris Grigorevich (*b.* 1958), a Russian, he was born in Moscow and was a member of the CPSU until August 1991. According to him he became a member of the Party to further his career and was never committed to its ideology. He estimated that about 20 per cent of Party members were convinced supporters. He graduated from the Moscow Institute of Finance as an economist. In 1980 he joined the main department for currency and economy of the USSR Central Bank as an economist and later became chief economist. While there, in 1985, he successfully presented his candidate dissertation in economics on the 'organization and economic role of present-day short-term exchange trading in developed capitalist countries' (PhD (Econ)). From 1987 to 1989 he was a senior research member of the Institute of World Economy and International Relations of the USSR Academy of Sciences. In 1990 he successfully presented his doctoral dissertation in economics on the 'loan capital market in the economies of developed capitalism' (DSc (Econ)). From 1980 to 1990 he was also consultant to the socio-economic department of the Party Central Committee. He became a member of the group around Academicians SHATALIN and PETRAKOV, and Grigory YAVLINSKY, who drafted the 500-day economic programme in the summer of 1990. This programme envisaged a transition in the Soviet Union from a planned to a market economy in 500 days. President Mikhail GOR- BACHEV declined to endorse it in the autumn of 1990. In July 1990 Fedorov became RSFSR Minister of Finance in the government headed by Ivan SILAEV. However, he resigned in December 1990 because of the lack of commitment of the Silaev government to market reform. In 1991 he became Russian representative in the European Bank for Reconstruction and Development (EBRD) in London and played an important role in framing the bank's policy towards Russia and the successor states of the Soviet Union. He gained valuable experience at the EBRD in macroeconomic policy and financial services. Russians liked to refer to him as 'their man in the City'. He turned down the opportunity to become chair of the Russian Central Bank, believing that as it was subordinate to the Russian parliament his room for manoeuvre would have been limited (this turned out to be a misjudgement). He also acted as executive director of the Russian Federation in the International Bank of Reconstruction and Development in Washington. He is a fluent English speaker, partly gained from his postgraduate studies at the University of London. He is the author of a Russian–English dictionary of currency and credit terminology. An able economist, he is in favour of strict monetary policies to move Russia to a market economy as quickly as possible. Able and ambitious, he has not found it easy to make the transition from economist to politician. He supports the concept of 'shock therapy' so as to move Russia to a market economy as quickly as possible. After the failure of Egor GAID- AR to be confirmed as Prime Minister at the VIIth Congress of People's Deputies, in December 1992, the road was open for a pro-reform economist to enter the government to oversee the reform process. Viktor CHERNOMYRDIN, the new Prime Minister, accepted Fedorov as his deputy responsible for macroeconomic reform and finance. This was a great boost for the economic reform lobby. Fedorov quickly established himself as the main decision maker on economic affairs and proposed economic reforms in March 1993 which were severe but offered some concessions to the population and the regions. In March 1993 Fedorov was also appointed Russian Minister of Finance, succeeding Vasily BARCHUK. A battle developed between him and Viktor GERASHCHENKO, head of the Russian Central Bank, over monetary policy. Fedorov was determined to bring the bank under government control. The Democratic Russia movement warmly welcomed Fedorov's appointment and offered its support. Fedorov regards the battle against inflation as a major priority and envisages new currency mechanisms and monetary policy based on a freely convertible currency. Enterprise should be free to enter foreign markets and to trade without hindrance. He is married with a son and a daughter and lives in Moscow.

Fedorov, Svyatoslav Nikolaevich (b. 1927), a brilliantly successful eye surgeon who has political ambitions to lead Russia. A Russian, he was born in Ukraine; his father had a fine military record but was declared an enemy of the people, 1937, and sent to the camps. Fedorov was a member of the Communist Party until August 1991. He graduated as a doctor from the Medical Institute, Rostov-on-Don, and became a Doctor of Medicine (DSc). He was a professor and a corresponding member of the USSR Academy of Sciences (Russian Academy of Sciences, from 1991) and the USSR Academy of Medical Sciences (the Russian Academy of Medical Sciences, from 1991). After graduation he worked as an ophthalmologist in various hospitals, and in 1957 became head of the clinical department of the branch of the Gelmgolts Scientific Research Institute of Eye Diseases, Cheboksary. In 1960 he was the first eye surgeon to place an artificial crystal in a patient's eye. The Soviet medical establishment condemned him for this and he had to stop practising but later he moved to the Arkhangelsk Medical Institute. He continued his work of implanting artificial plastic and then silicon crystals and by 1965 he had performed sixty-two such operations. He was head of a Moscow institute, 1967–74, director of the Moscow Scientific Research Laboratory for Experimental and Clinical Eye Surgery, 1974–80, and director of the Moscow Scientific Research Institute of Eye Microsurgery, 1980–6. In 1986 Fedorov met Nikolai RYZHKOV, the USSR Prime Minister, and made a great impression on him. With Ryzhkov's support, by a joint decree of the Party Central Committee and the USSR Council of Ministers, the institute was transformed into an interbranch scientific research complex for eye microsurgery with Fedorov as its director. In 1991 he was appointed a member of the Higher Consultation Co-ordination Council of the Russian Federation Supreme Soviet and in 1992 he became vice-president of the Russian Club (for those who had arrived in Russian society). He was elected to the USSR Congress of People's Deputies, March 1989, and became a member of the Supreme Soviet. In June 1990 he was elected president of the Russian Federation union of Lessees and Entrepreneurs. In August 1991 Fedorov ordered mobile medical equipment and cars of food to be sent to the White House. He left the Communist Party, August 1991, and

joined Democratic Russia. He has published over 400 scientific papers.

Filatov, Sergei Aleksandrovich (*b.* 1936), a leading democrat who worked closely with YELTSIN. He was born into a Russian family in Moscow and graduated from the Institute of Energy, 1964. He was a power generation specialist in Cuba, 1966–8. In 1969 he began working at the Tselikov All-Union Scientific Research and Project Design Institute of Metallurgical Machine Building where he became head of a department. He successfully presented his candidate dissertation in technical sciences (PhD (Eng)). He was elected to the RSFSR Congress of People's Deputies and the USSR Supreme Soviet and during the elections was supported by the Democratic Russia 90 electoral bloc. In January 1991 he became secretary of the Presidium (the key body which agreed the next day's agenda) of the Russian Supreme Soviet and then became involved in organising Yeltsin's presidential campaign. In August 1991 he was chief of staff of the deputies in the White House. In November 1991 he was elected first deputy speaker of the Russian parliament with Ruslan KHASBULATOV as speaker. Filatov was a member of the Security Council and a representative of Democratic Russia (DemRossiya). His differences with Khasbulatov surfaced at the VIth Congress of People's Deputies, April 1992, with Filatov taking a strongly pro-Yeltsin line. Relations degenerated into bitterness and in August 1992 Filatov was removed from his position in violation of parliamentary regulations. In January 1993 he was made chief of staff of the President.

Frunze, Mikhail Vasilevich (1885–1925), a leading Red commander during the Civil War, Frunze was born in Pishpek, now known as Bishkek, in Kyrgyzstan. Pishpek was renamed Frunze in 1926. His father was Moldovan and his mother

Russian, and he attended school in Verny, later Alma Ata and Almaty, Kazakhstan where he first encountered revolutionary ideas. When he moved to St Petersburg to study at a polytechnic in 1904 he joined the Bolshevik faction of the RSDRP. He was soon expelled from the polytechnic for taking part in a demonstration and he moved later to Ivanovo-Voznesensk where he became one of the leaders of the textile workers' strike there in 1905. The town also formed the first soviet in Russia. He participated in the Moscow uprising of December 1905 and was sentenced to ten years' hard labour in Siberia. In 1917 Frunze played a key role in Minsk and Belorussia. In October 1917 he led workers and soldiers in the struggle for Moscow. He was then dispatched to the Urals where he led the southern group of the Red Army in 1919. His troops inflicted a severe defeat on Admiral KOLCHAK'S White forces and Frunze took over command of the eastern front. He then turned his attention to Turkestan (Central Asia) and disposed of the local Muslim leaders, including the Emir of Bukhara. He led the Reds who routed General WRANGEL in Crimea in November 1920. He became People's Commissar for War in January 1925 when TROTSKY resigned. He sided with STALIN against Trotsky on military affairs. Frunze was the author of the 'unitary military doctrine' which envisaged that the military should be trained for offensive action and dedicated to carrying out one of the goals of the Communist Party, world revolution. This meant disposing of the ex-Tsarist officers whom Trotsky, out of necessity, had recruited during the Civil War. Frunze helped lay the foundations of the efficient Soviet military machine by introducing conscription and standardising military formations and uniforms.

Furtseva, Ekaterina Alekseevna (1910–74), under KHRUSHCHEV, she became the first woman to be elected to the Politburo and thus was the exception to the rule that only males could make it to the top. She was a special favourite of Nikita Sergeevich and progressed from being first Party secretary of a Moscow raion from 1942 to 1950, when she was made second secretary of the capital city. Khrushchev made her first secretary of Moscow city Party organisation in 1954 (until 1957). This was a formidable position for a woman to occupy. In 1952 she had been elected a candidate member of the Central Committee and in 1956 a full member. The same year she was elected a secretary of the Central Committee and a candidate member of the Presidium (Politburo), attaining full membership of the highest Party organ the following year. Her career nose-dived in 1960 when she lost her secretaryship of the Central Committee and was made USSR Minister of Culture. In 1961 she also lost her Presidium membership. Reported to have attempted suicide but found in time, she stayed in office under BREZHNEV and died in office in November 1974. This testifies to her conservative, conformist views on culture and indicates that her main function was to keep the cultural intelligentsia in line. Artists and intellectuals used to complain that the Soviet Union had a minister of culture who had no culture. This was unfair; she did like the circus.

G

Gabo, Naum (né Pevsner, Naum Nee-mya) (1890–1977), a leading Russian sculptor, born in Bryansk, he studied natural sciences and engineering in Munich. One of the fathers of constructivist sculpture, Gabo worked in Germany and elsewhere, before returning to Russia in 1917. He came from a talented artistic family and changed his name to Gabo so as not to be confused with his brothers and cousins. Nikolaus Pevsner, the well-known British architectural historian was a relative. Gabo participated fully in the early Bolshevik period and when LENIN visited his workshop, the Soviet leader, after viewing his work, remarked, 'I've no idea what this means, but carry on.' However, this tolerance did not last and Gabo emigrated to live and work in Germany, France, Britain and the United States.

Gagarin, Yury Alekseevich (1934–68), the first man in space, Gagarin made his stunning flight on 12 April 1961 in Vostok-1 for 108 minutes. He was born near Smolensk, the son of a collective farmer, and joined the Soviet Air Force in 1955, graduating from the Chkalov Military Aviation School, 1957. He became a fighter pilot and in 1960 was selected as a possible future cosmonaut. After his sensational orbiting of the earth he became a world celebrity and KHRUSH-CHEV revelled in this first in world science. Gagarin became a member of the Party in 1960 and was also elected a USSR Supreme Soviet deputy. He travelled the world as an ambassador for Soviet science and technology. At home he helped train a new generation of cosmonauts and was a test pilot. During a test flight in March 1968 he crashed and was killed. The reason for the crash may have been that his aircraft strayed into the slipstream of another jet.

Gaidar, Egor Timurovich (*b.* 1956), a leading Russian economist, he was born into a Russian family in Moscow. His father is a retired rear-admiral and a military journalist who was special correspondent of *Pravda* in Cuba and Yugoslavia. Gaidar's grandfather was Arkady Gaidar, a Red commissar and author of children's books, and his mother is a noted historian specialising in the eighteenth century. Gaidar left secondary school (part of it spent in Belgrade) with a gold medal. He entered the faculty of economics of Moscow University in 1973 and graduated in 1979 with distinction. He successfully presented his candidate dissertation in economics (PhD (Econ)), his supervisor being Academician Stanislav SHATALIN, in 1981. He followed this in 1988 with a doctorate in economics (DSc (Econ)). Gaidar was one of a brilliant group of mathematical economists who came into their own under GORBACHEV. ANDROPOV had brought them together (they included Anatoly CHUBAIS) to suggest solutions to the slowdown in economic growth. When the All-Union Scientific Research Institute of Systems studies split in 1985 into the Central Mathematical Economics Institute (under Academician PETRA-KOV) and the Institute of Economics and Forecasting of Scientific Technical Progress (under Shatalin), Gaidar remained with Shatalin. In 1987 Gaidar was invited by Aleksandr YAKOVLEV to become editor for economics of *Kommunist,* the Party's theoretical journal, then edited by Otto LATSIS. In 1990 Gaidar moved to *Pravda* and became a member of its board. In the autumn of 1990 he was appointed director of the Institute of Economic Policy, USSR Academy of Sciences. He was a member of Shatalin's team who helped draft the 500-day programme for Gorbachev but the latter found it too radical to implement. Gaidar then established contact with YELTSIN and after the abortive coup of August 1991 vied with YAVLINSKY to fashion a new market-oriented Russian economy. Gaidar won the battle and became deputy Prime Minister of the Russian Federation in November 1991, launching his 'shock therapy' in January 1992. It did not succeed and Gaidar had to retreat from government in December 1992, giving way to Viktor CHERNOMYRDIN as Prime Minister.

Galich, Aleksandr Arkadevich (pseudonym. Ginzburg) (1919–77), born in Ekaterinoslav (now Dnepropetrovsk), Galich moved with his family to Moscow and attended the Stanislavsky Studio there. He entertained the forces during the war and afterwards began writing film scripts and songs. He became a very popular singer of satirical ballads, accompanying himself on the guitar. It was the era of the tape recorder and this ensured his fame, as clandestine recordings circulated. One of his listeners was Yury ANDROPOV and Galich was expelled from the Union of Writers and the Union of Cinematographers in 1971, being forced to emigrate in 1974. He worked with Radio Liberty and became a regular broadcaster to the east. He electrocuted himself accidentally in Paris while trying to set up his stereophonic equipment. A great satirist, his time came again under glasnost and he was rehabilitated in 1988.

Galiev, Sultan Mirsaid (1880–1940), the most famous Muslim national Communist in the Soviet Union, he attempted to graft on aspects of Islamic teaching to Marxism–Leninism, thereby giving it a distinctly non-European national face. He favoured an autonomous Islamic Communist Party, the setting up of a Muslim Red Army with a Muslim High Command, the coming into being of a Muslim state, the Republic of Turan, to which all the Turkic peoples of the Volga and Central Asia would belong (this was later developed into an autonomous Islamic Soviet Socialist Republic), the formation of a Colonial International, separate from the Comintern, which would be mainly concerned with peasant-dominated countries. He was born in present-day Bashkortostan and taught and published in Ufa. He participated in the Muslim Congress in Russia in May and July 1917, joined the Russian Communist Party in November 1917 and was made chair of the Central Muslim Commissariat when it was set up in January 1918. He was also a member of the inner collegium of the Commissariat of Nationalities where he worked closely with STALIN. However, in 1919 he began to stress increasingly pan-Islamic and pan-Turkic ideas. His views were a direct threat to Moscow's goal of hegemony and in May 1923 he was arrested and accused of 'national deviation', mainly at the instigation of Stalin. International pressure led to his release. In November 1923 he was rearrested and sentenced to ten years' hard labour for treason. He was rearrested in early 1938, sentenced to death in December 1939 and executed in January 1940.

Gamsakhurdia, Zviad Konstantinovich (1939–94), the first President of the Republic of Georgia after the collapse of communism, his unalloyed nationalism alienated non-Georgians, contributed to the armed conflict in Abkhazia and South Ossetia, and eventually led to his removal as President by the military council in January 1992. His father was a leading Georgian literary figure and obtained a doctorate in (west European) philology from Tbilisi State University. He was the editor of samizdat journals and newspapers and was imprisoned between 1977 and 1979. In 1990 he was elected the speaker of the Georgian Supreme Soviet and in 1991 Georgia's first President. He saw Georgia as the republic of the Georgians and found most support among his fellow Mingrelians in west Georgia. Under his authoritarian rule there were constant armed clashes. After his removal he took refuge in Chechnya but could not dislodge Eduard SHEVARDNADZE, the new Georgian leader.

Gapon, Father Georgy Apollonovich

(1870–1906), an Orthodox priest who became an influential trade union leader at the instigation of the St Petersburg police. The goal was to counter the influence of the rising Marxist movement among the rapidly expanding working population of the capital. This phenomenon became known as police socialism, within which workers pressed for improved wages and conditions within a tightly regulated framework. Gapon's organisation, the Assembly of Russian Workers, founded in 1903, was soon penetrated by social democrats and this created a tension within it as regards goals. The radicals advocated strikes and other forms of agitation but this ran counter to Gapon's inclinations. In December 1904 the assembly became involved in a mass strike after some of its members had been dismissed. Gapon then drew up a manifesto to the Tsar appealing for more social justice, expressed in a mixture of religious and secular language. It proved immensely popular and had soon collected over 150,000 signatures. On Sunday 9 January 1905 Gapon headed a long procession of workers whose goal was to present the petition to Tsar Nicholas II in the Winter Palace. The police overreacted and fired on the demonstrators, killing over a hundred. Known as Bloody Sunday, the incident sparked off the 1905 revolution and exploded the myth that the Tsar was the loving father of the people. The incident shocked and radicalised Gapon but the police again contacted him and the Socialist Revolutionaries executed him as an agent provocateur.

Gdlyan, Telman Khorenovich (b. 1940),

an Armenian lawyer, born in Georgia, Gdlyan became famous under GORBACHEV as a terrier-like investigator of corruption among the ruling nomenklatura. He headed a group attached to the USSR Procurator's Office and it collected material on, for instance, Yury CHURBANOV, BREZHNEV's son in law, who was sentenced for corruption. Gdlyan became a celebrity and in 1989 was elected to the USSR Congress of People's Deputies where he found a platform for his eloquence and fearlessly levelled his accusations at the high and mighty, including Egor LIGACHEV. The establishment rallied against him and accused him and his associate Nikolai IVANOV of scandalmongering and using extra-legal methods in their search for evidence. The Congress censured them both in 1990 and they were also expelled from the Party but they were not deprived of their people's mandate. Had they been, they would have faced criminal charges.

Gerashchenko, Viktor Vladimirovich

(b. 1937), one of the Soviet Union's top bankers, Gerashchenko became notorious under YELTSIN as chair of the Russian Central Bank, declining to implement the government's anti-inflation policy. He was educated at the Moscow Finance Institute and began working in the USSR State Bank (Gosbank) in 1960, moving to the USSR Vneshtorgbank (Bank for Foreign Economic Trade) in 1961. In 1965 he moved to London as director of Moscow Narodny Bank and in 1967 to Beirut for the bank. In 1972 he returned to Moscow as deputy manager of USSR Vneshtorgbank. In 1974 he was appointed chair of the Soviet Bank in West Germany. In 1977 he became manager of a department of the Moscow Narodny Bank in Singapore. In 1982 he returned to Moscow as deputy chair of the board of USSR Vneshtorgbank. He became chair of the board of USSR Gosbank in 1989 and in 1992 chair of the Russian Central Bank. He was a member of the Communist Party, 1963–91 and a member of the Central Committee, 1990–1.

Gerasimov, Gennady Ivanovich (b. 1930), one of the most colourful representatives of glasnost under GORBACHEV as head of the press department of the USSR Ministry of Foreign Affairs, Gerasimov, a professional journalist, was always looking for the quotable phrase. He turned Frank Sinatra to good use by saying the Soviet Union was doing things its way. A Russian, born in Kazan, he worked on newspapers such as *Trud* and journals such as *World Marxist Review* before being recruited by Yury ANDROPOV, head of the Secretariat's department for liaison with communist and workers' parties in socialist states, as a consultant. He returned to journalism in 1967 and was editor-in-chief of *Moskovskie Novosti (Moscow News)*, 1983–6, although it did not flower until Egor YAKOVLEV succeeded Gerasimov as editor. Gerasimov then moved to the Foreign Ministry and remained as principal press spokesman until 1990. His removal was an indication that more conservative forces were becoming influential in Moscow. He went off to Lisbon as Soviet Ambassador to Portugal and in 1992 became Russian ambassador there. In Lisbon he felt isolated and missed the contact with the world's press. An American organisation once named him communicator of the year, something which gratified him deeply.

Gidaspov, Boris Veniaminovich (b. 1933), the man who succeeded Yury SOLOVEV as first secretary of Leningrad obkom in July 1989 after the latter had been defeated in elections to the USSR Congress of People's Deputies. Disliked by Leningrad democrats as a conservative and determined to put the brake on glasnost in the second Russian capital, he disappeared for a time during the attempted coup of August 1991. He trained as an industrial chemist in Kuibyshev, becoming general director of the State Institute of Applied Chemistry in 1977, and in 1985 general director of the State Institute of Applied Chemistry Production Association. From 1988 to 1989 he was also chair of the board of the Tekhnokhim Inter-branch State Association in Leningrad. He was elected a member of the department of general and industrial chemistry, USSR Academy of Sciences. He had also been developing his Party career as secretary of his workplace and in July 1989 became first secretary of Leningrad obkom and from November 1989 to April 1990, first secretary of Leningrad gorkom as well. In 1992 he reverted to working in Tekhnokhim as a consultant. He was elected to the USSR Congress of People's Deputies in 1989. Gidaspov joined the Party in 1962 and became a member of the Central Committee in July 1990, also being elected a CC secretary. He was a member of the group which worked on overcoming the consequences of the Chernobyl disaster.

Gilels, Emil Grigorevich (1916–85), a great Soviet pianist of the post-war era, Gilels was born in Odessa and studied with Berta Reyngbald at the Odessa Conservatory, graduating in 1935, and then with Genrikh Neugauz at the Moscow Conservatory. He won first prize at the Moscow Competition in 1933 and the Ysaye Competition in Brussels in 1938. He became a professor at the Moscow Conservatory and won an international reputation. He was a USSR People's Artist and an honorary member of the Royal Academy of Music, London.

Ginzburg, Abram Moiseevich (1878–1938), a leading economist after the October Revolution in the Supreme Council of the National Economy (VSNKh), he fell foul of STALIN's desire to accelerate economic growth and place his supporters in top economic posts. He was arrested in 1930, along with other leading ex-Menshevik economists, and was sentenced to ten years' imprisonment, probably being shot in 1938. He joined the Mensheviks in 1905 but gave up underground political activity and became leader of the Union of Metalworkers in 1906. He worked in local government in Kiev and became a specialist on the co-operative movement. He strongly opposed the Bolshevik seizure of power and was a member of the Ukrainian Rada in Kiev during the Civil War. He joined VSNKh in 1922 as deputy head of the economic division and was praised by DZERZHINSKY when the latter was head of VSNKh. Ginzburg was chair of the special commission for the preparation of the first Five Year Plan for industry. This turned out to be too modest for KUIBYSHEV, Stalin and other Bolsheviks. Naum Jasny: *Soviet Economists of the Twenties,* Cambridge, 1972.

Ginzburg, Aleksandr Ilich (*b.* 1936), a leading human rights activist who was in and out of prison in the 1960s and 1970s. He was born in Moscow and studied journalism at Moscow State University, editing three issues of the samizdat journal *Sintaksis.* He was arrested and jailed for two years (1960–2). In 1966 he gathered material on the trial of SINYAVSKY and DANIEL (*White Book*), was arrested a year later and sentenced to five years in a strict-regime camp. In 1972, together with Aleksandr SOLZHENITSYN, he organised a fund to help political prisoners and their families. In 1976 he founded the

Moscow branch of the Helsinki Monitoring Group but was arrested again in 1977 and was sentenced in 1978. In 1979 he and Eduard Kuznetsov were exchanged for two Soviet spies held by the Americans. He moved to Paris and became active in Russian émigré literary life.

Ginzburg, Evgeniya Semenovna (1904–77), she became famous in the west for her memoirs of her eighteen years in STALIN's camps. She was born in Moscow and graduated in history from Kazan State University. One of her two sons is the novelist, Vasily AKSENOV. Her husband, a senior Party worker, was arrested in 1937 and she followed as the wife of an enemy of the people. She was released and rehabilitated in 1955. She began writing about her experiences in *Yunost* in 1965–6 but her fame rests on two powerful works, translated into English as *Journey into the Whirlwind,* 1967, and *Within the Whirlwind,* 1979. They were published in the Soviet Union in 1988.

Glazunov, Ilya Sergeevich (*b.* 1930), a famous and controversial artist in the last decade of the Soviet Union, Glazunov was born in Leningrad but lost his parents during the siege of 1941–4. He graduated from the Repin Art Institute, Leningrad, in 1958 and the year before he staged a one-man exhibition of his works in Moscow. He was attracted to Russian themes and became known as a graphic artist and illustrator. He had an exhibition in Italy in 1963. He achieved the zenith of Soviet recognition by staging a one-man exhibition at the Manezh in Moscow in 1964 which attracted large crowds. He was attacked by the conservatives and the intelligentsia but was permitted to travel abroad and sell his works to foreign diplomats, a rare privilege. He became a Soviet millionaire and painted portraits of famous western politicians.

Glushko, Valentin Pavlovich (1908–89), a Ukrainian, born in Odessa, he became one of the most famous Soviet rocket designers. He graduated from Leningrad State University in 1929 and then began his association with the Gas Dynamics Laboratory in Leningrad. He developed the first Soviet liquid fuel rocket engine, 1930–1, and throughout the 1930s he worked on other rocket engines. Among these was the multi-barrelled Katyusha rocket. Arrested in 1938 along with KO-ROLEV, sentenced to eight years, he was one of many leading scientists to work under a prison regime. In 1974 he became head of the former Korolev Design Bureau in Kaliningrad, outside Moscow. This bureau played a key role in developing the Soviet space programme. He was elected a member of the USSR Academy of Sciences in 1958. He joined the Party in 1956 and was a member of the Central Committee from 1958 until his death. He was the recipient of many state awards.

Golikov, Marshal Filipp Ivanovich (1900–80), a master military political officer who as head of the GRU, military intelligence, ignored evidence about an imminent German attack on the Soviet Union in June 1941. He joined the Red Army and Bolshevik Party in 1918 as a political commissar. He graduated from the Frunze Military Academy in 1933. He participated in the Soviet–Finnish War, 1939–40, as deputy Chief of the General Staff to General MERETSKOV. He then became head of the GRU and received but disregarded information from Richard SORGE, the German communist spy in Tokyo, Soviet sources and German defectors, about preparations for a German attack. He may have done this since he thought Germany had first to knock out Great Britain or because he sensed that STALIN did not wish to have his illusions about his pact with Hitler exploded. Despite this, his career flourished. He was sent on a mission when war broke out to Washington and Lon-

don to negotiate aid for the Soviet Union. On his return he was made commander of the 10th Army and he participated in the relief of Moscow in December 1941. He then took over command of the Bryansk Front which was part of the disastrous Kharkov offensive personally ordered by Stalin. He told Stalin that he could not hold the front and was dismissed but was reinstated in time to take part in the counter-offensive to relieve Stalingrad. He then took over command of the Voronezh Front. He was appointed head of personnel and deputy People's Commissar for Defence, 1943–5, and ceased to hold a field command. KHRUSHCHEV, in his memoirs, states that he was eyewitness to Golikov's cowardice at Stalingrad. Golikov later denounced his commander Marshal EREMENKO. Stalin ignored the denunciation, recalled Golikov to Moscow and promoted him. He became head of the Soviet repatriation commission in 1944, responsible for locating and returning all Soviet refugees. He became commander of the Armed Forces Academy, 1950. He ingratiated himself with Khrushchev who made him head of the Political Administration of the Soviet Armed Forces, 1958–62, with a brief to restore the role of the political officers in the military after they had been eliminated by Marshal ZHUKOV when the latter was USSR Defence Minister. He was made Marshal of the Soviet Union in May 1960. He was a member of the Central Committee of the Communist Party, 1961–6. He demonstrated consummate political skill in rescuing his career on several occasions. Despite Khrushchev's contempt for his behaviour at Stalingrad, he appointed him to the key political post in the military. Golikov had obviously convinced Khrushchev that he was his man.

Gorbachev, Mikhail Sergeevich (b. 1931), if LENIN was the father of the Soviet Union, Gorbachev was its grave digger. A remarkable man for the Party to produce and then to entrust with power, he perceived that Stalinist socialism was doomed and set about democratising the system, including ending the Party's monopoly on power. He remains convinced that had it not been for the attempted coup in August 1991 he could have fashioned a Union of Sovereign States out of the moribund Soviet Union. There is some truth in this but the Baltic states would have done their utmost to recover their independence. The key to the Soviet Union's fate after August 1991 rested not with Gorbachev but with Boris YELTSIN of Russia and Leonid KRAVCHUK of Ukraine. If Russia decided it was in its interests to go it alone, no successor state to the Soviet Union was viable. If Ukraine also sided with Russia, no Gorbachev-inspired solution was feasible. Yeltsin's desire to be the boss in the Kremlin doomed Gorbachev to political oblivion. Gorbachev was born into a Russian peasant family in Privolnoe, Stavropol krai, and experienced hardship during the brief German occupation of his village in 1941–2 and afterwards. During the summer he worked with his father on the collective farm and he was awarded the Order of the Red Banner of Labour in 1949 for his part in bringing in a record grain harvest. This helped him to gain admission to the law faculty of Moscow State University in 1950. Before he graduated in 1955 he married RAISA MAKSIMOVNA Titorenko in 1953; their daughter Irina was born in 1957. Gorbachev became a full member of the Communist Party in 1952. He returned to Stavropol to begin a legal career but soon tired of the law and switched to Komsomol work, rising rapidly to become first secretary of Stavropol krai. He moved across into Party work in 1962 and in 1966 was first secretary of Stavropol gorkom. In 1970 be became first secretary of Stavropol kraikom. A year later he was elected a member of the Central Committee. At the age of forty he had become a member

of the Soviet élite. His progress was helped by having three influential patrons, Fedor KULAKOV, his predecessor in Stavropol who moved to Moscow to become Central Committee secretary for agriculture, Mikhail SUSLOV, the chief ideologist in the Politburo, and Yury ANDROPOV, then head of the KGB. When Kulakov died in 1978 Gorbachev took over as Central Committee secretary for agriculture. When BREZHNEV died in 1982 Gorbachev was firmly on Andropov's side as successor and expanded his responsibilities. However, it was Konstantin CHERNENKO who took over from Andropov in February 1984. With the strong backing of Andrei GROMYKO Gorbachev became Party leader in March 1985. The Gorbachev era can be divided into three periods: 1985–8 when he believed that the planned economy and Communist Party could be reformed from within. Reform from above, perestroika, was then accompanied by reform from below, glasnost. In 1988, at the XIXth Party Conference, the Party lost its key role as manager of the economy. The second period, 1988–90, saw rapid institutional change as Gorbachev sought to revitalise the soviets. The election of the USSR Congress of People's Deputies and its inner core, the USSR Supreme Soviet, in 1989, brought into being a functioning parliament. Economic reform began to lay the foundations of a market economy. These reforms shattered élite consensus about reform and led to fierce intra-élite conflict which culminated in the attempted coup of August 1991. Gorbachev made himself executive President in 1990 in an effort to overcome conservative opposition to reform. Even more contentiously the Party lost its monopoly on political power, enshrined in article 6 of the Constitution. Gorbachev needed an institution to manage the economy and which would implement top decisions. The Council of the Federation and the Presidential Council came into being to supplement the Cabinet of Ministers, the new style government being subordinate to the President. The period 1990–1 was characterised by the gradual breakdown of the economy and government as Gorbachev desperately searched for a successor state to the Soviet Union. Glasnost fuelled rising nationalism and republican elections in 1990, especially in the Baltic states, and produced parliaments dominated by national fronts whose objective became independence. The draft agreement on a Union of Sovereign States was ready for signing when the coup plotters struck. Mikhail Gorbachev: *Perestroika: New Thinking for Our Country and the World,* New York, 1988; *Memoirs,* London, 1996; Archie Brown: *The Gorbachev Factor,* Oxford, 1996.

Gorbacheva, Raisa Maksimovna (née Titorenko) (*b.* 1932), a highly intelligent, strong-willed woman who carved out for herself a political role in a male-dominated political system, she aroused jealousy inside the Soviet Union. On the one hand, male Communists took umbrage at her influence over Mikhail GOR-BACHEV and, on the other, many Soviet women bridled at her access to expensive western clothes and cosmetics. Mikhail and she met as students at Moscow University where she was in the philosophy faculty. She wanted to break off the relationship but he prevailed and they were married in 1953, their daughter Irina being born in 1957. She obtained a doctorate researching village life and pursued her own academic career which petered out when the family moved to Moscow in 1978. She was closely involved in a foundation for the preservation of Russian culture, headed by Academician Dmitry LIKHACHEV. She found house arrest at Foros during the attempted coup very stressful and suffered a mild stroke, taking about two years to recover fully. Raisa Gorbachev: *I Hope,* New York, 1991.

Gorbunovs, Anatoliis (Gorbunov, Anatoly Valerianovich) (1942–), a brilliant example of a Communist who made his career being loyal to the CPSU in Moscow and then, when he perceived that nationalism was on the rise, changed sides and became a national Communist. A Latvian, he graduated from the Riga Polytechnic Institute as a civil engineer in 1970, having joined the Communist Party of Latvia in 1966. He then moved into the Komsomol and Party apparatuses, becoming secretary of the Central Committee, Communist Party of Latvia, in 1985, and in October 1988 chair (speaker) of the Latvian Supreme Soviet. He maintained good relations with the popular front and in 1990 was elected chair of the Supreme Council of the Republic of Latvia in 1990. He changed his name back into the Latvian form, dropping the Russian orthography, and was rewarded by being elected the first President of the Republic of Latvia after independence in 1991.

Gordievsky, Oleg Antonovich (*b.* 1939), he was probably the most successful double agent ever recruited by British intelligence until his cover was blown by the CIA in 1985. As a KGB officer he was responsible for Great Britain and Scandinavia, specialising in 'illegals', KGB agents infiltrated in foreign countries to operate under cover. He was posted to Copenhagen in 1966 as a press attaché at the Soviet embassy and it was probably during his time there that he was recruited. He left in 1970 but returned in 1972, becoming first secretary of the embassy in 1978. In June 1982 he moved to the Soviet embassy in London and in 1984 became *Rezident,* or head of the KGB there. When his cover was blown by a CIA agent he was recalled to Moscow but managed to escape back to Britain. He provided much information on Soviet agents but more importantly on how the KGB operated. Oleg Gordievsky (with Christopher Andrew):

The KGB: The Inside Story, London, 1990.

Gorky, Maksim (né Peshkov, Aleksei Maksimovich) (1868–1936), regarded by many critics as the father of Soviet literature, Gorky was born into a Russian family in Nizhny Novgorod (renamed Gorky 1932–90) and spent his time as a wanderer, turning his hand to many trades. These experiences provided him with valuable material for his novels and plays as he knew Russian life from the bottom up. His first stories of the vagabond life were published in 1898 and made him popular. He became known world wide with the appearance of the play *Lower Depths* in 1902. He joined the Bolshevik Party and was active during the 1905 revolution. He left for a lecture tour of the United States in 1906 and caused a scandal by cohabiting with the actress Mariya ANDREEVA, not at that time his wife. He lived on Capri from 1906, put up the money for a Bolshevik Party school, and remained on close terms with LENIN. He published his autobiography in three volumes: *Childhood,* 1913, *In the World,* 1916, and *My Universities,* 1922. Gorky returned to Russia in 1913 and opposed violent revolution in 1917. ZINOVIEV and KAMENEV published their reservations about an armed seizure of power in October in his newspaper, *Novaya Zhizn.* After the revolution he was critical of Bolshevik excesses but kept many members of the intelligentsia alive by providing them with translation work. He fell out with Zinoviev, the Party boss of Petrograd, and left Soviet Russia in 1921, living in Sorrento, 1924–31. He became the most famous communist writer in the world while, ironically, living in Mussolini's Fascist Italy. He returned to the Soviet Union in 1931 and was proclaimed as the father of socialist realism. Unlike his criticisms of Lenin's Russia, he was quiet about STALIN'S excesses, especially forced collectivisation. His death may have been

due to the consequences of shooting himself through the lung in an attempted suicide attempt during his youth. On the other hand, Stalin may have been involved as Gorky may have been on the point of changing his mind about the type of state that Stalin was fashioning.

Gorshkov, Admiral Sergei Georgevich (1910–88), the father of the Soviet Blue Water Fleet, Gorshkov convinced KHRUSHCHEV that the Soviet Navy had to be transformed from being a coastal defence force into a global fleet. This was hugely expensive and imposed a greater and greater burden on the Soviet budget. By 1985 defence was accounting for about 40 per cent of the budget, denuding other sectors, such as education, of funds. GORBACHEV determined to reduce defence spending by changing the emphasis on security, arguing that military might alone did not guarantee a nation's security. His new political thinking ended the glory days of the Soviet Navy. Gorshkov joined the navy in 1927 and saw service in the Black Sea and Soviet Far East. He spent much of the Great Fatherland War in the Black Sea, the Danube and backing up the Red Army in the Sea of Azov, where he first worked with Leonid BREZHNEV. Khrushchev made him first deputy commander-in-chief of the Soviet Navy in 1955 and, in January 1956, commander-in-chief. His thinking about the role of the navy was presented in *Naval Power of the State,* 1976. In late 1985 Gorshkov was abruptly ousted and replaced by CHERNAVIN, a submariner.

Grachev, General Pavel Sergeevich (*b.* 1948), he rose to prominence as an Afghan War hero and switched to YELTSIN's side during the attempted coup of August 1991. He was born into a Russian family in Tula oblast and graduated with distinction from the Ryazan Higher Airborne Officers' Technical School, 1969, with distinction from the Frunze

Military Academy, 1981, and with distinction from the Academy of the General Staff, 1990. He joined the Communist Party in 1972. He was a combat officer with airborne troops, commanding the 103rd Vitebsk airborne division in Afghanistan in 1985, and becoming a major general in 1986. In May 1988 he was made a Hero of the Soviet Union in recognition of his record in Afghanistan. After Afghanistan he rose to become commander of Soviet airborne troops, December 1990. During the attempted coup of August 1991 he pursued a dual policy of carrying out superior orders but establishing contact with Yeltsin, and he promised to order the military not to use weapons. He was distrusted by some politicians as there were rumours that he was involved in plans to storm the White House. Nevertheless, on Yeltsin's recommendation, President Mikhail GORBACHEV appointed Grachev chair of the RSFSR state committee on defence and security. He also became first deputy USSR Minister of Defence and was promoted colonel general. However, Grachev did not attend the sessions of the state committee and was not involved in attempting to reform the military. In April 1992 he was appointed Russian Minister of Defence and in May 1992 he became Minister of Defence with the rank of general of the army.

Grechko, Marshal Andrei Antonovich (1903–76), a commanding military figure during the BREZHNEV years when the armed forces enjoyed unprecedented influence over security and foreign policy. He joined the Red Army in 1918 and participated in the Civil War. He graduated from the Frunze Military Academy in 1936 and from the Academy of the General Staff, 1941. He was given command of various armies, including that of the Voronezh Front in 1943. He then became commander of the 1st Guards Army, 1943–5. He led the armies which liberated Kiev and then Lvov and finally

pushed into Czechoslovakia. He was commander of the Kiev military district, 1945–53. He then became commander of the Soviet forces in (East) Germany, 1953–7. He was then promoted to commander of the Ground Forces and deputy USSR Minister of Defence, 1957. He was made commander-in-chief of the Warsaw Pact forces in 1960. He was USSR Minister of Defence from 1961 to his death in 1976. He was a member of the Central Committee of the Communist Party, 1961–76, and a member of the Politburo, 1973–6. He was Minister of Defence at the apogee of Soviet power, including the recognition by the Americans that there was parity on nuclear weapons between the superpowers.

Grigorenko, Petr Grigorevich (1907–86), after an outstanding military career which made him a major general, Grigorenko, a Ukrainian, fell rapidly from grace after criticising STALIN and KHRUSHCHEV at a Party meeting in 1960. He lost his post at the Frunze Military Academy and was expelled from the Communist Party. He was sent to the Soviet Far East in 1963 and imprisoned in a psychiatric hospital. He became a key figure in the emerging human rights movement in the Soviet Union and espoused the cause of the Crimean Tatars, expelled by Stalin in 1944 for allegedly collaborating with the German Wehrmacht, and rehabilitated by Khrushchev but not permitted to return to their ancestral homes. Grigorenko spent the years 1969–74 incarcerated in a psychiatric hospital and when he went to the United States in 1977 to visit relatives he was deprived of his Soviet citizenship and barred from returning. He then travelled widely, campaigning for human rights in his homeland. Petr Grigorenko: *Memoirs,* London, 1983.

Grishin, Viktor Vasilevich (b. 1914), known as the Moscow Godfather, Grishin once boasted that no one could touch him and he was in the running for the top Party post in March 1985 but was pipped at the post by Mikhail GORBACHEV. Within a year Gorbachev had brought his political career to an end. Grishin was born into a Russian railwayman's family in Serpukhov, near Moscow, and he followed in his father's footsteps. He rose to become a member of the Central Committee, 1952, and was chair of the Soviet trade union movement, 1957–67. He was elected a candidate member of the Presidium (Politburo), 1961 and a full member, 1971. In 1967 BREZHNEV chose him to head the Moscow city Party organisation (gorkom). He loved luxury and allowed those around him to take bribes until the city organisation became corrupt. Gorbachev gave Boris YELTSIN the task of cleaning up the capital city in late 1985 but he found the Moscow nomenklatura too tough a nut to crack and resigned two years later. Grishin lost his Politburo place in 1986 and departed the political scene.

Groman, Vladimir Gustavovich (1874–1937), an outstanding economist and statistician whose life and work were cut short by STALIN. His father was German and his mother Russian but he never mastered the German language. He was attracted early to Marxism, becoming a Menshevik in 1905 and remaining so until his death. While exiled in Tver guberniya he developed statistical methods to analyse economic trends. He served on the Special Committee on Food during the First World War and began thinking of a national economic plan under the provisional government. He joined Gosplan in 1922 and was the driving force behind the *kontrolnye tsifry* (*control figures*), a balance sheet of the Soviet economy in the 1920s. He favoured equilibrium but Stalin did not, the latter favouring going for the impossible. Groman was arrested in July 1930 and tried with many other Mensheviks in

the Menshevik trial of March 1931, being sentenced to ten years.

Gromov, General Boris Vsevolodovich (*b.* 1943), an Afghan War hero who was the last Soviet soldier to leave (on foot) Afghanistan. He was born into a Russian family in Saratov and graduated from the Kalinin (Tver) Suvorov Military School, 1963, the Leningrad Higher Military Officers' School, 1965, the Frunze Military Academy with distinction, 1972, and the Academy of the General Staff with distinction and a gold medal, 1984. He joined the Communist Party in 1966. His early career was with motorised rifle platoons and from February 1980 to August 1982, Gromov's division, part of the 40th Army, was in Afghanistan. He favoured severe measures against the mujahidin and to pacify the civilian population. He served again in Afghanistan, March 1985–April 1986. From 1987 to 1989 Gromov was commander of the 40th Army and the senior Soviet military officer in Afghanistan. As such he organised the withdrawal of Soviet troops. He was elected to the USSR Congress of People's Deputies, 1989, and belonged to a group of deputies who vigorously opposed the democratic forces in Russia and the national liberation movements in the republics. In December 1990 Gromov was appointed first deputy USSR Minister of Internal Affairs, under PUGO, but remained in the army. He was directly involved in ordering the internal forces to act against democrats in Russia and the Baltic states, January–March 1991. According to the evidence of the commission investigating the actions of the Emergency Committee, Gromov was actively involved and ordered the seizure of the White House. However, he also established relations with the Russian leaders. He returned to his army duties, September 1991, and was appointed deputy commander-in-chief, land forces. In June 1992 he was made deputy Russian Minister of Defence.

Gromyko, Andrei Andreevich (1909–89), known as grim Grom (he always looked as if he had toothache) and Mr Nyet (he was wont to say no), Gromyko personified Soviet foreign policy for almost three decades. When Mikhail GORBACHEV became Party leader in 1985 he wanted to implement the new political thinking and Gromyko became the unacceptable face of Soviet foreign policy. He was replaced in mid-1985 by the Georgian, Eduard SHEVARDNADZE, a more compliant, flexible official. Gromyko was born into a peasant family in Belorussia and studied agricultural economics, joining the economics journal *Voprosy Ekonomiki* in 1936. He was brought into diplomatic work in 1939 and became Soviet Ambassador to the United States in 1943. This revealed the modest standing of the Soviet embassy in Washington in STALIN'S eyes. However, Gromyko took to America and became very knowledgeable about US affairs, getting to know every American President from Roosevelt to Reagan. Gromyko was present at the founding of the United Nations and at the Yalta and Potsdam conferences, in 1945. He headed the Soviet mission at the UN, 1946–8, and in 1949 became first deputy USSR Minister of Foreign Affairs. He was downgraded in 1952 to become Soviet Ambassador at the Court of St James in London. He returned to Moscow after Stalin's death to become first deputy Foreign Minister again. Gromyko succeeded MOLOTOV in 1957 when the latter (a leading member of the Anti-Party Group) took on KHRUSHCHEV but lost. Khrushchev treated Gromyko with scant respect and once told de Gaulle, in Gromyko's presence, that if he asked Andrei Andreevich to take off his trousers and sit on a block of ice he would obey. Would de Gaulle's Foreign Minister, Couve de Murville do the same? Gromyko became a member of the Politburo in 1973 and gradually dominated decision making in foreign policy. He cannot be classified as a successful Foreign Min-

ister because tension increased between the superpowers and the arms race accelerated. He was much taken by Gorbachev and enthusiastically proposed him for the Party leadership in March 1985. He was reported as having stated that Gorbachev had a nice smile but teeth of steel. Gromyko overlooked that he might be bitten and he was moved upstairs in June 1985 to become Soviet President. In 1988 Gorbachev decided to become President himself. So Gromyko had to go. Had he known what Gorbachev's agenda was in 1985 he would have thought twice about recommending him for the top post. Gromyko spoke beautiful Russian and enjoyed a wide culture, being especially well read in English literature. A British ambassador on one occasion was taken aback, after delivering a protest note from the British government, to hear Gromyko's response – he recited a Kipling poem flawlessly. Gromyko also had a sense of humour but he never practised this gift in public.

Gromyko, Anatoly Andreevich (*b.* 1932), the son of Andrei GROMYKO, he followed in his father's footsteps and entered the diplomatic service, becoming first secretary at the Soviet embassy in London, 1961, and remaining until 1965. He then moved into the Institute of Africa of the USSR Academy of Sciences in 1966 before returning to work in what became the Institute of the United States and Canada, 1969–76. He then became director of the Institute of Africa. He was elected a corresponding member of the USSR Academy of Sciences in 1981.

Grossman, Vasily Semonovich (1905–64), he was born into a Jewish family in Berdichev, Ukraine, and graduated from Moscow University, 1929. During the 1930s he became a successful novelist writing about workers in the Donbass, and also joined the Communist Party. He became famous as a war correspondent with *Krasnaya Zvezda* and visited

Treblinka concentration camp. EREN-BURG and he drew up an account of the Nazi persecution of the Jews but it was not published in the Soviet Union and appeared as *The Black Book*, 1980, in Israel. The first volume of a huge novel on Stalingrad, *Za Pravoe Delo (For a Just Cause)*, 1952, was rejected by the Soviet authorities and his second volume puts Hitler and STALIN on the same plane. It was published in Moscow in 1988 as *Zhizn i Sudba (Life and Fate)* and was an overnight sensation. Another novel he wrote in secret, *Vse Techet (Always Flowing)*, is an insider's condemnation of forced collectivisation and was eventually published in the Soviet Union in 1989. He was viewed as a conformist Stalinist writer until the 1950s and his reputation has grown over time.

Guchkov, Aleksandr Ivanovich (1862–1936), a successful industrialist, an Old Believer and freemason, head of the Octobrist Party, but he harboured a low opinion of the TSAR and the Tsarina ALEKSANDRA. No democrat, he sided with STOLYPIN over the dissolution of the Second Duma in June 1907 and the introduction of a much more restrictive franchise. This made him a target for the ire of democratic politicians and in their eyes he never lived down his 'reactionary' habits. He was speaker of the Third Duma (1907–12). An early target in his conflict with the Romanovs was the role of Father Grigory RASPUTIN. In 1912 Guchkov launched a vitriolic attack on Rasputin in the Duma, got hold of earlier correspondence between the Tsarina and her children to Rasputin and circulated it clandestinely. The Tsarina quickly brought her wrath down on Guchkov's head, advising her husband, when in an agitated mood, to hang the recalcitrant politician. Guchkov became a prominent member of the Progressive Bloc in the Duma (1915–17). He influenced the development of the war economy as chair of the Duma committee on military and naval affairs and then, in 1915, as chair of the Central War Industries Committee, which was an initiative by industrialists, frustrated by the inefficiency of the government war effort. The February Revolution afforded Guchkov the opportunity to encourage the Tsar to abdicate. In March 1917 he and V. V. Shulgin travelled to Pskov to arrange the abdication of the Tsar in favour of his son, Aleksei. In the first provisional government, Guchkov was an obvious Minister of War and the Navy but the publication of Order no. 1 by the Petrograd garrison, which among other things undermined the authority of the officers, led to sharp disagreements with radical soldiers. He resigned along with the other members of the first provisional government on 2 May 1917 and bowed out of political life. The chances for his brand of centre right politics finding support in Russia in 1917 were wafer thin and he and his class were swept away by the Bolshevik tide. He joined many other Russian exiles in Paris.

Gumilev, Nikolai Stepanovich (1886–1921), a Russian, he was born in Kronstadt, the son of a naval doctor; he attended school at Tsarskoe Selo and Tbilisi. He studied at the Sorbonne, 1907–8, and went on the first of many trips as an explorer to Africa. He married Anna AKHMATOVA, 1910, and their son, Lev, was born in 1911. Gumilev became a well-known literary figure and founded the Acmeist group of poets in St Petersburg. He served in the First World War with distinction. He was active after the revolution and was elected chair of the Petrograd Union of Poets in 1921 but he and others were arrested in August 1921 by the Cheka and accused of being members of an anti-Bolshevik monarchist plot and executed. He was an unperson in the Soviet Union until the arrival of Mikhail GORBACHEV when the centenary of his birth was celebrated with great enthusiasm.

H

Helfand, Aleksandr Lazarevich (also Helphand, Parvus, Israel) (1867–1924), aptly called the merchant of revolution by his biographers, Helfand was the most successful financially of the many who sought their fortune acting as a go-between for those who wished to promote revolution and the practitioners of the art. He was born into a Jewish family near Minsk, studied at the University of Basle in 1887 and came to know PLEKHANOV, AXELROD and Zasulich. He collaborated with Karl Kautsky and the German social democrats and worked with TROTSKY in St Petersburg during the 1905 revolution. Incarcerated in the Peter and Paul Fortress, he was exiled to Siberia, slipped away and made for Germany where he became GORKY's literary agent, collecting his royalties wherever they could be found. The Bolsheviks accused him of keeping much of the money for himself and depriving them of Gorky's funds which, at that time, were an important part of their finances. A Party court found him guilty and he had to quit Germany in 1907. He lived in Constantinople, 1910–15, and channelled resources from the German government to the Young Turks, becoming wealthy in the process. His business empire expanded as a result and he moved to neutral Denmark to handle his German–Russian contacts. He was the go-between for German money for LENIN and the Bolsheviks, and the KERENSKY government thought that they could prove conclusively that Lenin was on the Germans' payroll. Unfortunately, they failed to prevent the press reporting this and the incriminating evidence was lost. Helfand slipped away to Switzerland just before Germany collapsed in 1918 and returned to his Berlin villa later where he died of a heart attack. Z. Zeman and R. Scharlau: *The Merchant of Revolution*, London, 1965.

I

Ignatev, Semen Denisovich (*b.* 1903), he succeeded ABAKUMOV as USSR Minister of State Security in 1951 and stayed in this very dangerous post until STALIN'S death. He joined the Communist Party in 1926. He was a prominent supporter of Stalin and the purges during the 1930s as Party secretary in Buryatia, 1938. He was Party secretary in the Bashkir ASSR, 1944–7. Ignatev was associated with Andrei ZHDANOV and in the wake of the Leningrad Affair BERIA and MALENKOV managed to remove Ignatev from the Belorussian Party secretariat, 1949, and pack him off to Uzbekistan. However, Ignatev was elected to the Politburo at the XIXth Party Congress, 1952, before being removed in 1953. The Doctors' Plot, fabricated by Ignatev and his deputy, Ryumin, was launched in January 1953. This alleged that a group of doctors, mainly Jewish, had been aiming to reduce the lifespan of leading Soviet officials. Among the so-called victims had been Zhdanov. Ignatev was dismissed from his ministerial post after Stalin's death but, as a KHRUSHCHEV protégé, the latter managed to have him elected a secretary of the Central Committee, March 1953, despite the fact that he was a bitter enemy of Beria. In July 1953 Ignatev was reinstated as a member of the Central Committee, surprising given the fact that the Doctors' Plot had been dropped before Stalin died. This underlines that Khrushchev was protecting Ignatev. During his Secret Speech at the XXth Party Congress, 1956, Khrushchev stated that Ignatev had acted on Stalin's personal orders. Ignatev was first Party secretary again in the Bashkir ASSR, 1954–7 and then in the Tatar ASSR, 1957–60.

Ilf, Ilya Arnoldovich (né Fainzilberg) (1897–1937), Ilf and Evgeny Petrovich Petrov (né Kataev) (1903–42) are the most famous satirists of the Soviet period. They both came from Odessa but met only in Moscow in 1925 and immediately collaborated on writing witty sketches. Their account of the wheeling and dealing of a very successful operator and fixer during NEP, published as *Dvenadtsat Stulev* (*Twelve Chairs*), 1927, and *Zolotoi Telenok* (*Golden Calf*), 1931, became instant classics and have remained so ever since.

Ilyushin, Sergei Vladimirovich (1894–1977), a brilliant Soviet aeronautical engineer who gave his name to various civil and military aircraft. He joined the Red Army in 1918 and the Bolshevik Party in 1919 and he graduated from the Zhukovsky Air Force Academy in 1926. He became leader of an aircraft design bureau in 1931 and he won the Stalin Prize in 1942, 1943 and 1946. He was made a Hero of Socialist Labour on three occasions, received many other state awards and was elected an academician in 1968. He designed one of the Red Army's most successful warplanes, the IL-2 Shturmovik, and its successor the much faster IL-10 which entered service at the end of the war. He also designed the main Soviet long-range bombers, the DB-3 and the IL-4.

Ioffe, Adolf Abramovich (1883–1927), born into a Jewish merchant family in

Crimea, Ioffe joined the RSDRP in 1902. This prevented him from attending a Russian university so he studied medicine and law at the universities of Berlin, Vienna and Zürich. He returned to Russia during the 1905 revolution but had to flee back to Berlin. He linked up with TROTSKY and together they published *Pravda* in Vienna. He was caught distributing the newspaper in Russia in 1912 and was exiled to Siberia until the February Revolution freed him. He was a member of Trotsky's mezhraionka (inter-borough) group – it also included LUNACHARSKY – and they collectively joined LENIN's Bolsheviks in July 1917. Ioffe was elected to the Central Committee. As a member of the Military Revolutionary Committee, he played an important role in the October Revolution and afterwards became one of the first diplomats (partly because of his knowledge of western languages) who attempted to implement a revolutionary agenda. He headed the Soviet delegation which attempted to negotiate a peace with imperial Germany and Austria. He supported Trotsky's view that 'neither peace nor war' was the best policy because the Germans were judged incapable of launching a successful offensive in Russia. There was also the point that addressing the German proletariat over the heads of their leaders would hasten revolution there. He, like Trotsky, declined to support the peace treaty they had negotiated. He became the first Soviet representative in Berlin (April–November 1918) but used the embassy to agitate for revolution. Evidence was fabricated by the German police and he was expelled. Ioffe worked in Ukraine during the Civil War and then headed the Soviet delegation negotiating peace agreements with the Baltic states in 1920 and Poland (the Treaty of Riga) in 1921. He was also an important member of the Soviet delegation which concluded the surprise treaty with Germany at Rapallo (1922). The following year he became Soviet Ambassador to China. He served in London and Vienna (1924–5). He became rector of the Chinese University in Moscow but as he shared Trotsky's view of STALIN as the 'gravedigger of the revolution' time was running out for him. He perceived that Trotsky lacked the steely resolve and political cunning necessary to outwit Stalin. The expulsion of Trotsky and ZINOVIEV from the Communist Party in November 1927 filled him with deep despair and he took his own life rather than admit defeat.

Iskander, Fazil Abdulovich (*b.* 1929), An Abkhazian, born in Sukhumi, Iskander graduated from the Gorky Literary Institute, Moscow. He came to prominence in the 1960s with *Sozvezdie Kozlotura* (*The Kozlotura Constellation*), a satire on KHRUSHCHEV's agricultural campaigns. Another humorous novel, *Sandro iz Chegema* (*Sandro from Chegem*), 1973, was only published in part at the time in the Soviet Union but under GORBACHEV it was published in full.

Ivanov, Nikolai Venyaminovich (*b.* 1952), Ivanov, a Russian lawyer, together with Telman GDLYAN, became a celebrity under GORBACHEV for his investigations of corruption among the ruling élite. Among their high-profile cases was the Uzbek Affair, which included false reporting of the Uzbek cotton crop, involving the whole Uzbek leadership and Yury CHURBANOV, BREZHNEV's son in law. Churbanov and many others were found guilty and sentenced to jail. Ivanov's popularity showed in 1989 when he was elected to the USSR Congress of People's Deputies and found there a platform to carry on his campaign against the high and mighty in the land, including Egor LIGACHEV. The establishment rallied against him and Gdlyan and accused them of scandalmongering and using extra-legal methods in their search for evidence. The Congress censured them both in 1990 and they were also expelled from the Party but they were not deprived of their people's mandate. Had they been, they would have faced criminal charges.

Ivashko, Vladimir Antonovich (*b.* 1932), when it was decided to appoint a deputy General Secretary of the Party at the XXVIIIth Party Congress, GORBACHEV, according to his *Memoirs,* regarded the appointment of a Ukrainian as natural. He was a Russian so his deputy should be a Ukrainian. Before this could happen, Egor LIGACHEV, the nominee of the conservative opposition to Gorbachev, had to be disposed of and this was done very effectively. However, Ivashko was a terrible disappointment as he sided with the Emergency Committee in August 1991. Gorbachev's comment is that Ivashko was just not up to the job. He graduated as a mining engineer but made his career in the Party in Kharkov. His career took off dramatically in 1986 when he was appointed secretary of the Central Committee, Communist Party of Ukraine. The following year he became first secretary, Dnepropetrovsk obkom, then in 1988 second secretary (to SHCHERBITSKY), Communist Party of Ukraine. In September 1989 he succeeded Shcherbitsky as first secretary and Party leader in Ukraine. He became a full member of the CPSU Politburo in December 1989.

K

Kaganovich, Lazar Moiseevich (1893–1991), one of the hard men around STA-LIN, Kaganovich was ruthless with his subordinates. The only Jew to remain a member of Stalin's inner group until the end, Kaganovich was too conservative for KHRUSHCHEV, who had previously worked closely with him, and his career ended with the defeat of the Anti-Party Group in 1957. He was born in Kiev guberniya into a poor family and joined the Bolsheviks in 1911. He proclaimed Soviet power in Gomel, Belorussia, and fought against DENIKIN during the Civil War. Stalin made him head of the organisational department of the Central Committee, 1922, and shortly after he became general secretary. Stalin made him first secretary of the Communist Party of Ukraine, 1925–8, and then recalled him to the Party Secretariat in Moscow. In 1926 Kaganovich was elected a candidate member of the Politburo and in 1930 a full member. In 1930 he became first secretary, Moscow gorkom, and as such oversaw the construction of the Moscow Metro but also demolished many fine Moscow cathedrals (including the cathedral of Christ the Saviour whose rebuilding was completed in 1996) and churches. During collectivisation he acted as a fireman and stamped out opposition on various missions, revealing gross brutality. This faded into the background during the purges when he accomplished his brief regardless of the human cost. He did not speak up for his brother, Mikhail, USSR Minister of the Aviation Industry, who committed suicide on hearing that BERIA intended to arrest him and have him shot. Jews com-plained of Kaganovich's anti-Semitism. He headed several ministries after 1935 and the reason for his appointment was always the same: the industry had become a bottleneck. Kaganovich broke the bottleneck. He became Minister for the Building Materials Industry, 1944, and then, in 1947, returned to Ukraine where he replaced Khrushchev as Party leader. After Stalin's death Kaganovich was one of the Party élite but misjudged Khrushchev. He was packed off to manage a cement factory in the Urals in 1957 and after Khrushchev's removal he reapplied for Party membership but was turned down. He retired to Moscow where during the GORBACHEV era he could be seen sitting on park benches. When asked about his past, he denied that he was a Jew and stoutly defended Stalin.

Kalashnikov, Mikhail Timofeevich (*b.* 1919), designer of the famous rifle, adopted by the Soviet Army in 1949, it became the most successful of all time. He was born in the Altai and was a tank NCO during the Great Fatherland War. His Avtomat Kalashnikova (AK) 7.62mm assault rifle was exported to the Third World and gained a world-wide reputation. He also designed machine guns (PK, PKS) and tank machine guns. He joined the Party in 1953 and was a people's deputy, USSR Supreme Soviet, 1966–89, and the recipient of many state prizes. After 1991 he lived on a small pension outside Moscow.

Kalinin, Mikhail Ivanovich (1875–1946), born into a peasant family in Tver guberniya, Kalinin joined the RSDRP in

1898 and was active during the 1905 and 1917 revolutions. He took over from SVERDLOV as chair of the Central Executive Committee of the Soviets in 1919 and in 1938 became chair of the Presidium of the USSR Supreme Soviet (in both posts nominal head of state). He was elected a member of the Politburo in 1925. Unkindly called STALIN's pet peasant, he was always smiling and with his goatee beard looked and was called a village elder. Politically of no consequence, he was useful to Stalin as an Old Bolshevik who knew to keep his mouth shut. His wife spent time in the Gulag. Tver was renamed after him and reverted to its former name in 1990. Königsberg, the capital of German East Prussia, became Kaliningrad in 1945 and the northern part, which passed to the Soviet Union, Kaliningrad oblast. In 1991 statutes and plaques commemorating him were removed.

Kalugin, General Oleg Danilovich (b. 1934), he became an overnight celebrity by accusing the KGB of being a bulwark of Stalinism while appearing to support perestroika. He travelled the world, promoting radical change in the Soviet Union. He was born into a Russian family in Leningrad and graduated from the university there before entering the KGB. He was an exchange student at Columbia University, 1958–9. His cover was that of a journalist in Moscow and the United States and he was promoted major general in 1974. KRYUCHKOV, head of the KGB, dismissed him as a troublemaker and he lost his rank and position. Kalugin provided information on defections from the KGB in the 1980s and also stated that the KGB had been involved in the murder of Georgi Markov, a Bulgarian working for the BBC in London. He became a security adviser to Boris YELTSIN in 1990.

Kamenev, Lev Borisovich (né Rosenfeld) (1883–1936), the eternal moderate of the Bolshevik Party, Kamenev was born into a Moscow Jewish family, briefly studied law at Moscow University but discovered that being an active social democrat was more exciting. He moved to western Europe in 1907 and became a member of the Bolshevik centre, a leading Bolshevik journalist and a close collaborator of LENIN. He returned to St Petersburg in 1914 to supervise the activities of *Pravda* but was arrested the following year. After the February Revolution Kamenev situated himself on the moderate wing of the Bolshevik Party, supported co-operation with the provisional government and revolutionary defensism, advocated some form of fusion with the Mensheviks and accepted that the socialist revolution was a long way off, only becoming possible when capitalism had matured in Russia. Conflict with Lenin was inevitable when the Bolshevik leader managed to get back to Petrograd. When Lenin launched his April Theses – a clarion call for the taking of power by the proletariat and the poorer strata of the peasantry – Kamenev was appalled and wrote in *Pravda* that these were the personal views of Comrade Lenin and not those of the Bolshevik Party. He advocated caution in the run up to the October Revolution and went so far as to publish an article in GORKY's newspaper, *Novaya Zhizn*, warning against revolutionary adventurism. This was treason – he was revealing that the Bolshevik Party was seriously contemplating seizing power – but it blew over and Lenin forgave him. Kamenev advocated a broad socialist coalition because of the narrow support base of the Bolsheviks. However, Lenin would not consider sharing power and Kamenev resigned as chair of the Central Executive Committee (CEC or VTsIK) of the soviets. Lenin welcomed this as he regarded Kamenev as too soft for the role. Instead Yakov SVERDLOV, one of the hard men of the Bolshevik Party, took over and transformed the CEC and then the Congress of Soviets into compliant bodies. Kamenev became chair of the Moscow soviet after the revolution and remained there until ousted by STALIN. He was a leading light in the Politburo and often chaired meetings when Lenin was too ill to attend. He was Lenin's deputy as chair of Sovnarkom and chair of the council of labour and defence. As a moderate, he was always opposed to TROTSKY's radicalism and he joined Stalin and ZINOVIEV to form the triumvirate whose aim was to prevent Trotsky succeeding Lenin, even though this was Lenin's wish. Ironically, Kamenev's wife was Trotsky's sister. Later Kamenev sided with Trotsky and Zinoviev against Stalin. He lost his place on the Politburo in 1925 and was dispatched to Rome as Soviet Ambassador to Italy (1926–7). He suffered the same fate as Zinoviev in being expelled several times from the Party, being readmitted when he had made the ritual obeisance to Stalin. Kamenev and Zinoviev, and a supporting cast of minor officials, had the dubious honour of starring in the first great show trial in Moscow in August 1936. Kamenev confessed to having been behind the murder of Sergei KIROV in 1934 and given the opportunity would have killed Stalin as well. All this was nonsense but Kamenev had understood that confessions would spare his own and his family's lives. They did not and the whole Kamenev household perished. Kamenev was rehabilitated under GORBACHEV on 13 June 1988.

Kandinsky, Vasily Vasilevich (1866–1944), one of the founders of abstract art, Kandinsky, born in Moscow, graduated from Moscow University in law and economics, but abandoned these disciplines to study art in Munich in 1897. He was a co-founder of the Berlin group, Der Blaue Reiter. His paintings began as abstract impressionism and then developed geometrical designs. He became famous in Germany and Russia and returned to his home-

land in 1914. He was influential in the early revolutionary era and was the first chair of the Institute of Artistic Culture in Moscow in 1920 and a co-founder of the Academy of Artistic Sciences, 1921. He returned to Germany in 1921 and when Hitler came to power in 1933 was forced once again to move, this time to France.

Kapitonov, Ivan Vasilevich (*b.* 1915), an archetypal Brezhnevite Party official, conservative, cautious but unable to stem the increasing corruption within the ranks of the nomenklatura, Kapitonov was born in Ryazan oblast into a Russian peasant family and joined the CPSU in 1939. He rose to become first secretary of Moscow gorkom, 1952–4, and Moscow obkom, 1954–9. KHRUSHCHEV was not satisfied with his performance and he was moved to head the Ivanovo obkom. When BREZHNEV took over the Party in 1964 Kapitonov's star rose and in 1965 he became a secretary of the Central Committee for organisational Party work (Party cadres) until 1983 and then for light industry until 1986. In that year he lost his membership of the Central Committee, becoming one of the many cadres brushed aside by GORBACHEV.

Kapitsa, Petr Leonidovich (1894–1984), an outstanding Soviet physicist who worked with Rutherford and won the Nobel Prize for Physics in 1978. He was born in Kronstadt, the son of a military engineer. He worked at the Cavendish Research Laboratory, Cambridge, from 1921–34 but STALIN decided he should not return to England after spending a holiday in the Soviet Union. He was elected a Fellow of the Royal Society, 1929, and a member of the USSR Academy of Sciences, 1939. He was often in conflict with the Soviet authorities and his laboratory was moved to Moscow, becoming later the Institute of Physical Problems. He was director until 1946 when he was arrested but continued working. He was released after Stalin's death and returned to his institute.

Kaplan, Fanny (Dora) (1893–1918), a member of the Socialist Revolutionary Party who objected to the signing of the Treaty of Brest-Litovsk, she shot LENIN several times as he left the Mikhelson factory in Moscow on 30 August 1918. She was immediately arrested and executed. Rumours persisted that she had not fired the shots but the Cheka used the attempted assassination to act against potential opponents.

Karakhan, Lev Mikhailovich (1889–1937), an Armenian, his full name was Karakhanyan, he was born in Georgia and became a leading Soviet diplomat. He joined the RSDRP in 1904 in Tbilisi but was also active in Kharbin and Vladivostok. He studied law at St Petersburg University (1910–15) and became a member of TROTSKY's Mezhraionka (Inter-borough). His opposition to the war led to exile to Tomsk but the February revolution permitted him to return to the capital where he was elected to the presidium of the Petrograd Soviet of Workers' and Soldiers' Deputies. Like other members of the Mezhraionka he joined the Bolsheviks in July 1917. He was active in the October Revolution as a member of the Military Revolutionary Committee. He became secretary of the Soviet delegation to the Brest-Litovsk peace talks in November 1917 and remained in diplomatic service for the rest of his life. He was the leading Soviet specialist on Asian affairs. He was a deputy People's Commissar for Foreign Affairs between 1918–20 and between 1925–34. He penned the 'Karakhan manifestos' of 1919 and 1920, apparently on his own initiative, which turned diplomacy on its head by repudiating the Tsarist 'unequal' treaties. This was the utopian phase of Soviet diplomacy – in 1921 it became more concerned with protecting national interests. He served as Soviet Ambassador to Poland just after the Treaty of Riga (1921) at a tense time in Polish–Soviet relations. He moved to China as ambassador in 1923 and stayed until 1927. He negotiated with all sides in China and also helped promote the rapprochement with Japan which resulted in diplomatic relations being established in 1925. He then returned to Moscow and together with Maksim LITVINOV played a key role in shaping Soviet diplomacy. He moved to Ankara in 1934, revealing that his position in Moscow was no longer secure. In 1937 he was recalled as Soviet Ambassador to Turkey, accused of treason and executed. He was rehabilitated after the XXth Party Congress in 1956.

Karimov, Islam Abduganievich (*b.* 1938), an Uzbek, born in Samarkand, Karimov became the main beneficiary of the purge of the Uzbek leadership in the 1980s as a result of the cotton scandal (the falsification of production data), which involved practically all the top Party and state officials. He graduated as an aeronautical engineer and worked in the Tashkent Aviation Enterprise, 1960–6, and then moved into the Uzbek Gosplan, 1966–83. He was then appointed Minister of Finance of Uzbekistan and in 1986 first secretary of Kashkadarya obkom. In June 1989 he was elected first secretary of the Communist Party of Uzbekistan and in 1990 he was elected the first President of Uzbekistan. At the XXVIIIth Party Congress in July 1990 he was elected to the Central Committee and the Politburo. During the attempted coup of August 1991 Karimov supported the Emergency Committee but after its collapse he declared Uzbekistan independent and continued in power. Since 1991 he has built up a reputation as a conservative but economically reform-minded leader and under his leadership Uzbekistan has attracted much foreign direct investment.

Karpov, Anatoly Evgenevich (*b.* 1951), a great Soviet chess player who came to personify the official face of the Soviet state in the 1980s. He graduated from the University of Moscow in economics. He became world youth champion in 1969 and world champion in 1975 by default, the only person to have become world champion in this manner. The American Bobby Fischer had won the title in 1972 and then put forward proposals to Fide, the international chess federation. When they were rejected he declined to defend his title. Karpov won two fiercely contested matches, in 1978 and 1981, against Viktor KORCHNOI to retain his title. A grandmaster, he met his match in Gary KASPAROV in 1985. To many, Karpov, the Russian, represented the Soviet establishment and Kasparov, a Jew, the opposition, at a turning point in Soviet history. Kasparov's victory was celebrated world wide. The intense Karpov, as a member of the Communist Party and president of the Soviet Peace Foundation, felt the defeat keenly, but, try as he might, was unable to overcome Kasparov.

Karpov, Vladimir Vasilevich (*b.* 1922), a high-profile writer and literary figure during the GORBACHEV years, he was born into a Russian family in Orenburg, was arrested in 1940 and then served in a penal battalion, winning the Soviet Union's highest decoration for bravery, Hero of the Soviet Union, in 1944. He graduated from the Frunze Military Academy, 1947, and the Moscow Literary Institute, 1954. His novels and prose were on military themes. He was made editor-in-chief of *Novy Mir* in 1981 and in September 1986 he became secretary of the USSR Union of Writers and a candidate member of the Central Committee. He had joined the Communist Party in 1943. He was elected a USSR people's deputy in 1984. Karpov tried to steer a middle course in the battles between the conservatives and the radicals under glasnost.

Kasparov, Gary Kinovich (né Vainshtein) (*b.* 1963), a great world chess champion, Kasparov is hugely popular because of his handsome appearance, flamboyant manners, liberal politics and fluency in English. He became keenly interested in mathematics when four years of age and became a Soviet grandmaster at eighteen. He won the world youth tournament in Dortmund, Germany, in 1981. He won gold medals at Malta (1980) and Lucerne (1982). In 1975 Anatoly KARPOV had become world chess champion by default when Bobby Fischer declined to defend his title after a dispute with Fide, the ruling international body. In late 1984 the contest between Karpov and Kasparov got under way. The world champion swept irresistibly into an early lead but gradually Kasparov fought his way back. In February 1985, after forty-six games in Moscow, Kasparov began to look like the eventual winner. Then the president of Fide flew into Moscow and declared the match over, stating that there would be another match later in the year. Kasparov had already made himself unpopular by criticising the Filipino president and now swore to destroy him and Fide. There was a widespread belief that Kasparov had been cheated out of the title. Kasparov exacted his revenge in November 1985 when he defeated Karpov and became world champion at the age of twenty-two. He defeated Karpov again in 1989 to retain his title, again playing with panache and brilliance. In 1993 Nigel Short (Great Britain) won the right to challenge Kasparov for the world title and Fide decided it should be staged in Manchester, without consulting either player. Kasparov and Short then decided to break away from Fide and founded a new professional organisation.

Kataev, Valentin Petrovich (1897–1986), a very popular Soviet writer, he was born in Odessa and was the elder brother of the famous satirical writer, Evgeny Petrov. He fought for the Reds during the

Civil War and became known in 1927 through the publication of his novel, *The Embezzlers*. He produced a socialist realist novel in 1932, *Vremya, Vpered (Time, Forward)*, which describes workers beating a concrete pouring record. His breakthrough came in 1936 with *Beleet Parus Odinoky (A Lonely White Sail Shines White)* about children in Odessa during the 1905 revolution. In 1956 he was appointed editor of *Yunost,* the leading youth literary magazine, and published many talented young writers, including Anatoly Kuznetsov and Vasily AKSENOV. He left in 1962 and continued writing novels which gradually moved away from his previous, conformist style.

Katukov, Marshal Mikhail Efimovich (1900–76), he joined the Red Army and fought in the Civil War. After graduating from the Military Academy of the Red Army, 1935, he was a tank commander and commanded various tank armies near Moscow, 1941, on the Voronezh Front, 1942–3, and in Belorussia and Ukraine, 1944. He was commander of tank forces in (East) Germany, 1948.

Katushev, Konstantin Fedorovich (*b.* 1927), a leading Party and economic official, he was born in Nizhny Novgorod oblast and graduated from the Gorky Polytechnic Institute, 1951. He then joined the Gorky Automobile Plant (GAZ) and became secretary of the Party organisation. He moved into the Gorky obkom Party apparatus in 1959, becoming first secretary in 1965. He was elected a member of the Central Committee in 1966. He was made a secretary of the Central Committee in 1968 and was responsible for the department for liaison with communist and workers' parties of socialist countries. This was the year when the Soviet-led invasion of Czechoslovakia aroused great protest. In 1977 he was made the Soviet Union's permanent representative to Comecon and a deputy chair of the USSR Council of Ministers.

In 1982 he fell from grace and was sent to Cuba as ambassador. His career took off again under GORBACHEV and in 1985 he was chair of the state committee for foreign economic relations. In 1988 he was appointed USSR Minister of Foreign Economic Relations.

Kazannik, Aleksei Ivanovich (*b.* 1941), he became well known in 1989 for standing down in favour of Boris YELTSIN in elections to the USSR Supreme Soviet. Kazannik had been elected but Yeltsin not, so Kazannik announced to GORBACHEV, chairing the USSR Congress of People's Deputies, that he wished to cede his place to Yeltsin. Gorbachev could not find anything in the rules preventing this and Boris Nikolaevich's passage was assured. Kazannik was born in Chernigov oblast, Ukraine, into a Ukrainian family, and never joined the Communist Party. He graduated in law from Irkutsk State University, successfully presented his candidate dissertation in law (LLM) and began teaching in the department of labour, economic and agricultural law, Omsk State University, 1975. He came to the conclusion that state law was merely the servant of the dominant ideology and that lawyers were restricted to producing commentaries on the Marxist–Leninist classics and contemporary figures. He abandoned law and switched to ecology. In 1991 he successfully presented his doctoral dissertation on the legal protection of the environment in the USSR (LLD). He was elected to the USSR Congress of People's Deputies, 1989, and he worked in the USSR Supreme Soviet committee on ecology and the rational use of natural resources. In Kazannik's view the wars against Finland and the Baltic states, 1939–40, the intervention in Hungary, 1956, Czechoslovakia, 1968, and Afghanistan, 1979–89, were Party crimes against the world. The mass repression of the STALIN era was a crime against humanity. He served for a time as Russian Minister of Justice under Yeltsin but became very disillusioned with Boris Nikolaevich's behaviour and policies.

Kebin, Ivan Gustavovich (Käbin, Johannes, in Estonian) (*b.* 1905), a typical Sovietised Balt who returned to his ancestral home after the Red Army took over and thereafter served Moscow well. An Estonian, he was born in St Petersburg and joined the Communist Party in 1927. He worked in various Russian cities and also as an academic before becoming first secretary of the Communist Party of Estonia in 1950. He presided over the Sovietisation of Estonia and thereby laid the foundation for the upsurge of nationalism there under GORBACHEV. In 1978 Kebin became chair of the Presidium of the Estonian Supreme Soviet (head of state) and retired in 1983.

Keldysh, Mstislav Vsevolodovich (*b.* 1911), a brilliant Soviet scientist who contributed to the space programme, Keldysh was born in Riga, the son of Vsevolod Keldysh, a prominent military engineer; his elder brother is the musicologist, Yury Keldysh. He graduated in mathematics from Moscow University in 1931 and worked in aerodynamics afterwards, being elected to the USSR Academy of Sciences in 1943. He was appointed director of the Institute of Applied Mathematics in 1953 and was president of the USSR Academy of Sciences, 1961–75. He was elected to the Central Committee in 1961.

Kerensky, Aleksandr Fedorovich (1881–1970), the great loser in twentieth-century Russian politics, Kerensky was blamed by an army of critics for the seizure of power by the Bolsheviks in October 1917. This weighed heavily on him and until his dying day it was impossible to carry on an objective conversation with him about the events of 1917. He was liable to fly into a rage if his role was brought into question. His father was headmaster of the school in Simbirsk

(Ulyanovsk) where LENIN and his elder brother Aleksandr (executed for attempted regicide in 1887) studied. He studied history and law at St Petersburg University and in 1905 joined the Socialist Revolutionary Party (several of his wife's relatives were in the party). He was arrested and exiled in 1905 but returned to the capital the following year and developed into a flamboyant, silver-tongued defence lawyer. He specialised in defending political activists and travelled to Siberia to investigate the Lena gold massacre in 1912. He was elected to the Duma in 1912 as a Trudovik. Despite the boycott of the Duma by the Socialist Revolutionaries, Kerensky managed, not for the last time, to drive a coach and four through official party policy. The publication of Duma debates promoted Kerensky's name and policies and he became the most popular deputy in the eyes of workers. Like many other top politicians, he became a freemason. The Trudoviks abstained in the debate on war credits in July 1914. The February Revolution afforded him centre stage and he became the most important non-Bolshevik politician in 1917. In the first provisional government Kerensky was Minister of Justice and when GUCHKOV resigned as Minister of War and the Navy, Kerensky succeeded him. This gave him a stage for his rhetoric and he toured the fronts attempting to enthuse the troops to victory. He created a very positive image while there but it soon dissipated. The lack of clarity in his dealings with General KORNILOV about suppressing Bolshevism and restoring army discipline led to Kornilov, who fondly believed that he was executing Kerensky's will, to make his disastrous move on Petrograd. This was the kiss of death for Kerensky. It confirmed Lenin's prognosis that there would be a coup from the right and any legitimacy which the provisional government had enjoyed in August 1917 was wiped away. He escaped arrest in the Winter Palace on 25

October 1917 by dressing up as a female nurse, and then attempted to rally loyal troops. He travelled to London and Paris for the Socialist Revolutionaries to advocate allied intervention on the side of Russian democrats. When the Allies supported Admiral KOLCHAK's forces, Kerensky denounced intervention. He spent many years of his exile in Paris and, after 1940, in the United States. Alexander Kerensky: *The Kerensky Memoirs: Russia and History's Turning Point*, New York, 1965; Richard Abraham: *Alexander Kerensky, the First Love of the Revolution*, New York, 1987.

Khachaturyan, Aram Ilich (1903–78), an Armenian composer and conductor who will probably be best remembered in the west for his ballet music, *Spartakus*, 1953. It was used on British television as the theme music of a popular series. He was born near Tbilisi, Georgia, and studied at the Gnesin Technical School of Music, Moscow, 1922–9, and at the Moscow Conservatory, 1929–34, graduating with distinction. He began his career as a conductor in 1950 and conducted his own works in the Soviet Union and abroad. His music reveals his interest in Armenian, Azerbaijani, Georgian and Russian folk music. He composed symphonies, a violin concerto and a cello concerto, among others. In 1948, together with SHOSTAKOVICH and PROKOFIEV, he was accused of allowing bourgeois tendencies to surface in his music by the Communist Party and admitted his guilt. After STALIN's death in 1953 he refuted his confession and condemned the accusations levelled at him and the others. He was awarded the Lenin Prize in 1959. His wife and nephew are also composers.

Khasbulatov, Ruslan Imranovich (*b.* 1942), a volatile Chechen who began as a YELTSIN supporter and eventually became a bitter foe, playing a leading role in the conflict which resulted in armed violence in Russia in October 1993. Born in Grozny, he was deported along with the Chechen and Ingush nations to Kazakhstan in 1944. STALIN's accusation that they had collaborated with the German Wehrmacht was rescinded by KHRUSHCHEV but Khasbulatov decided not to return to his homeland. He entered the law faculty, Kazakh State University, in Alma Ata (now Almaty), 1960, and remarkably transferred to the law faculty of Moscow State University, 1962, graduating in 1965. He obtained his doctorate in economics on the Canadian economy, 1970, following this with a DSc (Econ), again on the Canadian economy, 1980. In 1990 he was elected as a people's deputy for Grozny to the RSFSR Congress of People's Deputies and he became deputy speaker of the RSFSR Supreme Soviet, on Yeltsin's recommendation. When Yeltsin, the speaker, became Russian President in June 1991 Khasbulatov could not obtain a majority of votes to succeed him until October 1991, after the attempted coup. The break with Yeltsin came early. Already in December 1991 Khasbulatov was criticising Yeltsin and GAIDAR for adopting shock therapy. The gulf between them widened in April 1992 and thereafter relations deteriorated rapidly. The reasons for the split are difficult to assess but it may have been due to Yeltsin's unwillingness to offer Khasbulatov a top post in his government. After all Khasbulatov (cognate with the word Hezbollah) was a Chechen and a Muslim.

Khrushchev, Nikita Sergeevich (1894–1971), an intelligent, cunning, rumbustious Soviet leader who broke the Stalinist mould but was eventually removed by the nomenklatura. Khrushchev became the first Soviet leader to visit the United States and to promise that communism was round the corner in his homeland. He was born in Kalinovka, Kursh guberniya, into a Russian peasant family, and received only a modest education before moving with his family to Yuzovka (now Donetsk), Ukraine. He joined the Communist Party in 1918 and fought in the Civil War. He moved into the Ukrainian Party apparatus in 1924 and he supported Lazar KAGANOVICH and STALIN in the factional struggles of the period. Khrushchev was bowled over by Stalin's modesty and folksy manner and later admitted that he had been naïve. In 1929 Khrushchev managed to obtain a place at the Industrial Academy in Moscow, a breeding ground for future leaders. He was brought into the Moscow Party organisation by Kaganovich and was soon his number two. In 1934 Khrushchev was elected a member of the Central Committee and the following year first secretary of Moscow gorkom and obkom. In 1938 Stalin sent him back to Ukraine as first secretary. The same year he became a candidate member of the Politburo and in 1939 a full member. Khrushchev was a political officer during the war and in 1944 was appointed Prime Minister and first secretary of Ukraine with the task of rebuilding the shattered republic. In 1946 Khrushchev was replaced by Kaganovich as first secretary but in 1948 he was back again as Party leader. Stalin brought him back to Moscow in 1949 to head the Moscow Party organisation and he also became a secretary of the Central Committee. This made him a key player after Stalin's death in March 1953 and by June 1957 he had outmanoeuvred BERIA, MALENKOV and MOLOTOV to become a dominant, national leader. The defeat of the Anti-Party Group in June 1957 allowed Khrushchev to stack the Politburo with his appointees and marked the dominance of the Party apparatus over the government. This situation prevailed until the XIXth Party Conference in June 1988 when GORBACHEV removed the Party as the manager of the economy. In 1961 Khrushchev launched a new Party programme and expected the foothills of communism (to each according to need)

to be reached by 1980. He was later to be the butt of much ridicule for this utopian prediction. In many ways his reforms presage those of Gorbachev. Like the future Soviet leader he came to the conclusion that the Party apparatus was a brake on the economy and split it in 1962 into industrial and agricultural wings. As with Gorbachev, he wanted to afford industrial managers more latitude. There were considerable differences, however. Khrushchev never questioned the leading role of the Party and would not contemplate any market-oriented reforms. Arguably, in doing so, he doomed himself to failure. In foreign policy Khrushchev was very innovative but a high-risk taker. The XXth Party Congress demolition of Stalin infuriated Mao Zedong, who felt he should have been consulted beforehand. This led on to the Hungarian Revolution of 1956 and weakened the communist edifice world wide. The greatest crisis occurred in October 1962 when the superpowers almost began a nuclear war. In agriculture he launched the virgin land programme, a vast expansion of the cultivated area, which increased output but at great expense. By 1963 he was importing grain from the United States. He was removed by the nomenklatura whom he had almost totally alienated by October 1964. Nikita Khrushchev: *Khrushchev Remembers*, vol. 1, translated and edited by Strobe Talbot, Little, Brown, Boston, 1970; *Khrushchev Remembers, The Last Testament*, vol. 2, translated and edited by Strobe Talbot, Little, Brown, Boston, 1974; *Khrushchev Remembers, The Glasnost Tapes*, with a foreword by Strobe Talbot, translated and edited by Jerrold Schecter and Vyacheslav V. Luchkov, Little, Brown, Boston, 1990; Martin McCauley (ed.): *Khrushchev and Khrushchevism*, Macmillan, London, 1987; *The Khrushchev Era 1953–1964*, Longman, 1995; William J. Tompson: *Khrushchev: A Political Life*, Macmillan, London, 1995.

Khrushchev, Sergei Nikitich (*b.* 1935), the son of NIKITA SERGEEVICH, he graduated as an engineer and worked on rocket research. One of his father's supporters reported to him that BREZHNEV and others were planning a coup against his father. He informed Khrushchev of this but the latter refused to believe it. After the coup he lost his position as a rocket scientist. He played an important role in securing the publication of his father's memoirs in the west. His own book provides fascinating insights into the Khrushchevian political world. Sergei Khrushchev: *Khrushchev on Khrushchev: An Inside Account of the Man and his Era*, Little, Brown, Boston, 1992.

Kirichenko, Aleksei Illarionovich (1908–75), a Ukrainian, he reached the heights under KHRUSHCHEV but fell suddenly into oblivion. He graduated in agriculture and entered the Ukrainian Party apparatus in 1938, becoming first secretary of Odessa obkom, 1945, then second secretary, Communist Party of Ukraine, 1949, then first secretary, 1953. He was elected a member of the Politburo in 1955. He supported Khrushchev against the Anti-Party Group in June 1957 and was rewarded in December 1957 with a secretaryship of the Central Committee, becoming responsible for Party cadres. However, in January 1960 he was removed and sent to Rostov obkom as first secretary but lost even this in May 1960.

Kirilenko, Andrei Pavlovich (1906–90), a Russified Ukrainian who was at the top in Soviet politics for over two decades. He joined the Communist Party in 1931, beginning his Ukrainian Party career in 1938 in Zaporozhe and in 1950 succeeding BREZHNEV as first secretary, Dnepropetrovsk obkom. In 1955 KHRUSHCHEV moved him to Sverdlovsk to become first secretary there. This revealed that Khrushchev knew him personally from his days in Ukraine. Kirilenko was elected a member of the CPSU Central Committee at the XXth Party Congress, 1956, and in 1957 a candidate member of the Presidium (Politburo), becoming a full member in 1962. In the same year he was made first deputy chair of the Russian Bureau of the CPSU and in 1966 he became a secretary of the Central Committee, responsible for Party cadres. In 1964 he had joined Brezhnev and the other plotters against Khrushchev and developed a close relationship with the new Soviet leader. However, towards the end of the Brezhnev era Konstantin CHERNENKO pushed Kirilenko aside and assumed responsibility for Party cadres. When ANDROPOV died it was Chernenko who took over the supreme office. Kirilenko was a typical conservative, Brezhnevite official, the type whom Mikhail GORBACHEV found so uncongenial.

Kirov, Sergei Mironovich (1886–1934), the circumstances of his assassination in December 1934 are still unclear but the suspicion lingers on that STALIN was behind it. Kirov had been approached by some delegates at the XVIIth Party Congress, earlier in the year, to stand against Stalin as General Secretary. He declined, reported this to Stalin and this may have sealed his fate. He was born near Vyatka and brought up in an orphanage. He joined the Bolsheviks in 1904 and was active as a Party organiser in the north Caucasus, especially Vladikavkaz. He was elected a candidate member of the Central Committee, 1921, and a full member in 1923. In 1926 he became first secretary of the Leningrad organisation and his popularity there grew over time. In the same year he was elected a candidate member of the Politburo and became a full member in 1934 as well as a member of the Secretariat and Orgburo. As such he became Stalin's rival. After his murder many were executed and this may have been due to Stalin's desire to secure his position in Leningrad, always a troublesome city for Moscow Bolsheviks.

Klimov, Elem Germanovich (*b.* 1933), under glasnost he became the best-known satirical film maker. Born in Volgograd, he graduated as an aeronautical engineer and worked on helicopter design. Later he graduated from the State Institute of Cinematography and made films which were transparently satires of Soviet bureaucratic life, for instance, *Adventures of a Dentist*, 1967. His best-known film, *Agony*, about RASPUTIN and the demise of the Russian empire was complete in 1975 but was first shown abroad in 1984 and then in the Soviet Union in 1985. It became an overnight sensation everywhere as it dealt with subjects hitherto regarded as taboo. In 1986 he was elected first secretary of the Union of Film Makers and immediately began releasing all the films which had been held back over the previous thirty years.

Kokoshin, Andrei Afanasevich (*b.* 1945), a leading academic authority on the Soviet military and national security under GORBACHEV. He was born into a Russian officer's family in Moscow and graduated from the Moscow Bauman Higher Technical College, 1969, and then worked in the Institute of the USA and Canada, USSR Academy of Sciences, becoming a specialist on international, military and security questions. He successfully presented his candidate dissertation in history on the use of forecasts in the formation of US foreign policy (PhD) in 1973. He published prolifically on the domestic and foreign policy of the USA, the theory of international relations, arms reduction and disarmament. In December 1987, at the age of forty-two, he became one of the youngest corresponding members of the USSR Academy of Sciences. He was active and influential in interpreting the new political thinking of the Gorbachev era and

he owed his promotion primarily to Academician Georgy ARBATOV and General Vladimir Lobov. He actively co-operated with officers involved in the military for democracy and those who were advocating fundamental reforms of the armed forces. He was a front runner to take over as USSR or later Russian Minister of Defence, should a civilian take over the armed forces. In April 1992 he was appointed deputy Russian Minister of Defence and has been influential in restructuring the military economy.

Kolbin, Gennady Vasilevich (*b.* 1927), Kolbin, a Russian, took over from the dismissed Dinmukhamed KUNAEV as first secretary, Communist Party of Kazakhstan, 1986, and this provoked riots in Alma Ata (now Almaty) and other Kazakh cities. Kazakhs were demonstrating against a Russian being imposed on them. In his memoirs, GORBACHEV states that Kunaev favoured a Russian as his successor in order to prevent Nursultan NAZARBAEV obtaining the top post. Gorbachev gave Kolbin the task of eliminating corruption in the republic but most Kazakhs saw his appointment as an attempt to enforce Russian domination in Kazakhstan. Kolbin stayed until 1989 when Nazarbaev succeeded him. Kolbin graduated from the Urals Polytechnic Institute in 1955 and was second secretary of Sverdlovsk obkom, 1971–5, and then second secretary, Communist Party of Georgia, until 1983. He was first secretary of Ulyanovsk obkom, 1983–6, before moving to Kazakhstan. He was elected a candidate member of the CPSU Central Committee in 1975, and a full member in 1981.

Kolchak, Admiral Aleksandr Vasilevich (1873–1920), the leading White commander during the Civil War, he was nevertheless, as an admiral, like a fish out of water when leading land armies. He had a brilliant naval career in the Imperial Navy during the wars against

Japan and Germany. In 1916 he became commander-in-chief of the Black Sea Fleet, cleared the Black Sea of Turkish and German ships and closed the Bosphorus by laying mines. He resigned his commission in June 1917. Kolchak was lecturing in the United States in October 1917 and spent a year in the Far East waiting for the Trans-Siberian Railway to be cleared so that he could move back to the centre of Russia. In Omsk, in November 1918, he became, as the most senior officer, Minister of War in the provisional all-Russian government, which claimed to represent the disbanded Constituent Assembly. After a coup by right-wing officers later the same month, Kolchak was proclaimed Supreme Ruler of Russia. He was a poor military leader and lacked political acumen. Despite being a Crimean Tatar he had no feeling for nationality affairs. Like most Whites he failed to grasp that the Civil War was political as much as military. In November 1919 he retreated eastwards from Omsk but was caught by Czech troops who handed him over to the Socialist Revolutionaries and Mensheviks in Irkutsk, on the orders of General Janin, head of the allied military mission, in January 1920. He was moved on to the Bolsheviks who executed him in February 1920.

Kollontai, Aleksandra Mikhailovna (née Domontovich) (1872–1952), the 'femme fatale' of the Russian Revolution, she scored many firsts in Europe: the first woman to join a government and the first woman ambassador. She will probably be remembered for her role as a pioneer feminist and advocate of free love than for her revolutionary record. Her father was a general and her mother the daughter of a Finnish timber merchant. A formative influence on her was Elena Stasova (1873–1966) who aroused an interest in Russian women workers in her and this led on to Marxism. She travelled widely in Russia to acquaint herself with the condition of women. She abandoned her husband (she was later married to Paul Dybenko, the first People's Commissar for the Navy, from 1918 to 1923) and made for western Europe where she met Rosa Luxemburg, Karl Kautsky, Georgy PLEKHANOV, and finally LENIN. Until 1915 she belonged to the Menshevik group around the journal, *Nashe Slovo*, but later joined the left around LENIN in Berlin, writing tirelessly against the war. On the national question, she took an international position, and thereby clashed with Lenin. She spent the war in Scandinavia and the United States but always maintained close contact with Lenin. After returning to Petrograd after the February Revolution she supported Lenin's April Theses. In July 1917 she was elected to the Central Committee of the RSDRP. She supported the Left Communists around Bukharin who opposed the Treaty of Brest-Litovsk as treason and a betrayal of internationalism. This cost her her position on the Central Committee. She supported the Workers' Opposition and belonged to the first Sovnarkom for a short time but as head of the women's section of the Central Committee from 1920 she exercised influence over policy towards women, families and health. She was elected deputy head of the international women's commissariat of the Communist International (Comintern). The defeat of the Workers' Opposition left her isolated and she lost her post as head of the women's section of the Central Committee. Many of her progressive innovations were reversed by STALIN. In those days high-profile defeated political opponents were moved out of the country by giving them diplomatic functions. In 1923 Kollontai was sent to Oslo as Soviet representative, to Mexico (1926), then again to Norway (1927). She was well suited to this type of activity as she was an excellent linguist. In 1930 she was posted to Stockholm and in 1943–5 she was Soviet Ambassador to Sweden. During the war many attempts were made by Germany to float peace proposals and Stockholm was the main point of contact. In order to ensure that Kollontai was not inveigled into accepting any of these proposals for transmission to Moscow, Stalin dispatched one of his top young diplomats who acted as her minder. Kollontai had to accept that Stalin's Russia was male chauvinist and that the position of women declined over time. The most important liberating aspect was access to higher education and this was seized by women. Politically they were marginalised until 1991.

Kondratieff, Nikolai Dmitrievich (Kondratev) (1892–1938), a world-famous economist who discovered long cycles, named after him. He graduated from the University of St Petersburg (he was a pupil of Tugan-Baranovsky) and worked with CHAYANOV in the Union of Zemstvos during the First World War. After the February Revolution he became deputy Minister of Food responsible for providing peasants with industrial consumer goods. His great interest was in agriculture and he founded and was the first director of the Moscow Konyunkturny (Fluctuation) Institute, 1920–8. He regarded private agriculture as inherently more efficient than state-run agriculture. He was arrested in 1930 and was an important witness in the Menshevik trial of March 1931 as he had been an opponent of GROMAN and others. Kondratieff was never put on public trial. He was rehabilitated in July 1987 and the Supreme Court stated that the accusation that he had organised a counter-revolutionary party was baseless. Naum Jasny: *Soviet Economists of the Twenties*, Cambridge, 1972.

Konev, Marshal Ivan Stepanovich (1897–1973), one of the most successful Red Army commanders during the Great Fatherland War. He joined the Red Army and the Bolshevik Party in 1918 and participated in the Civil War. He graduated from the Frunze Military Academy, 1926. He fought in the Smolensk sector in August 1941 and from October 1941–December 1942 he was commander of the Kalinin Front. In July 1943 he held up the German advance and then moved on to liberate Orel, Belgorod and Poltava. In 1943–4 he commanded the Steppe Front (renamed the 2nd Ukrainian Front) and they took Kirovograd in January 1944. He scored one of the great Red Army victories over the Wehrmacht at Korsun-Shevchenko. He took over the 1st Ukrainian Front and recaptured Lvov. He became a Marshal of the Soviet Union in February 1944. His front advanced from the Vistula to the Oder and then Berlin. He continued to Torgau where he linked up with US forces. His forces then moved south and entered Prague in May 1945. He became first deputy People's Commissar for Defence and commander of Soviet ground forces, 1946–50 and 1955–6. He was commander-in-chief of the Warsaw Pact forces, 1956–60. He criticised Marshal ZHUKOV after the war hero was dismissed as USSR Minister of Defence in 1957. He was commander of Soviet forces in (East) Germany, 1961–2. He was a member of the Central Committee of the Communist Party, 1952–73. He represented the Soviet Union at the funeral of Sir Winston Churchill in London in 1965. Many monuments were erected in his honour in eastern Europe after the war but they were all taken down after 1989 and returned to the Soviet Union.

Korbut, Olga Valentinovna (*b.* 1955), she became a world celebrity at the Munich Olympic Games, 1972, when she won two gold and two silver medals. Her impish demeanour and grace captivated audiences. She had considerable influence on the development of gymnastics as she was a great innovator and risk taker. The Korbut loop on the asymmetrical bars ensures her immortality.

She was born in Grodno into a Belorussian (Belarusian) family and graduated from the Grodno Pedagogical Institute, 1977. She performed with the Minsk Armed Forces team from 1978. She was Soviet champion, 1970, 1974 and 1975 and world champion in 1974. Concerned about the fallout from Chernobyl (which seriously affected parts of Belarus) and the inability of Soviet athletes to augment their modest salaries with commercial appearances, she and her husband Leonid, a painter and musician, and son Robert moved to Atlanta, USA, in 1991. They had difficulties initially in adjusting to American life as neither spoke English. Olga then began a career as a teacher of gymnastics in Atlanta schools. Her three sisters and father still live in Belarus.

Korchnoi, Viktor Lvovich (*b.* 1931), a great Soviet chess player who never quite scaled the heights of some others. He is best known for two titanic struggles against Anatoly KARPOV, in 1978 and 1981, when he challenged the official face of the Soviet establishment for his world crown. Korchnoi had defected in 1976 to the Netherlands and hence his contests with Karpov had an added political dimension. After struggling for years to get his family out of the Soviet Union, he eventually succeeded. GORBACHEV offered him his Soviet citizenship back in 1990 but Korchnoi refused it.

Kornilov, General Lavr Georgevich (1870–1918), 'He had the heart of a lion but the brain of a sheep': this unflattering portrayal of Kornilov reflects his outstanding military career, which included undercover work, but also his disastrous lack of feel for politics. His father was a Cossack and his mother Buryat, and he spent his early military career in Turkestan, acquiring some of the languages. He had a good war against Japan and then served as military attaché in China, 1907–11. In March 1917 GUCHKOV,

Minister of War and the Navy, appointed Kornilov commander-in-chief of the Petrograd garrison. He quickly fell out with the provisional government which refused to sanction force to restore civil peace in the capital. He asked to be transferred again to the front and commanded the Eighth Army on the Southwest Front but was as unsuccessful as other Russian commanders. He took the law into his own hands and executed Russian looters, displaying their bodies as a warning to others. He successfully lobbied for the restoration of the death penalty in the army and the banning of political meetings at the front. In July 1917 he was made Supreme Commander-in-Chief, obtaining a free hand from the provisional government. He advocated the death penalty in the rear, vigorous action against the Bolsheviks in Petrograd and militarisation of the factories and railways. The Allies hoped KERENSKY would adopt Kornilov's programme but as usual he was indecisive. Through an intermediary, V. N. Lvov, Kornilov requested Kerensky's presence at Mogilev. Kerensky construed this as an ultimatum but it is probably more accurate to say that he had developed cold feet. Kerensky declared Kornilov a rebel and the general played into the politician's hands by issuing an appeal to the Russian people. Kornilov was arrested but escaped later to the south to become a White commander. The Kornilov episode destroyed the Kerensky government and opened the way for LENIN. Kornilov was killed by a shell near Ekaterinodar (now Krasnodar) in April 1918. George Katkov: *Russia 1917: The Kornilov Affair: Kerensky and the Break up of the Russian Army*, London, 1980; Alexander Kerensky: *The Prelude to Bolshevism: The Kornilov Rebellion*, London, 1919.

Korolev, Sergei Pavlovich (1907–66), the father of Soviet space rocketry, Korolev was not identified as such until after his death. His work merited the Nobel Prize but the Soviet authorities declined it since they did not wish to name him. He was born in Zhitomir, Ukraine, on 12 January 1907 and graduated from Odessa Technical Designers' School, the Moscow Higher Technical School and the Moscow School of Aviators. Always passionately interested in aircraft, he was a design engineer from 1930 and worked with Tsiolkovsky. They had a common interest in space flight and helped develop Soviet ballistic missiles. He was arrested in June 1938 by the NKVD and accused of selling information to a German company. He was sentenced to ten years, was dispatched to Kolyma, and from 1940 he worked in special prison laboratories on jet engines. He was thus one of a remarkable band of scientists who did pioneering work while in prison. STALIN's attitude was that if these specialists did not succeed, they would simply be shot. Korolev was released in July 1944. He was a member of the team which assessed German rocket technology after the Red Army had overrun Pennemünde. He contributed greatly to the design of many Soviet rockets, including Vostok, Voskhod, Elektron, Molniya-1 and Kosmos. After Stalin's death in 1953, he was rehabilitated and was elected a corresponding member of the USSR Academy of Sciences, becoming an academician in 1958. He also became a member of the CPSU in 1953. His prison experiences made him suspicious of strangers and few colleagues got to know him well. He often preferred to remain silent. His first marriage did not survive the camps and he married one of his assistants. She was also aware that his consuming passion was space travel. He died of cancer and is buried in the Kremlin wall.

Korotich, Vitaly Alekseevich (*b.* 1936), a Ukrainian, who qualified as a doctor, wrote poetry in Ukrainian, and in 1986 became editor of *Ogonek*, transforming it into the mouthpiece of glasnost. He was born in Kiev and practised as a doctor, 1959–66. He then became secretary of the Ukrainian Union of Writers and he also translated English-language poets and writers into Ukrainian. He joined the Communist Party in 1967. *Ogonek*, under his editorship, published many sensational articles about the STALIN period and crimes. This material was too hot for the professional historians to handle and literary journals began to debate the past. In 1989 he was elected to the USSR Congress of People's Deputies for Kharkov oblast and he was a regular commentator for the western media on Soviet affairs during the GORBACHEV era, always fully committed to reform. After the attempted coup of August 1991 he abandoned *Ogonek*, moved to the United States and teaches at a university there.

Kosygin, Aleksei Nikolaevich (1904–80), KHRUSHCHEV turned him down as his Prime Minister but he took over after Khrushchev's removal in 1964 and remained as government leader until he retired due to ill health in 1980. Had he become Prime Minister earlier he might have brought some order into Khrushchev's confused economic thinking. In 1965 he launched reforms geared to increasing the decision-making role of enterprises, including shedding surplus. These reforms petered out after the Soviet-led invasion of Czechoslovakia in August 1968 led to a recentralisation of decision making. Until 1968 Kosygin took the lead in representing the Soviet Union abroad but afterwards he conceded primacy to PODGORNY. Kosygin was a technically highly competent manager of Soviet industry but he was continually frustrated by the leading role of the Party in economic affairs. He was born in St Petersburg into a Russian working-class family, joined the Red Army in 1919 and fought in the Civil War. He worked in co-operatives during the 1920s and in 1930 entered the Leningrad Textile Institute, graduating in 1935. In 1938 he was elected chair of the Leningrad city soviet (mayor) and in January 1939 he became People's Commissar for the Textile Industry. The main reason for such extraordinarily rapid promotion was the slaughter of so many top officials during the purges. He became a deputy Prime Minister in 1946 as well as Minister of Finance but the death of ZHDANOV (his base was Leningrad) and the purge afterwards almost cost him his life. He weathered the storm (probably because he had been a technocrat and had not belonged to any political faction) and was a member of the Politburo, 1948–52, then of the new Presidium of the Central Committee. In 1957 Kosygin again became deputy Prime Minister. GORBACHEV found him cool, if not cold. This may be due to the fact that as a survivor of the purges of the 1930s and 1948 he avoided factional politics like the plague. When informed of the coup against Khrushchev his first question was about the position of the KGB. When told it was for, he said he was also for the coup.

Kozlov, Frol Romanovich (1908–65), regarded by KHRUSHCHEV as his likely successor, Kozlov suffered a stroke in 1963 and opened up the way for BREZHNEV. He was born into a Russian peasant family in Ryazan guberniya and graduated as an engineer from the Leningrad Polytechnic Institute, 1936. He then moved into Party work in Izhevsk and worked in the Central Committee during the war. He returned to Leningrad in 1949 and in 1953 became first secretary of Leningrad obkom. He became a full member of the Presidium (Politburo), 1957, then became RSFSR Prime Minister, moving up to become first deputy USSR Prime Minister in March 1958. In May 1960 he replaced KIRICHENKO as secretary for cadres in the Central Committee Secretariat and became effectively number two to Khrushchev, remaining so

until his stroke in April 1963 incapacitated him.

Kozyrev, Andrei Vladimirovich (*b.* 1951), Russian Foreign Minister before and after the collapse of communism in 1991, he came to personify the pro-western school of thought among Russian policy makers. He was born into a Russian family in Brussels, Belgium, graduated from the Moscow State Institute of International Relations of the USSR Ministry of Foreign Affairs, 1974, and successfully presented his dissertation in history on the role of the UN in the development of détente (PhD), 1977. He was in the department of international organisations of the ministry, 1974–86, ending up as first secretary of the department. By 1990 he was head of the administration of international organisations and was also a member of the Soviet delegation to the UN. He never served at a Soviet embassy abroad. In October 1990 Ivan SILAEV, RSFSR Prime Minister, invited him to leave the USSR Ministry of Foreign Affairs and become Russian Minister of Foreign Affairs. Previously this would have meant a demotion but in 1990 Russia was a rising power. He quickly established himself as a supporter of Russian sovereignty and during the autumn of 1991 he helped to draft the agreement which eventually set up the Commonwealth of Independent States. He was a member of the Communist Party until 1991. As Russian Foreign Minister he was savagely attacked in the RSFSR Congress of People's Deputies for not defending Russians in the ex-Soviet republics (called the near abroad) and being too pro-western. This was known as the Atlanticist view as opposed to the Eurasian view of the Russian nationalists.

Krasin, Leonid Borisovich (1870–1926), one of the few technical specialists who sided with the Bolsheviks. He was already involved in revolutionary student activity in 1890 and his activities prevented him from graduating as an electrical engineer until 1900. While working as an engineer in various parts of Russia, he engaged in radical politics. He was called LENIN's trusted aide, Party financier and bomber. He participated in the IInd Congress of the RSDRP in 1903 and was elected to the Central Committee. During the 1905 revolution Krasin was elected to the St Petersburg Soviet. He moved abroad in 1908 and sided with Lenin's left group. However, in 1909 he decided to devote his talents to his career and he joined Siemens and Schuckert in Berlin, later becoming manager of their enterprise in Moscow, then in St Petersburg, until 1914. During the First World War he managed part of the Siemens factory which the Russian state had taken over. After the October Revolution he placed himself at the disposal of the new authorities and was reconciled with Lenin. He played an influential role in industrial policy and attracted bourgeois specialists to Russia. He was a member of the Supreme Council of the National Economy, was People's Commissar for Transport, 1919–20, and was a member of the Council for Labour and Defence. He was indefatigable in negotiations to re-establish political and economic links with the rest of Europe and he participated in all major conferences. He was made People's Commissar for Trade in 1918. He was head of the Soviet trade mission in London 1920–3, successfully negotiating the Anglo-Soviet Trade Agreement (March 1921), and then moved to France in 1924. Since the Soviet state did not enjoy diplomatic relations with these countries, his mission served a dual purpose, commercial and political. They were also used by the successors of the Cheka for spying. At the XIIth Party Congress in 1923, Krasin sharply attacked Party interference in the economy. He was re-elected to the Central Committee but lost his post as a people's commissar in 1925. He remained Soviet representative in London where he died

in 1926. He played a key role in breaching the political and economic boycott of Soviet Russia by the major European powers. It was almost inevitable that Krasin, a first-class engineer, would evince little sympathy for STALIN's ambitions to expand Party control over the economy.

Kravchuk, Leonid Makarovich (*b.* 1934), the first President of independent Ukraine, Kravchuk transformed himself from being a communist apparatchik fighting Ukrainian nationalism into a Ukrainian nationalist. He was born into a peasant family in Rovno oblast in the traditionally national region of western Ukraine. He graduated in economics from Kiev State University and moved into Party work in 1960. He gained rapid promotion in the Ukrainian Party Central Committee apparatus in the 1970s and 1980s, becoming secretary for ideology in 1989. He was elected to the Politburo of the Ukrainian Party and was second secretary of the Party in June 1990. In July 1990 he was elected to the Central Committee of the CPSU. In the new Ukrainian Supreme Soviet, elected in March 1990, Kravchuk became chair (speaker). During the attempted coup of August 1991 Kravchuk sat on the fence until it was clear that the plotters had lost. He was elected President of the Republic of Ukraine on 1 December 1991, the same day Ukraine voted to become independent.

Kropotkin, Prince Petr Alekseevich (1842–1921), the most famous Russian anarchist, Kropotkin came from an old Moscow aristocratic family. In the early 1870s he agitated among workers and peasants, hoping to stimulate a social revolution which would sweep away all state authorities. He was arrested in 1874 but escaped abroad in 1876 and became an internationally famous anarchist, developing the theory (or rather the concept) of anarchist communism based on the need for mutual aid in revolution. He returned to Russia in 1917 but never exerted much influence due to his support for the war effort and the provisional government. The Bolsheviks made tactical use of the anarchists before the October Revolution but came down hard on them afterwards. Kropotkin served as the conscience of the anarchist movement and protested against the allied intervention and the growing excesses of the new regime. His funeral was the last great anarchist demonstration and his home became a shrine and a museum until 1938.

Krupskaya, Nadezhda Konstantinovna (1869–1939), LENIN's wife but not his love, she came from a poor noble family and was early attracted to education and women's questions. She first encountered Lenin in St Petersburg social democratic circles in 1894. They were both arrested in 1895–6 and in Siberian exile, Lenin proposed that she join him, informing the police that she was his fiancée. The police agreed, providing they marry immediately she arrived. They had to go through an Orthodox church ceremony in July 1898, much to Lenin's embarrassment, but it was a small price to pay for a companion and help-mate. There is no passion in his letters to her (unlike his correspondence with Inessa ARMAND). Krupskaya faithfully followed Lenin into exile and around Europe (1901–16). She played an important role as his secretary in building up and maintaining contacts with Bolsheviks. She returned with Lenin to Petrograd in April 1917 but she evinced little enthusiasm for early insurrection. She concentrated on education, women and youth themes. She did not accompany Lenin when he escaped to Finland after the July Days but did visit him twice in Helsinki. She was not an important emissary for Lenin – STALIN was already playing that role. They were reunited after the October Revolution but there was really no political role for her to play. She became deputy People's

Commissar for Enlightenment under LUNACHARSKY. She was devoted to Lenin but lacked the resolve or the cunning to deal with Stalin who treated her badly, deploying his command of coarse Russian to her. After Lenin's death Stalin warned her that the Party was quite capable of designating someone else as Lenin's widow. She appears to have feared Lenin's successor and retreated into herself. An illness left her with protruding eyes. Her reminiscences of Lenin are remarkable for their lack of political insight and acumen. Nadezhda Krupskaya: *Memories of Lenin*, New York, 1930; R. H. McNeil: *Bride of the Revolution: Krupskaya and Lenin*, Ann Arbor, 1972.

Krylenko, Nikolai Vasilevich (1885–1938), a leading Bolshevik military and legal specialist, Krylenko joined the social democrats in 1904 and became active in both Moscow and St Petersburg and a member of the Party's military organisation. He studied history and philosophy at St Petersburg University and law at Kharkov University. He was in the military from 1911 to 1913. He then joined the editorial board of *Pravda*. He was in Switzerland, on Party business, until the summer of 1915, but on his return to Russia he was arrested. He became an officer in the army on the South-east Front in 1916. He was quickly elected to several military committees after February 1917. In June 1917 he was elected to the Central Executive Committee (CEC) of the Ist Congress of Soviets. In October 1917 he was a member of the Military Revolutionary Committee. He was a founding member of Sovnarkom on 26 October 1917. Together with V. A. ANTONOV-OVSEENKO and P. E. Dybenko, he made up the committee on military and naval affairs (LENIN declined to entrust such a sensitive area of policy to one individual). They were joined the following day by N. I. Podvoisky. Krylenko was eventually made commander-in-chief of the army and People's Commissar for Military Affairs. Disagreements with TROTSKY over the latter's military policy led to Krylenko abandoning military affairs and as a qualified lawyer he moved to the Commissariat for Justice in March 1918. He helped draft the RSFSR Constitution of 1918 and the USSR Constitution of 1924. As chair of the supreme tribunal of the CEC and Procurator General of the RSFSR between 1922 and 1931, he presided over all the trials of the period, including those against the SRs and Mensheviks in 1921–22 and the Shakhty trial of 1928. During this period he refined his technique as a devastatingly sarcastic and ruthless prosecutor, treating the accused as already guilty. He became Commissar for Justice in the RSFSR in 1931 and USSR People's Commissar for Justice in 1936. He wrote several books on Soviet law and procedure but regarded torture and forced confessions as quite legitimate weapons against 'enemies of the people'. The concept of a 'fair' trial was alien to him and he practised legal terror in the courtroom. He was arrested in 1937 and executed in July 1938 without a public trial. The system which he had helped to create had devoured him. He was rehabilitated during KHRUSHCHEV's de-Stalinisation campaign and his contribution to the development of Soviet law was acknowledged at a time when Khrushchev was stressing socialist legality.

Kryuchkov, Vladimir Aleksandrovich (b. 1924), one of the many top officials misjudged by GORBACHEV who appointed him chair of the KGB in 1988. Kryuchkov became one of the leaders of the attempted coup of August 1991. He was born into a Russian working-class family in Volgograd and joined the Communist Party in 1944. He gained a legal diploma by correspondence in 1949 and worked in the Procuracy. In 1955 he was transferred to the diplomatic service

and was sent to the Soviet embassy in Budapest where the ambassador was Yury ANDROPOV. On his return to Moscow in 1959 Kryuchkov moved into the department for liaison with communist and workers' parties of socialist countries whose head was Andropov. When Andropov was appointed head of the KGB in 1967 he took Kryuchkov with him. Kryuchkov became deputy chair of the KGB in 1978. He was elected a member of the Central Committee in 1986. When Gorbachev was able to remove CHEBRIKOV as KGB chief in 1988, he chose Kryuchkov to succeed him. He became a member of the Politburo in September 1989 and a member of the Presidential Council in March 1990. Gorbachev remains very bitter about being betrayed by Kryuchkov.

Kuibyshev, Valerian Vladimirovich (1888–1935), a prominent economic functionary during the early stages of industrialisation, he was born into a Russian officer's family in Omsk and graduated in law from Tomsk University, 1910. He had joined the Bolsheviks in 1904 and was expelled from medical school in 1905 for revolutionary activity. After the February Revolution he played the leading role in capturing Samara for the Bolsheviks. He was a political commissar during the Civil War and was elected a secretary and member of the Central Committee, 1922. The following year he became chair of the Central Control Commission and Rabkrin. When DZERZHINSKY died in 1926 he took over as chair of the Supreme Council of the National Economy (VSNKh). He was elected to the Politburo, 1929, and became head of Gosplan, 1930, when that body began to play a dominant role in the economy. His promotion revealed that he was an ally of STALIN. When he died from heart disease there were rumours that he had been murdered by the Trotskyites. Samara was named after him but reverted to its original name in 1991.

Kulakov, Fedor Davydovich (1918–78), one of GORBACHEV's patrons, his move to Moscow in 1964 opened up the way for Gorbachev to succeed him as first secretary of Stavropol kraikom in 1970 and his death in 1978 led to Gorbachev moving to Moscow to replace him as Central Committee secretary for agriculture. He graduated in agriculture and was acknowledged as technically proficient. He joined the Communist Party in 1940 and was engaged in Komsomol and Party work during the war. In 1944 he moved to Penza and became chair of Penza oblast soviet. In 1955 he was made RSFSR Minister of Agriculture and later Minister of Grain Production. In 1960 KHRUSHCHEV transferred him to Stavropol as first secretary of the kraikom, in November 1964 he was promoted to Moscow to become head of the department of agriculture of the Central Committee and in September 1965 he was made Central Committee secretary for agriculture. In 1971 he was elected a full member of the Politburo.

Kulikov, Marshal Viktor Georgevich (b. 1921), the commander-in-chief of the Warsaw Pact forces from 1977 until GORBACHEV removed him in February 1989 for not moving with the times, Kulikov was born into a Russian peasant family and joined the Red Army in 1939. He graduated from the Frunze Military Academy, 1953, and the Academy of the General Staff, 1959. In 1967 he was appointed commander of Kiev military district and in 1969 became commander of Soviet Forces in (East) Germany. He was elected a member of the Central Committee, 1971, and in the same year Chief of Staff of the Soviet Armed Forces and first deputy USSR Minister of Defence. He headed the Warsaw Pact during a stressful period when the Soviet Union found it more and more difficult to match American defence spending. The advent of Gorbachev changed the situation with his emphasis on arms control and reduction.

Kunaev, Dinmukhamed Akhmedovich (b. 1912), his close association with BREZHNEV led to Kazakhstan gradually loosening Moscow's reins of control and riots greeted his dismissal by GORBACHEV in December 1986. A Kazakh, he was born in Alma Ata (now Almaty) and graduated from the Moscow Institute of Ferrous Metallurgy and Gold Mining, 1936. He joined the Communist Party in 1939. He worked in engineering until 1955 when he was appointed chair of the Kazakh Council of Ministers, becoming a member of the CPSU Central Committee in 1956. It was at this time that he had got to know Leonid Brezhnev when the latter was first secretary, Communist Party of Kazakhstan. He lost his position as Prime Minister in 1960 but in 1962 KHRUSHCHEV chose him as first secretary, Communist Party of Kazakhstan. However, in 1962 he was demoted to the position of Prime Minister. Khrushchev had evidently found his economic record unsatisfactory. However, when Brezhnev took over in 1964 Kunaev was restored as first Party secretary and remained in that position until sacked by Gorbachev. In 1966 Kunaev had been elected a candidate member of the Politburo and in 1971 a full member. He was always a loyal member of Brezhnev's team. One of the reasons why Gorbachev dismissed Kunaev was corruption, but in the eyes of the Kazakhs, Kunaev had been reclaiming the republic for them.

Kuptsov, Valentin Aleksandrovich (b. 1937), one of the leaders of the Russian Communist Party who never adjusted to perestroika and found it difficult to come to terms with the reality of post-communist Russia. He was born into a Russian family in Vologda oblast and began his career working on a kolkhoz. In 1958 he began working in Cherepovets as a sheet-metal worker and as an external student graduated as a metallurgical engineer from the North West Polytechnic Institute, 1966. He was elected deputy secretary of the Party committee of his enterprise. In 1974 he was appointed second, then first secretary of the Cherepovets city Party committee (gorkom) and became second secretary, Vologda obkom in 1984. In 1985 he moved to Moscow to become an inspector of the Central Committee but returned the same year to become first secretary, Vologda obkom. At the XXVIIth Party Congress, 1986, he was elected to the Central Committee and in 1988 he graduated from the Higher Party School, Leningrad. He was elected to the USSR Congress of People's Deputies, 1989, and from December 1989–June 1990 he was a member of the Russian Bureau, Party Central Committee. In March 1990 he was elected chair of the Vologda oblast soviet executive committee. In April 1990 he became head of the department for social and political organisation, Party Central Committee, and at the XXVIIIth Party Congress, July 1990, he was elected a secretary of the Central Committee. When the Communist Party of the Russian Federation was set up in July 1990 he was elected secretary. After the attempted coup the party was banned but later legalised·and Kuptsov played an important role as one of its leaders. The Russian Communist Party assumed the mantle of Russian nationalism and became a staunch supporter of the Orthodox Church.

Kurchatov, Igor Vasilevich (1903–60), the father of Soviet nuclear power, he was born into a Russian family near Chelyabinsk and graduated in physics from the Tauride University in Simferopol, Crimea. When STALIN decided to attempt to build an atomic bomb, Kurchatov was appointed scientific director of the project and he established a laboratory in Moscow (which became known as the Kurchatov Institute of Atomic Energy) in 1943, and he also became a member of the USSR Academy of Sciences the same year. He was subordinate to BERIA and

very skilfully handled administration and research. Kurchatov joined the Communist Party in 1948. He supervised the first atomic bomb test, 1949, and the first hydrogen bomb test, 1953. After Stalin's death he tried to promote collaboration with western scientists and protected geneticists (the discipline had been banned as a bourgeois pseudo-science in 1948), informing KHRUSH-CHEV that LYSENKO was a charlatan. However, Khrushchev was deaf to reason where Lysenko was concerned. The 104th element of the periodic table is called kurchatovium after him. David Holloway: *Stalin and the Bomb*, New Haven and London, 1994.

Kurochkin, General Pavel Alekseevich (1900–89), he participated in the storming of the Winter Palace in October 1917, joined the Red Army in 1918 and fought in the Civil War as a cavalry commander. He graduated from the Frunze Military Academy, 1932, and the Academy of the General Staff, 1940. He took part in the Soviet–Finnish War, 1939–40. In May 1941, when commander of the Trans-Baikal military district, he was nominated commander of the 20th Army and transferred to the west of Moscow. The German invasion intervened and he was made commander of the North-west Front by the end of 1941. In January 1942 he attacked and encircled German troops at Demyansk. In 1944 he became commander of the 2nd Belorussian Front but after failing to take Kovel he was dismissed. However, he was given the command of the 60th Army on the Czechoslovakian Front and took Opava in April 1945. He occupied senior positions after 1945, including that of head of the Frunze Academy and in the Supreme Command of the Warsaw Pact forces.

Kuusinen, Otto Vilgelmovich (1881–1964), a Finn who played an important role in the Comintern and later in the

Presidium (Politburo) under KHRUSH-CHEV. He joined the RSDRP in 1905 and was head of the Communist Party of Finland which attempted to seize power in 1918. He moved to Moscow in 1930 and was a loyal supporter of STALIN who had him down to take over Finland after the Soviet–Finnish War, 1939–40. He was made chair of the Presidium of the Karelo-Finnish Republic, 1940–56, which was to unite with Finland under communist rule but this never happened and the republic was downgraded to an autonomous republic within the Soviet Union. In Karelia Kuusinen came into contact with Yury ANDROPOV. He joined Khrushchev's Presidium in 1957 and was also a secretary of the Central Committee until his death.

Kuznetsov, Admiral Nikolai Gerasimovich (1902–74), a leading Soviet sailor, he was commander-in-chief of the navy and a member of Stavka during the Great Fatherland War. He joined the Red Navy in 1919 and participated in the Civil War. He graduated from the Naval Academy in 1932 and was a captain, 1934–6. He was the Soviet naval attaché in Spain during the Civil War, 1936–7. He had no operational command during the war but was present at all planning meetings and participated in the Yalta and Potsdam conferences, 1945. He then fell out of favour and in 1947 STALIN ordered that he be put on trial for providing allied navies with Soviet sea maps during the war. He was demoted and dispatched to the Pacific Fleet. He was eventually found not guilty and was appointed USSR Minister of the Navy, 1951. He became commander-in-chief of the USSR Navy after Stalin's death, 1953, and also first deputy USSR Minister of Defence, until 1956. He was a member of the Central Committee of the Communist Party, 1939–56.

Kuznetsov, General Vasily (1894–1964), one of the new generation of Red Army generals who emerged during the Great Fatherland War, in the company of KONEV, Govorov, ROKOSSOVSKY, KATUKOV and VLASOV. He was one of the defenders in the vain attempt to hold Kiev in 1941 and was blamed for this disaster which deflected responsibility from Marshal BUDENNY. Kuznetsov commanded the 1st Guards Army at Stalingrad. He was deputy commander of the South-west Front, 1942–3, and participated in the battles in the Donbass, Warsaw, eastern Pomerania and Berlin.

L

Landau, Lev Davydovich (1908–68), a brilliant Soviet theoretical physicist, who was born into a Jewish family in Baku and graduated from Leningrad State University in 1927. He studied in Denmark, England and Switzerland and in 1932 he moved to the Physicotechnical Institute, Kharkov. In 1937 he joined a theoretical group at the Institute of Physical Problems, Moscow. He fell foul of the authorities and was imprisoned, 1938–9. He worked with Petr Kapitsa and became a member of the USSR Academy of Sciences. He was awarded the Nobel Prize for Physics in 1962. David Holloway: *Stalin and the Bomb*, New Haven and London, 1994.

Landsbergis, Vytautas (*b.* 1932), the first President of the Republic of Lithuania after it had regained its independence, Landsbergis however concentrated too much on politics and neglected the economy so that he lost his position in 1993. He was born in Kaunas and his father was a famous architect. Landsbergis became a musicologist at the Conservatory. Under glasnost, a Lithuanian national movement, Sajudis, emerged. Landsbergis was elected its first chair in November 1988 and when independence was declared in March 1990 he was elected its first president. The declaration of independence was suspended but the demise of the Soviet Union in December 1991 led to world-wide recognition of Lithuanian independence. Landsbergis engaged in a self-defeating confrontation with Moscow and when the first democratic elections after independence were held in September 1992, the former Communists, led by Algirdas-Mikolas BRAZAUSKAS, swept the board. Landsbergis's comment was that the electorate were stupid. Presidential elections were held in February 1993 and Brazauskas won 60.1 per cent of the vote. Lithuania thus became the first post-communist state to elect ex-Communists back into power in democratic elections.

Latsis, Otto Rudolfovich (*b.* 1934), one of the leading economic journalists of the perestroika period, Latsis was born in Moscow and is of Latvian origin. He graduated from Moscow State University in journalism, 1956, began his journalistic career on a Sakhalin newspaper and joined the Communist Party in 1959. He worked on *Izvestiya* as an economic observer, 1964–71, and then worked in Prague on *World Marxist Review*, until 1975. He transferred to the Institute of Economics of the World Socialist System, USSR Academy of Sciences, becoming head of a department. He also acquired his doctorate in economics (PhD). In 1986 he moved to *Kommunist* and contributed to the renaissance of the Party's theoretical journal, strongly supporting reform. In 1987 he became its deputy editor. He was a member of the Central Committee, July 1990–August 1991.

Lebed, Aleksandr Ivanovich (*b.* 1950), one of the Russian military officers whose career took off rapidly after the failure of the August 1991 coup. He was born in Novocherkassk into a Ukrainian family. He graduated from the Ryazan Higher Air Force Officers' Technical College, 1973, and the Frunze Military

Academy, 1985. He joined the Communist Party in 1972. He began his career as a commander of a student platoon at the Ryazan Technical College (the company commander was the future General Pavel GRACHEV). He served in Afghanistan, 1981–2, as the commander of a paratroop battalion of the 40th Army. He was known for his severity during his missions against the mujahidin and civilian population. He was commander of an airborne division in Tula, 1988–91. In February 1991, as a protégé of Pavel Grachev, he was appointed deputy commander of airborne troops for training and education. On the evening of 19 August 1991 he arrived with his armed troops to defend the leaders of Russia. He was extremely rude to the members of the defence staff, stressing that he was willing to carry out any order whatsoever. Other sources state that his real purpose was to attack the White House from the rear during a possible storming and not the defence of the Russian leadership. He was made commander of the 14th Russian Army in Moldova and became a high-profile officer, defending the interests of the local Russian and Slav population. He exceeded his command brief and actively participated in politics, stressing the need for law and order, the protection of Russians outside Russia and the great power status of Russia. He always felt that he was born to lead Russia and that one day he would be President. After coming third in the Russian presidential election of June 1996, he became a key ally of President YELTSIN in the second round in July 1996.

Lenin, Vladimir Ilich (né Ulyanov) (1870–1924), one of the key political actors of the twentieth century, Lenin has left an indelible mark on Russian, European and world politics. Vladimir Ilich Ulyanov adopted many pseudonyms but Lenin, probably from the River Lena in Siberia, took over in 1901. A utopian Marxist socialist, he came to believe that will could triumph over everything else. A brilliant polemicist and tactician, Lenin had an unrivalled ability to analyse a political situation and evolve tactics to promote his party's ends. He was better at tactical than strategic thinking but a major weakness was his inability to read the characters of his closest cohorts. He was deadly in dissecting and exploiting the weaknesses of his political opponents but he failed singularly to grasp the essence of STALIN or TROTSKY. He lost his hair early and this contributed to his sobriquet as the 'old man' because of his seriousness and single-minded devotion to revolution. He was personally modest and hated close adulation. A member of the service nobility and a graduate in law at St Petersburg University, he nevertheless hated the intelligentsia – they were to him the chattering classes who never moved from word to deed. Another hatred was religion – he had been religious as a teenager. In private life he could be charming among his supporters but he could be as deadly as a viper towards his enemies. He was as bloodthirsty as a vampire during the early years of the revolution but mellowed in 1921. His declining years, partly due to the after-effects of a failed assassination attempt in August 1918 and advancing arteriosclerosis, were painful and deeply frustrating. He died a saddened and worried man. Lenin's first contact with radical thinking was at the University of Kazan and this cost him his place. He was permitted to take his law degree (first class) as an external student at the University of St Petersburg in 1891. He practised law in Samara but moved to the capital in 1893. He soon became a professional revolutionary and travelled to western Europe for the first time in 1895, visiting Germany, France and Switzerland. He established contact with the Emancipation of Labour Group around Georgy PLEKHANOV. On his return to St Petersburg he set up a group with Yuly MARTOV which became known as the St Petersburg

Union of Struggle for the Emancipation of the Working Class. Lenin was arrested in 1895 and exiled to Siberia from February 1897 to February 1900. During this time he wrote *The Development of Capitalism in Russia*, his first major theoretical work. He married Nadezhda KRUPSKAYA in Siberian exile in July 1898. After completing his exile, he moved to western Europe (including Munich, London, Paris and Geneva) and together with Martov, Plekhanov, Vera Zasulich and others, they published *Iskra* (*Spark*), the organ of the RSDRP. In the newspaper he developed the ideas which became known as Leninism, including the concept of the professional Party. When the Party split in 1903, Lenin became the leading Bolshevik, but he lost the support of Plekhanov and control of *Iskra*. He established his own newspaper, *Vpered* (*Forward*), but Party unity was agreed at the 1905 Congress. He returned to St Petersburg in November 1905 but made little impact, moving to Finland in 1907 and then to western Europe until the February Revolution. The experience of 1905 led him to promote the immediate transition from the bourgeois to the socialist revolution. He engaged in continuous polemics with the Mensheviks and others and in 1912 achieved one of his goals, the expulsion of the Mensheviks from the RSDRP. At the outbreak of war he moved to Bern and Zürich where he hammered away at the 'social traitors' in Russia who supported the defence of their country against Germany. He wanted Russia's defeat, believing it would promote revolution. At the Zimmerwald (1915) and Kienthal (1916) conferences in Switzerland he called for the development of the 'imperialist' war into a socialist revolution. He negotiated a deal with the German government and set off for Petrograd in March 1917 in the famous 'sealed train' (the doors were sealed). On his arrival in Petrograd on 4 April, he proclaimed the April Theses, one of the key political documents of the

era: it is a major contribution to Marxism–Leninism. He called for the transition from the first stage of the revolution to the second, the socialist stage, immediately. Russia would be administered by soviets and implacable hostility was to be shown to the provisional government. Few supported him at the time but the Bolsheviks grew until they had the majority in the St Petersburg Soviet by September. After the July Days Lenin had to disguise himself as a mute Finnish railway fireman (he knew no Finnish) to move to Finland. He continued to urge insurrection (Lenin never referred to the events of October as a revolution) and eventually the Central Committee agreed. Trotsky's view that the opening of the IInd Congress of Soviets on 25 October 1917 should be the moment for the declaration of Soviet power was accepted. The Bolshevik take-over was therefore a soviet revolution which ushered in Soviet Russia. Lenin became chair of Sovnarkom and developed a passion for governmental detail. He never occupied a top Party post but was the acknowledged leader. However, if a commissar lost the argument in Sovnarkom, he was permitted to appeal to the Central Committee, from 1919, the Politburo. Lenin lost quite a few arguments, the most serious one being over the advisability of the Treaty of Brest-Litovsk. Eventually he had his way but it led to the attempt on his life in August 1918. Lenin's lack of administrative experience – he thought, for instance, that the structure of government was less important than those who occupied leading positions – led to the resurrection of practically the old imperial governmental structure. He railed against the increasing bureaucratisation of Soviet life but this was the inevitable consequence of growing centralisation, the Civil War and the desperate struggle for survival. He was honest enough in 1921 to admit that the industrial proletariat had ceased to exist. The tactical retreat of the New

Economic Policy in 1921 revealed that he had lost none of his political guile. His flawed legacy was only recognised by the Communists in the late GORBACHEV era. Robert Service: *Lenin: A Political Life*, 3 vols, London, 1985–95; Dmitri Volkogonov: *Lenin: Life and Legacy*, London, 1984.

Liberman, Evsei Grigorevich (1897–1983), he shot to prominence in 1962 after the publication of an article on affording more autonomy for enterprises appeared in *Pravda*. Presumably KOSYGIN had supported the publication of the article as Liberman's ideas were woven into Kosygin's 1965 reforms. Liberman was a seven-day wonder with *Time* going overboard by describing him as the harbinger of capitalism in the Soviet Union which he certainly was not. He was born into a Jewish family in Kharkov and spent his whole working life there. Evsei Liberman: *Economic Methods and Effectiveness of Production*, London, 1971.

Ligachev, Egor Kuzmich (*b.* 1920), Ligachev and GORBACHEV were moderate reformers, 1985–8, but then they parted company when Gorbachev became a radical reformer. Whereas until 1988 reform had been intra-systemic, it then began to unpeel the existing system. Ligachev found all this very disturbing, insisting on the leading role of the Party, the collective ownership of land and the dominance of the state in the economy. To his credit, Ligachev did not join the coup plotters in August 1991, even though he judged Gorbachev's policies to be disastrous to the socialist system. He was born near Novosibirsk and graduated from the Moscow Aviation Institute, 1943. He then returned to Novosibirsk to work in an enterprise building fighter planes. His father-in-law, an army general, was executed in 1937 after a ten-minute trial, so Ligachev was related to a family which was classified as an enemy of the people. His father-in-law

was rehabilitated under KHRUSHCHEV. Ligachev joined the Communist Party in 1944 and soon left the aviation factory for full-time work in the Komsomol. He says he had no choice and refusal would have meant imprisonment. He had a close shave in 1949 when, as first secretary of Novosibirsk oblast Komsomol committee, he was accused of Trotskyism but got away with just being sacked. His Party career took off under Khrushchev when he was Party secretary of a Novosibirsk raion, 1958, where the Academy of Sciences town (Akademgorodok) was to be built. In 1959 he became first secretary of Novosibirsk obkom. He worked in the Central Committee apparatus in Moscow, 1961–5, as deputy head of the propaganda department, and then of Party personnel for the Russian Federation, but was then posted to Tomsk as first secretary of the obkom where he remained until 1983. In his memoirs he states that he asked for the transfer but not why he should exchange life at the centre of the Party apparatus for life in the sticks. It may have been due to his distaste for the BREZHNEV administration, well known for its liking of cutting corners and doing deals. Ligachev's incorruptibility evidently so irritated the Kremlin that an attempt was made to dispatch him into exile as a Soviet ambassador, but he refused to go. Ligachev was elected a candidate member of the Central Committee, 1966, and a full member, 1976. In Tomsk he conducted an anti-alcohol campaign and no hint of corruption surrounded him. ANDROPOV brought him to Moscow and in 1983 he became a secretary of the Central Committee. He was *de facto* number two to Gorbachev after March 1985, chairing meetings of the Secretariat. He was widely believed to be behind Nina ANDREEVA's letter to *Sovetskaya Rossiya* in March 1988 which YAKOVLEV called an anti-perestroika manifesto, but Gorbachev accepted that this was not true. Ligachev's attempt to become

Gorbachev's deputy at the XXVIIIth Party Congress, July 1990, was stymied by the General Secretary himself. He was then not elected to the new-look Politburo which contained only Party functionaries. Had Ligachev been more ruthless and ambitious he might have become an extremely dangerous opponent for Gorbachev. Egor Ligachev: *Inside Gorbachev's Kremlin: The Memoirs of Yegor Ligachev*, Boulder, Co., 1996.

Likhachev, Dmitry Sergeevich (*b.* 1906), a revered Russian cultural figure, who was imprisoned in Solovki (1928–32) and then became the leading specialist on early Russian literature. He was greatly admired by Raisa Maksimovna GOR-BACHEVA, who became his deputy when he was made head of the Soviet Cultural Foundation, 1987. He was born in St Petersburg and graduated from Leningrad State University, joining the Institute of Russian Literature (Pushkinsky Dom) in 1938. He was elected a member of the USSR Academy of Sciences in 1970. He refused to condemn Academician SAKHAROV in 1975 and was beaten up, presumably by the KGB. He strongly advocated the preservation of Russia's cultural past and the return of artefacts taken out of Russia. He was elected to the USSR Congress of People's Deputies in 1989.

Litvinov, Maksim Maksimovich (1876–1951), one of the top Soviet diplomats, Litvinov was sacrificed by STALIN in May 1939 when his rapprochement with Hitler had reached an advanced stage. He came from a middle-class Jewish family (né Vallakh or Wallach) and became an RSDRP activist in 1900. He was soon arrested and eventually escaped to Switzerland where he worked on the editorial board of *Iskra*. He supported LENIN from 1903 onwards. In 1905, together with KRASIN, he founded *Novaya Zhizn*, the first legal social democrat newspaper (financed by Maksim GORKY). After the

failure of the revolution he reached London in 1907 and worked there as a clerk but was also secretary of the London Bolsheviks. He was on the prohibited list of practically every country in Europe in 1917. After the October Revolution he was a Soviet diplomat in London but he was arrested in September 1918 and exchanged for the British diplomat Robert Bruce Lockhart. As a member of the collegium of the People's Commissariat for Foreign Affairs, he negotiated agreements with the Baltic states on the repatriation of prisoners (1919), with Britain on the exchange of prisoners, and with other west European states. He became Soviet plenipotentiary and trade representative in Estonia in 1920, deputy People's Commissar for Foreign Affairs and deputy leader of the Soviet delegation at the Hague Conference in 1922. He participated in the drafting of trade treaties with several west European states (1924–7) and in drafting Soviet proposals on disarmament at the disarmament conferences of the League of Nations (1926–9). He played an important role in the successful conclusion of the Briand–Kellogg Pact in February 1929 which involved the Soviet Union, for the first time, in a joint security pact with the major powers. As People's Commissar for Foreign Affairs (1930–9) Litvinov pursued a similar line, that of collective security in Europe. Several agreements were signed and in 1933 diplomatic relations were established with the United States. The Soviet Union joined the League of Nations in 1934 and Litvinov led the Soviet delegation (1934–8). Treaties were signed with France and Czechoslovakia. Litvinov was elected to the Central Committee of the Party at the XVIIth Congress in 1934 and the XVIIIth Congress in 1939. In the run up to the Stalin–Hitler Pact, Litvinov had to cede to MOLOTOV. This signalled the negation of Litvinov's foreign policy and he lost his position in the Central Committee. However, he became deputy

Commissar for Foreign Affairs (1941–6) and from 1941 to 1943 he was Soviet Ambassador to Washington. He escaped the purges which ravaged the Commissariat of Foreign Affairs despite having a British wife (née Low) who retained her British citizenship. Regarded by some as arrogant and overbearing, the fact that he was not close to any in the Soviet leadership may have saved him. His lack of influence at the end of the war meant he could do nothing to halt the emergence of the Cold War.

Lobov, Oleg Ivanovich (*b.* 1937), a member of the Sverdlovsk (Ekaterinburg) group (some would say mafia) around YELTSIN, he never quite climbed to the top. He was born in Kiev into a Russian family, graduated from the Institute of Railway Engineers, Rostov-on-Don, and successfully presented his candidate dissertation in technical sciences (PhD (Eng)). He joined the Communist Party in 1971. He began working as an engineer in Sverdlovsk in 1960 and in 1972 moved into the Sverdlovsk Party obkom (headed by Yeltsin) as deputy head of the construction department, becoming head in 1975. In 1982 he was appointed secretary and in 1983 second secretary, Sverdlovsk obkom. In 1985 he became chair (mayor), Sverdlovsk oblast soviet executive committee and in 1987 he became an inspector of the Party Central Committee and then a deputy chair, RSFSR Council of Ministers. In 1989 GORBACHEV chose him as second secretary, Communist Party of Armenia, at a time of great nationalist fervour there, and he remained there until 1991. He was elected to the USSR Congress of People's Deputies, 1989, and at the XXVIIIth Party Congress, July 1990, he was elected a member of the Central Committee. He and Ivan POLOZKOV vied for the post of first secretary, Communist Party of the Russian Federation, when it was set up in June 1990 but Polozkov won. Lobov returned from

Armenia in April 1991 and became first deputy chair, RSFSR Council of Ministers, (under SILAEV) and held the post until November 1991. In August 1991 he was head of the shadow Russian government which President Yeltsin sent underground. Later Lobov became secretary of the Russian Security Council.

Lukin, Vladimir Petrovich (*b.* 1937), an influential diplomat who became Russian Ambassador to the United States. He was born into a Russian family in Omsk and his parents were both arrested in 1937 but were freed after EZHOV was dismissed. He graduated from the Moscow State Pedagogical Institute in history and successfully presented his candidate dissertation on social democracy in South and South-east Asia (PhD) at the Institute of World Economics and International Relations, USSR Academy of Sciences. He worked on the *World Marxist Review* in Prague and developed good relations with some of those around Alexander Dubcek, 1965–8. He then joined the Institute for the Study of the United States and Canada and published several books on international affairs. He specialised on US relations with Asia and successfully presented his doctoral dissertation (DLitt). In 1987 he joined the USSR Ministry of Foreign Affairs and in 1989 he moved into the Secretariat of the USSR Supreme Soviet as head of the centre for analysis and information for deputies. He was a strong supporter of the move towards democracy under GORBACHEV and signed a letter of protest in January 1991 against the events in Vilnius in which several people had been killed. He was elected to the RSFSR Congress of People's Deputies and the RSFSR Supreme Soviet, 1990, and was chair of the Supreme Soviet committee on international affairs and foreign economic relations. He stood for speaker in July 1991 but was not elected. During the attempted coup of August 1991 he maintained contacts with foreign countries on behalf of the Russian leadership. In January 1992 he was appointed Russian Ambassador to the United States.

Lukyanov, Anatoly Ivanovich (*b.* 1930), regarded by GORBACHEV as one of the leaders of the attempted coup against him in August 1991 (which Lukyanov denies), Gorbachev and he were fellow students in the law faculty, Moscow State University, and worked together in the Komsomol there. Lukyanov joined the Communist Party, 1955, and unlike Gorbachev decided on a law career, becoming an adviser to the USSR Council of Ministers, 1956–61, when he moved into the Secretariat of the Presidium of the USSR Supreme Soviet, eventually becoming head of the Secretariat in 1977. He spent the year 1976–7 in the Central Committee Secretariat. ANDROPOV brought him into the Central Committee Secretariat again in 1983 and made him first deputy head of the general department which works very closely with the General Secretary. In March 1985 Gorbachev promoted him to head of the general department. In 1987 he became a secretary of the Central Committee and head of the administrative organs department which supervised the armed forces, the KGB and the legal agencies. He was elected a candidate member of the Politburo, 1988, and also Gorbachev's deputy in the USSR Supreme Soviet Presidium (in effect deputy head of state). When Gorbachev became President of the Soviet Union in 1990, Lukyanov succeeded him as speaker (chair) of the USSR Congress of People's Deputies and Supreme Soviet. During the attempted coup, he had the power to convene the USSR Congress of People's Deputies but declined to do so until after the coup, when that body decided to consign itself to oblivion. The first Duma amnestied all coup plotters in early 1994 and Lukyanov was free to recommence his political career, becoming an influential member of the Russian Communist Party. Gorbachev remains bitter about his betrayal by Lukyanov.

Lunacharsky, Anatoly Vasilevich (1875–1933), the most important figure in Soviet culture during the first decade after the October Revolution, Lunacharsky was a writer, critic and playwright who was passionately interested in education and the arts. He joined a Marxist group while still at school in Kiev and later studied at the University of Zürich where he met Rosa Luxemburg. In 1896 he returned to Russia, joined a social democratic group, was arrested and exiled to Kaluga, where he encountered the philosopher A. A. BOGDANOV. Bogdanov was a kindred spirit because both of them were trying to achieve a synthesis of Marxism and empirio-criticism. Lunacharsky first met LENIN in Paris in 1904 and sided with the Bolsheviks. However, Lenin was suspicious of Lunacharsky's search for spiritual values (the denigratory term of 'God-seeker' was used) in philosophy in order to merge them with Marxism. Lunacharsky returned to St Petersburg in 1905 and helped edit *Novaya Zhizn*, the first legal social democrat newspaper. When Lenin demolished the God-seekers and Marxist 'deviants' in his *Materialism and Empirio-criticism*, an open breach developed between Lenin and Lunacharsky with the latter giving up the Bolshevik cause. TROTSKY, MARTOV and Lunacharsky edited the fiercely internationalist, anti-war newspaper, *Nashe Slovo*, in Paris until 1915 when the French authorities expelled Trotsky, Lunacharsky repairing to Switzerland. He accompanied Lenin in the 'sealed train' to Scandinavia and Petrograd. Lunacharsky then linked up again with Trotsky and his Mezhraionka (Inter-borough). All of them fused with the Bolshevik Party in August 1917. He proved a powerful orator and became deputy mayor of Petrograd. Culture was not in the forefront of Bolshevik minds after the October Revolution but Lunacharsky strove manfully to reform education and the arts during Civil War, disease and hunger. Reform really got under way under the New Economic Policy when primary and secondary schools were fused and pupils were also to acquire vocational skills. There was a desperate rush to train new élites, especially technical and administrative, and one of the short cuts adopted were the Workers' Faculties (Rabfaks), which aimed, but often failed, to move from primary-school knowledge to diploma-level knowledge in two years. One area of outstanding success, however, was the campaign to eliminate adult illiteracy. Culture flourished during the 1920s and there was considerable experimentation. Lunacharsky did not participate in the struggle for Lenin's mantle. He simply ignored STALIN and engrossed himself in original work. He was appointed LITVINOV's deputy at disarmament conferences and in 1930–2 he was with him at the League of Nations in Geneva. He was appointed Soviet Ambassador to the Spanish Republic in 1933 but died en route in Paris. Sheila Fitzpatrick: *The Commissariat of the Enlightenment: Soviet Organization of the Education and the Arts under Lunacharsky*, Cambridge, 1970.

Luzhkov, Yury Mikhailovich (*b.* 1936), together with Gavriil POPOV he personified the new Moscow of the late GORBACHEV and early YELTSIN eras. He was born into a Russian family in Moscow and graduated from the Gubkin Oil Institute, Moscow. In 1964 he became head of a department of the USSR Ministry of the Chemical Agro-Industry and in 1974 became head of a research bureau in the same ministry. He was general director of Neftekhimavtomatika, 1980–6. He was elected a deputy of Moscow city soviet 1977, but perestroika enticed him into full-time politics and he became first deputy chair, Moscow soviet executive committee in 1987. In April 1990 he

was made chair of Moscow city soviet and in June 1991 Popov and Luzhkov stood for the posts of mayor and vice-mayor of Moscow and won. Luzhkov was also named Prime Minister of the government of Moscow. In August 1991 Luzhkov played a leading role in the city in resisting the decrees of the Emergency Committee. After the coup President Gorbachev made Luzhkov responsible for the agro-industrial complex, fuel, foreign economic relations and social questions of the Soviet Union; he also remained Prime Minister of Moscow. When Gavriil Popov resigned as mayor of Moscow in June 1992, Luzhkov took over and became immensely influential and powerful.

Lvov, Prince Georgy Evgenevich (1861–1925), the provisional government's first Prime Minister, he was a landowner and Constitutional Democrat (Kadet). The quintessentially modest, mild-mannered, reasonable politician (his detractors called him a spin-doctor whose words hid a shallowness of mind), Lvov was caught up in the whirlwind after the February Revolution. He came to the fore in 1915 as head of the All-Union Union of Zemstva. He attempted to merge the efforts of the zemstva and the war industry committees which sprang up everywhere in 1916. A liberal at a time of revolutionary change, he had neither the mettle nor the appetite for the increasingly fractious politics of the time. The first government was brought down by its desire to see Russia acquire territorial concessions at the end of hostilities. He headed the first coalition government in May 1917, which saw Mensheviks and other socialists joining the government. The July Days brought home to him the threat posed by Lenin but his government resigned on 8 July. After the October Revolution he emigrated to France where he continued to oppose the Bolsheviks through an émigré organisation.

Lysenko, Trofim Denisovich (1898–1976), the greatest charlatan of the STALIN and KHRUSHCHEV eras, Lysenko cost Soviet agriculture dear. He founded agrobiology, a pseudo-science, in the 1920s, and promised to raise yields rapidly and cheaply. A passionate patriot, Lysenko's tragedy was that he lacked a rigorous scientific training and he fell victim to his ambition to make the Soviet Union bloom and himself the leading scientist. He was born into a Ukrainian peasant family, near Poltava, and graduated from the Kiev Institute of Agriculture, 1925. He was a disciple of Michurin and espoused the Lamarckian theory of acquired characteristics, rejecting the chromosome theory of heredity. Lysenko thought that plants could be moulded by their environment. He was a gifted politician and won over Stalin with his arguments against the scientific establishment of the day. He was made head of the USSR Academy of Agricultural Sciences, 1938, and targeted those geneticists who opposed him, especially NIKOLAI Vavilov, a leading world scientist at the time. Vavilov was arrested in 1940 and died in prison later. Lysenko became virtual dictator of Soviet biological science and conduced campaigns against genuine scientists, many of whom were dispatched to the Gulag. He reached his apogee in 1948 when genetics was banned with Stalin playing close attention to the arguments used. Khrushchev was as blind as Stalin and would not listen to criticism of Lysenko. His nefarious influence extended to China where Mao, in 1958, was much taken by his ideas such as planting deeply and densely on less land, grafting vegetables with fruit, and the killing of all insect-eating birds. These ideas contributed to the Great Chinese famine of 1959–61 when between 30 and 60 million peasants died. It was only in 1965 that Lysenko was dethroned and genetics rehabilitated. Soviet scientists were later able to demonstrate that he had falsified his results. David Joravsky: *The Lysenko Affair*, Cambridge, Mass., 1970; Roy Medvedev: *The Rise and Fall of T. D. Lysenko*, New York, 1969.

M

Maisky, Ivan Mikhailovich (né Lyakho-vitsky) (1884–1975), 'Pussy face' Maisky was a very popular Soviet Ambassador to the Court of St James, 1932–43. He joined the social democrats at the turn of the century, was expelled from St Petersburg University, 1902, and exiled to Omsk. He sided with the Mensheviks when the Party split in 1903. He moved to Switzerland and later graduated from the University of Munich, 1912. He lived in England until 1917 and studied the trade union movement. He returned to Russia after the February Revolution, left the Menshevik Party in 1920 and joined the Bolshevik Party, 1921. He joined the diplomatic service in 1922. He was Soviet Ambassador to Finland, 1929–32, then in London until 1943. He was ambassador during the difficult days of the Nazi–Soviet Pact, informed STALIN that Britain would fight on alone and provided him with information about the impending German attack – which Stalin ignored. His main task after June 1941 was to press the Allies to open a second front in Europe against the Germans. He persuaded Harry Hopkins, Roosevelt's personal representative, to go to Moscow and the result was the US–USSR Lend-Lease Agreement. Maisky also negotiated with the various governments-in-exile in London. His days of influence ended in June 1943 when Stalin recalled him to Moscow to become deputy People's Commissar for Foreign Affairs. He was a member of the Soviet delegation at the Yalta and Potsdam conferences, 1945, and was also chair of the Allied Reparations Commission in Moscow, 1945. He was one of the outstandingly successful Jewish diplomats who promoted the image of the Soviet Union as a 'normal' state before 1945.

Makashov, General Albert Mikhailovich (b. 1938), he gained notoriety at the XXVIIIth Party Congress by berating GORBACHEV and calling for a return to traditional values. He was born into a Russian family in Voronezh oblast and he graduated with distinction from the Tashkent All-Arms Command Technical College, from the Frunze Military Academy with a gold medal and from the Academy of the General Staff. He was commander of the Urals military district, January–September 1989, and commander of the Volga–Urals military district, September 1989–September 1991. He was a member of the Communist Party. He was elected to the USSR Congress of People's Deputies, for a constituency in Sverdlovsk oblast. During the election campaign he opposed the transformation of the army into a standing (professional) army and the deferment of students in higher education until their studies were completed because this would lead to an army of workers and peasants. During the XXVIIIth Congress he embarrassed Gorbachev by attacking perestroika and glasnost and called on the General Secretary to return to the principles of LENIN. He was loudly supported by other military and KGB delegates, all in uniform. He stood for President of the Russian Federation in 1991 and came fifth of six candidates. He supported the attempted coup of August 1991 and after its defeat retired from the armed forces.

He was elected to the Central Committee, Communist Party of the Russian Federation (CPRF), when it was established in June 1990, and in 1992 he was elected to the Central Committee, Russian Communist Workers' Party. The latter party is to the left of the CPRF and espouses traditional Marxist–Leninist views. Makashov was also one of the leaders of the National Salvation Front, a Russian nationalist organisation.

Makhno, Nestor Ivanovich (né Mikhnenko) (1889–1935), the leading Ukrainian anarchist partisan military leader, Makhno was used tactically by LENIN to pursue Bolshevik aims in Ukraine. He was early attracted to anarchist politics and was arrested for violent behaviour in 1908. He was sentenced to death in 1910 but reprieved because of his youth and served his time in Moscow. The February Revolution afforded him liberty and he returned to Ukraine to become a leading agitator among workers and peasants. He developed cavalry tactics, based on mobility, and fought against the Germans, Austrians, the Ukrainian nationalists and for and against the Bolsheviks, depending on the circumstances. His goal was a Ukraine run by peasants, workers and soldiers without outside interference but given the strategic significance of Ukraine this was naïve. He promoted a social revolution but developed no coherent counter to Bolshevik Marxism. He played an important role in the defeats of SKOROPADSKY, Petlyura, DENIKIN and WRANGEL. These were also the enemies of the Bolsheviks so when they were defeated it was inevitable that Moscow would turn on Makhno. By the end of 1920 he had to flee and moved to Romania, eventually ending up in Paris where he wrote three volumes of memoirs, among other things. Michael Malet: *Nestor Makhno in the Russian Civil War*, London, 1982.

Malenkov, Georgy Maksimilianovich

(1902–88), the GORBACHEV of his era, he promoted new political thinking at home and abroad as Prime Minister, 1953–5. He was a member of the group around STALIN which displayed great tactical skill but after Stalin's death was rather easily outmanoeuvred by KHRUSHCHEV. He joined the Red Army and was commissar in Turkestan, 1919. He joined the Bolshevik Party in 1920 and graduated from the Higher Technical Institute, Moscow, 1925. He became a Party official in the 1920s and was a protégé of KAGANOVICH during the 1930s. He was responsible for Party cadres and as such was deeply involved in the purges. He was a member of the Central Committee of the Communist Party from 1941. When war broke out he became a member of the State Defence Committee (GKO), responsible for technical supplies to the army and air force. He was actively involved in transferring Soviet industry to the east – when about one-third of enterprises were moved to the rear to avoid enemy occupation. During the early years of the war he was also political commissar on various fronts. He became chair of the committee for the rehabilitation of formerly occupied territories in 1944. In 1946 he was elected a secretary of the Central Committee and deputy Prime Minister. This underlined his considerable administrative talents and his political skill. He was a member of the Politburo from 1946 to 1957. Stalin came to regard him as his number two during the last years of his life and he was, among other things, responsible for Party organisation. In the cut and thrust of the late Stalin era Malenkov proved ruthless in defending his own position and this earned the undying hatred of Khrushchev, who was later to accuse him of dirty deeds during the Leningrad Affair, 1949, when many leading Leningrad politicians perished. On Stalin's death in March 1953, Malenkov became head of the Party and Prime Minister but was soon forced to give up one of these posts. He chose to remain Prime Minister and thus opened up the way for Khrushchev to challenge him for supremacy by using the Party as his base. Malenkov ushered in a period of détente at home and abroad, promoting a more consumerist approach to economic growth. At first, BERIA and he worked closely together, but Khrushchev managed to attract Malenkov away from Beria. After Beria's arrest in June 1953 the contest between Malenkov and Khrushchev got under way in earnest. There ensued the first open conflict over the direction of economic policy in the USSR since the 1920s. Malenkov took the line that less emphasis should be placed on heavy industry and greater stress on light and consumer industries. Khrushchev counter-attacked and defended the 'metal lobby' – mainly defence – while openly contradicting Malenkov on agriculture. Malenkov had to resign in February 1955. He sided with the Anti-Party Group (so called because they opposed the Party having a major say in running the economy) in July 1957 and their defeat meant the end of his active political career. He was dispatched to Ust Kamenogorsk, Kazakhstan, to manage the hydro-electric plant there. Khrushchev's mild treatment of his defeated political foes in 1957 established a precedent. The executions of Beria and several Ministry of Interior officials in 1953 were the last political executions in the Soviet Union. Malenkov soon returned to Moscow and he lived privately. There were reports that he attended Orthodox services. News of his death took some time to emerge as relatives had asked for the information to be withheld.

Malinovsky, Marshal Rodion Yakovlevich (1898–1967), a successful Red Army commander during the Great Fatherland War, he later succeeded the brilliant but abrasive Marshal Georgy ZHUKOV as KHRUSHCHEV's Minister of Defence. He acted as a Bolshevik organ-

iser when in France with the Russian Expeditionary Corps during the First World War. He joined the Red Army in 1919 and participated in the Civil War. He graduated from the Frunze Military Academy, 1930, and took part in the Spanish Civil War. He commanded an army in Odessa in June 1941 and in December was made commander of the South-west Front. At Stalingrad (December 1942) Malinovsky prevented Manstein freeing Paulus's encircled 6th Army. In 1943 and 1944, as commander of the South-west Front and then the 3rd Ukrainian Front, Malinovsky defeated the Wehrmacht in the Donbass and western Ukraine. In late 1944 he assumed command of the 2nd Ukrainian Front, and together with TOLBUKHIN invaded Romania, and destroyed the German armies. Malinovsky's forces entered Hungary and took Budapest in February 1945. Then they took Slovakia in April 1945. Malinovsky then moved to Manchuria and routed the Japanese there. Khrushchev, who knew him from the war, chose him as USSR Minister of Defence in 1957. The Soviet leader was looking for a soldier who would take orders from politicians and would not attempt original thinking. Malinovsky was his man and he stayed in the post until his death. He was a member of the Central Committee of the Communist Party from 1956 until 1967.

Malinovsky, Roman Vatslavovich (1876– 1918), one of the most successful Okhrana (imperial secret police) spies in the Russian social democrat camp. A Russian Pole by birth, he was a trade union leader (the Metalworkers' Union), but was arrested in Moscow in 1910 and turned. The Okhrana encouraged him to re-establish his earlier links with the Bolsheviks and in 1910 and 1911 he provided the police with numerous reports which revealed Party pseudonyms, meeting places and where illegal Party literature was stored. Malinovsky attended the

VIth RSDRP Conference in Prague as a delegate. LENIN was impressed by Malinovsky's trade union career and self-confidence and had him elected to the Party's Central Committee and Russian Bureau. He was also keen that Malinovsky be elected to the Fourth Duma as a Moscow worker representative. Not surprisingly, Malinovsky was elected to the Duma in October 1912. He displayed considerable eloquence in the Duma and quickly established himself as the leader of the Bolshevik Duma faction of six deputies. His Party career prospered and he even served on a commission to identify and eliminate police spies within the Party. The Okhrana ordered him to split the Bolshevik Duma faction, which he did, but eventually Malinovsky became such an embarrassment to the police because of his agitational skills that they instructed him to resign his seat. Rumours abounded about him but a Party tribunal, presided over by Lenin, decided that his 'political honesty' was not in question but that he should be stripped of all his Party positions for abandoning his seat in the Duma. He was captured by the Germans in 1915 and in a prisoner-of-war camp they facilitated the renewal of contacts with Lenin. Malinovsky helped spread Leninist anti-war propaganda among other prisoners. In October 1918, despite the fact that his treachery to the Bolsheviks had been revealed by the Okhrana archives, he returned to Russia voluntarily and was tried by a revolutionary tribunal. He was condemned to death and executed for 'bringing the revolution and its leaders into disrepute'.

Mandelstam, Nadezhda Yakovlevna (née Khazina) (1899–1980), the widow of the poet Osip MANDELSTAM, she became world famous in the 1970s after publishing two volumes of memoirs, *Hope against Hope*, 1970, and *Hope Abandoned*, 1972. She was born near Saratov, grew up in Kiev and studied painting

with Aleksandra Ekster. She met Mandelstam in 1919, they married soon after and she shared his exile in various cities. As an enemy of the people she was not allowed to live in Moscow and kept her husband's literary heritage alive. She was also a friend of Anna AKHMATOVA.

Mandelstam, Osip Emilovich (1891–1938), one of the most famous Russian poets of the twentieth century, Mandelstam was born into a Jewish merchant's family in Warsaw and grew up in St Petersburg. He was a major post-symbolist poet before the First World War and during the Civil War continued to stress human values and the importance of human dignity. The political culture of communist Russia was alien to him and he published two novels as well as poetry during the 1920s. His boldness in criticising STALIN was his undoing. He recited a poem, written in November 1933, at a gathering and Stalin got to hear of it. He disparagingly refers to Stalin as a mountaineer, Stalin's cockroach whiskers leer, and every killing is a treat for him. Mandelstam was arrested in May 1934 and died in the Gulag.

Martov, Yuly Osipovich (1873–1923), the gentle revolutionary, LENIN always had a soft spot for him. He was born into the Jewish middle-class Tsederbaum family in Constantinople. Lenin and he founded the St Petersburg Union of Struggle for the Emancipation of the Working Class in 1895. They also founded the *Iskra* journal and group to campaign for the unification of social democracy. Martov parted company with Lenin at the IInd Congress of the RSDRP in 1903 and became the *de facto* leader of the Mensheviks. He worked tirelessly to block Lenin's take-over of the Party. In 1905 he sided with PLEKHANOV's view that the upcoming revolution was bourgeois and that social democrats should not attempt to achieve power. Their main task would be opposition to the post-revolutionary bourgeois government. After 1905 Martov lived mainly in Paris and engaged in extensive literary work, including editing the Menshevik journal. He was one of the editors, together with TROTSKY and N. V. ANTONOV-OVSEENKO, of *Golos*, a stridently internationalist, anti-war journal in Paris (it was later renamed *Nashe Slovo*). He helped to vitiate Lenin's attempts at the Zimmerwald (1915) and Kienthal (1916) conferences to transform the socialist peace movement into a Bolshevik vehicle to promote revolutionary civil war. He returned to Russia in May 1917 but could not prevent the Menshevik leadership joining the provisional government. He headed a small group of Menshevik-Internationalists who opposed the war and the coalition. He could never convince a majority of Mensheviks that the party should abandon its coalition with the bourgeois provisional government. He advocated the establishment of a broad socialist coalition government after the October Revolution and when this failed he led a small fearless Menshevik opposition party. He supported Soviet power against the Whites and allied intervention but on practically every other issue he strongly opposed Soviet policy, especially terror. He gave up and moved abroad in 1920, much to Lenin's relief, and edited *Sotsialistichesky Vestnik*, which quickly established itself as a leading journal on the left wing of European social democracy. He was appalled at events in Soviet Russia but he never supported revolutionary or military action against the Bolsheviks, fearing this would promote counter-revolution. He was caught in a cruel dilemma, a revolutionary with moral and ethical views against a Bolshevik leader to whom everything was relative – everything that strengthened Soviet power was good. Israel Getzler: *Martov: Political Biography of a Russian Social Democrat*, Cambridge, 1967.

Masherov, Petr Mironovich (1918–80), party leader in Belorussia during the BREZHNEV era, Masherov was born in Vitebsk oblast and graduated as a teacher. During the Great Fatherland War he was a partisan leader in Belorussia and headed the Komsomol in Belorussia, 1947–54, after which he moved into the Party apparatus in Minsk and Brest. In 1962 he became second secretary of the Communist Party of Belorussia and, in 1965, first secretary. He was elected to the CPSU Central Committee in 1964. His death in a car crash in 1980 led to speculation that it had not been an accident.

Maslennikov, Arkady Afrikanovich (*b.* 1931), a highly successful Soviet journalist who made an almost effortless transition to the market economy. He was born into a Russian family in Kostroma oblast and graduated in economics from Moscow State University, 1954. He worked in the Institute of World Economy and International Relations, USSR Academy of Sciences, 1954–65, and successfully defended his candidate dissertation in economics (PhD (Econ)). In 1965 he became a *Pravda* correspondent in India, then in Pakistan and Great Britain, with his articles arousing great interest as a barometer of glasnost. In 1989 he was appointed head of the press service of the USSR Supreme Soviet and in April 1990 press secretary to President Mikhail GORBACHEV. In late 1991 he became editor-in-chief of the newspaper *Birzhevye Vedomosti* and he was later elected chair of the supervisory board of the All-Russian Exchange Bank.

Maslyukov, Yury Dmitrievich (*b.* 1937), the last head of Gosplan before its demise, Maslyukov was born into a Russian family in Leninabad, Tajikistan, and graduated as an engineer from the Leningrad Mechanics Institute in 1962. He joined the Communist Party in 1966. He worked in research institutes and then moved into the USSR Ministry of Defence. He was first deputy Minister of the USSR Defence Industry, 1979–82, and then moved to Gosplan as first deputy chair, responsible for the defence sector. He was elected a member of the Central Committee, 1986, a candidate member of the Politburo, February 1988, and was a full member of the Politburo, September 1989–July 1990. In 1988 he also became first deputy chair of the USSR Council of Ministers and in March 1990 a member of the Presidential Council. Maslyukov was a highly successful official at a time of rapid economic decline in the Soviet Union and after the collapse of the Soviet Union remained loyal to the Party, becoming a leading member of the Russian Communist Party.

Mayakovsky, Vladimir Vladimirovich (1893–1930), an enthusiastic supporter of the October Revolution and proletarian culture, Mayakovsky was born in Georgia and educated in Kutaisi and Moscow, the family having moved to Moscow in 1906. He was involved in revolutionary activity and as a poet liked to scandalise society. During the First World War his anti-war poetry gained him many admirers. During the Civil War he supplied brilliant captions to cartoons and was a natural adman. He was the leader of the Left Front in Art (LEF) and his '150,000,000', 1920, and 'Vladimir Ilich Lenin', 1924, glorified the deeds of the Bolsheviks. He travelled widely but gradually lost faith in the revolution, which to him was a revolution in the arts. He shot himself in Moscow and a new myth began to surround him as the greatest poet of the revolution. In the STALIN era he became an icon and in PASTERNAK's words he was 'planted everywhere like potatoes'.

Mazurov, Kirill Trofimovich (1914–89), a leading Belorussian official who also played a prominent role at the all-Union level. Mazurov fought in the partisan movement in the Great Fatherland War and afterwards became first secretary of the Belorussian Komsomol. He was made chair of the Belorussian Council of Ministers, 1953, and then first secretary of the Communist Party of Belorussia, 1956–65. He was elected a candidate member of the Presidium (Politburo) before falling out with KHRUSHCHEV in 1964, but he was not dismissed. Under BREZHNEV he became first deputy chair, USSR Council of Ministers, in 1965 and a full member of the Politburo and remained in these posts until 1978 when he was dropped like a stone.

Medvedev, Roi Aleksandrovich (b. 1925), a Leninist, he became the most penetrating critic of Stalinism and published many influential historical works. He was born in Tbilisi, the son of a Red commissar who later died in the Gulag. He graduated in philosophy from Leningrad State University and he worked in various research institutes of the USSR Academy of Sciences but was expelled from the Communist Party in 1969 after publishing *K Sudu Istorii,* which appeared in English as *Let History Judge* (revised edition, 1989). Despite not having an official position, he continued research and published many books abroad, among which are *On Socialist Democracy,* 1975, and *Khrushchev,* 1982. While his twin brother Zhores emigrated he remained in Moscow and came into his own under GORBACHEV. He was elected to the USSR Congress of People's Deputies and the USSR Supreme Soviet, 1989, and proved a good parliamentarian, defending Gorbachev, human rights and minorities.

Medvedev, Vadim Andreevich (b. 1929), a high-placed official during the GORBACHEV era, he was born into a Russian family in Yaroslavl and graduated from Leningrad State University, 1951, joining the Party in 1952. He taught economics at the Leningrad Institute of

Railway Transport and the Leningrad Technological Institute, 1956–68. He then entered the Leningrad Party gorkom and in 1970 moved to the Secretariat of the Central Committee as deputy head of the department of propaganda. He was rector of the Academy of Social Sciences of the Central Committee, 1978–83, and then rejoined the Central Committee Secretariat as head of the department of science and education. Under Gorbachev he advanced rapidly (he had worked with Aleksandr YAKOV-LEV in the Secretariat, 1970–3), becoming Central Committee secretary for liaison with communist and workers' parties of socialist countries, 1986, and a full member of the Politburo, 1988. At the XXVIIIth Party Congress, in July 1990, however, he lost his secretaryship and his membership of the Central Committee and Politburo. Nevertheless, he became a member of the Presidential Council in July 1990.

Meretskov, Marshal Kirill Afanevich (1897–1968), he was Chief of the General Staff when war broke out in June 1941 but proved inadequate and was soon succeeded by Marshal ZHUKOV. He joined the Bolshevik Party in 1917 and the Red Army in 1918, acting as a political commissar in the Civil War. He graduated from the Military Academy in 1921 and participated in the Spanish Civil War, 1936–7. During the Soviet–Finnish War, 1939–40, he commanded the 7th Army which broke through the Mannerheim Line at Vyborg. He commanded the Volkhov Front during the siege of Leningrad, 1941–4 and is credited with helping to save Leningrad in December 1941 by driving the Germans out of Tikhvin, thus keeping supply lines open. In January 1942 General Govorov and he re-established railway traffic between Leningrad and Moscow. Meretskov became commander of the Karelian Front in February 1944 with a mission to drive the Wehrmacht out of Finland. He was a deputy People's Commissar for Defence, 1941–5. In August 1945 he assumed command of the 1st Far Eastern Front to occupy Manchuria and northern Korea.

Mesyats, Valentin Karpovich (b. 1928), a leading Party agricultural official who was out of temper with GORBACHEV's agrarian reforms. He was born into a Russian family in Kemerovo and graduated from the Timiryazev Agricultural Academy, Moscow, 1953. He worked in the Moscow obkom and as deputy RSFSR Minister of Agriculture until BREZHNEV sent him to Kazakhstan in 1971 as second secretary. He returned to Moscow in 1976 and was appointed USSR Minister of Agriculture. Gorbachev was not one of his admirers (he had been Central Committee secretary for agriculture) and in November 1985 Mesyats was made first secretary of Moscow obkom.

Meyerhold, Vsevolod Emilevich (1874–1940), one of the giants of the Russian theatre, who also enjoyed a world-wide reputation as a producer, he was born into a German Jewish family near Penza and on his conversion to Orthodoxy was given the name Vsevolod. He was a pupil of Stanislavsky, 1898–1902, and worked as an actor in various theatres. He joined the Bolshevik Party, 1918, and LUNACH-ARSKY made him supremo of all Moscow theatres. He was given his own theatre in Moscow in 1920 but it was closed after KRUPSKAYA complained that it was a madhouse. He produced several of MAYAKOVSKY's plays but by 1930 his revolutionary commitment had vanished as Soviet cultural life became conservative and conformist. His theatre was closed in January 1937, he was arrested in June 1939 and shot on 2 February 1940.

Mikoyan, Anastas Ivanovich (1895–1978), a master politician who exhibited great tactical skill, he managed always to

stay at the top, be it STALIN, KHRUSH-
CHEV or BREZHNEV who was in control.
An Armenian, he, like Stalin, received a
theological education, but joined the
Bolsheviks in 1915. After the February
Revolution he was a Bolshevik organiser
in the Caucasus, doing battle with the
nationalists. When the Bolsheviks had to
flee, twenty-six commissars were captured and shot. He was the twenty-
seventh commissar and it still remains
unclear how he managed to save his skin.
He formed a close alliance with Stalin
early on and after the Civil War one of
his tasks in the newly liberated areas was
to ensure that TROTSKY's supporters
were eased out. He was a Party official in
Nizhny Novgorod (Gorky), Rostov-on-
Don and the north Caucasus. He was
elected a member of the Central Committee of the Communist Party in 1923.
He occupied many ministerial posts from
the 1920s onwards: People's Commissar
for Trade, 1926–30; People's Commissar
of Supplies, 1930–4; People's Commissar
for Food, 1934–8. He was deputy chair of
Sovnarkom (later USSR Council of Ministers), 1937–55. He was also People's
Commissar for Foreign Trade, 1938–49,
and was a member of the Politburo from
1935. There were many stories of his as-
tuteness as Comrade Commerce. He is
negotiating with Henry Ford and is
offered one of the new Ford models. He
enquires about the price and is told it is
50 cents. He takes one but Ford apolo-
gises for not having 50 cents' change.
Mikoyan, quick as a flash, replies:
'That's alright, I'll take two!' During the
war he was chair of the committee of
supply for the Red Army. He chose wise-
ly in allying himself with Khrushchev
after Stalin's death and was USSR Minister of Trade, 1953–5, then, after
MALENKOV's resignation as Prime Minister, he was first deputy Prime Minister,
1955–64. Khrushchev sent Mikoyan to
Cuba and he fell in love with Castro's
revolution there, saying that it reminded
him of his youth. In October 1964 he

rang Khrushchev in Pitsunda, Crimea,
summoning him to a Politburo meeting
to be dismissed. He had changed sides
but he remained a friend. Mikoyan proposed Khrushchev be given an honorific
Party title which Brezhnev rudely turned
down. Khrushchev confided to Mikoyan
that he was ready to go and would not
put up a fight. After defeat, Mikoyan
kissed Khrushchev goodbye and they
never met again. Mikoyan was chair of
the Presidium of the USSR Supreme Soviet (President), 1964–5. His son, Sergo,
kept the information about Khrushchev's
death from him, but he read about it in
Pravda. He managed to send a wreath to
the funeral. He had an extraordinary
career, was awarded five Orders of Lenin,
wrote many volumes of memoirs but
bore part of the guilt for the tragic history of twentieth-century Russia. In 1988
Sergo Mikoyan was the first of the children of the old élite to acknowledge
openly the responsibility of their parents
for the terrible past.

**Mikoyan, Major General Artem Ivano-
vich** (1905–70), brilliant aeronautical
engineer who developed, with Gurevich,
the MiG fighter aircraft. His brother was
Anastas MIKOYAN. He graduated from
the Zhukovsky Air Force Academy in
1936. M. I. Gurevich, a mathematician,
and he designed the MiG-1 high-altitude
fighter which first flew on 5 April 1940.
The plane evolved into the MiG-3, of
which over 3,000 were produced before
production was halted in the middle of
the war. It was of great importance in the
early part of the war for interception and
air-to-air combat, due to the fact that it
was compact, light, manoeuvrable, with
a range of 1,200 kilometres and un-
equalled at altitudes above 5,000 metres.
Mikoyan was elected an academician in
1968.

Mikulin, Aleksandr Aleksandrovich
(1895–1985), brilliant aeronautical engineer who designed some of the most

important Soviet engines. He began as a designer of car engines, 1923, and then moved to aircraft engines, 1929. One of his engines powered CHKALOV when he flew over the North Pole to the United States in 1937. His AM-35A engine was installed in the MiG-1 when it made its maiden test flight in 1940. He was elected an academician and designed some of the most successful Soviet jet engines (for the TU-104 and other aircraft) in recent times.

Mil, Mikhail Leontovich (1909–70), brilliant aeronautical engineer who became the foremost designer of helicopters in the Soviet Union. He graduated from the Novocherkassk Aviation Institute, 1931. From then until his death he designed and participated in the design of a wide range of Soviet helicopters (Mi series and others). First in his field, his helicopters held over sixty world records of various kinds, at various times.

Miller, General Evgeny Karlovich (1867–1937), white general, allied to the British Expeditionary Corps in northern Russia, 1919, but defeated, then moved to France where he continued his anti-Bolshevik activities. He was of Baltic German origin but served the TSAR loyally. He was Russian military attaché in Belgium, the Netherlands and Italy, 1898–1907. He was chief of staff of the Moscow military district in 1912 and later fought in the First World War. He was wounded by revolutionary soldiers during the February Revolution before being appointed commander of the Northern Front forces by Admiral KOLCHAK in 1919. After the British left Arkhangelsk he carried on but had to evacuate his forces in February 1920. In exile in France, he chose General WRANGEL as his chief of staff. Later he became the deputy leader of the White Civil War veteran association and took over as head in 1930 after the previous head had been kidnapped by Soviet agents. He disappeared in September

1937 and it was assumed that he had been kidnapped. He was later found dead.

Milyukov, Pavel Nikolaevich (1859–1943), the leading liberal in Russia between 1905 and 1917, Milyukov was a brilliant intellectual, was widely read and travelled, but was lost in the maelstrom of Russian politics in 1917. He was dismissed as a lecturer at Moscow University for criticising the regime. In January 1905 he was in Chicago and decided to return to Russia. He regarded the Tsarist regime as beyond redemption and he dominated the founding conference of the Party of Constitutional Democrats (Kadets). He regarded the October Manifesto as inadequate and pressed for a Constituent Assembly, linking up with the revolutionaries. This was too radical for most liberals who feared anarchy. He was a sharp critic of the government in the Third and Fourth Dumas, criticising the regime's handling of the war effort, and became a member of the Progressive Bloc which demanded a say in managing the war economy. He became notorious in November 1916 in a thunderous speech in which he catalogued the government's failings and then queried whether this was due to treason or incompetence; the clear inference being that the government could not lead the country to victory. He was appointed Minister of Foreign Affairs in the first provisional government. He supported the war effort and wanted to preserve the monarchy as an institution. This proved his political downfall as in a note to the Allies dated 18 April (1 May) he stated that he hoped that means would be found to 'obtain those guarantees and sanctions which were indispensable for the prevention of sanguinary conflicts in the future'. This sounded like imperialist aggrandisement to the socialists and demonstrations brought down the government. He watched the disintegration of the provisional government from the sidelines and after October helped form the Volunteer Army under General Alekseev. He moved to France where he was active in Russian émigré politics and wrote prolifically. William G. Rosenberg: *Liberals in the Russian Revolution: The Constitutional Democratic Party 1917–1921*, Princeton, NJ, 1974.

Moiseev, General Mikhail Alekseevich (*b*. 1939), chosen by GORBACHEV to succeed the formidable Marshal Sergei AKHROMEEV as Chief of the General Staff and first deputy USSR Minister of Defence in December 1988, his appointment was read as the Soviet President's desire to introduce younger officers to high command. It also reduced the authority of the post. Moiseev, a Russian, was the first Chief of the General Staff since 1945 not to have participated in the Great Fatherland War. Marshal YAZOV, USSR Minister of Defence, was his patron. Moiseev graduated from the Frunze Military Academy, 1972, and the Military Academy of the General Staff, 1982. In January 1987 he succeeded Yazov as commander-in-chief of the Far East military district. After the attempted coup in August 1991 he succeeded Yazov as USSR Minister of Defence but was replaced by Marshal SHAPOSHNIKOV in September 1991.

Molotov, Vyacheslav Mikhailovich (né Scriabin) (1890–1986), like many other true-red Bolsheviks, he came from a middle-class family and was related to the composer Skryabin. He joined the Bolsheviks soon after the 1905 revolution and quickly identified with LENIN and later STALIN. Only in the Anti-Party Group against KHRUSHCHEV in 1957 did he emerge as a leader in his own right. Until then he had been the eternal bridesmaid and never the bride. He was an incongruous figure: a Bolshevik with pince-nez. Obdurate, humourless (at least in public), he personified the unattractive side of Soviet foreign policy, especially in the immediate post-war years. His pseudonym, Molotov, means hammer and this was apt. He displayed great political skill in his relations with Stalin and always kept his head. Molotov's wife was a Jewess and served time in the camps while her husband represented Moscow in foreign affairs. He did not bring the matter up with Stalin. On one occasion Stalin said to him, 'Vyacheslav Mikhailovich. I'm told you are a Jew.' Molotov could get out about one sentence before he began to stutter. 'Oh, no, comrade Stalin, you have been misinformed,' he replied fluently. Stalin looked at him in his penetrating manner and offered him some advice. 'Vyacheslav Mikhailovich, you should think about it.' (The moral of this story is that Stalin had the power to decide if you were a Jew.) In retirement at Peredelkino, just outside Moscow, he was recognised while shopping by a woman who screamed at him, 'Why is this Stalinist criminal still at liberty?' Molotov did not utter a word but slowly turned, left the shop and Peredelkino for ever. Conversations with him were published in the 1980s but are disappointing. He never wavered in his conviction that everything Stalin had done was correct. When he was readmitted to the Party in July 1984, the in-joke was that CHERNENKO was smoothing the path for his successor! Molotov was a member of the Military Revolutionary Committee during the October Revolution and afterwards he rose in the Party organisation, especially after the Civil War when he and others, such as KAGANOVICH, planted pro-Stalinist officials in the newly Bolshevised territories. He became a member of the Politburo in 1925. Stalin chose him as chair of Sovnarkom in 1930 and he replaced LITVINOV as People's Commissar for Foreign Affairs in 1939. Stalin became Prime Minister himself in 1941. The Soviet–German Non-aggression Treaty of August 1939 is often referred to as the Molotov–Ribbentrop Pact. He was at Stalin's side during all the wartime conferences and at Potsdam. Ernest Bevin, the British Foreign Minister, developed a great dislike of him, mainly because of his defensive, distrustful foreign policy stance. He was replaced in 1949 as Minister of Foreign Affairs by Andrei VYSHINSKY but on Stalin's death in March 1953 he returned to the foreign ministry. Khrushchev used him to outmanoeuvre BERIA but Molotov was too conservative for the innovative Khrushchev. In 1957 Andrei GROMYKO took over the Foreign Ministry. Molotov led the Anti-Party Group (so called because they resisted the Party assuming primacy in the state) in July 1957 and had the guts, in defeat, to refuse to acknowledge that he had been wrong. He was packed off to Ulan Bator as Soviet Ambassador to Mongolia and later to Vienna as Soviet representative to the Atomic Energy Agency. He was vilified during the de-Stalinisation period and was expelled from the Party in 1964.

Mukhitdinov, Nuritdin Akramovich (b. 1917), the first Central Asian Muslim to become a member of the Presidium (Politburo) and to play a role in the Party at the centre. An Uzbek, he served in the Red Army from 1939 to 1946. In December 1955 he became first secretary, Communist Party of Uzbekistan, and at the XXth Party Congress, 1956, he was elected a candidate member of the Presidium. After the defeat of the Anti-Party Group, June 1957, Mukhitdinov became a Central Committee secretary and a full member of the Presidium but was like a fish out of water in Moscow. He was dropped from the Presidium and lost his secretaryship, 1961, and served as Soviet Ambassador to Syria, 1968–77.

Murakhovsky, Vsevolod Serafimovich (b. 1926), he worked closely with GORBACHEV in Stavropol krai and succeeded him as first secretary in 1978. Mura-

khovsky, a Ukrainian, served in the Red Army, 1944–50, and joined the Communist Party in 1946. He graduated from the Stavropol Pedagogical Institute, 1954, and then moved into Komsomol work, later into Party work, with Gorbachev. In 1975 he was made first secretary of Karachaevo-Cherkess obkom and was recalled to Stavropol as first secretary of the kraikom when Gorbachev moved on to Moscow. He was elected a full member of the Central Committee, 1981, and when Gorbachev took over in 1985 he brought Murakhovsky to Moscow as first deputy chair, USSR Council of Ministers, and chair of Gosagroprom (state committee for the agro-industrial complex). Predictably Murakhovsky failed to make Soviet agriculture more efficient and Gosagroprom was abolished in 1989.

Mutalibov, Ayaz Niyazi Ogly (b. 1938), an Azeri, he was born in Baku and graduated as an engineer. In 1982 he became chair of Gosplan in Azerbaijan and in 1989 chair of the Azerbaijani Council of Ministers. After the disorders in Baku in January 1990 which led to many fatalities, Mutalibov took over as first secretary, Communist Party of Azerbaijan. At the XXVIIIth Party Congress, July 1990, he was elected to the CPSU Central Committee and the Politburo. He also became the first President of pre-independent Azerbaijan. During the attempted coup of August 1991 he appeared to be on the side of the plotters but after it failed he reverted to Azeri nationalism and was elected the first President of the Azerbaijan Republic, 1991.

Mzhavanadze, Vasily Pavlovich (1902–88), the godfather of Georgia until he was replaced by Eduard SHEVARDNADZE as Party boss. Mzhavanadze was born in Kutaisi, graduated from the Lenin Military Political Academy, 1937, and served in the Main Political

Administration in the Red Army during the Great Fatherland War. He was made first secretary, Communist Party of Georgia, 1953, because he was not a member of any political group. He was elected a candidate member of the CPSU Presidium (Politburo), 1957, and a full member, 1966. He lost his positions in 1972 when Shevardnadze was brought in to clean up Georgia.

N

Nasriddinova, Yadgar Sadykovna (*b.* 1920), the most prominent Muslim woman in the post-STALIN era in the Soviet Union, Nasriddinova, an Uzbek, graduated from the Tashkent Institute of Railway Engineering, 1941, and joined the Communist Party in 1942. She became vice-chair, Uzbek Council of Ministers, 1955, and was elected to the CPSU Central Committee at the XXth Party Congress, 1956. In 1959 she became nominal head of state of Uzbekistan as chair of the Presidium of the Uzbek Supreme Soviet. This also made her *ex officio* vice-chair of the Presidium, USSR Supreme Soviet. In 1970 she was elected chair of the Soviet of Nationalities, USSR Supreme Soviet. This prominence made her a national figure and she also travelled abroad. However, her propensity to use state funds for her own pleasure led to her removal in 1974. She was almost expelled from the Party in 1976 for corruption but the inevitable happened under GORBACHEV and she was finally expelled, in the wake of the Uzbek cotton and other scandals.

Nazarbaev, Nursultan Abishevich (*b.* 1940), an astute, authoritarian Kazakh politician who came to the fore in the late GORBACHEV era and was elected the first President of the Republic of Kazakhstan. He was born near Alma Ata (now Almaty) and graduated from the technical college in Dneprodzerzhinsk, Ukraine, 1960, from the Higher Technical College of the Karaganda Integrated Steel Complex, 1967, and from the CPSU Central Committee's Higher Party School, 1976, as an external student. He worked in the Karaganda steel enterprise from 1960 and in 1969 moved into Party work with the Communist Party of Kazakhstan. In 1977 he was elected secretary and, 1977–9, second secretary of the Karaganda Party obkom. In 1984 he was appointed chair of the Kazakh Council of Ministers and he was a member of the CPSU Central Committee from 1986 until August 1991. Mikhail Gorbachev chose him to succeed Gennady KOLBIN as first secretary, Communist Party of Kazakhstan in 1989. The reason why Nazarbaev did not succeed Dinmukhamed KUNAEV, sacked in December 1986, may have been linked to Kunaev's desire to prevent Nazarbaev's succeeding him. He told Gorbachev that a Russian was preferable. Nazarbaev was elected to the USSR Congress of People's Deputies and the USSR Supreme Soviet in 1989. He became President of Kazakhstan in February 1990 in an uncontested election. In 1992, after the establishment of the Republic of independent Kazakhstan, Nazarbaev became President of independent Kazakhstan.

Neizvestny, Ernst Iosifovich (*b.* 1926), despite fundamental disagreements with KHRUSHCHEV on art, the Soviet leader developed a respect for the sculptor, and his widow Nina Petrovna commissioned Neizvestny to sculpt the memorial to Khrushchev in Novodeviche Cemetery, Moscow. He was born in Sverdlovsk (Ekaterinburg) and was severely wounded during the Great Fatherland War, afterwards becoming a famous sculptor.

He had a famous confrontation with Khrushchev in the Manezh, Moscow, in 1962, over his work. He was expelled several times from the USSR Artists' Union for artistic reasons and also for his support of human rights. He emigrated first to Switzerland and then to the United States. His Soviet citizenship was restored in 1991.

Nemchinov, Vasily Sergeevich (1894–1964), a leading Soviet economist and statistician and one of the fathers of mathematical economics in the Soviet Union, Nemchinov developed statistical methods to calculate differences in agrarian economies and independently provided STALIN with information on the grain harvest of 1928. He worked in the Agricultural Academy and was director, 1940–8. He stood up to LYSENKO in 1948 when the latter enjoyed Stalin's support and was forced to resign his post. After Stalin's death his work led to the founding of the Central Mathematical Economics Institute. He was elected a member of the USSR Academy of Sciences in 1946.

Nemtsov, Boris Efimovich (b. 1959), one of the most successful new pro-market men in Russian politics, he was born in Sochi and graduated in radio physics from Gorky (Nizhny Novgorod) State University where he later successfully defended his candidate dissertation (PhD (Eng)). From 1981 he worked in the Scientific Research Radio Physics Institute and in 1991 was appointed representative of the President of Russia in Nizhny Novgorod oblast. In December 1991 he became head of the Administration (governor) of Nizhny Novgorod oblast. He was elected to the RSFSR Congress of People's Deputies in 1990. He is a strong advocate of agrarian reform and private farming.

Nikonov, Viktor Petrovich (b. 1929), GORBACHEV's choice as Central Committee secretary for agriculture (a post he had himself held since 1978) in 1985 but eventually he proved too conservative for the Soviet leader. He was born into a Russian family in Rostov oblast and joined the Communist Party in 1954. His early experience was in agriculture and he was second secretary, Tatar obkom, 1961–7, and first secretary Mari obkom, 1967–79. In 1983 Nikonov was appointed RSFSR Minister of Agriculture and in 1985, CC secretary. He was elected to full member of the Politburo in June 1987 but in September 1989 he retired from public life.

Niyazov, Saparmurad Ataevich (b. 1940), a Turkmen who was born in Ashkhabad, grew up in a children's home and later became President of Turkmenistan. He joined the Communist Party, 1962, and graduated from Leningrad Polytechnic, 1967, and from the CPSU Central Committee Higher Party School, 1976, as an external student. He began working in Leningrad then returned to Turkmenistan in 1967. He transferred to Party work in 1970 and in 1980 was appointed first secretary of the Ashkhabad Party gorkom. In 1985 he became chair of the Turkmen Council of Ministers. In December 1985 he was elected first secretary, Communist Party of Turkmenistan, and in January 1990 he was also made chair (speaker) of the Turkmen Supreme Soviet. He was elected a member of the CPSU Central Committee, 1986, and the Politburo, July 1990. He was also a member of the USSR Congress of People's Deputies and the USSR Supreme Soviet. On 27 October 1990 he became President of Turkmenistan and in June 1992 was elected the first President of the Republic of Turkmenistan. He is an example of a member of the communist nomenklatura who has successfully adjusted to the post-communist era. He is authoritarian and holds sway over a stable state which is potentially quite rich.

Novikov, Marshal Aleksandr Aleksandrovich (1900–76), a leading Soviet airman during the Great Fatherland War who fell foul of STALIN afterwards. He joined the Red Army in 1919 and fought in the Civil War. He graduated from the Frunze Military Academy in 1930. He was Chief of Staff of the Air Force on the Leningrad Front, 1938–40, and Chief of Staff of the Air Force on the Karelian Front during the Soviet–Finnish War, 1939–40. He was commander-in-chief of the Soviet Air Force (VVS), 1942–6, and a deputy People's Commissar for Defence. Novikov was appointed by Stalin to undertake a major reorganisation of the air force after the initial heavy defeats by the Luftwaffe. He attended most Stavka meetings during the war and was in command of air operations during the battles of Stalingrad, Kursk, Belorussia and Königsberg. He then moved to command the Soviet Air Force in Manchuria. He was arrested in 1946, together with the Minister for Aviation Shakhurin, allegedly after Stalin's son, Vasily, had complained to his father at the Potsdam Conference that American planes were superior to Soviet planes. Allegedly BERIA extorted a confession from Novikov under torture and tried to use this against Marshal ZHUKOV. Novikov was sentenced to fifteen years in a labour camp but was released after Stalin's death. He recommenced his air car-

eer and was Commander of Strategic Aviation, 1953–6.

Novozhilov, Viktor Valentinovich (1892–1970), one of the founders of mathematical economics in the Soviet Union, he was born in Kharkov, graduated from Kiev University, 1915, and taught statistics before moving to teach in Leningrad. One of his innovations was to attempt to calculate the efficiency of capital investment but this work only developed after STALIN's death. He was internationally known and respected. Viktor Novozhilov: *Problems of Cost-benefit Analysis in Optimal Planning*, New York, 1970.

Nureyev, Rudolf (1938–93), a world-famous ballet dancer and choreographer, he was born into a Tatar family in Ufa, now Bashkortostan. He first trained in Ufa, then moved to Leningrad, 1955, and graduated in 1958, revealing great talent. He was an overnight sensation at the Kirov and in Vienna, 1959. In 1961 in Paris he was ordered back to Moscow and immediately sought political asylum. He became a firm favourite in the west and danced with many leading ballerinas, including being Margot Fonteyn's partner for several years. He was also a choreographer and was director of the Paris Opera Ballet, 1982–9. He returned to the Soviet Union in November 1987 and danced again at the Kirov in November 1989.

O

Oborin, Lev Nikolaevich (1907–74), a pianist and highly respected teacher, one of whose pupils was Vladimir ASHKENAZY. He was born in Moscow and studied at the Gnesin Music School and Moscow Conservatory where he was a pupil of Konstantin Igunnov. He won first prize in the first Chopin International Pianists' Competition in Warsaw, 1927, and was also the first Soviet pianist to take part in an international competition. He became a professor at the Moscow Conservatory and became a USSR People's Artist in 1964.

Ogarkov, Marshal Nikolai Vasilevich (*b.* 1917), a formidably intelligent and technically competent Chief of the General Staff, Ogarkov proved too thrusting for the Soviet leadership and he was removed so as to prevent him from possibly succeeding Marshal Dmitry USTINOV as Minister of Defence. Ogarkov became internationally known in the aftermath of the Soviet shooting down of Korean Airlines 007 in September 1983. He became the first Chief of the General Staff since Marshal TUKHACHEVSKY to give a press conference (the Soviet leader Yury ANDROPOV was incapacitated) and he expressed no remorse about the disastrous chain of events which had led to the downing of the aircraft. His brilliantly technical performance sent shivers down many foreign spines. The cover-up split the Politburo and Ogarkov was sacked in September 1984 and was given a non-operational command as commander of the western theatre of military operations; he held this post until November 1988. He was born into a Russian peasant family in Kalinin (now Tver) oblast, joined the Red Army, 1938, graduated from the Kuibyshev Military Engineering Academy, 1941, and served throughout the war. He graduated from the General Staff Academy, 1959, and was commander of the Volga military district, 1965–8. He was elected a candidate member of the Central Committee, 1966, and a full member, 1971. He was appointed Chief of Staff and first deputy USSR Minister of Defence, January 1977. He argued vigorously for increased defence spending but recognised the futility of piling up more and more nuclear arms, putting his faith in the development of conventional weapons of enormous destructive power.

Oistrakh, David Fedorovich (1908–74), a violinist who gained a world-wide reputation, he was born into a Jewish family (the name is derived from the German for Austrian) in Odessa and received his musical training there and in Moscow, becoming a member of staff at the Moscow Conservatory, 1934, and later a professor. He won first prize at the All-Union Violinists' Competition in Leningrad, 1935, and at the Ysaye Competition in Brussels, 1937. He joined the Communist Party in 1942. He toured widely and became internationally known through his concerts and recordings. He was awarded an honorary doctorate in music by the University of Cambridge in 1969.

Okudzhava, Bulat Shalvovich (*b.* 1924), he was the first pop star in the Soviet Union and had an impact comparable to the Beatles in Great Britain. A poet, he accompanied himself on the guitar and became immensely popular during the 1960s through clandestine tape recordings. He was born in Moscow, his father was Georgian and his mother Armenian. Both parents were Party officials, and his father was shot and his mother spent nineteen years in the Gulag. Okudzhava served in the Red Army during the Great Fatherland War and graduated from the University of Tbilisi in 1950. He moved to Moscow, joined the Communist Party, 1955, after the rehabilitation of his parents (his father posthumously). His songs were not anti-establishment and were thus tolerated.

Olesha, Yury Karlovich (1899–1960), he became famous in 1927 with the publication of his novel, *Zavist (Envy)* in which the representatives of the new order are rather soulless and the good lines are reserved for the bad characters. This was to cause him trouble after 1934 when socialist realism became the ruling orthodoxy, Olesha having made a speech defending humanism at the Congress of Soviet Writers. He grew up in Odessa and joined the Red Army, 1919, while his parents fled to Poland. A novel for children, *Three Fat Men*, came out in 1924 (filmed in 1961) and he collaborated with MEYERHOLD. He was arrested in 1934 and spent many years in the Gulag, reappearing in the KHRUSHCHEV era.

Ordzhonikidze, Grigory Konstantinovich (Sergo) (1886–1937), a prominent Georgian revolutionary who was influential in the 1930s during industrialisation. He was born in Kutaisi guberniya, joined the RSDRP, 1903, and sided with the Bolsheviks, participated in the 1905 revolution and then moved to Germany. He returned in 1907 and was politically active

in Baku but was arrested, sent to Siberia, escaped and made for Paris, 1910. There he encountered LENIN at the Longjumeau School, and was made a member of the Bolshevik Central Committee, 1912. He participated in the Civil War as a political commissar and helped to secure Soviet rule in Armenia and Georgia. He was a supporter of STALIN and in 1926 moved to Moscow to become chair of the Central Control Commission and Rabkrin (responsible for discipline among Party and state officials). In 1930 he became chair of the Supreme Council of the National Economy (VSNKh) and in January 1932 Commissar for Heavy Industry, the core of industrialisation. In 1926 he had been elected a candidate member of the Politburo and in 1930 a full member, revealing that he was a member of Stalin's inner group. He fell out with Stalin over the purges, his brother was tortured and shot, and all around him were being arrested. He died suddenly, officially of a heart attack, but it is widely believed that he committed suicide.

Ostrovsky, Nikolai Alekseevich (1904–36), the author of the classic socialist realism novel, *Kak Zakalyalas Stal (How the Steel Was Tempered)*, 1932–4, which describes and glorifies the role of youth in industrialisation. The novel's hero, Pavel Korchagin, begins as a roughneck and is then gradually transformed into a model communist worker, finally dying as a tragic hero from a terminal illness. It was obligatory reading for all schoolchildren until 1987 when it was dropped and is now completely ignored. He was born in Rovno, Ukraine, and served in the cavalry during the Civil War, was a Komsomol official during the 1920s, and joined the Communist Party in 1924. He became blind and died prematurely.

P

Pankin, Boris Dmitrievich (*b.* 1931), siding with GORBACHEV during the attempted coup of August 1991, he became his Foreign Minister and later Russian Ambassador to London. He was born into a Russian family in Frunze (Bishkek), Kirgizia (Kyrgyzstan), the grandson of a kulak (well-off peasant) exiled by Stalin. He graduated from the faculty of journalism, Moscow State University, 1953, and was a journalist until 1973. He was elected a member of the USSR Union of Writers, 1970, and later became a member of its board. Pankin became editor-in-chief of *Komsomolskaya Pravda*, 1965. When the All-Union Copyright Agency (VAPP) was established in 1973 he became chairman of its board. Vladimir VOINOVICH accused Pankin, in an open letter, of acquiring publishing rights for VAPP, thus depriving authors of their royalties, but Pankin stayed in the post until 1982 when he went to Stockholm as Soviet Ambassador to Sweden. In 1990 he was posted to Prague as Soviet Ambassador to Czechoslavakia. He was one of the few diplomats who refused to support the attempted coup, expressing support for Russian Federation President YELTSIN and calling for the release of Mikhail Gorbachev. After the collapse of the coup Gorbachev phoned him and offered him the post of USSR Minister of Foreign Affairs, replacing Aleksandr BESSMERTNYKH who had been passive during the attempted coup. He never really appeared at ease as Foreign Minister and when the Soviet Union collapsed he became, in January 1992, the first Russian Ambassador to the Court of St James since 1917.

Pashukanis, Evgeny Bronislavovich (1891–1937), the leading Soviet legal thinker until he fell foul of STALIN's entourage, he was of Lithuanian origin and studied law at the universities of St Petersburg and Munich, being obliged to complete his studies in Germany because of his revolutionary politics. He joined the Communist Party, 1918, and acted as a people's judge, becoming a legal adviser to the RSFSR People's Commissariat of Foreign Affairs. He gained fame in 1924 with the publication of his *General Theory of Law and Marxism*. 'Sale and purchase is a bourgeois institution ... socialism does not recognise sales and purchases. It recognises only direct supply,' wrote Pashukanis in 1929. Since crime and litigation were the result of class conflict, it followed that the ending of private property presaged the end of crime. Pashukanis and his followers developed the theory of commodity-exchange which would lead to the withering away of law. This was because it was believed that all law emanated from capitalism, hence under socialism there would be no socialist law. However, in 1931–2 Pashukanis was obliged to confess that law served the state's interests. The Stalin Constitution of 1936 was the death blow to Pashukanis's theories as socialism required rigorous criminal laws to protect state assets. In January 1937 Pashukanis was arrested, tried and executed. This may have been due to his struggle with VYSHINSKY who emerged the victor. Pashukanis was rehabilitated in March 1956.

Pasternak, Boris Leonidovich (1890–

1960), world famous for his novel *Dr Zhivago* which was turned into a successful film in the west, Pasternak was born in Moscow into a Jewish family which was very artistic, his father being a painter. He studied at the universities of Moscow and Marburg. He published his first poems in 1913 and proved a fine lyric poet. He wrote prose also but gradually found STALIN's Russia more and more uncongenial. Pasternak turned to translation, including Goethe and Shakespeare. His *Dr Zhivago* (Old Church Slavonic orthography; it would be *Dr Zhivogo* in modern Russian) hinted at spiritual values and the search for freedom. It was published in Italy in 1957 and Pasternak was awarded the Nobel Prize in 1958. He was treated as a traitor by the Soviet establishment and had to decline the Nobel Prize. One doctor stated that the book was an insult to the medical profession, without having read it. The scandal shortened his life and KHRUSHCHEV, in his memoirs, regretted not having read the work himself at the time. *Dr Zhivago* was published in the Soviet Union in 1988, thus completing his rehabilitation as one of the great Russian poets and writers of the twentieth century.

Pavlov, General Dmitry Grigorevich (1897–41), the highest-ranking victim of STALIN in his search for scapegoats in the wake of the catastrophic Red Army losses during the initial assault by the Wehrmacht in June 1941. He joined the Red Army and the Bolshevik Party in 1919 and participated in the Civil War. He graduated from the Frunze Military Academy in 1928 and participated in the Spanish Civil War, then in the Soviet–Finnish War, 1939–40, on the Mannerheim Line. He came to the conclusion that tanks would play a subsidiary role to infantry. He was appointed commander of the Western military district (renamed the Western Front on 23 June 1941) which embraced north-east Poland, the Bialystok and Brest-Litovsk regions. Pavlov's tanks and infantry were devastated during the surprise German attack and he was replaced by EREMENKO on 28 June 1941. He was summoned to Moscow by Stalin, court-martialled and shot, together with his chief of staff and Korobkov, commander of his 4th Army, for incompetence. In the GORBACHEV era it was admitted that he was not primarily to blame, his orders could not have been fulfilled by any officer.

Pavlov, Ivan Petrovich (1849–1936), a famous Russian physiologist who became the first Russian to win the Nobel Prize in 1904. He was born in Ryazan into a Russian priest's family and graduated from St Petersburg University, 1875. His early work was on animal physiology and he was the professor of physiology at the Military Medical Academy, 1896–1924. He was elected to the Russian Academy of Sciences, 1907, and headed its Institute of Physiology, 1925–35. During the Civil War LENIN, who was very keen to keep Pavlov working in Russia, authorised the sale of gold abroad to feed Pavlov's experimental dogs and his staff. During the 1920s Pavlov was very critical of the regime's anti-religious policy – he was himself a believer – and its constraints on artistic and scientific freedom. His international reputation ensured that no action was taken against him. He is known in the west for his theory of conditioned reflexes, working with chimpanzees and dogs. He was a hero to the Soviet rulers as his theories appeared to confirm the materialist views of mankind.

Pavlova, Anna Pavlovna (1881–1931), the greatest ever Russian prima ballerina and arguably the greatest ballet dancer the world has ever seen. She made her début at the Mariinsky Theatre, St Petersburg, in 1899 and became prima ballerina in 1906. She became an international star in 1908 when she toured widely. She joined

Diaghilev's Ballets Russes in Paris in 1909 in *Les Sylphides*. She fell out with Diaghilev in 1911 when he wanted her to dance STRAVINSKY's *Firebirds*, and then set up her own ballet company. She danced with this company throughout the world from 1913. With various partners, including Laurent Novikov and Pierre Vladimirov, and companies, she was a peripatetic missionary for her art. Those who witnessed her performances were left with a lasting memory of disciplined grace and poetic movement. She was married to Victor Dandre whose tangled financial affairs (charges of fraud) prevented the couple returning to Russia. Her home, Ivy House in Hampstead, London, became famous for the ornamental lake with swans, symbolic of her most famous role, Mikhail Fokine's Dying Swan, which she performed about 4,000 times. On her deathbed in The Hague, she is reported to have said, 'Prepare my swan costume.' Her body was brought to Golders Green Crematorium, London, and cremated. Her remains now rest in a marble urn there. Controversy erupted in 1996 when Jean Thomassen, a Dutch painter, in a book, claimed that Pavlova's dying wish had been to return to Russia once communism had fallen. He accuses Dandre (whom he maintains was never married to her) of manipulating Pavlova, of forcing her to dance until her death, of plundering her London bank account, of falsifying her dying wish to return to Russia. As an Orthodox believer, Thomassen maintains, Pavlova would never have consented to being cremated. Pavlova, a marshmallow and meringue confection topped with whipped cream, is named after her.

Pelshe, Arvid Yanovich (1899–1983), of the many Latvians who served the Bolshevik cause, living in the Soviet Union after the defeat of the revolution in their own country, then returning to his homeland to Sovietise it. He was born into a peasant family in Bauska district, Latvia, joined the Bolshevik Party in 1915 and met LENIN in Switzerland in 1916. He was elected to the Petrograd Soviet of Workers' and Soldiers' Deputies, joined the Cheka, 1918, and was sent by Lenin to Latvia to prosecute the revolution there. After defeat he returned to Russia and worked in various military training schools. He was a committed participant in the brutal collectivisation campaign of the early 1930s. The annexation of Latvia by the Soviet Union saw him return there and he was a secretary of the Communist Party of Latvia until 1959 when he became first secretary. In 1966 BREZHNEV brought him to Moscow and he became chair of the committee of Party control and a full member of the Politburo. He was intolerant of ideological deviation but was quite unable to cope with increasing corruption within the Party. A terrible joke was told about him after Brezhnev's death. Pelshe visits Brezhnev when he is dying and asks him how he is feeling. He replies 'aargh', again and again as the question is repeated. Finally he scribbles something down and expires. The note states, 'You fool, you are sitting on my oxygen supply.'

Penkovsky, Oleg (1912–63), one of the most successful spies recruited by western intelligence in the Soviet Union. He was the nephew of a high-ranking Soviet general and worked in military intelligence (GRU), specialising in NATO nuclear capacity. According to some reports he decided to pass information to the west after becoming profoundly disillusioned with KHRUSHCHEV's behaviour which he judged to be potentially lethal to world security. He was arrested in October 1962, tried and shot for treason. His memoirs were later published in the west. He may have been the most valuable senior Soviet military officer ever turned by the west.

Pervukhin, Mikhail Georgevich (1904–78), one of the officials who played a role in the development of the Soviet atomic bomb, he was born in Yuryuzan and joined the Communist Party in 1919. He graduated in electrical engineering and worked in various power plants before becoming People's Commissar for the Electrical Power Industry, 1939, and deputy chair of Sovnarkom, 1940. As such he became involved in atomic research as KURCHATOV, the father of the project to develop an atomic bomb, reported to him in 1943 that intelligence information had saved Soviet scientists much fruitless endeavour. He was People's Commissar for the Chemical Industry during the war. In 1945 Pervukhin became a member of the Scientific Technical Council of Sovnarkom whose task was to catch up with the Americans whatever the cost. In 1952 he was elected a full member of STALIN's Presidium (Politburo) and was reluctant to support KHRUSHCHEV in his coup against BERIA in July 1953 since he had worked closely with the latter, especially on the atomic project. Pervukhin did not side with the Anti-Party Group against Khrushchev in June 1957 but, nevertheless, his career declined afterwards. In that year he lost his membership of the Politburo and he was USSR Minister for Medium Machine Building (the ministry concerned with atomic weapons) only from 1957 to 1958. He later served as Soviet Ambassador to the GDR.

Peters, Yakov (Ekabs) Khristoforovich (1886–1938), a leading light in the early years of the Cheka, he earned a reputation as a merciless defender of the revolution. He joined the Latvian Social Democratic Party in 1904, was imprisoned but settled in London in 1909 and worked as a tailor. He was an active member of the London Bolshevik Group, joined the Labour Party and married an Englishwoman. He was arrested in December 1910 in connection with murders committed by Latvian anarchists but released due to problems of identifying him. He returned to Russia after the February Revolution and became a member of the Central Committee of the Latvian Social Democratic Party, which supported LENIN. One of the many Latvians who joined the Cheka when it was founded in December 1917 and helped save the Bolshevik regime. He played an important role in dealing with the Left Socialist Revolutionary violence of July 1918 (the Left SRs strongly opposed the Brest-Litovsk Treaty). He became acting head of the Cheka in July–August 1918 when DZERZHINSKY was suspended. He was deputy to Dzerzhinsky from August 1918 to early 1919. In 1920–2 he was Cheka boss in Turkestan. He was a senior member of the prosecution during the Bruce Lockhard and Sidney Reilly trials. He presided over the secret trial of Fanya KAPLAN who had attempted to assassinate Lenin in August 1918. In 1922–8 he was head of the Eastern Department of the Cheka but played other roles as well. He was a member of Rabkrin. He was ruthless, involved in mass executions, reprisals, hostage taking, torture and the other appurtenances of terror. He was head of the Kremlin Guard in 1937 but was arrested in December 1937 and executed in April 1938. He was posthumously rehabilitated and portrayed as a model Chekist.

Petrakov, Nikolai Yakovlevich (b. 1937), one of the leading reform economists under GORBACHEV, he was born into a Russian family in Moscow and graduated from the economics faculty, Moscow State University, 1959, and later defended successfully his candidate dissertation in economics (PhD (Econ)), then his doctorate (DSc (Econ)). He was elected a corresponding member of the USSR Academy of Sciences (since 1992 the Russian Academy of Sciences). He worked in the USSR State Committee for Chemistry, 1959–61, and in the

Economics Institute of USSR Gosplan, 1961–5. He then moved to the Central Mathematical Economics Institute, USSR Academy of Sciences, becoming deputy director, 1965–90. He then became the first economist to serve as an aide to Gorbachev, 1990–1. In 1991 he was invited to become the first director of the Institute for Market Problems, USSR Academy of Sciences. He was elected to the USSR Congress of People's Deputies in 1989.

Petrosyan, Tigran Vartanovich (1929–84), one of the greatest chess players ever produced by the Soviet Union, he was world champion from 1963 to 1968. The Armenian grandmaster took the title from Mikhail BOTVINNIK in 1963 and the latter was never able to challenge him successfully again for the title. Petrosyan was, perhaps, fortunate to be at the height of his powers when Botvinnik was near the end of his illustrious career. However, Petrosyan was a worthy successor to the former master.

Petrov, General Ivan Efimovich (1896–1958), a successful Red Army commander during the Great Fatherland War, he joined the Red Army and the Bolshevik Party, 1918, and participated in the Civil War. In June 1941 his task was to defend Odessa but when this became impossible he was evacuated to Crimea. He was in charge of the defence of Sevastopol after the remainder of Crimea had fallen and managed to hold up the Wehrmacht for several months before the Germans took it in July 1942. During the winter of 1942–3 he commanded the Black Sea Front but made little headway. However, his troops managed to take Novorossiisk and the Taman and Kerch peninsulas in September–October 1943. (BREZHNEV was a political commissar during these engagements and later exaggerated his own role.) He was made commander of the 2nd Belorussian Front but was

quickly moved to the 4th Ukrainian Front, August 1944–April 1945. His troops crossed the Carpathians and moved into Ruthenia in October 1944, before moving west into Slovakia. In January 1945 he moved north into Poland and took part of that country. He was first deputy commander of Land Forces, 1955, and chief inspector of the USSR Ministry of Defence, 1956. He became chief scientific consultant to the deputy USSR Minister of Defence in 1957.

Plekhanov, Georgy Valentinovich (1856–1918), the founding father of Russian Marxism, Plekhanov graduated from populism to Marxism. He joined Zemlya i Volya (Land and Liberty) in 1876 but when it split in 1879 over the tactical use of terrorism, he joined the non-violent Black Repartition minority. He moved abroad in January 1880, abandoned populism and embraced Marxism, taking as his model the German SPD. Possessed of a lucid prose style, Plekhanov exerted a powerful influence over young educated Russians. He co-founded the Liberation of Labour Group in 1883, in Geneva, the aim of which was to promote the 'ideas of scientific socialism' in Russia. He adopted moderate German Marxism and feared that a premature seizure of power in Russia by socialists could lead Russia back to despotism. Somewhat ironically it was on Plekhanov's initiative that the expression 'dictatorship of the proletariat' was added to the 1902 draft programme of the RSDRP. He originated the concept of dividing the coming revolution in Russia into two phases: the first, the bourgeois-democratic phase, during which the proletariat would help to place the bourgeoisie in power, and it in turn would develop liberal institutions which would promote capitalism and the Europeanisation of backward Russia. Under capitalism, the growing working class, guided by members of the intelligentsia, armed with socialist theory, would gradually develop political consciousness (meaning it would come to realise that Marxism was its destiny) to be able to take power, possibly aided by the peasantry. The first stage of the revolution, the bourgeois-democratic phase, would be relatively short due to the fact that Russian capitalism was underdeveloped, the Russian bourgeoisie was small and the working class was strong. Thus Marxists had to discipline themselves during this stage not to attempt to seize power prematurely. If power were seized by a socialist minority the result would be disaster and would be akin to 'patriarchal authoritarian communism'. Socialism could not be built from above but only by the workers themselves. Plekhanov's vision electrified many young Russians who had been seeking a way out of Russia's backwardness. Plekhanov now offered them the opportunity of joining the mainstream of European development, armed with a European ideology. He made an original contribution to European Marxism and may have coined the expression 'dialectical materialism'. At times he sided with LENIN and the Bolsheviks, at other times he sided with the Mensheviks, and this lack of consistency was held against him. His theories about the development of Russia prepared the way for Lenin's views on the introduction of socialist consciousness from without: it could be endogenously imparted. It also institutionalised the role of the Marxist intellectual in the Party. His influence petered out after the 1905 revolution when Lenin and TROTSKY built on his views to develop their own concepts of revolution. He returned to Russia in March 1917 but was accepted by neither the Bolsheviks nor the Mensheviks. Lenin turned the tables on Plekhanov in January 1918 when he dispersed the Constituent Assembly, quoting from Plekhanov's 1903 speech in which the latter had justified any action which protected the revolution. Everything he had

warned socialists not to do was being put into practice before his eyes. He died a disillusioned man.

Pliushch, Ivan Stepanovych (*b.* 1941), he is a typical peasant product of post-war social mobility in Ukraine and rose to become speaker of parliament. He was born in Chernigov oblast and educated at the Ukrainian Agricultural Academy and at the Academy of Social Sciences of the CPSU Central Committee. He worked on sovkhozes (state farms), 1967–74, and was responsible for agriculture in Kiev Party obkom, 1975–81. He then moved into the Kiev oblast soviet and became chair, 1984–90. In June 1990 Pliushch was elected first deputy chair (speaker), Ukrainian Supreme Soviet. After Leonid KRAVCHUK, a close ally, was elected the first President of the Republic of Ukraine, Pliushch replaced him as speaker of the Supreme Soviet. He was a member of the Communist Party of Ukraine from 1962 until August 1991, when Ukraine declared its independence.

Podgorny, Nikolai Viktorovich (1903–83), a member of the triumvirate which took over from KHRUSHCHEV in 1964 (the others were BREZHNEV and KOSYGIN) Podgorny was an influential figure until 1977 when he fell out with Brezhnev. He was born into a Ukrainian family in Karlovka, Poltava oblast, and worked in the Ukrainian sugar industry, 1931–9. Then he became a deputy Ukrainian People's Commissar for the Food Industry and in 1940 held the same position in the USSR People's Commissariat. He became first secretary, Kharkov obkom, 1950, and second secretary, Communist Party of Ukraine, 1953. His career flourished under Khrushchev and he became a member of the CPSU Central Committee, 1956, a candidate member of the Presidium (Politburo), 1958, and a full member 1960. He moved to Moscow in 1963 to become a secretary of the Central Committee. He sided with

Brezhnev in 1964 but in 1965 he lost his secretaryship and was made chair of the Presidium of the USSR Supreme Soviet, or head of state. He exercised more influence as head of state than most former incumbents but it was not a real power base. When Brezhnev wanted to become head of state himself in 1977, he offered Podgorny the deputy's job, which the latter turned down flat. Podgorny was dismissed and also removed from the Politburo without a word of thanks for his long service. No pretence was made about his having resigned for reasons of health.

Pokrovsky, Mikhail Nikolaevich (1868–1932), the leading Soviet Marxist historian of the 1920s, Pokrovsky attempted to produce a Marxist counter-blast to the writings of Klyuchevsky. He joined the RSDRP in 1905, met LENIN for the first time and participated in the December 1905 uprising in Moscow. He attended the Vth Party Congress in 1907 and was elected to the Central Committee. In order to avoid persecution Pokrovsky emigrated to France in 1909. He devoted himself to developing a Marxist Russian historiography, emphasising economic and social themes. Nine volumes on Russian nineteenth-century history were published in and after 1907 and another five volumes on Russia since its origins. He was on the left of the Bolshevik Party and by 1914 was close to Lenin. He returned to Russia in August 1917 and became chair of the Moscow Soviet, a member of the Military Revolutionary Committee and editor of *Izvestiya*. He was a member of the Bolshevik delegation which negotiated the Brest-Litovsk Treaty but sided with the Left Communists in opposing it. He was appointed deputy Commissar for Enlightenment (under LUNACHARSKY) in May 1918 and remained in that post until his death. By the 1920s he had produced a formidable body of historical work from a Marxist point of view. In 1925 he founded the Society of Marxist Historians whose major task was to debunk the works of bourgeois historians. He participated wholeheartedly in the persecution of non-Marxist historians in the Soviet Union in and after 1928. However, his days as the leading historian were numbered as nationalism, the role of leadership and will asserted themselves. The Party wanted narrative history which glorified Russian achievements and emphasised the role of political, military and diplomatic leadership. History had to become Party history. Pokrovsky's castigation of Russia for its past imperialism and conservatism were falling out of favour. He died before he could be disgraced and was rehabilitated in 1956. His work was denigrated as 'vulgar Marxism'.

Polozkov, Ivan Kuzmich (*b.* 1935), against GORBACHEV's wishes he was elected the first secretary of the Russian Communist Party at its founding Congress in June 1990. He was born into a Russian peasant family in Kursk oblast and graduated from the All-Union Finance and Economics Institute, as an external student, from the Higher Party School of the CPSU Central Committee and from the Academy of Social Sciences, CPSU Central Committee. He moved into Party work in 1962 in Kursk obkom, becoming in 1983 a secretary of Krasnodar kraikom and in 1985 first secretary. In April 1990 he was also elected chair of Krasnodar Soviet executive committee. He was elected to the USSR Congress of People's Deputies, 1989, and the RSFSR Congress of People's Deputies, 1990. He joined the Communist Party, 1958, and was a member of the Central Committee, 1986–91. In June 1990 he was elected to head the Russian Communist Party and in July 1990 he was elected to the CPSU Politburo. Polozkov was a great disappointment as he proved a colourless conservative apparatchik, close to the line pursued by

LIGACHEV. His party was banned by President YELTSIN in November 1991.

Poltoranin, Mikhail Nikiforovich (*b.* 1939), an influential journalist who supported YELTSIN during the last years of the Soviet Union and the early years of independent Russia. He was born into a Russian family in Leninogorsk, Kazakhstan, and his father was killed during the Great Fatherland War. He joined the Communist Party in 1961. He graduated in journalism from the Kazakh State University, Alma Ata (Almaty), 1968, and from the Higher Party School, CPSU Central Committee, 1970. He joined *Pravda* and was its correspondent in Kazakhstan, 1975–86. He became widely known in 1986 after publishing a series of articles in *Pravda* on abuse of power by Party workers, police and the KGB in Voroshilovgrad (Lugansk), Ukraine. In January 1987 he became editor-in-chief of *Komsomolskaya Pravda,* strongly supported by Boris Yeltsin who at the time was first secretary of Moscow Party gorkom. Poltoranin was one of the few members of the Moscow Party organisation who did not turn against Yeltsin after the latter's dismissal in November 1987 and he was sacked as editor-in-chief of *Komsomolskaya Pravda* in January 1988 as a result of the direct intervention of Lev ZAIKOV, Yeltsin's successor as first secretary, Moscow gorkom. He then began working for *Novosti* as a political observer. He was elected to the USSR Congress of People's Deputies and the USSR Supreme Soviet, 1989, as a nominee of the USSR Union of Journalists. Close to Yeltsin, he was appointed RSFSR Minister of the Press and Media in July 1990. After the failure of the attempted coup in August 1991 he stated that the main task of his ministry was the depoliticisation of the media but clearly supported some large publishing houses because he found their output congenial. This led to continuing altercations with Ivan SILAEV, the Russian Prime Minister,

which only ended when Silaev resigned. Poltoranin called on all democrats to combat the old nomenklatura by making use of the radio, television and print media to propagate their views. Eventually President Yeltsin was forced to compromise with his opponents and he sacked Poltoranin in November 1992.

Polyansky, Dmitry Stepanovich (*b.* 1917), a leading politician under KHRUSHCHEV and for part of the BREZHNEV era, he was an agricultural expert, born into a peasant family in Ukraine and having graduated from Kharkov Agricultural Institute in 1939. He worked his way up in the Party apparatus and Khrushchev chose him as chair, RSFSR Council of Ministers, 1958, where he stayed until 1962. Khrushchev promoted him to full membership of the Presidium (Politburo) in 1962. Under Brezhnev Polyansky became first deputy chair, USSR Council of Ministers, 1965–73, the Prime Minister being Aleksei KOSYGIN. He was then demoted to USSR Minister of Agriculture, 1973–6, and then dispatched as Soviet ambassador to various countries.

Ponomarev, Boris Nikolaevich (*b.* 1905), a conservative ideologist who played a leading role in supervising communist parties outside the Soviet Union, he was born into a Russian family near Moscow and graduated from Moscow State University in 1926. He was deputy director of the Institute of Red Professors, 1932–6, and then moved to the Comintern until its dissolution in 1943. He was director of the Marx–Engels Institute, 1943–4, and became head of the international department when it was established in the Central Committee Secretariat in 1955, and remained there until 1985. He was elected to the Central Committee, 1956, and as a candidate member of the Politburo, 1972, but never became a full member before he departed in 1986. This would suggest that he had enemies, one of whom was probably Yury ANDROPOV. He was ill at ease under perestroika and GORBACHEV sacked him in 1986 and replaced him with Anatoly DOBRYNIN, previously the long-serving Soviet Ambassador to Washington.

Popov, Gavriil Kharitonovich (*b.* 1936), a leading economist and politician of the GORBACHEV era, he was born in Moscow into a family of Greek origin, he graduated in economics from Moscow State University, 1959, joined the Communist Party, 1959, and taught in the university, 1963–88, becoming dean of faculty in 1977. He campaigned for the introduction of business studies and was eventually successful. He then became editor of *Voprosy Ekonomiki*. He was elected to the USSR Congress of People's Deputies in 1989, and became a leader of the Inter-Regional Group, a reform-minded group within the CPSU. In April 1990 he was elected chair of Moscow city council and he left the Communist Party in July 1990. He was elected mayor of Moscow in June 1991 (with Yury LUZHKOV as his deputy) and thereby became a prominent figure. He was a leading member of the Democratic Russia (DemRossiya) movement and was also chair of the All-Union Society of Soviet Greeks and the president of the USSR Baseball and Softball Federation. He resigned as mayor of Moscow in June 1992.

Popov, General Markian Mikhailovich (1902–69), a competent general during the Great Fatherland War, his star rose and declined. He joined the Red Army, 1920, and the Bolshevik Party, 1921, and participated in the Civil War. He graduated from the Frunze Military Academy in 1936. He was commander of the Leningrad military district (renamed the Northern Front later in 1941) when war broke out and was a commander of Armoured Divisions during the Battle of Stalingrad. His troops took Kharkov in

February 1943 but they were driven out by a massive German counter-offensive. In July 1943, during the Battle of Kursk, Popov's forces attacked the Germans near Orel and scored a decisive victory. He then advanced from Orel to Bryansk in August 1944. He was then given command of the 2nd Baltic Front but made little progress due to the fortifications he encountered. On failing to take Riga, STALIN sacked him and replaced him with EREMENKO. After the war he was head of the military training administration and first deputy commander-in-chief of Soviet Land Forces from 1956.

Popov, Pavel Ilich (1872–1950), the founding father of Soviet statistics who was commissioned by LENIN to establish the Central Statistical Administration and was its first head, 1918–26. He was born into a Russian family in Irkutsk and became involved in revolutionary activity during the 1890s but did not join the Communist Party until 1924. He worked in various statistical offices before the revolution. He lost his position in 1926 after a dispute with STALIN and thereafter occupied minor positions.

Potresov, Aleksandr Nikolaevich (1869–1934), he was a co-founder, with LENIN and MARTOV, of the St Petersburg Union of Struggle for the Emancipation of the Working Class. Imprisoned and exiled, he moved abroad in 1900 and linked up again with Lenin and Martov to develop an underground network in Russia and the Party newspaper, *Iskra*. He fell out with Lenin, finding him unprincipled and intolerant of opposing views. He joined the Mensheviks after 1905. He condemned the October Revolution because it did not conform to the 'laws of history' and advocated a coalition with the Kadets to overthrow the Bolsheviks. He was out of temper with the Menshevik view that opposition to the Bolsheviks should only be pursued by legal means, was sympathetic to the allied intervention and shared the allies' view that there were two enemies: Germans and Bolsheviks. He emigrated in 1924 and died in Paris.

Preobrazhensky, Evgeny Aleksandrovich (1886–1937), one of the leading Soviet economists until the late 1920s when STALIN's rise meant his fall. He was born into a Russian Orthodox priest's family in Bolkhoz, Orel guberniya, and was a believer until the age of fourteen, then switching to Marxism. He began working for the Bolsheviks in 1903 and became close to LENIN from 1912. He helped to establish Soviet power in the Urals and fought against KOLCHAK. He returned to Moscow to work on *Pravda* and help draft the 1919 Party Programme. He was chair of the finance committee of the Central Committee and a member of the presidium of the Communist Academy. He and BUKHARIN wrote the *ABC of Communism* and he was firmly on the left of the Party, siding with TROTSKY against STALIN. He developed the concept of the primitive accumulation of capital, to be provided by the peasants. As such he was out of tempter with NEP and favoured the introduction of a socialist economy. These policies were not acceptable to Stalin and the right before 1927 but Trotsky's defeat meant that Stalin could move to the left and steal Preobrazhensky's ideas. He was expelled from the Party, 1927, and lost all his other positions as well. He recanted and was readmitted to the Party, was a witness for the prosecution against ZINOVIEV in 1936 but was arrested in 1937, tried and executed.

Prezent, Isaak Izrailovich (1902–70), a notorious philosopher who allied himself to LYSENKO and conducted a war against geneticists, thereby causing enormous damage to Soviet science and agriculture. Born into a Jewish family, he joined the Communist Party in 1921. He moved into biology about 1930 and thereafter provided Marxist–Leninist theory for Lamarckian biology. He taught at Leningrad State University, 1931–48, and played an important role in the August 1948 Party session which came down in favour of Lysenko and his so-called agrobiology and against genetics. He was active in the All-Union Lenin Academy of Agricultural Sciences, 1951–6, but fell out with Lysenko and disappeared from public view well before the demolition of Lysenko's reputation in 1965.

Primakov, Evgeny Maksimovich (*b.* 1929), an astute politician who rose to prominence under GORBACHEV and then played an even more important role in YELTSIN's Russia. He was born in Kiev and is partly of Jewish origin. His military father was executed. He graduated from the Moscow Institute of Oriental Studies, 1953, as an Arabist. He began postgraduate studies at Moscow State University, 1956, and successfully defended his candidate dissertation (PhD) and his doctoral dissertation (DLitt), 1969. He was elected a member of the USSR Academy of Sciences in 1979. He began his journalistic career in 1956, working in Gosteleradio (state television and radio). From 1962 to 1970 he was on the staff of *Pravda* and was their Middle East correspondent from 1966. In 1970 he was appointed deputy director of the Institute of World Economy and International Relations, USSR Academy of Sciences. In 1977 he became director of the Institute of Oriental Studies, USSR Academy of Sciences and in 1985 he returned to the Institute of World Economy as director. In 1986 he was elected a candidate member of the Central Committee and in 1988 became the first head of a department for world economy and international relations in the USSR Academy of Sciences. His progress was very rapid thereafter: in April 1989 he was made a full member of the Central Committee and in September

1989 a candidate member of the Politburo. In 1989 he was elected to the USSR Congress of People's Deputies (nominated by the Communist Party) and the USSR Supreme Soviet and from June 1989 to March 1990 he was chair (speaker) of the Soviet of the Union, one of the two houses of the USSR Supreme Soviet. In March 1990 he was made a member of Gorbachev's Presidential Council. He was a frequent visitor to Iraq and some observers believe he had foreknowledge of Iraq's plan to invade Kuwait. From December 1990 to January 1991 he travelled to Baghdad and negotiated with Saddam Hussein in an effort to stave off the Gulf War. He also travelled to Baghdad during the war in an attempt to broker a settlement. In January 1992 President Yeltsin appointed him head of the Main Intelligence Administration (GRU) and in January 1996 he became Russian Foreign Minister, succeeding Andrei KOZYREV.

Prokofiev, Sergei Sergeevich (1891–1953), he was among the artists who emigrated from the Soviet Union after the October Revolution and from 1918 lived in the United States, Germany and France. He returned to give concerts in 1927, 1929 and 1932 in the USSR and returned for good in 1933. Prokofiev accepted the new Stalinist cultural policy of socialist realism, which involved disciplining composers and politicising artistic life. When the Party rejected 'bourgeois modernism', it also rejected a significant part of his previous work. Prokofiev was willing to pay a price to be able to have his music brought to a wide public and to co-operate with other artists (he composed the screen music to Eisenstein's film, *Ivan the Terrible*). He composed symphonies, piano concertos, operas and ballets. He became a People's Artist of the RSFSR in 1947 and was awarded several Stalin Prizes. He was not well informed about the top political functionaries and on encountering ZHDANOV in 1948

he asked the main critic of the cultural intelligentsia who he was, whereupon Zhdanov pointed to portraits of himself with STALIN and MOLOTOV. 'Don't you recognise my portrait?' Prokofiev's rejoinder was typical of his attitude to bureaucrats. 'So what!' The Central Committee decree of February 1948 condemned Prokofiev, as well as SHOSTAKOVICH and KHACHATURYAN, for cacophony, decadence and anti-popular formalism. However, no punishment was meted out to Prokofiev as he acknowledged the accuracy of the accusations. The accusations were withdrawn by the Party in 1958. He was awarded the Lenin Prize in 1957 for his Seventh Symphony. A brilliantly versatile, innovative composer, his popularity grew at home and abroad after his death.

Prunskené, Kazimiera Danuté (*b.* 1943), a Lithuanian economist who shot to prominence in the late GORBACHEV era but who was too moderate for Lithuanian nationalists. She graduated from Vilnius University and lectured there, 1965–85, becoming a professor. She successfully defended her candidate dissertation (PhD (Econ)) and her doctoral dissertation (DSc (Econ)). She was a member of the Communist Party of Lithuania and also of the council of Sajudis, from 1988. She was appointed deputy chair of the Lithuanian Council of Ministers in 1989 and was elected to the USSR Congress of People's Deputies in 1989. From March 1990 to 1991 she was Prime Minister of the Republic of Lithuania.

Pryanishnikov, Dmitry Nikolaevich (1865–1948), one of the leading Soviet agricultural chemists who made a huge contribution to agricultural science in the Soviet Union. He was born into a Russian family and graduated from Moscow University, 1887, where one of his teachers was K. A. Timiryazev. In 1895 he joined the staff of the Moscow

Agricultural Institute (renamed the Timiryazev Agricultural Academy, 1923) and he remained there for the rest of his life. He was elected a full member of the USSR Academy of Sciences in 1929. N. I. VAVILOV was one of his pupils and together they helped to found the All-Union Lenin Academy of Agricultural Sciences. He worked with Gosplan on the use of fertilizers in agriculture but survived the STALIN times unscathed.

Pugo, Boris Karlovich (1937–91), one of the many Latvians to attain high political office in the Soviet Union. He was born in Kalinin (now Tver), the son of the Latvian communist émigré, Karlis Pugo. His father was one of the Latvian communists who secured the Sovietisation of their homeland and he died in Riga in 1955. Pugo graduated from the Riga Polytechnic Institute in 1960. He was first secretary of the Latvian Komsomol, 1969–70, then secretary of the All-Union Komsomol until 1974. He was first secretary, Riga Party gorkom, 1975–6, and then he was made first deputy chair of the Latvian KGB, 1977–80, and chair, 1980–4. Yury ANDROPOV had chosen him for these posts. Pugo was appointed a KGB major general in 1981. Then from 1984–8 he was first secretary, Communist Party of Latvia, became chair of the All-Union Committee of Party Control and in September 1989 was elected a candidate member of the CPSU Politburo. In December 1990 he replaced Vadim BAKATIN as USSR Minister of Internal Affairs. His appointment was regarded by liberals at the time as a bad omen and this turned out to be true as Pugo was one of the plotters in August 1991.

Immediately after its failure he committed suicide by shooting himself. He was one of the many GORBACHEV appointments which proved ill-judged and the main reason appears to be that Gorbachev relied on personnel promoted by his patron Andropov.

Pyatakov, Georgy Leonidovich (1890–1937), he was born into a Russian sugar merchant's family, flirted with anarchism, joined the Bolshevik Party, 1910, and was always on the left of the Party, supporting BUKHARIN against LENIN and TROTSKY against STALIN. Lenin regarded him as someone he could not rely on in a political tight corner. He was a member of the Left Communists, led by Bukharin, 1918, which advocated revolutionary war against Germany. He was a member of the presidium of the Supreme Council of the National Economy and was chair of the tribunal which sentenced SR leaders in 1922. RADEK and he were sent to Germany in 1923 to help the revolutionary cause there. He sided with Trotsky against Stalin after Lenin's death in 1924 and was expelled from the Party but readmitted when he decided to support Stalin's industrialisation policy. He was deputy chair, then chair of the State Bank, 1928–30, and deputy People's Commissar for Heavy Industry (under ORDZHONIKIDZE), 1932–6. He joined the chorus demanding the death penalty for ZINOVIEV and KAMENEV but this did not save him and he was later accused of being the head of a Trotskyist centre. He was the chief defendant in the second great show trial of 1937, was found guilty and shot. He was rehabilitated during perestroika.

R

Radek, Karl Berngardovich (né Sobelsohn) (1885–1939), a Polish Jew from Austrian Galicia, he was active in Polish and German social democracy before 1914. He was a convinced internationalist during the war and opposed all attempts to break up the international workers' movement. He became an adherent of TROTSKY's theory of permanent revolution and as such opposed LENIN over the Brest-Litovsk Treaty. He moved to Petrograd during the summer of 1917 and joined the Bolsheviks. He was elected to the Central Committee of the Communist Party in March 1919 but he never came to terms with developments within the Party and Russia. He sided with the Left Communists in their demands for instant socialism in the economy and opposed the Brest-Litovsk Treaty, favouring international revolution. His area of interest was observing international developments which could lead to socialist revolution. As secretary, from 1920, of the Communist International (Comintern), he was well informed and devoted great attention to the German left. The language of the Comintern under Lenin was German and when Lenin was lost for a German word, Radek, who was crouched under the podium, would come up with the relevant term. He was present at the founding of the KPD (Communist Party of Germany) and during the autumn of 1923 (the last opportunity for a revolution in Germany) he was active in promoting revolution. STALIN skilfully blamed Trotsky and Radek for the failure of the left in Germany; Radek supported Trotsky against Stalin and was expelled from the Party in 1927 but was readmitted in 1929 after he had repented of his mistakes. He then became a passionate promoter of Stalin. However, his days of influence in the Comintern and in Soviet foreign policy were over. He was again expelled from the Party in 1936 and arrested. In 1937 he was sentenced to ten years' imprisonment during the show trial against the Anti-Soviet Trotsky Centre. He gave evidence against some of the other accused and this saved him from the executioner's bullet. He died in a labour camp and was rehabilitated in 1988.

Rakhmaninov, Sergei Vasilevich (1873–1943), the last great Russian romantic composer and a gifted pianist, one of the great virtuosi of his day, was born on the family estate near Lake Ilmen and was destined for a military career like his father. However, his father lost the entire family fortune through speculation and Sergei was sent to Moscow to study under Nikolai Zverev. He graduated from the Moscow Conservatory, 1892, with a gold medal. His first concerto was performed in the same year but he was subject to bouts of depression if his work was not well received, for example, his first symphony. His second piano concerto was very successful and still is. He made his first visit to the United States in 1909 and remained abroad after the October Revolution, settling in the United States in 1935.

Rakovsky, Khristian Georgievich (1873–1941), a Bulgarian whose family fortune permitted him to study medicine and travel around Europe at will. He was a revolutionary from 1889 and published in both LENIN's and TROTSKY's periodicals. He favoured a Balkan union of nations to promote their independence. The October Revolution appeared to offer the best hope for revolution in the Balkans and he threw in his lot with the Bolsheviks. Lenin recruited him in 1918 and he was put in charge of negotiations between the soviets and the Ukrainian Rada. In January 1919 he was appointed head of the Ukrainian Soviet government. He was also in charge of the Party and army, remaining until 1923. He was a founding member of the Comintern in March 1919, was elected to the Central Committee of the Bolshevik Party in March 1919 and participated in negotiations with Britain and France which led to the establishment of relations. He became Soviet Ambassador to Paris in 1925 but was expelled from the Party in 1927 as a Trotskyist. He was exiled to Astrakhan and Barnaul but was readmitted to the Party in 1934, having recanted his anti-Stalinist views. He was made head of the Soviet Red Cross in 1935 but was arrested in January 1937 and sentenced to twenty years in a labour camp for treason in 1938. He was shot in September 1941 during the advance of German forces on Moscow. He was rehabilitated in 1988.

Rashidov, Sharaf Rashidovich (1917–83), the godfather of Uzbekistan in many Moscow eyes, he waxed during the easygoing BREZHNEV years and died in office before GORBACHEV came to power and wielded his broom. He was a journalist before the war, was severely wounded and invalided out of the army, 1942, and returned to journalism. In 1954 he was elected to the bureau (the equivalent of the CPSU Politburo), Communist Party of Uzbekistan and, in 1959 KHRUSHCHEV made him first secretary of the Uzbek Party and he remained the ruler of Uzbekistan until his death. He was a member of the Presidium (Politburo)

from 1961 until 1983. What Gorbachev regarded as corruption the Uzbeks regarded as restoring control over their own republic.

Rasputin, Father Grigory Efimovich (né **Novykh**) (1872–1916), the most infamous Orthodox priest of his generation, he established contact with the Romanov family in 1905. The Tsarevich Aleksei suffered from haemophilia which he had inherited from his mother, who in turn had acquired it as a relative of Queen Victoria. Rasputin used hypnosis to staunch the internal bleeding, which caused excruciating pain. This led to the TSARINA regarding him as sent from God. Had he remained a healer, there would have been no scandal. However, he was a libertine (Rasputin is derived from this word) and he advocated sinning in order to experience repentance. The more sin there was in one's life, the more opportunities there are for repentance. His powerful presence made him very attractive to the noble women of the court and he engaged in sexual relations with many of them. (There is no conclusive evidence that he and the Tsarina were ever lovers.) His privileged position at court offered chances for financial and political gain and Rasputin was identified as early as 1912 as a baleful influence on the monarchy. When Tsar NICHOLAS II moved to Mogilev to assume command of the Russian armies in 1915 he left the Tsarina in Petrograd to cope with ministers. (The fact that the Tsar preferred to spend most of his time at Mogilev speaks volumes about their marital relations.) The Tsarina placed great faith in Rasputin's counsel and this led to ministers and their deputies being sacked and replaced at whirlwind speed. Russian military defeats led to rumours that there was a German faction at court, headed by the Tsarina. This was, in reality, nonsense but it was believed and damaged the royal family. Eventually, in December 1916, a relative of the Tsar conspired with others to poison – so much poison was administered that it worked as an antidote – then shoot Rasputin and drop him through a hole into the frozen River Neva. Rasputin lives on in many western films.

Rasputin, Valentin Grigorevich (*b.* 1937), a leading Russian novelist of the village prose school who championed the countryside and life and fought vigorously against environmental pollution. He was born into a Russian family in Irkutsk oblast and sets most of his works in Siberia, contrasting the glibness and shallowness of urban life and the open frankness of village people. He attracted notice in 1965 with his novel, *Money for Maria* and his most popular work is *Farewell to Matyora*, 1976, which describes life just before the island is drowned by a hydro-electric scheme. He campaigned ceaselessly and eventually successfully to protect Lake Baikal from industrial pollution. Egor LIGACHEV, when he was first secretary of Tomsk obkom, was much taken by him and they worked together to preserve some of the old wooden architecture of Tomsk. Rasputin was elected to the USSR Congress of People's Deputies, 1989, and became a member of GORBACHEV's Presidential Council, March 1990, being the only noncommunist member.

Ratushinskaya, Irina Borisovna (*b.* 1954), one of the finest poetesses of the late Soviet period, she was born into a Russified family of Polish gentry in Odessa and graduated in physics from Odessa University in 1976. She married Igor Gerashchenko, a scientist, and moved to Kiev. She published poetry in samizdat but was unable to publish in the USSR. She attempted to emigrate in 1980, and was arrested in Moscow after taking part in a human rights demonstration in 1981. She was rearrested in 1982 and sentenced to seven years' imprisonment in labour

camps and five years' exile. Her cause was taken up by supporters in the west and she was released in October 1986. She was subjected to a very harsh regime and her jailers failed to break her deep Christian faith. She emigrated, was stripped of her Soviet citizenship and settled in London. She published a novel in 1995 about youth life in Odessa but it was poorly received. Her ability to write poetry comparable to that of her Soviet period appears to be disappearing.

Razumovsky, Georgy Petrovich (*b.* 1936), one of the officials promoted rapidly by GORBACHEV in the early years of perestroika but who later parted company with the Soviet President. He was born into a Russian family in Krasnodar and graduated from the Kuban Agricultural Institute in 1958. He joined the Communist Party and moved into the Party apparatus in 1961 in Krasnodar kraikom. He worked in the Central Committee apparatus, 1971–3, then returned to chair the Krasnodar Soviet executive committee, until 1981. As such he would have had regular contact with Gorbachev in neighbouring Stavropol. Razumovsky worked in the agricultural administration of the USSR Council of Ministers, 1981–3, and then returned to Krasnodar as first secretary of the Party kraikom. When Gorbachev became General Secretary he chose Razumovsky to head the department of Party organisation work, Central Committee Secretariat. In other words, Razumovsky was now in charge of Party cadres. In November 1985 he became chair of the commission on legislative proposals, USSR Supreme Soviet, in March 1986 a Central Committee Secretary and in February 1988 a candidate member of the Politburo. In October 1988 Razumovsky, as a result of the reorganisation of the Central Committee Secretariat, was appointed chair of the commission on Party construction and cadres policy. However, in July 1990 he was not re-elected to the Central Committee and was sent off to China as a Soviet consul.

Reed, John (1887–1920), the most famous US Bolshevik, Reed was a Harvard graduate and a distinguished war correspondent. He gravitated to Russia in 1917 because of his radical sympathies and sided wholeheartedly with the Bolsheviks in October 1917. He was present at the storming of the Winter Palace. Together with other western Bolsheviks, he worked in the Bureau of International Revolutionary Propaganda, which later was renamed the Press Bureau of the Commissariat of Foreign Affairs (Narkomindel). In January 1918, the Bolsheviks proposed Reed as the Soviet consul in New York, replacing the provisional government's nominee. The US government turned down the request. However, he returned to the United States in February 1918 and wrote his famous first-hand account of the revolution, *Ten Days that Shook the World*, which was published in March 1919. He was a founder of the Communist-Labor Party which eventually became the Communist Party of the USA. He returned to Russia in 1919 and was elected to the Executive Committee of the Comintern. He also attended the IInd Comintern Congress and afterwards accompanied ZINOVIEV and others to Baku for the inaugural Congress of the Peoples of the East. He fell ill with typhoid in Baku and died soon after his transfer to Moscow. He is buried in front of the Kremlin wall.

Reilly, Sidney (né Rozenblum) (1874–1925), one of the most famous spies of the early revolutionary period, he was an agent for Britain and other countries and found the conspiratorial life irresistible. Born in Russia, he married an Irish widow in London in 1898 and changed his name to Reilly, thereby acquiring a British passport. He was a British intelligence officer in several countries and represented a German armaments company in St Petersburg until 1914. He was a British–Japanese double agent in the Far East. He was quite a society figure in St Petersburg and provided the Okhrana (Russian secret police) with information about revolutionaries, including, possibly, STALIN. He entered Russia in April 1918 on a Soviet passport given him in London by LITVINOV and, aided by Robert Bruce Lockhart, another British intelligence officer acting as a diplomat, established contact with the Cheka head of the Kremlin Guard. The latter, under Chekist orders, pretended the Latvian troops guarding the Bolsheviks were disillusioned. Reilly fed him funds to promote an anti-Bolshevik coup. He acquired a Chekist passport and attempted to arrest LENIN and DZERZHINSKY. He was also involved in joint British, American and French espionage and efforts to undermine the Bolsheviks but the Cheka was aware of what was happening and arrested many of the participants. Reilly, by now back in England, was sentenced to death *in absentia*. He was encouraged to return to Soviet Russia in 1925 by Chekist underground agents who were running a monarchist anti-Soviet organisation, called Trest. He crossed the Finnish–Soviet border in September 1925 and was immediately arrested by the Soviets. In 1966 a Soviet weekly stated that he had been executed in November 1925 in Moscow. Sam Neill played him in a British TV series.

Rokossovsky, Marshal Konstantin Konstantinovich (1896–1968), in an illustrious career, he was tortured after TUKHACHEVSKY's execution, proved himself a very able commander in the Far East and during the Great Fatherland War, and ended up as Minister of Defence in Poland. He fought in the First World War as an NCO, then joined the Red Army, 1918, and the Bolshevik Party, 1919, and participated in the Civil War as commander of a cavalry division.

He graduated from the Frunze Military Academy in 1929. During STALIN's slaughter of the high command after Tukhachevsky's arrest, Rokossovsky was arrested, tortured and imprisoned. After his release he led the first tank counterattack in Ukraine after the German invasion, was transferred north and helped two armies to escape encirclement near Smolensk in August 1941. He was very successful during the defence of Moscow in November and December 1941. In 1942 Rokossovsky was commander of the Don Front during the Battle of Stalingrad. His troops broke through the Romanian and Italian lines and enabled the Red Army to move south and encircle Field Marshal Paulus's 6th Army. He commanded the Central Front at the Battle of Kursk, July 1943, launching the initial attack (several hours ahead of the German plan) and holding his ground for a week until Field Marshal Kluge decided to go on to the defensive, leaving behind 50,000 German dead, 400 tanks and mobile guns and 500 aircraft. In June 1944 Rokossovsky was given command of the 1st Belorusian Front and he took Lublin and Brest-Litovsk. By July 1944 he had advanced to the outskirts of Warsaw but halted his offensive. Warsaw rose in August 1944, mistakenly believing that the Red Army would come to its aid. Stalin ordered Rokossovsky to wait until the Germans had crushed the uprising. (Stalin calculated that if Hitler killed the cream of Polish society, the communists would face little opposition when they took over.) Rokossovsky denied the use of Red Army airfields to allied planes which wished to aid the insurgents. In January 1945 the fronts were reorganised and Rokossovsky assumed command of the 2nd Belorusian Front, destroyed Warsaw, and swept through northern Poland to take Danzig (Gdansk) in late January. In May 1945 his troops made contact with British troops at Wittenberg, Germany. He commanded the victory parade in Red Square on 24 May 1945. He was then sent by Stalin to Poland (he was of Polish origin) where he assumed the posts of Minister of Defence and deputy Prime Minister. He was also made Marshal of Poland. The Poles always regarded him as a Soviet spy and his removal was high on the list of demands by Gomulka during the tense negotiations with KHRUSHCHEV and other Soviet leaders in Warsaw in October 1956. Khrushchev acceded to the Polish wish and Rokossovsky returned to Moscow where he was a deputy USSR Defence Minister until 1962.

Romanov, Grigory Vasilevich (b. 1923), a contender for the post of General Secretary in March 1985, his defeat by GORBACHEV ended his political career. He was born into a Russian peasant family in Novgorod oblast and served in the Red Army during the Great Fatherland War, joining the Communist Party in 1944. He graduated from the Leningrad Shipbuilding Institute in 1953, moved into the Leningrad Party apparatus in 1955 and rose to be first secretary, Leningrad obkom, 1970–83. He had the reputation of being a tough administrator and gained much defence investment for Leningrad. In 1973 he was elected a candidate member of the Politburo and in 1976 a full member. ANDROPOV called him to Moscow in 1983 and made him a secretary of the Central Committee, where he was responsible for the armed forces and defence industry. Romanov supported CHERNENKO against Gorbachev in 1984 and then GRISHIN in March 1985 (under Grishin he had the prospect of becoming heir apparent). Gorbachev moved quickly, informed Romanov that he had no future under him and he was sacked in July 1985. It was put about that he had been involved in corruption, drunken bacchanalias and orgies, a familiar tale related after a political leader has fallen.

Romanov, Nikolai Aleksandrovich (Nicholas II, Tsar of all Russia) (1868–1918), a mild-mannered, self-effacing, politically unimaginative, family-loving man, completely out of his depth as Tsar, especially at such a critical juncture in his nation's history. His father, Alexander III, died early of liver disease in November 1894, catapulting the young Tsarevich (Tsar's son) into responsibility for the Russian nation at a much younger age than expected. His mother was a daughter of the King of Denmark. A few weeks after ascending the throne, Nicholas married Princess Alix (ALEKSANDRA) of Hesse Darmstadt, whose mother, Alice, was a daughter of Queen Victoria. After four daughters, the most desired son, Aleksei, was born in 1904. However, joy mingled with tragedy; he was haemophiliac, inherited through the female line. Nicholas II's training, between 1885 and 1890, under the supervision of Konstantin Pobedonostsev, a conservative, ill-prepared him to cope with the rapid economic and social changes under way. He started off on the wrong foot by denouncing as 'senseless dreams' proposals to involve public bodies, such as the zemstva, in government. He shared the anti-Semitism which was prevalent at the court and did nothing to put a brake on the pogroms against Jews. He was forced into concessions during the 1905 revolution and he always resented WITTE's role in this, even though his autocratic powers were confirmed in the Fundamental Laws, April 1906. After the tercentenary celebrations of the Romanov dynasty, 1913, he even considered dissolving the Duma, even though it only enjoyed weak legislative powers. After the initial defeats of the Russian Army, he determined in August 1915 to move to Mogilev, the headquarters of the General Staff, to become commander-in-chief. His advisers told him this was ill-judged, since he lacked military experience and he would become personally associated with defeat. One reason why he insisted

on going may have been the desire to escape from the Tsarina. He was deaf to all pleas for a government of national confidence and it was only when he was abdicating, March 1917, that he conceded on this issue. His refusal to integrate those parties which accepted a constitutional monarchy as their goal, the Octobrists and Kadets, fatally weakened them during 1917. When he abdicated he noted in his diary that he read Caesar's *Gallic Wars*. (The Russian word Tsar is derived from Caesar.) He abdicated in favour of his son, Aleksei, but when informed that this would mean parting with him, he abdicated a second time in favour of his brother, Grand Duke Mikhail, who had the political foresight to state that he would only accept the throne if invited by parliament. After the February Revolution, the royal family were kept at Tsarskoe Selo (now Pushkino) for five months with KERENSKY enquiring if they had collaborated with the Germans. The British Prime Minister, David Lloyd George, offered them political asylum in Britain, but King George V would have none of it and the offer was withdrawn, thereby sealing their fate. In August 1917 they were moved to Tobolsk and in April 1918 they were taken to Ekaterinburg. When the Tsar's brother and other members of the royal family were executed by the Bolsheviks in June 1918, the future began to look bleak for Nicholas and his family. LENIN gave the go ahead to murder them to the Ekaterinburg Bolsheviks and on 17 July 1918 all were butchered in a cellar and their bodies thrown down a disused mine shaft. Boris YELTSIN, as first Party secretary, of Sverdlovsk region, gave the order to destroy the house where they were killed and pave over the area, a decision he regretted later. The remains of the Tsar and his family were dicovered in the mid-1970s and scientists confirmed that they were authentic in 1993. For many years a woman claimed that she was Anastasia, the youngest daughter, but after her death scientists demonstrated that this claim was false.

Romanova, Aleksandra Fedorovna (Tsarina) (1872–1918), the last tragic Tsarina who, despite her efforts, was never accepted at court or by the Russian people. She was a princess of Hesse Darmstadt and her mother, Princess Alice, was a daughter of Queen Victoria. She lived in England after her mother died when she was six and became a favourite of Queen Victoria who called her 'sunshine'. (However, she never mastered the English language and her memoirs, written in ungrammatical, unidiomatic English, have not helped her reputation.) She first travelled to Russia in 1884 where her elder sister, Elizabeth, married Grand Duke Sergei (brother of Alexander III). She met Nicholas (see ROMANOV), the heir to the throne, and he later fell in love with her and they married in 1894, despite strong opposition from the Russian royal family. She converted to Orthodoxy. After four daughters, her son Aleksei was born to great rejoicing but this turned into mourning when it was discovered that he was suffering from haemophilia, an hereditary disease transmitted through the female line. Her guilt at his subsequent suffering, especially from internal bleeding, led her into mysticism. The Siberian holy man, nicknamed RASPUTIN, was able to staunch Aleksei's bleeding, probably by hypnosis. After the initial Russian defeats at the hands of the Germans in 1914, she was seen as a German agent. This was quite unjustified but it increased her isolation. The decision of the Tsar to moved to Mogilev to take over day to day running of the war left her in charge in Petrograd. She was too easily influenced by Rasputin and acted on his suggestions, badgering her husband to make the changes she advocated. The Tsar usually took the line of least resistance and gave in. She lacked political judgement and self-confidence and when a minister contradicted her,

her normal course of action was to move to dismiss him. After the February Revolution King George V prevented the Russian royal family going into exile in England. KERENSKY sent them to Tobolsk and they were murdered by the Bolsheviks in Ekaterinburg, July 1918. The Ipatev house in which they were shot was demolished and the site concreted over by Boris YELTSIN when he was first Party secretary, Sverdlovsk oblast. Robert K. Massie: *Nicholas and Alexandra*, New York, 1967; Bernard Pares: *The Fall of the Russian Monarchy*, New York, 1939.

Rostropovich, Mstislav Leopoldovich (*b.* 1927), one of the great cellists of his generation, he was born in Baku, and graduated from the Moscow Conservatory in 1946. He won first prize in the International Cellists' Competition in Prague, 1950, and this launched his career as a solo performer. He was awarded the Lenin Prize in 1963. In the 1960s he gained a reputation also as a conductor. Later he also demonstrated that he was a first-class pianist. In the early 1970s he gave refuge to Aleksandr SOLZHENITSYN and this underlined the increasing tension between him and his wife, Galina VISHNEVSKAYA, and the Soviet cultural authorities. In 1974 he and his wife stayed abroad and in 1975 he was made conductor of the National Symphony Orchestra, Washington, DC, and music director, 1977. The couple lost their Soviet citizenship in 1978 but under perestroika they returned to an emotional welcome and had their citizenship restored in January 1990. Queen Elizabeth II conferred on him an honorary knighthood in 1987 in honour of his sixtieth birthday. He was in the Russian White House during the attempted coup in August 1991.

Rotmistrov, Marshal Pavel Alekseevich (1901–82), a successful Red Army tank commander during the Great Fatherland

War, he joined the Bolshevik Party and Red Army, 1919, and fought in the Civil War. He graduated from the Frunze Military Academy in 1931 and commanded tank forces during the Soviet–Finnish War, 1939–40. In December 1942, as commander of the 7th Tank Corps, he inflicted heavy losses on the Wehrmacht during the Battle of Stalingrad. At Kursk Rotmistrov commanded the 5th Guards Tank Corps. On 11–12 July he had to make a forced march of 380 kilometres to reach Prokhorovna which was executed brilliantly and so well camouflaged that the Germans did not perceive what was under way. Red Army units were under severe pressure and Rotmistrov had to attack the Germans on his own initiative. The Wehrmacht lost 10,000 men and 300 tanks in the engagement. In January 1944 he was in Ukraine and was promoted to Marshal of Armoured Troops and deputy commander of the Armoured Forces of the Red Army. After the war he commanded Soviet Tank Forces in (east) Germany and later in the Soviet Far East. He graduated from the Academy of the General Staff in 1953, and became a professor at the academy. He was head of the Academy of Tank Forces, 1958, and a deputy USSR Minister of Defence, 1964–8.

Rozhdestvensky, Gennady Nikolaevich (*b.* 1931), a conductor with a worldwide reputation, he was born into a Russian family in Moscow and was a pupil of the conductor Nikolai Anosov (his father) and the pianist Lev Oborin at the Moscow Conservatory, graduating in 1954. He was principal conductor of the Bolshoi Theatre 1965–70, of the Moscow Chamber Opera, 1974, conductor and artistic director of the USSR Gosteleradio Grand Symphony Orchestra, 1961–74, conductor of the Stockholm Philharmonic, 1974–7, guest conductor of the BBC Symphony Orchestra, 1978–81, and then chief conductor of the Vienna Symphony

Orchestra. He has made many recordings and is an influential teacher. His wife is the pianist Viktoria Postnikova.

Rumyantsev, Oleg Germanovich (*b.* 1961), a very active democrat who was elected co-chair of the Social Democratic Party of the Russian Federation (SDPRF) at its founding Congress in May 1990. At that time he was co-chair of the Democratic Perestroika Club in Moscow. He was born into a Russian family in Moscow, graduated from the geography faculty, Moscow State University, and then carried out postgraduate research at Budapest University. In 1983 he joined the Institute of Economics of the World Socialist System, USSR Academy of Sciences. He was secretary of the Constitution Commission of the RSFSR Supreme Soviet, 1990–1, then he became the responsible secretary of the Constitution Commission, Russian Supreme Soviet. He was elected to the RSFSR Congress of People's Deputies in 1990. During the attempted coup of August 1991 Rumyantsev organised support for President YELTSIN. He was deputy chair of the SDPRF, April–October 1992. In November 1992 the founding Congress of the Russian Social Democratic Centre, a group within the SDPRF, headed by Rumyantsev, was held in Moscow. His political views are quite nationalist and not in the mainstream of European social democracy.

Rusakov, Konstantin Viktorovich (1909–86), a conservative communist official with great experience in dealing with ruling communist parties, he was born in Tver guberniya, was trained as an engineer and joined the Communist Party in 1943. He developed into a specialist in the fish industry and was USSR Minister for the Fish Industry, 1950–2. He then became a diplomat in communist countries and was Soviet Ambassador to Mongolia, 1962–4. ANDROPOV then brought him into the department for liaison with communist and workers' parties of socialist countries, as deputy head under him, in the Central Committee Secretariat. In 1968 Rusakov took over as head of department and was elected a full member of the Central Committee in 1971. BREZHNEV then invited Rusakov to act as an aide, 1972–7, and when he returned as head of the department he was also elected a Central Committee secretary. Rusakov was synonymous with Soviet control over ruling communist parties but over time his ability to influence events declined. When GORBACHEV came to power he told communist leaders that they could choose their own path and this new approach to relations with eastern Europe required a new man in the Secretariat. Rusakov was replaced by Vadim MEDVEDEV in early 1986 and died later the same year.

Rutskoi, Aleksandr Vladimirovich (*b.* 1947), he became nationally prominent politically in 1989 when advocating the military virtues of discipline, and was chosen by Boris YELTSIN as his Vice-President for the Russian presidential elections of June 1991. He was a hero during the attempted coup of August 1991 and was with Yeltsin in the White House. He was born into a Russian family in Kursk and graduated from the Air Force Higher School, Barnaul, Altai krai, then from the Air Force Gagarin Academy, Moscow, and from the Academy of the General Staff, Moscow, 1990. He joined the Communist Party in 1970. From 1985 to 1986 he was commander of an air force regiment, Afghanistan, and in 1988 he was commander of the air force of the 40th Army, Afghanistan. He flew over 400 combat missions, was shot down twice, severely wounded, and was a prisoner of war of the mujahidin for six weeks in Pakistan. He returned to the Soviet Union a war hero and a Hero of the Soviet Union. In May 1989 he was elected deputy chair of the Moscow

society Otechestvo. He was elected to the RSFSR Congress of People's Deputies, March 1990, and the RSFSR Supreme Soviet. Ivan POLOZKOV proposed him for the Central Committee of the Russian Communist Party, but he declined the invitation. Rutskoi linked up with Yeltsin at the IIIrd RSFSR Congress of People's Deputies, March 1991, and saved Yeltsin from defeat at the hands of the Communists who were trying to remove him as speaker. Rutskoi formed his own faction, Communists for Democracy, at the Congress and voted with Democratic Russia (DemRossiya) to ensure victory for Yeltsin. Rutskoi was chosen as Vice-President in the June 1991 presidential elections. During the attempted coup he appealed to all 'officers, soldiers and sailors' not to act against the people and not to 'support the conspirators'. He organised a Russian national guard, composed of Afghan veterans, to defend the White House. He flew to Foros to 'liberate' GORBACHEV and the Soviet President promoted him to major general. In October 1991 the People's Party of Free Russia, headed by Rutskoi, was founded. Its programme revealed it to be essentially social democratic. Gradually relations between Yeltsin and Rutskoi cooled and the latter felt slighted that Yeltsin did not offer him a prestigious post. Gradually a gulf opened and it culminated in October 1993 with Rutskoi being sworn in as President by the Congress of People's Deputies. Rutskoi was among those arrested after the storming of the White House but was amnestied later by the Duma.

Rykov, Aleksei Ivanovich (1881–1938), STALIN's ally in his struggle with TROTSKY after LENIN's death, Rykov reaped the whirlwind later. He joined the RSDRP in 1901, and after 1903 he sided with the Bolsheviks. He worked as an underground agent for the Bolsheviks in his native Saratov region, Moscow and St

Petersburg. He participated in the 1905 revolution but became annoyed at Lenin's dictatorial method of leadership from abroad. He broke with Lenin's Bolsheviks in 1910 and formed his own Bolshevik group which was more conciliatory towards other socialists. He was in exile in Paris, 1910–11. On his return to Russia he was exiled to Siberia until freed by the February Revolution. Then Rykov became a member of the Moscow Soviet and, not surprisingly, came out against Lenin's April Theses. Despite the fact that he advocated moderation, he was elected, in September 1917, to the Bolshevik Central Committee and the Petrograd Soviet. During the Civil War he was responsible for supplies to the Red Army and Navy. His skill as an administrator overcame Lenin's lack of faith in him and he was People's Commissar of the Interior, 1917–18, and then chair of the Supreme Council of the National Economy (VSNKh), 1918–20 and 1923–4. He was also Lenin's deputy on Sovnarkom, chairing meetings of the government when Lenin was too ill to attend. On Lenin's death, he was the obvious candidate to succeed him and remained as head of government until he fell foul of Stalin in 1930. He was elected to the Politburo in 1922. Throughout the early Soviet period, Rykov maintained an independent, critical stance. He always favoured a coalition socialist government and opposed a narrow definition of the dictatorship of the proletariat. As a consequence he was one of the six Bolsheviks who resigned from the Central Committee and Sovnarkom to encourage Lenin to negotiate seriously with the Left SRs about a coalition government. Given his moderate line, it was not surprising that Rykov sided with BUKHARIN, TOMSKY and Stalin against Trotsky and ZINOVIEV after Lenin's death. He became a leading member of the right opposition, with Bukharin, against Stalin's policies, especially forced collectivisation. After the defeat of the

right opposition, Rykov became for a time People's Commissar for Post and Telegraph. In 1930 he was removed from all his posts and was expelled from the Politburo in December. He was arrested in 1937 and later tried for treason in the third great show trial, 1938. He was found guilty of having formed a terrorist group, in 1934, which had targeted Stalin, MOLOTOV, KAGANOVICH and VOROSHILOV. He was sentenced to death and executed on 15 March 1938. Stephen F. Cohen: *Bukharin and the Bolshevik Revolution: A Political Biography, 1888–1938,* New York, 1973.

Ryzhkov, Nikolai Ivanovich (*b.* 1929), an industrial manager, Ryzhkov was President GORBACHEV's Prime Minister and supported perestroika until it became economically too radical for him. He was born into a Russian family in Donetsk oblast, Ukraine, and graduated from the Kramatorsk Technical College and the Kirov Urals Polytechnic Institute. He began on the shop floor of Uralmash, in Sverdlovsk (now Ekaterinburg), 1950, and became general director of the Uralmash Production Association, 1971. He was made first deputy USSR Minister of Heavy and Transport Machine Building, 1975, and in 1979 was appointed first deputy chair, USSR Gosplan. In 1981 he was elected to the Central Committee and was a member of the Politburo, 1985–90. In 1982 he was elected Central Committee secretary and head of the economics department. In September 1985 Gorbachev chose him as chair of the USSR Council of Ministers where he remained until a heart attack forced him to retire in January 1991. He was a member of the Presidential Council until January 1991. He was elected to the USSR Congress of People's Deputies, 1989, as a nominee of the CPSU. In June 1991 he stood against YELTSIN in the Russian presidential elections, polled 16.9 per cent and came second. Ryzhkov was a moderate reformer whose industrial and planning experience gave him insights into the difficulties of moving to a market economy. He was never in favour of moving rapidly and opposed the SHATALIN–YAVLINSKY 500-day programme, proposing a more moderate variant, called the regulated market approach. He did not support the private ownership of land and did not favour Russia accepting western credits as this would lead to the west enslaving Russia.

S

Saburov, Maksim Zakharovich (*b.* 1900), born into a Russian family, he was a prominent economic official from joining USSR Gosplan in 1938 until he sided with the Anti-Party Group against KHRUSHCHEV in June 1957. He became chairman of Gosplan in 1941 and as such was an important official during the war. He was elected to the Presidium (Politburo) at the XIXth Party Congress, 1952. He did not become involved in factional infighting after STALIN's death in 1953 but he was blamed for the state investment problems which arose in December 1956. He predictably sided with the Anti-Party Group as Khrushchev was proposing that the Party become the dominant force in the state management of the economy.

Sakharov, Andrei Dmitrievich (1921–89), the father of the Soviet hydrogen bomb, he became the most famous dissident in the Soviet Union until recalled to Moscow by GORBACHEV where he devoted his last years to active support of democracy. He was born into a Russian family in Moscow and graduated in physics from Moscow State University in 1942. In 1945 he moved to the Lebedev Physics Institute, USSR Academy of Sciences, and successfully defended his doctoral dissertation in physical sciences (DSc). In 1948 he joined those working on the development of a hydrogen bomb and it was successfully tested in 1953. He was elected a member of the USSR Academy of Sciences in the same year. Sakharov supported the Soviet nuclear programme but became concerned about the problems of fall-out and began to advocate the ending of nuclear testing. This was adopted internationally in 1958 but in 1961 KHRUSHCHEV began preparing for more tests in connection with the building of the Berlin Wall. Sakharov warned Khrushchev at a meeting that this was inadvisable because it would set in train another round of the arms race and anti-missile defence systems. Khrushchev's reply was that foreign policy should be left to the experts. In the 1960s he became involved in the dissident movement through his second wife, Elena BONNER. He published an article in 1968 in the west advocating close Soviet–American co-operation and a convergence of the two social systems. This resulted in his removal from secret work but he carried on research at the Lebedev Institute on other matters. He actively supported human rights in the 1970s and was awarded the Nobel Peace Prize, 1975. He provided details of cases which could be used abroad to apply pressure on the Soviet authorities. He was a thorn in the flesh of Yury ANDROPOV but he could not be jailed as American scientists warned that such action would lead to a curtailment of scientific contacts between the two countries. Andropov came up with the astute solution of exiling Sakharov to Gorky (now Nizhny Novgorod) in January 1980, which, as a closed city, could not be visited by the western media. His wife acted as his conduit with the outside world. Gorbachev needed the intelligentsia on his side against the bureaucrats during glasnost and invited Sakharov back to Moscow in December 1986. Sakharov gave qualified support but wanted more radical reforms. The European Union founded the Sakharov Prize for the Defence of Human Rights in 1987. He was elected to the USSR Congress of People's Deputies and became a leading democrat, condemning, for instance, the war in Afghanistan. He enjoyed immense moral authority. His fellow scientists regarded him as often politically naïve. Andrei Sakharov: *Memoirs,* New York, 1990; *Moscow and Beyond*, New York, 1991; *Thoughts on Progress, Peaceful Co-existence and Intellectual Freedom,* London, 1968.

Semichastny, Vladimir Efimovich (*b.* 1924), always regarded as close to Aleksandr SHELEPIN, he was born into a Russian family in Ukraine and was first secretary, Ukrainian Komsomol, 1947–50. He then moved to Moscow to the All-Union Komsomol and forged close relations with Shelepin whom he succeeded as head of the Komsomol. His most important advancement was in 1961 when KHRUSHCHEV chose him to succeed Shelepin as head of the KGB. As such he was the controller of many Soviet spies, including George Blake. His willingness to side with BREZHNEV in 1964 sealed Khrushchev's fate but in 1967 he was demoted to become deputy chair of the Ukrainian Council of Ministers. This may have been connected with his closeness to Shelepin who was regarded as dangerously ambitious by Brezhnev. In the late 1980s Semichastny gave vent to his resentment against Brezhnev.

Serov, General Ivan Aleksandrovich (*b.* 1905), a blood-stained, ruthless political policeman who was personally responsible for many mass deportations and murders. He joined the Red Army in 1923, graduated from the Military Academy, transferred to the People's Commissariat of Internal Affairs (NKVD) in 1939 and was responsible for the mass deportations from the Baltic states after

they fell under Soviet control in 1940. He then became People's Commissar for Internal Affairs in Ukraine until 1941 under KHRUSHCHEV who trusted and valued him. As such he masterminded the deportation of about 3.5 million Ukrainians and Poles to labour camps in the east. In 1941 he was appointed deputy People's Commissar for State Security under BERIA and was responsible for the deportation of over fifty nationalities, including Chechens, Ingushi, Kabardins, Balkars and Crimean Tatars, to Kazakhstan and Siberia. They were accused of collaborating with the enemy (these charges were later judged unfounded and they were all rehabilitated, beginning in 1956). All, except the Crimean Tatars and Germans (deported in August 1941), were allowed to return to their previous homes. Serov was deputy supreme commander of Soviet Forces in (east) Germany, 1945–7, and head of the Smersh (death to spies) organisation. He played an important role in Stalinising eastern Germany (it is estimated that 43,000 east Germans perished in camps, 1945–50). Close to Khrushchev, he took part in the arrest of Beria in June 1953. Khrushchev then appointed him head of the KGB in March 1954, remarking in his memoirs that he turned down another candidate because he did not know him personally. Serov was sent ahead to London to prepare the ground for the BULGANIN and Khrushchev visit in 1956 but the British tabloid press gave him such a roasting (because of his unsavoury background) that he was hastily withdrawn. He played an important role in the suppression of the Hungarian Revolution of 1956. During Khrushchev's struggle with the Anti-Party Group in July 1957 Serov stayed loyal and helped to bring the First Secretary's supporters in the Central Committee to Moscow to overturn the anti-Khrushchev vote in the Presidium (Politburo). In December 1958 he was removed as head of the KGB, being succeeded by Aleksandr SHELEPIN, and made head of Soviet military intelligence (GRU). He lost his post as head of GRU in 1963 in the wake of the PENKOVSKY affair. According to one source, he was expelled from the Party in spring 1965, under BREZHNEV, for crimes committed during the STALIN and Khrushchev eras.

Shafarevich, Igor Rostislavovich (*b.* 1923), a brilliant mathematician who became involved in the human rights movement in the 1960s and was particularly concerned with the rights of believers. He was born into a Jewish family in Zhitomir, Ukraine, and graduated in mathematics from Moscow State University, 1940, at the age of seventeen. He began teaching algebra at Moscow State University, 1946, and was also senior scientific assistant at the Mathematics Institute, USSR Academy of Sciences, 1947–60. From 1960 he was also head of the department of algebra, Steklov Mathematics Institute, USSR Academy of Sciences. He successfully defended his doctoral dissertation in mathematical physics (DSc). He was elected a corresponding member of the USSR Academy of Sciences, 1958, but had to wait over thirty years to be elected a full member. He was awarded the Lenin Prize, 1959, and is a foreign member of the American National Academy of Science and the Royal Society, among others. A story circulated that he informed his class that three students had come to him and said that they actually understood his course. One was called Kazhdan and the other two Bernshtein. (All three later became prominent mathematicians.) In the mid-1960s Shafarevich was a member of the committee for the defence of human rights and worked closely with Andrei SAKHAROV and Aleksandr SOLZHENITSYN. He lost his position at Moscow State University in 1974. He wrote prolifically, including a study of Soviet law on religion and a history of socialism which described it as mankind's death wish: it was published

in France in 1977. His *Russophobia*, published in West Germany, 1988, is regarded by many critics as anti-Semitic. The Moscow mathematics community and others were appalled to find Shafarevich among the 'national patriots' and the most extreme anti-Semites. He was a member of the political council of the Russian nationalist Front for National Salvation.

Shaimiev, Mintimer Sharipovich (*b.* 1937), the first President of independent Tatarstan, he has proved a skilful politician in balancing the interests of his republic and Moscow. He was born into a Tatar family in Aktanyshsky raion, Tatarstan, graduated from the Kazan Agricultural Institute, 1959, and worked as an agricultural engineer. He joined the Communist Party in 1963. In 1967 he was an instructor and deputy head of the agricultural department, Tatar Party obkom, in 1969 he was appointed Minister for Amelioration and Water Economy of his republic and in 1983 he became first deputy chair, Tatar Council of Ministers. In September 1989 he became first secretary, Tatar obkom, or Party leader of his republic. He was elected to the USSR Congress of People's Deputies, 1989, and in April 1990 he was elected speaker of the Tatar Supreme Soviet. On 31 August 1990 the Supreme Soviet proclaimed the sovereignty of Tatarstan. On 12 June 1991 he was elected unopposed President of the Tatar Soviet Socialist Republic and as President issued a declaration during the attempted coup of August 1991 supporting the position of the Emergency Committee. Despite this he skilfully extricated himself and remained President, gradually becoming a staunch defender of Tatar interests *vis-à-vis* Moscow.

Shakhnazarov, Georgy Khosroevich (*b.* 1924), an Armenian, he became a close adviser of GORBACHEV during perestroika and was with him at Foros.

He was born in Baku, served in the Red Army during the Great Fatherland War and then studied at the Moscow Institute of Law. He successfully defended his candidate dissertation (LLM) and his doctorate in law (LLD) and was elected a corresponding member of the USSR Academy of Sciences in 1987. Fedor BURLATSKY and he advocated the development of political science in the Soviet Union and a greater flow of information to Soviet citizens. Shakhnazarov was elected president of the Soviet Association of Political Sciences, 1974, and was also vice-president of the International Political Science Association, 1974–88. His main career has been in the Central Committee Secretariat. He was brought into the department for liaison with communist and workers' parties of socialist countries by Yury ANDROPOV, was deputy head of the department between 1972 and 1986, and from 1986 to 1988, first deputy head. Then he became a full-time adviser to Gorbachev. He was elected to the USSR Congress of People's Deputies and the USSR Supreme Soviet. Karen Shakhnazarov, the film director, is his daughter.

Shakhrai Sergei Mikhailovich (*b.* 1956), a leading politician and lawyer of the later GORBACHEV era and independent Russia, he was born into a Russian family of Cossack background in Simferopol, Crimea, and graduated in law from Rostov-on-Don State University in 1978. He successfully presented his candidate dissertation (LLM) in 1981. He was a member of the law faculty, Moscow State University, 1982–4, specialising in the problems of federal, multinational states. From 1987 he had his own laboratory on legal information and cybernetics in the law faculty, Moscow State University. He invented the electronic voting system used by the USSR Supreme Soviet. He was elected to the RSFSR Congress of People's Deputies and the RSFSR Supreme Soviet

and in July 1990 was elected chair of the Supreme Soviet committee on law. When Boris YELTSIN was speaker of the RSFSR Supreme Soviet he nominated Shakhrai several times for the post of deputy speaker but he never received the requisite number of votes. He resigned from the Communist Party in August 1991. In December 1991 he was appointed deputy Prime Minister of the Russian Federation to supervise the Ministry of Justice, the agency of federal security, the Ministry of Internal Affairs and the state committee on nationality policy. Also in December 1991 he was made head of the state legal administration, subordinate only to the President. In November 1992 he succeeded Valery Tishkov as chair of the state committee on nationality policy.

Shaposhnikov, Marshal Boris Mikhailovich (1882–1945), a brilliant military thinker whose advice was consistently overruled by STALIN, to the Red Army's cost, during the Great Fatherland War. He graduated from the Academy of the General Staff in 1910 and rose to the rank of colonel during the First World War before joining the Red Army in 1918. He was commander of the Leningrad and Moscow military districts, 1925–8 and Chief of Staff of the Red Army, 1928–31. Then he became head of the Frunze Military Academy, until 1935. In 1937 he again became Chief of the General Staff. Unlike practically all other former Tsarist officers in the Red Army, he survived the purges and was elected a candidate member of the Central Committee of the Communist Party in 1939. In 1940 he became a deputy People's Commissar for Defence and head of Stavka (Staff Headquarters), with ZHUKOV as his deputy and in August assumed overall charge for fortifications. He proposed that the Red Army be withdrawn behind fortifications, the Stalin Line, rather than being thinly spread out. Stalin turned this down (fortifications had failed in 1914). Shaposhnikov was dismissed and replaced by MERETSKOV. In July 1941 Stalin reorganised Stavka and Shaposhnikov was again made Chief of the General Staff. Again he argued in favour of strategic withdrawal and again Stalin overruled him. After falling ill, he was replaced by VASILEVSKY but contributed to the defence of Moscow. In June 1942 Shaposhnikov again counselled against the Kharkov offensive, regarding it as premature, preferring strategic defence. Stalin pressed on with the offensive which turned into a disaster. Also in June 1942 he was again made a deputy People's Commissar for Defence. In June 1943 he became commandant of the Academy of the General Staff and died in that post. He wrote prolifically and had a considerable, if belated, influence on Soviet military thinking.

Shaposhnikov, Marshal Evgeny Ivanovich (*b.* 1942), a nephew of Marshal Boris SHAPOSHNIKOV, he supported President YELTSIN during the attempted coup of August 1991 and afterwards became USSR Minister of Defence. He was born into a Russian family in Rostov oblast and graduated from the Kherson Higher Military Aviation Technical School for aviation pilots, 1963, the Air Force Academy, 1969, and the Military Academy of the General Staff, 1984. He joined the Communist Party in 1963, and left in August 1991. He developed a reputation as an ace pilot and in 1988 was appointed first deputy commander-in-chief of the air force and in June 1990 commander-in-chief and deputy USSR Minister of Defence. He was elected to the Central Committee at the XXVIIIth Party Congress, July 1990. In August 1991 he refused to use the air force to implement the decisions of the Emergency Committee. After the failure of the coup he was appointed USSR Minister of Defence. In February 1992 he was appointed commander-in-chief of the Unified Armed Forces of the Commonwealth of Independent States.

Shatalin, Stanislav Sergeevich (*b.* 1934), the 500-day programme, drafted by Shatalin and YAVLINSKY, was the most radical attempt at economic reform in the perestroika era. A brilliant, independently minded economist, he was at the heart of efforts to improve the efficiency of the Soviet economy from KOSYGIN to GORBACHEV. He was born into a Russian family in Pushkino, Leningrad oblast and graduated in economics from Moscow State University in 1958. His father was a Bolshevik commissar and his uncle, N. N. Shatalin was a Central Committee secretary during the 1950s. Shatalin joined the Communist Party in 1962. He joined the scientific research department of USSR Gosplan, 1959, and he successfully defended his candidate dissertation (PhD (Econ)) in 1964, and his doctoral dissertation in 1971. In 1965 he was appointed deputy director of the Central Mathematical Economics Institute, USSR Academy of Sciences, and in 1969 he and B. Mikhailevsky forwarded to Aleksei Kosygin, USSR Prime Minister, an analysis of the Soviet economy but he was almost expelled from the Party for his efforts. In May 1970 he became head of the department of mathematical methods for economic analysis, Moscow State University, and exercised a considerable influence on new generations of economists. In 1974 he was elected a corresponding member of the USSR Academy of Sciences and in 1987 a full member. From 1976 he worked on systems modelling of social and economic processes. In 1978 he lost his position as deputy director of the All-Union Scientific Research Institute for Systems Research because too many of his assistants (twenty-four) had emigrated to Israel and the United States. In 1983 he became a member of the working group, set up by ANDROPOV, on improving the management of the national economy. In 1986 he delivered a paper at a conference on systems modelling and drew the conclusion that the Soviet system should change. He became personally acquainted with Mikhail Gorbachev in 1989 and in February 1990, at a Central Committee plenum, he criticised the economic programme of the CPSU, prepared for the XXVIIIth Congress. He was made a member of the Presidential Council in 1990. During the summer of 1990 he headed the working group which drafted the 500-day programme which envisaged moving from a planned to a market economy in that time. However, the programme was too radical for Gorbachev. After the tragic events of Vilnius in January 1991 Shatalin resigned from the CPSU. He acted as an agent for YELTSIN during the Russian presidential campaign and in June 1991 he joined the Democratic Party of Russia. In July 1991 he became co-chairman of the Movement for Democratic Reforms (International).

Shaumyan, Stepan Georgevich (1878–1918), born into an Armenian merchant's family in Tbilisi, Georgia, Shaumyan joined the RSDRP in 1901 while a student at Riga Polytechnic, being subsequently expelled for revolutionary activities. He was exiled to the Caucasus but soon made for Berlin where he continued his formal education. He also became involved in social democracy there but his meetings with PLE-KHANOV and LENIN in Switzerland led to him becoming a disciple of Lenin. Dubbed later the Lenin of the Caucasus, Shaumyan returned to Tbilisi and headed the Bolshevik organisation there. In 1907 he moved to Baku and played an active role in developing the workers' movement there. He was arrested in 1909 and was in and out of exile until 1914 when he was packed off to Saratov. After the February Revolution he returned to Baku and was elected chair of the Baku

Soviet. He was an ardent promoter of the Bolshevik cause in the Caucasus and played a leading role in the establishment of Soviet power there. He was chair of the Baku Military Revolutionary Committee, was chair of the Baku Sovnarkom and Commissar for Foreign Affairs. He was elected to the Central Committee of the Communist Party in 1918. He played a leading role in the establishment of the Baku Commune and the Republic of Azerbaijan. Shaumyan and the Bolsheviks were vigorously opposed by various factions, primarily the Mussavats who favoured a Muslim federation, linking up with Turkey. The situation became tense and the Baku Soviet, overruling the objections of Shaumyan and the Bolsheviks, appealed to British troops, stationed in north Persia, to come to their aid. Shaumyan and twenty-five other Baku commissars fled but were captured near Krasnovodsk by forces loyal to the Menshevik government of Trans-Caspia. The Menshevik authorities enquired of General Malleson, whose mission was 400 miles away at Meshed, what should be done with the prisoners. The general was ill at the time and decided that the Russian authorities themselves should decide the prisoners' fate. A more astute move on his part would have been to request their handing over to the British authorities to be used as hostages and exchanged for British prisoners. The Mensheviks executed the prisoners (only about half of them were commissars, the others being drivers and the like) in Krasnovodsk. Shaumyan was later glorified as a martyr to the Bolshevik cause in books and films.

Shchelokov, General Nikolai Anisimovich (1910–84), a close confidant of BREZHNEV. While head of the Ministry of Internal Affairs he became lax and permitted the spread of corruption, becoming himself embroiled in it. He was born into a Ukrainian family in Almaznaya, joined the Communist Party in

1931, and graduated from the Dnepropetrovsk Metallurgical Institute in 1933. He served as a political commissar in the Red Army, 1941–6, and moved in 1951 to Moldavia when Leonid Brezhnev was first secretary, Communist Party of Moldavia. He also worked with Konstantin CHERNENKO there. Shchelokov occupied many important positions in the Moldovian government and Party before Brezhnev called him to Moscow in 1966 to become USSR Minister for the Maintenance of Public Order; when the ministry was reorganised as the USSR Ministry of Internal Affairs in 1968 Shchelokov became the minister. He was elected a full member of the Party Central Committee in April 1968 and was promoted general in 1976. ANDROPOV, head of the KGB, was incapable of moving against Shchelokov until Brezhnev died. Shchelokov was forced into retirement in December 1982 (his son, who was a senior official in the Komsomol was also sent packing) and in June 1983 he was expelled from the Central Committee, with his past becoming the subject of an investigation. The ill Chernenko could not protect him and in November 1984 he was accused at a session of the USSR Supreme Soviet of bringing the rank of army general into disrepute and subsequently he was stripped of it. He died shortly afterwards, probably by his own hand.

Shcherbitsky, Vladimir Vasilevich (1918–90), a close ally of Leonid BREZHNEV, he was Party leader in Ukraine well into the GORBACHEV era. He was born into a Ukrainian family in Dnepropetrovsk oblast and graduated from the Dnepropetrovsk Institute of Chemical Technology, 1941, the year he joined the Communist Party. He then served in the Red Army until 1945. His Party career began in 1948 in Dnepropetrovsk (Brezhnev's home base) and in 1955 he became first secretary, Dnepropetrovsk obkom. He was elected a candidate

member of the Presidium (Politburo) but KHRUSHCHEV demoted him in 1963. However, when Brezhnev succeeded Khrushchev in 1964 things brightened and his candidate membership of the Central Committee was restored in 1965, becoming a full member of the Politburo in 1971. In 1972 he succeeded the less than strict Petr SHELEST as first secretary, Communist Party of Ukraine. He immediately moved against manifestations of Ukrainian nationalism but charges of corruption were not levelled at him later. When Gorbachev came to power in March 1985 Shcherbitsky was astute enough to support all the new leader's initiatives but there was little perestroika in Ukraine. Gorbachev was frustrated by the fact that Shcherbitsky's subordinates in Ukraine were mostly his appointees and feared that his removal would lead to their dismissal. It was only in September 1989 that Gorbachev was able to remove him as first secretary, less than a year before he died.

Sheinis, Viktor Leonidovich (b. 1931), a committed supporter of perestroika who became an active politician in independent Russia. He was born into a Jewish family in Kiev and graduated from Leningrad State University, 1953. He worked on the shop floor of the Kirov factory in Leningrad, 1958–64, following conflict with the authorities in his academic post. He then became a postgraduate in the department of economics of contemporary capitalism, Leningrad State University, and successfully presented his candidate dissertation (PhD (Econ)), 1966, and his doctorate (DSc (Econ)), 1982. He joined the Institute of the World Economy and International Relations, USSR Academy of Sciences, 1975, and wrote and published prolifically. He was elected to the RSFSR Congress of People's Deputies and the RSFSR Supreme Soviet in 1990. During the election Sheinis was supported by Democratic Russia (DemRossiya) and the Moscow

Memorial Society. He was one of the fifty-four deputies who collectively resigned from the Communist Party in July 1990.

Shelepin, Aleksandr Nikolaevich (1918–94), born on 18 August 1918, Shelepin was a ruthlessly ambitious politician, schooled under STALIN, who never hid his talents under a bushel. He became the archetypal Soviet politician, heavy handed, domineering and capable of arousing awe and revulsion in his subordinates and ideological foes. KHRUSHCHEV used him to bring the KGB under political control but he became one of the organisers of the coup which removed him in October 1964. Rumours circulated that Shelepin had been promised the post of First Secretary but this was eventually filled by Leonid BREZHNEV. If this is so he was double-crossed by Brezhnev and the other conspirators, who included the then head of the KGB SEMICHASTNY, on the grounds that he was potentially too dangerous to exclude from the plot. The Politburo was aware that Shelepin's reputation in the western world was similar to that of Genghis Khan and Himmler. As head of the Soviet trade unions he attended a get-together in Geneva in 1975 and Len Murray, TUC general secretary, invited him to Britain. Shelepin must have been mindful of the treatment handed out by the tabloid press to his KGB predecessor General Ivan SEROV when he had arrived in London to oversee preparations for the visit of BULGANIN and Khrushchev in 1956. The violent attacks on him resulted in his immediate recall. It is tempting to see Shelepin being thrown to the London lions by Brezhnev and his colleagues. The predictable happened and Shelepin was pinned in Transport House with the embarrassed Len Murray failing to raise the siege. When he returned to Moscow he was dismissed from the Politburo and disappeared into political oblivion. Given the opportunity to give his side of

the story in and after 1991 he chose to remain silent. A broken man, he had no fight or ambition left in him. Shelepin was born into a Russian family in Voronezh, south-east of Moscow. He studied at the Moscow Institute of History, Philosophy and Literature, 1936–9. He saw war service during the Soviet–Finnish War, 1939–40, and became a member of the Communist Party of the Soviet Union in 1940. He became first secretary of the Komsomol in 1952 and was responsible for the sixth World Youth Festival in Moscow in 1957 which made a lasting impression on many Russians. Khrushchev chose him to succeed Serov in 1958 as head of the KGB. He thus became the first non-professional political policeman to take over since the early Stalin days. As KGB chief Shelepin was keen to make the Soviet Union 'safe for socialist democracy' and was the scourge of the emerging Soviet dissident movement. He sent his hit men abroad and among their victims was BANDERA, the Ukrainian nationalist leader, in Munich. He also dispatched Rudolph ABEL to spy in the United States. Shelepin brought many university graduates into the KGB in an attempt to change its image. Khrushchev made him chair of the newly created Party-state control commission which oversaw the police, legal and juridical agencies in 1961. In 1963, thinking about a successor, Khrushchev decided Shelepin lacked industrial experience and offered him the Party leadership of Leningrad oblast. Shelepin turned it down, regarding it as a demotion. Khrushchev realised that he had misjudged the man. After Khrushchev was ousted Shelepin was a vigorous advocate of campaigns against political dissidents and Jews but in December 1965 the new regime cut the ground from under him. It abolished the Party-state control commission. He thereby lost his post as a deputy Prime Minister. Worse was to come at the XXIIIrd Party Congress in 1966. It failed to re-elect him as a secretary of the

Central Committee. His new post, chair of the All-Union Central Council of Trades Unions, was insufficiently senior for him to remain in the CC Secretariat. However, he retained his Politburo seat until 1975.

Shelest, Petr Efimovich (*b.* 1908), a close ally of KHRUSHCHEV, Shelest had to cope with the increasing resentment of the Ukrainian intelligentsia at what it regarded as Russification. Under Khrushchev this was not a problem but it became one under BREZHNEV who regarded Shelest as too lax in combating Ukrainian nationalism. Shelest was born into a Ukrainian family and joined the Communist Party in 1928. He occupied the responsible post of head of the industrial department, Chelyabinsk obkom, 1941 until 1954, when he moved to Kiev, becoming first secretary, Kiev gorkom, 1957. Khrushchev chose him as first secretary, Communist Party of Ukraine, 1963, and in December 1963 he was elected candidate member of the Presidium (Politburo), becoming a full member in November 1964. In the wake of the suppression of the Prague Spring, August 1968, Shelest came down hard on any manifestation of political dissent or democratic thinking but tried to compensate by being more accommodating in cultural affairs. This did not please Brezhnev and he replaced Shelest with SHCHERBITSKY, May 1972, and sacked him from the Politburo, April 1973.

Shenin, Oleg Semonovich (*b.* 1937), one of the top Party officials who sided with the plotters during the attempted coup of August 1991. He was born into a Russian family in Volgograd oblast and graduated from the Krasnoyarsk Mining Technical College, the Tomsk Construction Engineering Institute and the Academy of Social Sciences, CPSU Central Committee. He joined the Communist Party in 1969. He was a construction engineer in Krasnoyarsk krai until 1974

when he moved into Party work, eventually becoming first secretary, Krasnoyarsk kraikom and simultaneously chair, Krasnoyarsk krai soviet executive committee, until 1990. He was then elected a Central Committee secretary responsible for Party cadres. He was elected to the USSR Congress of People's Deputies and the USSR Supreme Soviet in 1989. He was a member of the Russian Bureau of the CPSU Central Committee, December 1989–June 1990, when he joined the newly founded Russian Communist Party. He was elected to the Politburo in July 1990. In his memoirs GORBACHEV admits that he completely misjudged Shenin and that his remarkably fast promotion was due to his ability to give the impression that he was a reformer. He was arrested after the failure of the coup but was later amnestied by the Russian Duma.

Shevardnadze, Eduard Amvrosievich (*b.* 1928), GORBACHEV's Foreign Minister who was responsible for implementing the new political thinking abroad until he resigned in December 1990, warning about the possibility of a right-wing coup. He was born into a Georgian family in Mamati, Georgia, and graduated from the Party School of the Georgian Central Committee, 1951, and the Kutaisi Pedagogical Institute, 1959. He joined the Communist Party, 1948, and in 1957 he became first secretary of the Georgian Komsomol. In 1961 he moved across into the Party apparatus: in 1964 he was appointed first deputy Minister, and the following year Minister for the Protection of Public Order (later titled Minister of Internal Affairs). This post involved combating crime (excluding political offences): a formidable task at a time when the first Party secretary, V. P. MZHAVANADZE, was the godfather of Georgia. Shevardnadze collected information on the godfather's activities, showed it to BREZHNEV and was rewarded by being given Mzhavanadze's post. He now acted swiftly against his predecessor's appointees and did his best to clean up the republic. He had had professional contacts with Gorbachev in neighbouring Stavropol krai since the 1960s. Shevardnadze was elected to the CPSU Central Committee, 1976, and a candidate member of the Politburo, 1978. In March 1985 he was a staunch supporter of Gorbachev and soon became a full member of the Politburo. Gorbachev astonished the world in July 1985 when Shevardnadze replaced Andrei GROMYKO as Soviet Foreign Minister. After all, Shevardnadze knew no foreign languages other than Russian and had no diplomatic experience. However, he soon proved an excellent advocate for the new political thinking. He was a welcome change from 'Grim Grom' Gromyko and added a dash of flair to diplomacy. He became a member of the Presidential Council, March 1990, but left the Politburo in July of that year, when it was reorganised to include only Party officials. He resigned from the Communist Party in June 1991 but remained loyal to President Gorbachev after the failed August 1991 coup and was reapppointed Soviet Foreign Minister in November 1991. However, the Soviet Union was dissolved the following month. He then returned to Georgia where he later became head of state. Eduard Shevardnadze: *The Future Belongs to Freedom*, New York, 1991.

Shevchenko, Valentina Semenovna (*b.* 1935), the first woman ever to be elected to the Bureau (Politburo) of the Communist Party of Ukraine (CPUk), she was born into a Ukrainian family in Kiev and graduated from Kiev University. After moving from the Komsomol to the Party apparatus she advanced in March 1985 to the Bureau of the CPUk and in 1986 she was elected to the CPSU Central Committee. She was elected to the USSR Congress of People's Deputies and the USSR Supreme Soviet

in 1989. She was chair of the Presidium of the Ukrainian Supreme Soviet (head of state) and vice-chair of the Presidium of the USSR Supreme Soviet (GORBACHEV was chair), 1989–91.

Shlyapnikov, Aleksandr Gavrilovich (1885–1937), a leading figure in the workers' opposition which advocated that industry should be under the control of the trade unions but led by Bolshevik workers. At the Xth Party Congress in 1921 it was branded a 'syndicalist and anarchical deviation' in the Bolshevik Party by LENIN and the propagation of its views was declared to be incompatible with membership of the Communist Party. The term workers' opposition was an insult hurled by Lenin at Shlyapnikov, KOLLONTAI (who had become Shlyapnikov's lover) and others. Shlyapnikov was one of the few leading Bolsheviks with impeccably proletarian credentials. He came from a family of Old Believers and lost his father at the age of two. He had little schooling but considerable ability. He became a skilled mechanic and, beginning in 1908, worked in France, Germany and Britain (where he worked in the Hendon aircraft works), learning reasonable French and some German and English. He had thrown in his lot early with the Bolsheviks and returned to the Russian capital as a Bolshevik organiser in 1914 but was dispatched to Stockholm in October 1914 to operate as courier between Switzerland and Russia. Shlyapnikov asked Lenin to move to Scandinavia to ease contacts with Petrograd but then he (and Kollontai) simply moved to Oslo and left the Bolshevik links with Petrograd in ruins. However, Shlyapnikov returned to Stockholm and continued his runs to Petrograd. He found the constant wrangling between Lenin and other Bolsheviks very irksome and was especially annoyed at Lenin's treatment of BUKHARIN. Shlyapnikov was one of the few Bolsheviks in Petrograd when the February Revolution broke out and the Russian Bureau of the Central Committee of the Bolshevik Party, guided by him, appealed for the formation of a provisional revolutionary socialist government and denied any support to the provisional government. This found little support and when STALIN and KAMENEV returned from exile and advocated conditional support of the provisional government, Shlyapnikov could do little but protest. Meanwhile, he was active in the trade union movement and became president of the Metalworkers' Union. He became the first Commissar for Labour but was in favour of a coalition socialist government. He was no match for Lenin as a theorist and administrator and his advocacy of the trade unions as the dominant force in the control of industry riled Lenin, leading them eventually to fall out. The devastating defeat of the workers' opposition at the Xth Party Congress effectively ended Shlyapnikov's political career. He followed the usual path for defeated politicians at that time and was dispatched to Paris to play the diplomat. He later published two books on 1917 which have retained their significance. He was expelled from the Party in 1933, arrested in 1935 and died in prison in 1937. Michael Futrell: *Northern Underground*, London, 1963; Leonard Schapiro: *The Origin of the Communist Autocracy*, London, 1955.

Shmelev, Nikolai Petrovich (*b.* 1936), one of the most radical economists during perestroika, he was born in Moscow and graduated from the economics faculty of Moscow State University. He successfully defended his candidate dissertation (PhD (Econ)), 1961, and his doctoral dissertation (DSc (Econ)), 1968. His first wife was the granddaughter of Nikita KHRUSHCHEV, who had lived with the Khrushchev family after her father was killed on active service during the war and her mother arrested. In 1958 he joined the Institute of Economics, USSR

Academy of Sciences, and in 1961 he moved to the Institute of Economics of the World Socialist System, USSR Academy of Sciences. He joined the Communist Party in 1962. In 1982 he moved to the USA and Canada Institute, USSR Academy of Sciences, headed by ARBATOV, and specialised in the impact of the United States on the world economy. Since his student days he had written fiction but the first short story, *Pashkov Dom* (*Pashkov's House*), was only published in *Znamya* in 1987. The same year he published a devastating critique of the Soviet planned economy and demolished the myth that it had been very successful. He was elected to the USSR Congress of People's Deputies and the USSR Supreme Soviet (on the USSR Academy of Scientists' list). He was a member of the SHATALIN-YAVLINSKY group which drafted the 500-day programme for GORBACHEV. Shmelev argued that anything that is economically effective is moral. In 1992 he moved to Sweden to work on the Russian and east European economies.

Shokhin, Aleksandr Nikolaevich (*b.* 1951), a very able economist who became an influential minister under YELTSIN. He was born into a Russian family in Arkhangelsk oblast and graduated in economics from Moscow State University, 1974, and then worked in a variety of scientific institutes, including the Gosplan Scientific Research Institute of Economics and the USSR State Committee on Labour. Finally he was head of the laboratory of the Institute of Economics and Forecasting of Scientific-technical Progress, USSR Academy of Sciences, where he worked with Egor GAIDAR. Shokhin successfully presented his candidate dissertation in economics (PhD (Econ)), and his doctoral dissertation in economics (DSc (Econ)) in 1989. In 1987 he became an adviser to Eduard SHEVARDNADZE, USSR Minister of Foreign Affairs, and was later made head of the foreign economic administration of the ministry. He became Russian Minister of Labour on 20 August 1991 in the government headed by Ivan SILAEV. In November 1991 he became Russian Minister of Labour and Employment, having been proposed by the Social Democratic Party of Russia, even though he was not a member. He accepted their nomination but informed the Social Democrats that he would not represent their interests as minister but would act as a non-party member of the government. Shokhin was appointed deputy Russian Prime Minister. He is a member of the dazzling group of economists around Gaidar who rose to prominence with the advent of a market economy. He was formerly a member of the Communist Party.

Sholokhov, Mikhail Aleksandrovich (1905–84), a highly successful Soviet author who will always be remembered for his novel, *Quietly Flows the Don*, and was awarded the Nobel Prize for Literature in 1965. He was born into a Russian family (even though he wrote about Cossacks he was not one himself) in Rostov oblast. After the October Revolution he helped confiscate grain from peasants. He emerged as a writer during the mid-1920s (*Donskie Rasskazy* (*Tales of the Don*), 1925). His masterpiece, *Quietly Flows the Don*, was written between 1928 and 1932, became a classic and made him a favourite of STALIN who ensured that he lived in splendour. It recounts the role of the Cossacks during the October Revolution and Civil War and is not totally biased in favour of the Reds. He joined the Communist Party, 1932, and was showered with awards, including the Lenin and Stalin Prizes. His novel *Virgin Soil Upturned*, was published in two parts, the first in 1932 and the second in 1960, because of problems of interpretation. Sholokhov accepted the Nobel Prize for Literature although he had attacked PASTERNAK for doing so in 1958. He also demanded the execution

of SINYAVSKY and DANIEL during their trial in 1965. Controversy surrounded the authorship of *Quietly Flows the Don* with some critics claiming that it had really been written by Fedor Kryukov.

Shostakovich, Dmitry Dmitrievich (1906–75), a great Russian composer, with an international reputation, who managed to continue composing Russian music while appearing loyal to the Stalinist regime. He was involved in many conflicts with the official cultural norms of the regime but managed to retain his creative talents undimmed. The Party expected great things from him including the glorification of the achievements of the Five Year Plans. He composed his first opera *The Nose* (based on Gogol's story) in 1928. His *Lady Macbeth of Mtsensk* (reworked as *Ekaterina Izmailova*) was attacked as a 'mess instead of music', probably the result of STALIN's anger on hearing the work. It was declared formalistic (and hence to be banned) and this led to a large-scale campaign against formalism and ideological deviation in all areas of culture. He was saved from imprisonment in 1937 by the arrest of his investigator. Shostakovich composed his great seventh symphony (the Leningrad Symphony) to commemorate the resilience of the city under German siege. 'My symphony is about the Leningrad Stalin destroyed and Hitler almost finished off,' he confessed in private. But nothing compared to his travails after the Party decree on music in 1948 which condemned him, KHACHATURYAN and PROKOFIEV, for antipopular formalism. Shostakovich's music was proscribed but he took some revenge by asking ZHDANOV to explain exactly what he meant, so that he could learn how to compose. One of the Party officials at a meeting mispronounced Rimsky-Korsakov's name and Shostakovich worked this into a playful review of Russian music. Only in 1958 were the accusations against him annulled. Despite his conflicts with the regime he was awarded Stalin Prizes in 1941, 1942, 1946, 1950 and 1952. He also received the Lenin Prize in 1958. In 1957 he was elected secretary of the USSR Union of Composers and was elected a deputy of the USSR Supreme Soviet several times. He finally joined the Party in 1960. He was made a People's Artist of the USSR in 1954 and a Hero of Socialist Labour in 1965. Many were disappointed when he signed a letter against Academician Andrei SAKHAROV in 1973. He received an honorary doctorate from the University of Oxford and was a sensitive, emotional man who was nevertheless a master of manoeuvre.

Shtemenko, General Sergei Matveevich (1907–76), a successful military career during the war led to demotion later but his career revived under KHRUSHCHEV. He was of Don Cossack origin and joined the Red Army, 1926, and the Communist Party, 1930. He graduated from the Mechanised Academy of the Red Army, 1937, and the Academy of the General Staff, 1940. He was in the General Staff operations office, 1940–2, and then STALIN promoted him to deputy chief of operations of the General Staff and deputy Chief of the General Staff, 1943–8. He was then promoted to Chief of the General Staff and USSR Minister of the Armed Forces. However, Stalin fell out with him and he was dismissed from his posts and sent to East Germany to be Chief of Staff of Soviet Forces in Germany. His career took off again under Khrushchev and he was Chief of the Main Staff of the Soviet Ground Forces, 1962–5, deputy Chief of the General Staff, 1965–8, and then first deputy Chief of the General Staff. As such he was responsible for the Warsaw Pact forces during their invasion of Czechoslovakia in August 1968.

Shukshin, Vasily Makarovich (1929–74), a multi-talented actor, writer and film director, he was one of the *derevensh-chiki* (village prose) writers who presented the virtues of rural life and morality and the conflicts and tensions which arose between rural and urban dwellers. He was born into a Russian family in Siberia and graduated from the State Film School, Moscow, 1960, as a director. He also acted and became famous for his short stories in *Novy Mir*. His most popular film was *Kalina Krasnaya* (*The Red Snowball Tree*), based on his own story and in which he also acted. It described the life of a criminal attempting to go straight by working on a collective farm. He published a novel about Stenka Razin, the famous rebel and Cossack leader and was very keen to turn it into a film but the authorities would never give permission. Perhaps this had to do with the title, *I Came to Give You Freedom*. His death, due to a heart attack, was felt as a national tragedy.

Shumeiko, Vladimir Filippovich (*b.* 1945), a pro-reform politician whose career rise since 1990 has been meteoric. He was born in Rostov-on-Don into a Russian family of Cossack origin and entered the Rostov Polytechnic Institute, 1963, before doing his national service in the Red Army, then returning to complete his studies, eventually successfully presenting his candidate dissertation in technical sciences (PhD (Eng)). In 1985 he became chief designer in the Krasnodar electrical measuring instruments enterprise and was elected general director in January 1989. He was elected to the RSFSR Congress of People's Deputies and RSFSR Supreme Soviet and was active in the Communists of Russia faction. He was deputy chair (speaker) of the Russian parliament. He resigned from the Communist Party in August 1991. From June–December 1992 he was first deputy Prime Minister of Russia.

Shushkevich, Stanislav Stanislavovich (Suskevic, Stanislau Stanislaujevic in

Belarusian) (*b.* 1939), together with Boris YELTSIN (Russia), Leonid KRAVCHUK (Ukraine), Shushevich (Belorussia) signed the document which dissolved the Soviet Union and established the Commonwealth of Independent States (CIS) in the Belovezh Forest (near Minsk) on 8 December 1991. Minsk was declared the capital of the CIS. He was born into a Belorussian family and his father was a famous poet who suffered imprisonment under STALIN. Shushkevich graduated in physics and mathematics from Minsk State University, 1957, and then became a postgraduate student at the Institute of Physics, Belorussian Academy of Sciences. He was pro-rector for science, Minsk Radiotechnical Institute, 1967–9, and pro-rector of the Minsk State University, 1986–90. He was elected to the Belorussian Supreme Soviet and became first deputy chair (speaker). In September 1991 he was elected speaker of the Supreme Soviet of the Republic of Belorussia. Since the republic had decided not to adopt a presidential system, Shushkevich was head of state. He was elected to the USSR Congress of People's Deputies and the USSR Supreme Soviet in 1989. He was a democrat who favoured Belorussia (it became Belarus after independence) developing as a democratic, market-oriented independent state. However, those who favoured a close relationship with Russia, led by Aleksandr Lukashenko, later took over.

Shvernik, Nikolai Mikhailovich (1888–1970), a tough Stalinist bureaucrat, he was born in St Petersburg, joined the RSDRP, 1905, and participated in the October Revolution. He was elected to the Central Committee, 1925, and became a candidate member of the Politburo, 1939. He was head of the Soviet trade union movement, 1930–44, and chair of the Presidium of the USSR Supreme Soviet (head of state), 1946–53. At the XIXth Party Congress, 1952, he was made a full member of STALIN's

enlarged Presidium (Politburo) but was downgraded to candidate status immediately after Stalin's death in March 1953. Shvernik was one of the panel that condemned Lavrenty BERIA to death in December 1953. He was chair of the Party Control Commission, 1956–66, and in 1957 was restored to full membership of the Presidium. He retired in 1966.

Silaev, Ivan Stepanovich (*b.* 1930), as Prime Minister of the Russian Federation, he sided with YELTSIN during the crucial year 1990–1. He was born in Gorky (now Nizhny Novgorod) oblast into a Russian peasant family, graduated from the Kazan Aviation Institute as an engineer in 1954 and joined the Communist Party in 1959. He began on the shop floor and rose to become director of the Gorky Aviation Enterprise in 1971. He was deputy USSR Minister of the Aviation Industry, 1974–7, first deputy USSR Minister of the Aviation Industry, 1977–80, USSR Minister for Machine Building and Instrument Making, 1980–1, USSR Minister of the Aviation Industry, 1981–5, chair of the bureau of the USSR Council of Ministers for machine building, 1985–90. He was chair of the RSFSR Council of Ministers, June 1990–September 1991. Then he became chair of the Inter-Republican Economic Committee, September–November 1991. From November–December 1991 he was chair of the Inter-State Economic Committee and Prime Minister of the Economic Community. In December 1991 he became the permanent Russian representative to the European Community in Brussels. He was a member of the CPSU Central Committee, 1981–91. His transfer to Brussels in December 1991 revealed that he was not enthusiastic about the shock therapy programme about to be launched in Russia by Egor GAIDAR.

Sinyavsky, Andrei Donatovich (pseudonym Terts, Abram) (*b.* 1925), together with his co-defendant, Yuly DANIEL, he was involved in a famous trial which marked the end of the post-Stalinist 'thaw' in Soviet literature. He was born in Moscow and graduated from Moscow State University, 1952. He was a well-established literary scholar and prose writer when he was arrested in 1965. He was the co-author of a study on the poetry of the early revolutionary years. Yuly Daniel and he sent satirical stories (one was *The Fantastic World of Abram Terts*) abroad under pseudonyms. Other influential works included *What is Socialist Realism*, 1959, and *The Trial Begins*, 1960. His writings fascinated readers but his identity eventually became known and he was arrested in September 1965. Sinyavsky and Daniel's trial became an international *cause célèbre* as it was very well documented and was the first time since the death of STALIN that writers were being sentenced for literary works. Sinyavsky got seven years in a labour camp, February 1966. He was released in 1971 and permitted to emigrate to France, 1973. He became a literary figure in Paris and published his prison journal, *A Voice from the Chorus*, 1973, but he aroused considerable controversy with his literary criticism of the Russian classics, *Walks with Pushkin*, and *In Gogol's Shadow*, 1973. He founded and edited, together with his wife Mariya Rozanova, the journal *Sintaksis*. Sinyavsky also holds the title of professor at the University of Paris, Sorbonne, and he returned to the Soviet Union, 1989, for Yuly Daniel's funeral.

Skokov, Yury Vladimirovich (*b.* 1938), a technocrat, he came to play an important role in Russian security after independence. He was born into a Russian family in Vladivostok where his father was a KGB officer. He graduated from the Leningrad Institute of Electrical Engineering and in 1961 he began working in the No. 2 Scientific Research Institute, USSR Ministry of Defence, Kalinin (Tver). He became a postgraduate student at the Leningrad Institute, 1963, and successfully presented his candidate dissertation in technical sciences on a classified subject (PhD (Eng)). In 1969 he moved to the All-Union Scientific Research Institute of the Sources of Current, Krasnodar, and was acting director of the institute's Saturn experimental enterprise, 1978–86. In 1986 he was appointed general director of the institute and chairman of the board of the Kvantemp Inter-branch Industrial Association, Moscow, the first association to link enterprises in fourteen cities and five Union republics. He was elected to the USSR Congress of People's Deputies and the USSR Supreme Soviet, 1989, but never made a speech. In June 1990 he was made first deputy chair, RSFSR Council of Ministers, and in August 1991 he was a member of YELTSIN's shadow government set up in the Urals. After the resignation of SILAEV's government in late 1991 Skokov was appointed an RSFSR state adviser on security and in May 1992 he was made secretary of the Security Council. He did not support many of President Yeltsin's policies and this led to his dismissal in May 1993.

Skoropadsky, Pavlo Petrovych (1873–1945), he was elected hetman (head of state) of Ukraine in April 1918 when it was under German occupation. Dependent on German help to stay in power, the collapse of Germany hastened his demise and he was defeated by left-wing Ukrainian forces, under Petlyura, in December 1918. Skoropadsky was born in Wiesbaden, Germany, and was descended from Ukrainian Cossacks. He participated in the Russo-Japanese War and was a lieutenant general during the First World War, receiving a commendation for bravery in combat with the Germans. The provisional government appointed him commander of the first Ukrainian corps. He was elected leader of the Ukrainian Free Cossacks in October 1917 which committed itself to the Central

Rada. After his defeat he returned to Germany where he spent the rest of his life.

Skvortsov-Stepanov, Ivan Ivanovich (1870–1928), an important Bolshevik theorist, he was editor of *Izvestiya* from 1925 and deputy editor of *Pravda* from 1927. He was a committed atheist and a natural foe of BOGDANOV and LUNA-CHARSKY and their attempts to retain aspects of the spiritual experience in Marxist ideology. Trained as a teacher, he became a social democrat in 1896. Bogdanov introduced him to the Bolshevik group in Geneva in 1904. He worked for the Bolsheviks in Russia between 1914 and 1917, editing several journals and becoming a leading Bolshevik literary figure. He became leader of the Bolshevik faction in the Moscow City Duma in June 1917 and was a member of the Moscow Revolutionary Committee. He sided with KAMENEV in withholding support for insurrection in October but was nevertheless offered the post of Commissar for Finance in the first Sovnarkom. He never acted as commissar and was replaced by N. R. Menzhinsky in February 1918. He preferred to engage in journalism. He sided with STALIN and BUKHARIN against TROTSKY and in 1925 opposed ZINOVIEV, being appointed editor of *Leningradskaya Pravda*, in Zinoviev's own fiefdom. He re-edited LENIN's works in such a way as to highlight Kamenev's and Zinoviev's disagreements with the Bolshevik leader. He translated and edited Marx's *Das Kapital*. He was elected to the Central Committee in 1925. He died of typhoid in 1928 and is buried in the Kremlin wall.

Slyunkov, Nikolai Nikitovich (*b.* 1929), a top economic official who eventually revealed little enthusiasm for perestroika. He was born into a Belorussian peasant family in Gorodets, Gomel oblast, and then graduated from a technical school. He joined the Communist Party in 1954.

He worked in industry and was director of the Minsk Tractor Plant, one of the largest in the Soviet Union, 1965–71. In 1972 he moved into Party work as first secretary, Minsk gorkom. In 1974 he was appointed deputy chair of USSR Gosplan, responsible for the machine building industry. In 1983 he returned to Belorussia to become first secretary, Communist Party of Belorussia. Slyunkov was elected a candidate member of the Politburo in 1986, in 1987 a secretary of the Central Committee and a full member of the Politburo. In July 1990 he was ousted from the Politburo and the Central Committee. He had worked with RYZHKOV in Gosplan and continued this relationship under GORBACHEV but he came to the same conclusion as Ryzhkov: a radical move to the market would not work. He was elected to the USSR Congress of People's Deputies and the USSR Supreme Soviet in 1989.

Smirnov, Georgy Lukich (*b.* 1922), a leading ideologist during perestroika, he was close to GORBACHEV and helped to introduce fresh ideas to Marxism–Leninism. He was born into a Russian family of Cossack origin in Volgograd oblast, joined the Communist Party, 1943, and began a career in the Komsomol, graduating from the Volgograd Pedagogical Institute, 1952, and from the Academy of Social Sciences, CPSU Central Committee, 1957. He successfully presented his candidate dissertation (PhD) and his doctoral dissertation (DLitt) in philosophy (Marxism–Leninism), 1971. He was a member of the editorial board of *Kommunist*, the Party theoretical journal, 1962–5. Then he joined the department for propaganda, Central Committee Secretariat, and he became head in 1974, succeeding Aleksandr YAKOVLEV as first deputy head. Smirnov was elected a candidate member of the Central Committee, 1976, became an aide to Gorbachev, 1985, and in January 1987 he was appointed director of the Institute of Marxism–Leninism, CPSU Central Committee.

Smyslov, Vasily Vasilevich (*b.* 1921), a great Soviet chess player who was world champion in 1957–8. He revealed precocious talent and became chess champion of Moscow at the age of seventeen. He came second in the world championship in 1948. In 1954 he challenged grandmaster Mikhail BOTVINNIK for the world title and drew with him. This meant that Botvinnik retained his title. However, in 1957 he beat Botvinnik but the latter defeated him the following year to regain his world title. In 1988 he was ranked twentieth in world listings.

Snechkus, Antanas Yuozovich (Snieckus, Antanas in Lithuanian) (1903–74), STALIN's man in Lithuania, he implemented the Sovietisation of his homeland and remained in power until his death, revealing considerable political skill. He was born into a Lithuanian family and joined the Communist Party, 1920 (after it had failed to seize power in Lithuania) and was the communist underground leader in independent Lithuania from 1926. He became first secretary, Communist Party of Lithuania, in 1940, after the incorporation of the republic in the Soviet Union. He was elected a candidate member of the CPSU Central Committee, 1941, and a full member, 1972. Some observers credit him with slowing down immigration into the republic during the post-war years, in striking contrast to the waves of Slavs who moved into Latvia and Estonia.

Snegur, Mircea Ion (*b.* 1940), the first President of independent Moldova who toyed with the idea of union with Romania. He was born into a Moldovan family, graduated from the Kishenev (Chisinau) Agricultural Institute, 1961, and joined the Communist Party of Moldavia, 1964. He successfully presented his candidate dissertation in natural sciences (PhD). He was head of the main administration of the Moldavian Ministry of Agriculture, 1973–8, and was general director of the Selektsiya Scientific Production Association, Ministry of Agriculture, 1978–81. In this post he would have had contact with Mikhail GORBACHEV, who was then Central Committee secretary for agriculture. Snegur moved into the Party apparatus in 1981 and in May 1985 he became a secretary of the Central Committee, Communist Party of Moldavia. In 1989 the Moldavian Supreme Soviet elected Snegur president of the Supreme Soviet Presidium. In this new post Snegur presided over fundamental changes in Moldavia, including making Moldovan/Romanian, in the Latin script, the state language of the republic, August 1989, and declaring sovereignty, June 1990. The Supreme Soviet had taken over from the Communist Party as the leading institution and in April 1990 the Supreme Soviet elected Snegur President of the republic for a five-year term. On 8 December 1991 he was elected President of the Republic of Moldova, receiving over 98 per cent of the votes cast: he was the only candidate. The Popular Front in Moldova clamoured for union with Romania but Snegur bided his time. Nevertheless, the Slav population of the republic became alarmed and this led to the conflict in the Transnistria region.

Sobchak, Anatoly Aleksandrovich (*b.* 1937), he shot to prominence after being elected to the USSR Congress of People's Deputies and the USSR Supreme Soviet, for Leningrad, 1989, and established himself as an accomplished parliamentarian. He took advantage of the fact that the country was falling apart to challenge the establishment (for instance, Nikolai RYZHKOV, the Prime Minister), and his legal skills were put to forensic use. He was born into a Russian family in Chita, received his early education in Kokand and Tashkent, Uzbekistan, and graduated with distinction in law from Leningrad State University. In 1964 he successfully defended his candidate dissertation at Leningrad State University (LLM) and his doctorate (LLD) in 1983. In 1965 he began lecturing in law at the Leningrad Special School of the Militia, USSR Ministry of Internal Affairs, and the Leningrad Technical Institute for the Paper Industry, and then joined the faculty of law at Leningrad State University, becoming a professor. In 1989, after election to the new Soviet parliament, he joined the Inter-Regional group of deputies, among whose other members was Boris YELTSIN. In May 1990 he was chair of the Leningrad city soviet. In June 1991 he was elected mayor of Leningrad and during the summer of 1991 he was one of the founders of the movement for democratic reforms. During the attempted coup of August 1991 he appealed to all not to implement the decisions of the Emergency Committee and arranged with the military commander for forces to leave the city. He then declared there was no state of emergency in the city. In August 1991 he was made a member of GORBACHEV's Presidential Council and headed USSR delegations to Estonia and Ukraine. In September 1991 he was appointed head of administration (governor) of St Petersburg by President Yeltsin. He was a member of the Communist Party, 1988–July 1990. Anatoly Sobchak: *For a New Russia*, New York, 1992.

Sokolovsky, Marshal Vasily Danilovich (1897–1968), very successful military career which spanned active operations, the General Staff and governmental duties. He joined the Red Army in 1918 and participated in the Civil War as commander and chief of staff to a division. He graduated from the Military Academy of the Red Army in 1921. In February 1941 he became deputy Chief of the General Staff. He was General Konev's chief of staff on the Western

Front, 1941–3. He commanded the Western Front at the Battle of Kursk, July 1943. His Western Front then took Smolensk in September 1943. He was Chief of Staff of the 1st Ukrainian Front but was held responsible for the failure to move north from the Pripet Marshes. Nevertheless, in April 1945, he was appointed deputy commander of the 1st Belorusian Front, under ZHUKOV, in the final attack on Berlin. He was commander of Soviet forces in (east) Germany, 1946–9, and was Chief of the General Staff, 1952–60. Sokolovsky was a member of the Central Committee of the Communist Party, 1952–6, and a candidate member of the Politburo, 1961–8. Among his many decorations were eight Orders of Lenin and a British OBE. He is buried in the Kremlin wall.

Solomentsev, Mikhail Sergeevich (b. 1913), a conservative official who was a member of the top élite for over two decades. He was born into a Russian peasant family in present-day Lipetsk oblast and graduated from Leningrad Polytechnic Institute, 1940, the year he joined the Communist Party. He began as a collective farm worker and then worked in factories in Chelyabinsk oblast, 1940–54. He then moved into the Party apparatus, becoming a full member of the Central Committee, 1961. In 1966 he was promoted to a secretaryship of the Central Committee and in 1971 he became a candidate member of the Politburo. He ceased to be a Central Committee secretary on becoming chair of the RSFSR Council of Ministers. He gave up this post in June 1983 when ANDROPOV made him chair of the Committee of Party Control. In December 1983, after waiting twelve years, he became a full member of the Politburo. This reveals he was not a member of BREZHNEV's inner circle but obviously had supported him. He was one of the many senior Party officials who never took to perestroika and glasnost with any enthusiasm and as chair of the Committee of Party Control he was not very sympathetic to those who were seeking readmission to the Party. GORBACHEV finally managed to send him into retirement in September 1988, along with many others.

Soloukhin, Vladimir Alekseevich (*b.* 1924), one of the most influential and popular writers of the *derevenshchik* (village prose) school. He was born into a Russian peasant family in Alepino, Vladimir oblast, and graduated from the Gorky Literary Institute, 1951. He published his first book of poems in 1953 and attracted great attention in 1957 with the appearance of his *Vladimirskie Proselki* (*Vladimir Country Roads*). It describes his wanderings down the devastated and impoverished Russian countryside and raises the problem of the neglect of Russia's cultural heritage. He wrote of village life before collectivisation. After the collapse of communism he became chairman of the fund for the restoration of the cathedral of Christ the Saviour in Moscow. Its restoration was completed in 1996.

Solovev, Yury Filippovich (*b.* 1925), the most famous casualty of the elections to the USSR Congress of People's Deputies in 1989, Solovev, the first secretary of Leningrad obkom, was rejected by the Leningrad voters. He was soon replaced as first secretary and also lost his candidate membership of the Politburo. He was born into a Russian family in Kuibyshev oblast, served in the Red Army, 1943–4, and was invalided out. He graduated from the Leningrad Institute of Railway Engineering, 1951, and joined the Communist Party, 1955. Among the projects he worked on in Leningrad was the Metro. He was deputy chair of the Leningrad city soviet executive committee, 1973–4, and then joined the city Party apparatus. In 1976 he became a member of the Central Committee and in 1978 he was elected first secretary,

Leningrad gorkom. In 1984–5 he was USSR Minister of Industrial Construction and was then appointed first secretary, Leningrad obkom. He continued in this post until his career came to an inglorious end through the ballot box.

Solzhenitsyn, Aleksandr Isaevich (*b.* 1918), the leading Russian writer of his generation. He was born on 11 December 1918 in Kislovodsk, north Caucasus, into a Russian family. His grandfather, Semen Efimovich Solzhenitsyn, owned almost 1,000 hectares and about 50,000 sheep. Aleksandr had three brothers and a sister. His father, Isai Semenovich Solzhenitsyn, took part in the First World War and returned home as an officer and with a wife. However, he fatally wounded himself while out hunting in 1918. Solzhenitsyn went to secondary school in Rostov-on-Don and loved to cycle during the holidays. On one of these trips he visited STALIN's museum in Gori, Georgia, and afterwards, he related, his first doubts about the Stalin cult formed. From youth onwards Solzhenitsyn was single-minded and disciplined. In his fourth year at school he was already compiling his *Complete Works*. At Rostov State University he studied mathematics and physics, and graduated the year war broke out, in 1941. During his third year he married his first wife, Natalya Alekseevna, née Reshetovskaya, who was studying chemistry. His passion for literature surfaced during his undergraduate days when he penned his first stories. He was immediately called up and, as a mathematician, graduated from the Artillery Technical School, specialising in acoustics. In May 1943 he was appointed commander of a battery, fought in the 3rd Army on the Bryansk Front, and was decorated twice. While on active service he continued to write and completed stories which were recommended for publishing but were never published. He rose to the rank of captain but was arrested in February

1945 in East Prussia and was sentenced to eight years in a labour camp. He had been unwise enough to criticise Stalin in letters to a friend. He was in many prisons, including Butyrki and Lefortovo, and was part of the labour force which built Lenin Prospekt, the prestigious Moscow street, and this provided material for his play, *The Republic of Labour*. As an acoustics specialist he was valuable to the Soviet Union and hence was better treated. In 1948, in Moscow, he was employed in a top-secret scientific research institute in its acoustics laboratory and this provided the material for his novel, *The First Circle*. Then, in 1950, he was exiled to Kazakhstan; this meant that he was no longer a prisoner and was free to engage in other activities but had to reside in a village in that republic. He became a conscientious teacher of mathematics, physics and astronomy in a secondary school. Already he was quite an impressive figure and the pupils were struck by the fact that he did not swear, smoke or drink and had acquired a wide knowledge, not only of the subjects he taught, but of history and literature. Much of this had been acquired in prison where it was normal for prisoners to give lectures on their speciality. Stalin's camps housed many highly educated men and women. Prison life, however, had left its physical mark on him. The index finger of his right hand had been crushed while there. In 1955, while still in Kazakhstan, he began work on *The First Circle*. In exile, he contracted cancer but remarkably, aided by sheer will power, he was completely cured. The experience is related in *The Cancer Ward*. His experiences in Kazakhstan also provided some background for *One Day in the Life of Ivan Denisovich*. His period of exile ended on 26 June 1956 and he was permitted to return to European Russia. Here he was reunited with his wife Natalya, who during his absence had assumed that he had perished and had remarried and had two children. In 1958

they moved to Ryazan, east of Moscow, where Natalya taught chemistry in an agricultural institute. Solzhenitsyn taught mathematics, physics and astronomy in a school. He was constantly under KGB surveillance and developed great ingenuity in outwitting them. This episode in his life is related in *The Calf and the Oak*. Solzhenitsyn became famous in 1962 when *One Day in the Life of Ivan Denisovich* was published in the prestigious literary journal, *Novy Mir*. No less a person than Nikita KHRUSHCHEV had given his approval to publication as he believed that it would harm Stalin and benefit himself. The novel was an overnight sensation and broke the taboo of not describing the reality of the Gulag. In 1963 two more stories were published in *Novy Mir*. He became friends with Mstislav ROSTROPOVICH, the cellist, his wife, Galina VISHNEVSKAYA, the singer, Kornei CHUKOVSKY, the author, and Aleksandr Men, the popular Orthodox priest. Solzhenitsyn carried on a campaign against censorship, and advocated religious freedom and, most significantly, the renaissance of traditional Russian values. His views became well known in samizdat (unofficial publishing) and circulated among the intelligentsia. The KGB and the official literary establishment regarded Solzhenitsyn as a subversive and after Khrushchev was removed in 1964 persecution was stepped up. In 1965 his archive was seized and the manuscript of *The First Circle* was discovered. He did not dare live at home and friends such as Chukovsky and Rostropovich put him up at their dachas. Natalya was prevailed upon to publish her diaries and this infuriated Solzhenitsyn and led to divorce. He then met Natalya Dmitrievna, a scientist, who later became his second wife. He was expelled from the USSR Union of Writers in 1969 which meant he could not publish officially in the Soviet Union. In 1970 he was awarded the Nobel Prize for

Literature but decided not to accept it in person, fearing that he would not be permitted to re-enter the Soviet Union. After the KGB had seized a copy of *The Gulag Archipelago*, Solzhenitsyn gave permission for its publication abroad. The Soviet authorities decided against imprisoning him because of the international furore it would have caused and instead stripped him of his citizenship in February 1974 and, in handcuffs, he was put on a special plane to Frankfurt-am-Main. His wife and four children followed about six weeks later and his archive also went west. He became the spokesperson for anti-communism and Russian nationalism in the west and wrote the *Letter to the Leaders of the Soviet Union* in which he advocated that Russia return to her European heartland and her traditional culture and religion, viewing her connection with the Muslim republics of central Asia and elsewhere as a millstone round her neck. He stayed a short time in West Germany and then moved to Zürich where he completed his *Lenin in Zürich*. In 1976 he moved to the United States, near Cavendish in Vermont, where he acquired a farm and about 20 hectares of woodland. A strict Orthodox Christian he and his family went to church every Sunday. He became a sharp critic of American democratic values and pointed out to Americans that they were arrogant in believing that their society was the ideal one to be copied by everyone. He continued to advocate that Russia slough off atheist communism and revert to its former Orthodox faith with local communities running themselves. Glasnost changed the country's attitude to him and his writings were published in the USSR in the late 1980s and early 1990s. He was, at last, recognised as the greatest living Russian writer. In August 1990 he was officially invited to return to the motherland and finally returned in 1994. His citizenship had been restored in September 1990. He is regarded as a great man of letters but politically he is a Russian nationalist and this has alienated many. He has never come to terms with the western concept of democracy. Fearless, industrious and opinionated, he has brought many subjects into the public arena, including the forced repatriation of Soviet prisoners of war in 1945. He played a leading role in encouraging the Russian Orthodox Church to lift its anathema on the Old Believers, thereby opening the way for the end of the schism.

Sorge, Richard (1895–1944), a very successful German spy in Japan but working for the Soviet Union. Among his ancestors was one of Karl Marx's private secretaries. He was born in Baku but his family returned to Germany and he served in the First World War. He joined the Communist Party of Germany (KPD) in 1919 and graduated from the University of Hamburg, 1920. He became an editor of a Party newspaper, taught in a school but was dismissed for promoting Marxism. He moved to Moscow in 1924. He joined the All-Russian Communist Party (later the CPSU) in 1925. He was already in intelligence and he attempted to organise networks as early as 1929. He returned to Moscow in 1933 and went to a military intelligence (GRU) school. He was sent to Shanghai to obtain information on Chaing Kai-shek's Nationalist Army. On returning to Germany, he established contacts with the Abwehr (German military intelligence) and the Gestapo, and joined the NSDAP (Nazi Party). He obtained a post in Tokyo as a correspondent for the *Frankfurter Allgemeine Zeitung* and other newspapers. In the Japanese capital he built up good relations with the German embassy and became a star reporter. In 1934 Sorge built up a network of agents throughout Japan and his main agent, Ozaki Hozumi, was a China expert and adviser to the Prime Minister. Some of this information was passed on to the German military attaché, Colonel Eugen Ott. The latter became German ambassador in 1935 and Sorge was press attaché at the embassy. He provided STALIN with details of Barbarossa and even the exact number of German divisions in June 1941; Stalin ignored him. His greatest contribution to Soviet security was the information that the Japanese had no intention of invading the Soviet Union, having decided to move south. This permitted Stalin to move his Siberian divisions in December 1941 to defend Moscow. One of Sorge's weaknesses was that he could not resist a beautiful woman and his personal life was surrounded by scandal. Japanese military counter-intelligence had intercepted the transmission of a signal and was aware of the network. They trapped him with the help of a cabaret dancer and he was arrested in October 1941. They had also arrested one of his organisers and he confessed, implicating Sorge and Hozumi. He was sentenced to death in September 1943 and Hozumi and he were hanged on 9 October 1944. The dancer was shot in a Tokyo street soon after, apparently by Soviet Smersh (death to spies) agents. Sorge was made a Hero of the Soviet Union in November 1964 and became a cult figure with a film and several books chronicling his exploits.

Soskovets, Oleg Nikolaevich (b. 1949), an industrialist who played an important role in Russian politics after independence. He was born into a Russian family in Taldy Kurgan, Kazakhstan. He worked in the Karaganda Metallurgical Combine and studied in its technical college. He successfully defended his candidate dissertation (PhD (Eng)) in the Institute of Steel and Alloys, Moscow, 1985. He was director of the Karaganda Metallurgical Combine in 1987–8, and general director of the enterprise, 1988–91. He was USSR Minister of Metallurgy in 1991. In January 1992 he was appointed deputy Prime Minister of the Republic of Kazakhstan, then Minister of Industry of the republic. He had previ-

ously been elected to the USSR Congress of People's Deputies and was a member of the Communist Party, 1972–91. He made a name for himself by advocating greater independence for enterprises.

Spassky, Boris Vasilevich (b. 1937), he became well known for his epic encounter with Bobby Fischer for the world chess title in 1972. He was born in Leningrad, became an international grandmaster, 1956, and graduated in journalism from Leningrad State University, 1959. He became Soviet youth chess champion in 1955 and was champion of the Soviet Union, 1962 and 1973. In the 1966 final Spassky lost to PETROSYAN but three years later defeated the world champion. He lost his title to Fischer by 12.5–8.5. He eventually left the Soviet Union and moved to Paris with his French wife.

Spiridonova, Maria Aleksandrovna (1885–1941), an unquenchable Left Socialist Revolutionary who, given the opportunity, used violence against the imperial regime. She was appalled by the violence against peasants in Tambov guberniya (she was a native of Tambov) during the 1905 revolution and volunteered to assassinate those responsible. In January 1906 she mortally wounded a general involved in the violence. Her maltreatment in prison became a *cause célèbre* and she was fêted during her journey into exile in Siberia. Another version has it that she shot her lover in a jealous fit and was sentenced to death, later commuted to exile for life. Lenin used her case to illustrate the cruelty of the Tsarist system. She was released after the February Revolution, became mayor of Chita and blew up the local prison. When she arrived in Petrograd in May her radicalism and passion soon made her a leader of the left wing of the Socialist Revolutionary Party, led by Viktor CHERNOV. This meant that she sided with the Bolsheviks in October and she became leader of the Party of Left

Socialist Revolutionaries, splitting from the SR Party. She chaired the IInd Congress of Peasant Soviets and was the Left SR–Bolshevik candidate for speaker of the Constituent Assembly. She prevaricated about accepting the Brest-Litovsk Treaty but eventually agreed with other Left SRs and participated in the anti-Bolshevik violence in July 1918. The Bolsheviks arrested DZERZHINSKY but did not know what to do with him, eventually setting him free, as a fellow revolutionary. Latvian Chekists then dealt swiftly with the insurrectionists. Spiridonova was exiled and moved from camp to camp. She was shot in Orel Prison in September 1941 by the NKVD, as were other prisoners, lest the advancing Germans capture her. I. Steinberg: *Spiridonova: Revolutionary Terrorist*, London, 1935.

Stakhanov, Aleksei Grigorevich (1906–77), he became famous in August 1935 when he mined 102 tonnes of coal in 5 hours and 45 minutes, or fourteen times the average, at a mine in the Donbass. The Stakhanovite movement was applied everywhere in Soviet industry to boost productivity. Books and films appeared to glorify his exploits. This made him a hero of the bureaucrats but not with many workers. It was later admitted that the Stakhanovite method of storming (working intensively for a short period to meet a target) was inefficient and socialist labour brigades replaced them. In October 1988 the Soviet press revealed that the whole exercise had been a fraud. Stakhanov had had first-class equipment, all of which worked, but also the efforts of his mates were added to his productivity.

Stalin, Iosif Vissarionovich (né Dzhugashvili) (1879–1953), one of the dominant political actors of the twentieth century who has left an indelible mark on Russia and the world. The system he spawned, Stalinism, lived after him. Short of stature, with a pock-marked face, Stalin did not speak Russian until the age of eleven. A Georgian by birth (his father was of Ossetian origin, the family name is Ossetian with a Georgian suffix), he came to dominate Soviet Russia in a manner that no communist leader did before or after him. He both craved for and was repelled by personal adulation. A French diplomat exclaimed, 'Mon Dieu', on beholding a huge portrait of Stalin being trailed across the sky. 'Precisely, monsieur', replied his companion. The Stalin cult was presenting Stalin as a god. He had slightly yellow eyes and could silence any Soviet general or politician by merely fixing them on him. He was very well read, possessed of an elephantine memory and never forgot a slight. He was highly intelligent and had a great facility to grasp an argument, draft memoranda and penetrate to the core of any matter. His Russian prose is clear and fluent and bears testimony to his days in a Georgian Orthodox seminary where he was being trained as a priest. He was a master of intrigue and a shrewd tactician. He was a Hercule Poirot when it came to detecting the human weaknesses of an opponent. Stalin then ruthlessly and mercilessly exploited his advantage. TROTSKY, intellectually more gifted, was nevertheless like a rabbit being mesmerised by Stalin the stoat. He acted according to the maxim: if in doubt, never trust anyone. However, he did trust Hitler, for some unfathomable reason, and lived to regret it. He never made the mistake of trusting a foreign politician again. LENIN identified Stalin as a coming comrade early and he was elected to the Central Committee of the RSDRP in 1912. He was a professional revolutionary and, among other things, robbed banks to augment Party finances. He was a delegate to several Party Congresses. The following year, Lenin commissioned Stalin to write an extended essay on Marxism and the nationality question, a subject of increasing significance at that time. He spent a month in

Vienna composing the work, with BUKHARIN helping him since he knew no German. He was exiled to north Siberia in 1913 (SVERDLOV was a fellow inmate but they did not get on) and the February Revolution liberated him. He immediately returned to Petrograd and after Lenin's arrival adopted his position and became one of his closest collaborators. Lenin made him Commissar for Nationalities (until 1923) in the first Sovnarkom and hence he became, with Lenin, responsible for policy towards non-Russians. He was deeply involved in military–political affairs during the Civil War and the first serious conflicts with Trotsky date from this period. Stalin used his activities to develop his network of friends and subordinates. He was made General Secretary of the Party in 1922 but no one at that time regarded the post as important. Stalin, as a member of the Politburo, Central Committee and Organisational Bureau (Orgburo), was the best-informed comrade in the Party. His relations with KRUPSKAYA, Lenin's wife, reached such a nadir that Lenin proposed in late 1922, in his Testament, that Stalin be shorn of his position as Party General Secretary. At Lenin's funeral he delivered a quasi-religious eulogy to the dead leader and thereafter claimed to be Lenin's chief pupil. His skill at coalition politics produced victories over the left-leaning Trotsky, KAMENEV and ZINOVIEV and finally the right-leaning Bukharin. This made Stalin the main political actor but Stalinism did not really take root until 1936. It can be defined as concentrating the decision-making process at the centre, mobilising the resources of the country and giving preference to defence-related heavy industries, eliminating the market mechanism, transforming education and culture into weapons in the great struggle to become the leading world power. Everyone and everything should serve the economic goals of the state. The phenomenon was dominated by the cult of

Stalin's personality. Extraordinary economic feats were recorded but at an appalling human cost – of no importance to Stalin. He decided that a pact with Germany would keep the USSR out of the coming European war and appears to have sought agreement with Hitler from 1936. The German invasion of June 1941 stunned him and MOLOTOV made the announcement of the attack to the Soviet people. He was very vulnerable and could have been removed but his comrades decided that he was an asset not a liability. It took him about two years to learn mechanised warfare but he became a popular and astute war leader. The wartime conferences with the Allies made him very popular in the west (he was known as Uncle Joe and it had to be explained to him that this was an affectionate sobriquet). The Russians acquired another empire after 1945, in eastern and south-eastern Europe and the rule was that the Party set up shop after the Red Army had finished its work. The only exceptions to this were Austria (Moscow withdrew in 1955) and northern Iran which they quit in 1946. Stalin did not want Mao Zedong and the Communists to take power in China until he had established some type of control over them. When Mao came to Moscow in 1950 to request aid Stalin attempted to humiliate him, eventually providing some aid but charging interest. However, to counterbalance this, Stalin revealed to Mao the names of the Chinese comrades working for him. Mao quickly liquidated them. Stalin fell out with Tito, the Yugoslav leader, in 1948 because he thought him too independent. He failed to develop good relations with the west after 1945 and the Cold War took hold in 1947. This began an arms race which eventually proved a great economic liability for Moscow. Stalin's declining years saw him withdraw from the public gaze and become erratic and indeed paranoid. One of his doctors advised him to retire but Stalin characteristically turned on him. His death was slow and painful. It was his custom to lock himself in his quarters for the night and he suffered a stroke during the night, only being found in the morning. There was still a record on the gramophone. Stalin had spent his last hours listening to Chopin, played by a Russian pianist. Robert Conquest: *Stalin: Breaker of Nations*, London, 1991; Robert H. McNeal: *Stalin: Man and Ruler*, London, 1988; Robert C. Tucker: *Stalin as Revolutionary 1879–1929*, New York, 1973; Adam B. Ulam: *Stalin: The Man and His Era*, New York, 1973; Dmitri Volkogonov: *Stalin*, London, 1994.

Stankevich, Sergei Borisovich (*b.* 1954), a highly successful academic turned politician in the late GORBACHEV era. He was born near Moscow into a family of Ukrainian origin. His father was a military lawyer. Stankevich graduated in history from the Moscow State Pedagogical Institute, successfully defended his candidate dissertation in history (PhD) and then worked in the Institute of General History, USSR Academy of Sciences. He was elected to the USSR Congress of People's Deputies and the USSR Supreme Soviet, rapidly established himself as a skilled parliamentarian and became a member of the Inter-Regional group of deputies. He was elected to the Moscow city soviet, 1990, and became deputy chair. As a good English speaker he became known internationally as a commentator on Soviet and Russian affairs. From July to November 1991 he was an RSFSR state counsellor on relations with social organisations. In September 1992 he became an adviser to President YELTSIN. He gradually developed forceful nationalist views, especially defending the rights of Russians living outside Russia in states of the former Soviet Union. He was also successful in business and is reputed to be very wealthy.

Starodubtsev, Vasily Aleksandrovich (*b.* 1931), one of the members of the attempted coup against GORBACHEV in August 1991, he was an agrarian specialist who was opposed to the concept of private ownership of land. He was born into a Russian family in Volovchik, Lipetsk oblast. He graduated as an extramural student from the All-Union Agricultural Institute and successfully presented his candidate dissertation in agriculture (PhD (Agric)). He began working in 1947 as a kolkhoznik (collective farm worker) and became the chair of various kolkhozes. In 1987 he became chair of the Novomoskovskoe Agro-Industrial Association. He was elected to the USSR Congress of People's Deputies in 1989, was chair of the Russian Farmers' Union, 1990, and chair of the USSR Peasants' Union, June 1990–August 1991. He was arrested after the failure of the coup but was released in June 1992. He was elected chair of the Peasants' Union of the Commonwealth of Independent States and the Russian Peasants' Union. He was a member of the Communist Party, 1960–91, and a member of the Central Committee, 1990–1.

Starovoitova, Galina Vasilevna (*b.* 1946), a liberal academic and politician and leading specialist on inter-ethnic relations in Russia, the tide of Russian nationalism has seen her influence wane. She was born into a Russian family in Chelyabinsk and grew up in Leningrad, the daughter of an enterprise director. She graduated in psychology from Leningrad State University and successfully presented her candidate dissertation in history (PhD) in 1980. She worked as a social psychologist and then moved to the Institute of Ethnography, USSR Academy of Sciences, 1974–91. She was a senior scientific assistant, Centre for the Study of Inter-ethnic Relations, Presidium of the USSR Academy of Sciences, 1989, was an RSFSR state counsellor, specialising in inter-ethnic problems, 1991 and an adviser to President YELTSIN on inter-ethnic relations, 1991–2. She was elected to the USSR Congress of People's Deputies and the USSR Supreme Soviet, 1989, for Erevan, and the RSFSR Congress of People's Deputies and the RSFSR Supreme Soviet, 1990. She supports national self-determination, a democratic law-governed state and a market economy. In 1991 she was elected to the co-ordinating council of the Democratic Russia (DemRossiya) movement and played a leading role in promoting democracy in Russia. She was removed as adviser to the President in November 1992 by those who wanted Russia to defend more aggressively its own national interests. She was the most prominent female politician to emerge in the late GORBACHEV and early Yeltsin eras.

Stolypin, Petr Arkadievich (1862–1911), had Tsar NICHOLAS II conferred the necessary power on him, he might have modernised Russia and saved the monarchy. He was no friend of democracy or the rule of law, believing that saving the state took precedence. He was a severe governor of Saratov guberniya in 1905, deploying force to suppress peasant disturbances in this agriculturally poor region. This earned him the undying hatred of democrats and revolutionaries but also led to his appointment as Minister of the Interior in April 1906. He became chair of the Council of Ministers, or Prime Minister, in July 1906. In Saratov he had come to the conclusion that the peasant commune (obshchina) was the major brake on agricultural development and in October and November 1906 he introduced legislation which permitted peasants to leave the commune and set up as individual farmers. This was called the wager on the strong. Repartition had led to more and more narrow pieces of land (strips), mainly due to increasing population, and consolidation now only required a

two-thirds majority of village voters (a simple majority in 1910) instead of unanimity. By 1916 only about 10 per cent of peasants had availed themselves of the opportunity of setting up on their own. Russia's tragedy was that war intervened in 1914 and held up the process which could have provided a solution to Russia's perennial problem of millions of small, uneconomic holdings. Thirty or forty years, at least, were needed to allow market relations to effect fundamental change in agriculture. Stolypin undermined the October 1905 Manifesto, which can be referred to as a constitution, by altering the electoral law in 1907, after the Second Duma, like the first, had been dissolved by the Tsar. Stolypin's law ensured that future Dumas would have a guaranteed conservative majority. He also attempted to introduce reforms in other policy areas but was resolutely opposed in conservative and court circles. He was assassinated at the opera in Kiev, also attended by the Tsar, in September 1911. Nicholas II did not hasten to visit him in hospital, underlining the loss of trust between the two. Dorothy Atkinson: *The End of the Russian Land Commune, 1905–1930*, Stanford, Cal., 1983.

Stravinsky, Igor Fedorovich (1882–1971), a great modern composer, his work had a revolutionary impact on musical thought before and after the First World War and his music epitomised modernism during his lifetime. He was composing at the age of eighteen but then went to the University of St Petersburg to study law and philosophy (1900–5). He impressed Rimsky-Korsakov and he accepted him as a private pupil. His first composition appeared in 1908 and then he worked for Diaghilev in Paris. He became internationally famous in 1910 and 1911 for the *Firebird* and *Petrushka*. The first performance of the *Rite of Spring* in Paris in 1913 occasioned one of the most famous riots in the history of music. Thereafter

Stravinsky was known as the 'destructive modernist'. He settled in Switzerland in 1914, moved to France in 1920 and then to the United States in 1939. He returned to the Soviet Union in 1962 and gave many concerts which were joyously received. He conducted his own music in a style reminiscent of a cat catching a mouse. The Soviet public was treated to his music which had been previously vilified. On completing a concert in Leningrad he addressed the audience and informed them that it was a moving experience for him to be back in the same hall (he pointed to the chair he had sat on) where, at the age of six, he had attended his first concert. He had been bowled over by Tchaikovsky's sixth symphony and afterwards met the composer.

Strumilin, Stanislav Gustavovich (1877–1974), a leading Soviet economist and who contributed considerably to the development of planning and labour economics. He was born in Dashkovtsy and graduated from the St Petersburg Polytechnic Institute where one of his teachers was M. I. Tugan-Baranovsky. He belonged to the Menshevik wing of the RSDRP and only joined the Communist Party in 1923. He was appointed to Gosplan on LENIN's recommendation when it was established in February 1921. He produced important studies on regional development and the effect of education and training on labour productivity.

Suslov, Mikhail Andreevich (1902–82), a desiccated ideological calculating machine, the *éminence grise* of Soviet ideology, the sea-green incorruptible of the Soviet establishment, all these fit the formidable guardian of Soviet political and moral orthodoxy. He was born into a Russian peasant family in the present-day Saratov oblast, was active in the Komsomol, 1918, and joined the Communist Party, 1921. He was sent to study at the Institute of Red Professors and at

the Plekhanov Economics Institute and then progressed in the Party apparatus. He played his role in the purges of the early 1930s and benefited from the high casualty rate of Party cadres, becoming a secretary in Rostov obkom, 1937, and then first secretary, Stavropol kraikom, 1939–44. He was elected to the Central Committee in 1941. He was a high-ranking NKVD officer, 1944, when he was given the task of incorporating Lithuania in the USSR. He was ruthless and supervised the deportation of thousands, mainly the intelligentsia. In 1946 he became a secretary of the Central Committee and head of the agitation and propaganda department. He retained these duties until his death. He was editor of *Pravda*, 1949–51. From 1955 to his death he was a Central Committee secretary and a full member of the Presidium (Politburo) and was therefore a major player in Kremlin politics. However, he never aspired to become top dog. He was a retiring man who preferred one to one conversations to addressing large groups. He was temperamentally unsuited to coexist with KHRUSHCHEV but managed it and was much more at home with BREZHNEV's more orthodox, conservative style. He gave the Czechoslovak communists a dressing down after the August 1968 Warsaw Pact invasion of their country. He did not seek the company of westerners and once at a Kremlin reception placed tables between himself and foreign diplomats. He and ANDROPOV were competitors and Suslov's death permitted Andropov to come back into the Central Committee Secretariat and challenge for leadership of the Party. He protested against the increasing corruption among the Soviet nomenklatura but could do little other than berate the perpetrators.

Sverdlov, Yakov Mikhailovich (1885–1919), a brilliant Bolshevik administrator who carried most of the information about Party members in his head, his early death allowed STALIN to take over as chief of the Party apparatus. He was one of the few Old Bolsheviks (Party members before 1917) and Jews whose reputation remained untarnished during the treacherous 1930s. He was born into a working-class family in Nizhny Novgorod and worked in the metal industry, becoming a social democrat in 1905. He was an active Party member, siding with LENIN, and used his phenomenal memory to file away comrades who could be relied upon. He was exiled to Siberia and did time with Stalin but they did not get on. After the February Revolution Lenin instructed him to build up the Party Secretariat. He was more a practical administrator than a theoretician and built up a network of Party officials around the country. They had all been known personally to him before 1917. He played an important organisational role during the October Revolution. A Jew, he opposed TROTSKY becoming Commissar for Internal Affairs because as a Jew he would have fuelled anti-Semitism in Russia (had he done so this would have been a case of the poacher becoming gamekeeper). He also did not favour Trotsky becoming head of the Party press and instead proposed him as Commissar for Foreign Affairs, the post he occupied in the first Sovnarkom. Lenin was unhappy with the lenient line adopted by KAMENEV as chair of the Central Executive Committee (CEC or VTsIK) of the Soviets and chose Sverdlov as his hard man. The latter then brought the CEC into line and, among other things, gave the Secretariat precedence. This inevitably weakened the CEC and the decline of the soviets was under way. Sverdlov then set about the task of establishing secretariats in local Party committees, all reporting to Moscow. Lenin and he became fast friends and their organisational views were remarkably similar. So good was Sverdlov at anticipating what Lenin wanted that on occasions he replied, 'Already done, already done', when the Bolshevik leader instructed him to do something. He contracted Spanish flu and died in March 1919. Had he lived the Party might not have gone through the organisational convulsions it experienced until 1921. Also he would have been the natural candidate for the post of General Secretary of the Party in 1922. How that might have changed history!

T

Tal, Mikhail Nekhemevich (1936–92), one of the greatest Soviet chess players, who, had it not been for indifferent health, might have won the world championship more than once. He came from Riga, Latvia, and was nicknamed the Riga Magician, because of his great talent, natural attacking skill and verve. He defeated Mikhail BOTVINNIK in 1961 to take the world title from the father of Soviet chess. He took the grandmaster completely by surprise and beat him comprehensively. However, Botvinnik prepared well for the rematch, in 1962, and identified certain psychological and technical weaknesses in his younger opponent, beating him, in turn, comprehensively. The result might have been different had Tal not been ill. He represented the Soviet Union successfully in many tournaments around the world.

Talyzin, Nikolai Vladimirovich (1929–91), he was chosen to take over USSR Gosplan in 1985 after GORBACHEV became Soviet leader but the demands of perestroika were beyond him and he was subsequently demoted. He was born into a Russian family, was an electrician, 1945–50, then graduated from the Moscow Institute of Electrical Engineering and Communications, 1955, and worked in the Research Institute of Radio Engineering, until 1965. He was appointed first deputy USSR Minister of Communications and was Minister, 1975–80. Then he became the Soviet Union's permanent representative to Comecon and a deputy chair of the USSR Council of Ministers. He was recalled from this post in October 1985 to head Gosplan and was also made first deputy chair of the USSR Council of Ministers. The post also led to his election as a candidate member of the Politburo, having been elected to the Central Committee in 1981. He never revealed any dynamism as the top planner and in October 1988 he was downgraded to his previous job in Comecon and in September 1989 he lost his Politburo seat and his Comecon post.

Tarkovsky, Andrei Arsenevich (1932–86), a film director who became internationally famous for his film *Andrei Rublev* which was completed in 1966 but which could not be shown in the Soviet Union until 1971. He was born into a Russian family in Moscow, his father was the poet Arseny Tarkovsky, and he graduated from the State Film Institute, 1961, and there studied under Mikhail Romm. His first film was *The Steam Roller and the Violin*, 1961, and his breakthrough came with *Andrei Rublev*, which was awarded the International Critics' Prize, 1969. It deals with the relationship of a painter with the environment and the limits of artistic expression. He made two more films but the Soviet public and critics found him difficult to comprehend. He moved abroad and made films in Italy (*Nostalgia*, 1983) and Sweden (*The Sacrifice*, 1985, which won a prize at Cannes). He defected in 1984 and was deprived of his Soviet citizenship. He had cancer and fought a brave battle against it, dying in Paris. Under glasnost he was recognised as a great director and all his films were shown.

Tereshkova, Valentina Vladimirovna (*b.* 1937), the first woman in space when she made her one and only space flight in Vostok-VI in June 1963 and became a world celebrity. She was born into a Russian family, her father was a kolkhoznik (collective farm worker), in Yaroslavl oblast, and worked in factories in Yaroslavl and was a parachutist at the local aviation club until selected for training as a cosmonaut in 1962. In 1963 she married fellow cosmonaut Adrian Nikolaev and took the name Nikolaeva-Tereshkova. When their daughter was born in 1964 she became the first child in the world whose parents were both cosmonauts. Tereshkova later divorced him, citing drunkenness. She played a leading role in the Soviet Committee for Women and was chair from 1968–87. However, she failed to be re-elected to the committee in 1987. She then became chair of the Soviet Society for Friendship and Cultural Relations with Foreign Countries. She joined the Communist Party in 1962 and was a candidate member of the Central Committee, 1971–90. As a cosmonaut she was a military officer and continued her education, graduating from the Zhukovsky Aviation Academy, 1969. In 1992 she was appointed chair of the Presidium of the Russian Association for International Co-operation. She was elected to the USSR Congress of People's Deputies in 1989. She represented the Soviet Union abroad at many conferences and was known as a formidable, businesslike woman. A crater on the reverse side of the moon is named after her.

Tikhonov, Nikolai Aleksandrovich (*b.* 1905), when GORBACHEV became Soviet leader in 1985 the Prime Minister was eighty years old, older than the Soviet Union itself. Tikhonov was a classic example of the rule of the gerontocrats, having succeeded KOSYGIN in 1980. He was born into a Ukrainian family in Kharkov and began work as a train driver. He graduated from the Dnepropetrovsk Metallurgical Institute, 1930, worked as an engineer, 1930–47, then as an enterprise director. He joined the USSR Ministry of Ferrous Metallurgy in 1955 and then in 1957 became chair of the Dnepropetrovsk Economic Council. In 1960 he became deputy chair of the State Scientific and Economic Council, USSR Council of Ministers and in 1963 deputy chair of USSR Gosplan. In 1965 he was one of the deputy chairs, USSR Council of Ministers, under Kosygin, and in 1976 he progressed to become first deputy chair. When Kosygin retired he took over. He only joined the Communist Party in 1945. He was elected a candidate member of the CPSU Central Committee, 1961, and in 1966 became a full member. In 1978 he was made a candidate member of the Politburo and a year later a full member. Gorbachev found him quite incapable of performing his state functions (he seemed more concerned about his future pension and perks) and pushed him aside in September 1985 to make way for Nikolai RYZHKOV.

Timoshenko, Marshal Semen Konstantinovich (1895–1970), he occupied many top military posts during the Great Fatherland War but it was his friendship with STALIN, which dated back to the Civil War, which saved him from retribution for failure. He joined the Red Army in 1918 and the Bolshevik Party in 1919 and fought in the Civil War. His experience was in cavalry and he participated in the occupation of eastern Poland, 1939, and in the Soviet–Finnish War, 1939–40. In May 1940 he was promoted Marshal and replaced Klimenty VOROSHILOV as Commissar for Defence with special responsibility for reorganising the Red Army and the training and discipline of recruits. Timoshenko became the first chair of Stavka (Soviet High Command) in June 1941. He was made commander of the Western Front when the Germans invaded but could initially do little to stem the advance and his army was even encircled near Smolensk. In September 1941 he was transferred to command the South-western Front but was helpless in the face of the German penetration to Stalingrad and the Crimea. He was unfortunate to be in command of the Kharkov Offensive in May 1942 which KHRUSHCHEV, for one, had attempted to dissuade Stalin from launching. The Germans were well prepared since they had intended to launch their own offensive shortly afterwards. The rout cost Timoshenko his command and he was moved to the North-western Front. This was his last operational command and during the rest of the war he was involved in planning and as Stavka representative in the Baltic and the Balkans. He was a member of the Central Committee of the Communist Party, 1939–52, and a candidate member, 1952–70. After the war he was commander of various military districts.

Titov, German Stepanovich (*b.* 1935), he became the first cosmonaut to complete a long flight in space on board Vostok-2 in August 1961, circling the earth over seventeen times. He completed his flight just after the historic first flight in space by Yury GAGARIN. He was born into a Russian family in the Altai krai and graduated from the Zhukovsky Air Force Academy and the Academy of the General Staff. In 1957 he became a fighter pilot in the Leningrad military district and was chosen for cosmonaut training, 1960. He worked in the USSR Ministry of Defence, 1976–91, and was first deputy head of the space section, USSR Ministry of Defence, 1991. Then in 1992 he became president of Kosmoflot. He was a member of the Communist Party, 1961–91. A crater on the moon is named after him.

Tolbukhin, Marshal Fedor Ivanovich (1894–1949), one of the most successful Red Army commanders, he commanded the troops which drove the Wehrmacht out of Crimea, Ukraine, Romania, Yugoslavia and Hungary. He was an officer in the Tsarist Army during the First World War, joined the Red Army, 1918, and fought in the Civil War. He graduated from the Frunze Military Academy, 1934. He commanded the 57th Army which defended Stalingrad, 1942–3. In 1943, as commander of the Southern Front, he liberated towns at the mouth of the River Donets. In April 1944, Tolbukhin, together with EREMENKO, recaptured Crimea. In August 1944, Tolbukhin and MALINOVSKY were given the task of driving the Germans from the Balkans. Together they defeated the Wehrmacht (with 200,000 troops) at Jassy-Kishinev and Tolbukhin was promoted to Marshal. In conjunction with Tito he captured Belgrade in October 1944. He then left Yugoslavia and moved north to link up with Malinovsky to lay siege to Budapest which they took in early 1945. Tolbukhin then drove the tenacious German 6th SS Panzer Army out of western Hungary into Austria, March 1945. He was made chair of the Control Commission in Bulgaria and Romania, 1944, and commander of the Southern Group of Armies, 1945–7.

Tolstoi, Aleksei Nikolaevich, Count (1883–1945), a member of the Tolstoi family, he became court writer to STALIN and was called Comrade Count. He began publishing stories and poems in 1907, writing especially about the aristocracy which had fallen on hard times. He was a war correspondent in Britain and France for *Russkie Vedomosti* during the war. Tolstoi emigrated after the October Revolution and lived in Berlin and Paris where he began writing his novels about White émigrés, *Road to Calvary*. He returned to Moscow in 1923, began adopting a more proletarian style and subsequent volumes of *The Road to Calvary* appeared to 1941. Tolstoi's return was a great propaganda coup for the Soviet Union, and especially Tolstoi represented Soviet letters abroad. He was astute enough to choose heroic Russian themes for his novels: he wrote two plays about Ivan the Terrible and an unfinished trilogy on Peter the Great. In reality he was writing about Stalin and how wonderful a leader he was. His reputation collapsed under glasnost.

Tolstykh, Boris Leontevich (b. 1936), a highly successful engineer who shot to prominence under GORBACHEV because he was technically competent and fitted perfectly into the ethos of perestroika. He was born into a Russian family in Voronezh and graduated as an engineer from Voronezh State University, 1959. He worked as an engineer in the Voronezh Elektronika enterprise complex which specialised in military aircraft and space technology. He became general director of the plant in 1977. While head, he completely modernised the factory. He was brought to Moscow in 1985 as deputy head of the State Committee for Science and Technology, becoming its head in 1987 as well as being appointed a deputy chair, USSR Council of Ministers. In 1989 he was appointed chair of the State Committee for Computer Technology and Information Science.

Tomsky, Mikhail Pavlovich (1880–1936), the only fully fledged worker among the top Bolsheviks after LENIN's death, Tomsky was a moderate who was drawn to BUKHARIN and perished with him. He became a social democrat in 1904 and was arrested in 1908 and 1909. After the October Revolution Tomsky was a leading trade unionist and resisted the notion that the unions should be mere transmission belts for conveying the Party's instructions to the working class. The number of strikes during the Civil War had convinced Tomsky that less not more pressure should be applied to workers. In this he clashed head-on with TROTSKY who wished to discipline the working class and argued that trade unions

should become production unions, chiefly concerned with raising labour productivity. In 1920 Tomsky became chair of the All-Russian Central Council of the Trade Unions. He followed Lenin's line on the trade unions but in 1921 Lenin fell out with him on the role of unions under the New Economic Policy, even demanding the exclusion of Tomsky from the Central Committee and the Party itself, in line with the resolution on Party unity passed at the Xth Congress. However, the matter was allowed to fade into the background. He was soon rehabilitated as Lenin no longer feared the trade unions could undermine NEP, and Tomsky was elected to the Politburo at the XIth Party Congress, 1922. He was one of the coffin bearers at Lenin's funeral. He led a Soviet trade union delegation to London, 1924. As a supporter of Bukharin, Tomsky lost his Politburo place at the XVIth Party Congress, 1930. Along with Bukharin and RYKOV, he should have played a starring role in the second great show trial but, no longer able to bear his changed circumstances, he shot himself in August 1936.

Trapeznikov, Sergei Pavlovich (1912–84), the guardian of conservative cultural and scientific orthodoxy under BREZHNEV, he was universally disliked and the academicians of the USSR Academy of Sciences, despite political pressure, rejected his candidature for full membership. He was born into a Russian family in Astrakhan and joined the Communist Party in 1930. He participated as a Party activist in the collectivisation campaign in Penza oblast, then worked in Party propaganda. He graduated from the Moscow Pedagogical Institute, 1946, and was head of the Party School, Communist Party of Moldavia, 1948–56, where he came in contact with Leonid Brezhnev and Konstantin CHERNENKO. Brezhnev brought him to Moscow in 1960 to become deputy rector of the Higher Party School, CPSU Central Committee. In

1966 he was made head of the Central Committee department of science, technology and culture. He remained in that position until ANDROPOV sent him into retirement. Under GORBACHEV it was admitted openly that his reactionary behaviour had harmed Soviet cultural and scientific life. His conservatism may have been linked to his own modest level of culture and technical knowledge. His two-volume history of Soviet collectivisation, published in the late 1960s, is a paean of praise to STALIN's policies and avoids mentioning any of the negative consequences of the ending of private agriculture.

Travkin, Nikolai Ilich (*b.* 1946), one of the reformers within the Communist Party who became frustrated and left to set up the Democratic Party of Russia. He was born into a Russian family in Moscow oblast and graduated from the Klin Construction Technical College and the extra-mural faculty of physics and mathematics, Kolomna State Pedagogical Institute. He was a successful builder and in 1987 he was appointed head of a construction association. He attended the Higher Party School of the Party Central Committee, 1988–9, was elected to the USSR Congress of People's Deputies and the USSR Supreme Soviet, 1989, and joined the Inter-Regional group of deputies. He was elected to the RSFSR Congress of People's Deputies, 1990, but although he stood three times for election to the RSFSR Supreme Soviet he was unsuccessful. In early 1990 Travkin joined the Democratic Platform within the Communist Party and in March 1990 he resigned from the Party and appealed for the foundation of a democratic party as an alternative to the CPSU. In May 1990 the Democratic Party of Russia was founded and Travkin became leader but it split in December 1990 when Gary KASPAROV, Gennady BURBULIS and others quit in protest, citing Travkin's authoritarian behaviour as the reason.

He was at odds with many democrats over the future of the Soviet Union: he argued strongly for the maintenance of the Soviet Union, seeing its break-up as a disaster. In November 1991 the Democratic Party left the Democratic Russia (DemRossiya) movement. Travkin continued to exert influence after 1991 but he shared the weakness of the other democrats, an inability to unite and present a common platform of reform.

Trifonov, Yury Valentinovich (1925–81), a leading Russian novelist who chronicled the decline and demoralisation of the Russian intelligentsia. He was born into a Russian family in Moscow and his father, a founder member of the Cheka, was executed in 1938. He graduated from the Gorky Literary Institute, Moscow, 1949, and became well known a year later when his novel of student life, *Studenty* (*Students*), appeared and was awarded a Stalin Prize in 1951. His *Dom na Naberezhnoi* (*House on the Embankment*), 1976, was an instant success, as was *Starik* (*The Old Man*), 1979. His last novel, *Vremya i Mesto* (*Time and Place*), 1981, is openly critical of STALIN and his legacy.

Trotsky, Lev Davidovich (né **Bronstein**) (1879–1940), the most gifted orator and writer among the Bolsheviks, he was second only to LENIN in October 1917 and afterwards, but the leader's illness from 1922 onwards also marks Trotsky's political demise. He was a great bridesmaid but was quite incapable politically of ever becoming the bride. Perhaps it was due to resentment of his Jewishness that a gulf opened up between himself and ordinary people. He singularly failed to build up his own political 'tail', despite widespread support for his Left Communist views. A comrade once remarked that one could understand everything that STALIN said, some of what Lenin was saying, but Trotsky, he was talking to the gods. He is the classic case of the intellectual in politics who is easily out-manoeuvred by the more mundane, Party machine man. His prose is the most brilliant of the revolution but only a small minority of those he addressed were educated. A talented organiser, he threw himself with immense energy into tasks which interested him, but these were followed by periods of lassitude. Stalin hated and feared him and relentlessly attempted to denigrate him in the eyes of Lenin. This gradually affected Trotsky's health – one is tempted to say that many of his post-1922 illnesses were psychosomatic – and he needed to take time off to recuperate in the south. His wife comments that on one occasion, after a tempestuous Party meeting, he returned home bathed in sweat. It was remarkable that Trotsky subordinated himself to Lenin after August 1917 since earlier there had been many bitter feuds with the Bolshevik leader. Trotsky always saw himself as a natural number one, never as a number two. He first met Lenin in London in 1902 and there was mutual respect but at the IInd RSDRP Congress in 1903 he violently criticised Lenin's organisational blueprint for the Party, regarding him as a dictator and reminiscent of the mad Robespierre. He was also ill-suited to the moderate views of the Mensheviks but in 1905 he was a leading figure in the St Petersburg Soviet. He alternated between arrest, exile and escape but eventually moved abroad and travelled widely, participating everywhere in social democratic affairs. He was in New York when the February Revolution broke out and got back to Petrograd in May 1917. He merged his own group, Mezhraionka, with the Bolshevik Party and set sail under Bolshevik colours. One reason why he was reconciled with Lenin was that the latter had adopted Trotsky's theory of permanent revolution. Trotsky, like Lenin, scented revolution in the air in the summer of 1917. As head of the Military Revolutionary Committee, the General Staff of the revolution, in Petrograd, Trotsky played a vital role in the Bolshevik success. He was Commissar for Foreign Affairs in the first Sovnarkom (he saw himself as the conductor of world revolution) and was given the distasteful job of negotiating a peace treaty with the Germans and Austrians. Convinced that revolution in Germany was imminent, Trotsky dragged out proceedings (had the Bolsheviks concluded peace in late 1917 they would have obtained much better conditions than in March 1918), always expecting a telegram informing that Berlin was red. The peace issue tore the Party apart. Lenin wanted peace at any price and BUKHARIN and the Left Communists would not conclude peace at any price. Trotsky, typically, came up with the slogan of neither peace nor war, based on the false premise that the Germans were militarily incapable of advancing on the Russian Front. He departed the foreign affairs scene in March 1918 and was appointed Commissar for War and president of the Supreme War Soviet. He organised the Red Army from scratch and mastered military theory on the hoof. This was a brilliant achievement and he played the key role in ensuring that the Bolshevik regime survived. During the Civil War he clashed repeatedly with Stalin. It later became clear to Lenin that the two comrades could not bear one another and this could have disastrous consequences for the Party. Lenin regarded Trotsky as his natural successor but declined to propose this to the Party. This permitted the others to organise against Trotsky. It was almost child's play to outmanoeuvre Trotsky and the master manipulator was Stalin. No Bolshevik saw Stalin's end game: to become leader. Trotsky sided with the left in economics and advocated aid to revolutionary movements outside Russia. Stalin, sensing the mood of the country, put the security of the revolution in Russia ahead of international adventures. He, therefore, supported socialism in one country, which Trotsky ridiculed. Trotsky resigned his last important state office, Commissar for War, in 1925, when he could have hung on. He had been one of the builders of the Party which permitted the leaders to silence their critics and, in desperation, he and his supporters took to the streets in November 1927 to publicise their opposition to Stalin and his policies. He was exiled in 1928 and eventually went abroad, surprisingly being allowed by Stalin to take his archive with him, and eventually found refuge in Mexico in 1937. He continued his bitter feud with Stalin but by now it was David against Goliath. Despite this Stalin was always nervous about Trotsky's potential influence and his political police attempted to murder Trotsky on several occasions. They eventually succeeded in August 1940. Trotsky's writings inspired a legion of disciples, especially in the universities of the capitalist world, but their influence waned after the 1970s. Isaac Deutscher: *The Prophet Armed*; *The Prophet Unarmed*; *The Prophet Outcast*, 3 vols, London, 1954–63; Baruch Knei-Paz: *The Social and Political Thought of Leon Trotsky*, Oxford, 1978; Leon Trotsky: *The History of the Russian Revolution*, London, 1965; *My Life*, New York, 1930; *The Revolution Betrayed*, New York, 1937; *Stalin: An Appraisal of the Man and His Influence*, London, 1941.

Tsereteli, Irakli Georgevich (1881–1959), a leading Menshevik and foe of LENIN, Tsereteli was swept away by the rising tide of radicalism in 1917. He was a Georgian, born in Kutaisi, and his father was a writer and radical politician. He studied law at Moscow University but was arrested in 1902 for leading student demonstrations and exiled for five years to Irkutsk. His exile ended in 1903 and he returned to Tbilisi and joined the RSDRP. He took issue with Lenin's centralising tendencies (this may have had a lot to do with the fact that he was a

Georgian and Lenin's plans implied Russian domination of the Party). He was elected as a social democrat to the Second Duma in 1907 and proved a powerful orator. After it was dissolved he was sentenced to five years' imprisonment and then exiled in 1913 to Irkutsk. After the February Revolution, he returned to Petrograd and was made a member of the Soviet Executive Committee. As a Menshevik he advocated co-operation with the provisional government and supported a defensive war effort. He was a leading figure in the Russian Central Executive Committee of the Soviets and joined the first coalition government in May as Minister of Posts and Telegraphs. He returned to Georgia after the October Revolution and was elected to the Constituent Assembly but decided not to attend after the Bolsheviks issued an order to arrest him. In Georgia, where the Mensheviks came to power, he was not a major player, but represented his country at the Paris Peace Conference. After the Bolshevik take-over of Georgia in 1921 he continued his opposition but emigrated in 1923 to Paris and later to the United States. Not even the Soviet victory in the Second World War softened his opposition and he refused to attend a reception in the Soviet embassy in Paris in February 1945 to drink STALIN's health.

Tsipko, Aleksandr Sergeevich (b. 1941), he became prominent under GORBACHEV as an innovative and daring political analyst. He was born into a Russian family in Odessa and graduated in philosophy from Moscow State University, 1968, where he successfully defended his candidate dissertation (PhD), 1972. He joined the Institute of Economics of the World Socialist System, USSR Academy of Sciences, 1972, and accepted an invitation in 1978 from the Institute of Philosophy and Sociology, Warsaw, to work there: he presented a dissertation on the 'Philosophical and Sociological Foundations for Understanding Real Socialism' but it was rejected. He was a consultant to the international department, CPSU Central Committee, 1980–90, when he returned to the Institute of Economics of the World Socialist System as deputy director (the director was Oleg BOGO-MOLOV). In 1992 he became director for political programmes at the Gorbachev Fund, Moscow. He was a member of the Communist Party until 1991. A fundamental thesis he developed in many publications was the doctrinal link between Marx, LENIN and the foundations of Stalinism.

Tsvetaeva, Marina Ivanovna (1892–1941), rated by many as the greatest Russian poet of the twentieth century, her life was tragic and her fame was posthumous. She was born into a Russian family in Moscow, her father was the founder of the Pushkin Museum, and she studied in Moscow, Switzerland, Germany and Paris. She published her first verse in 1910 and married Sergei Efron in 1912. She lived in Moscow after the October Revolution and published verse praising the Whites (her husband had become a White officer). They emigrated in 1922 and eventually settled near Paris. Her poetry had a distinctive voice and did not fit into any contemporary category. This led to her estrangement from the émigré community. Her husband became involved with the GPU (later KGB) and after the murder of a GPU defector, he fled to the Soviet Union. Her daughter had also gone over to the Communists and had already returned to the USSR. She returned to the Soviet Union with her son, 1939, but was isolated and not permitted to publish. In 1941 she was evacuated to present-day Tatarstan but committed suicide soon after arrival.

Tsvigun, Semon Kuzmich (1917–82), as first deputy chair of the KGB, he played an important role in permitting the growth of corruption within that organisation, previously regarded as almost incorrupt-

ible. He graduated from the Odessa Pedagogical Institute, 1937, and joined the NKVD (later KGB), 1939, becoming a Smersh (death to spies) officer during the Great Fatherland War. He was deputy Minister of State Security and deputy chair of the NKVD–KGB in Moldavia, 1951–5, working with Leonid BREZHNEV and Konstantin CHERNENKO there. Then he moved to Tajikistan and was KGB chief, 1957–63, then KGB head in Azerbaijan, 1963–7. He was Brezhnev's brother-in-law and when Yury ANDROPOV was appointed chair of the USSR KGB in 1967, Brezhnev brought Tsvigun to Moscow as first deputy to Andropov. Tsvigun was a candidate member of the CPSU Central Committee, 1971–81, and then a full member. Brezhnev protected him against Andropov's evidence of corruption but Andropov struck and began an investigation when Brezhnev's health failed. Tsvigun shot himself as a result.

Tukhachevsky, Marshal Mikhail Nikolaevich (1893–1937), one of the architects of the Red Army, Tukhachevsky's brilliant career was cut short by suspicions about his loyalty to the Soviet Union. He was of aristocratic Polish background and graduated from military school in 1914. He was an officer in the First World War, was captured by the Germans in 1915 (Charles de Gaulle was a fellow prisoner) and escaped to Russia after the February Revolution. He joined the nascent Red Army and the Communist Party in 1918. He had a brilliant Civil War and led the Red Army invasion of Poland where he crossed swords for the first time with STALIN. There were serious differences of opinion and Stalin was partly blamed for the Soviet defeat on the Vistula. He headed the troops who crushed the Kronstadt revolt and the peasant uprising in Tambov guberniya. He was made head of the military academy in 1921 and this permitted him to begin the comprehensive retraining of the Red Army. He recognised early the significance of tanks and armoured vehicles, and was a major influence in developing tactical and strategic concepts, especially mobility of forces. Soviet military doctrine became offensive, the next war was going to be fought on someone else's territory. He was Chief of the General Staff, 1925–8. He then became commander of the Leningrad military district. In 1931 he was appointed deputy chair of the Revolutionary Military Soviet and in 1934, deputy; from 1936 he was first deputy Commissar for Defence and head of the administration for military training. He was very popular in the military and became a Marshal of the Soviet Union in 1935. He was elected a candidate member of the Central Committee at the XVIIth Party Congress in 1934. In January 1936 he was head of the Soviet delegation to the funeral of King George V in London and afterwards visited France (where he was able to practise his fluent French) and Germany. Stalin, who never trusted the top military, obtained information about Tukhachevsky's alleged treachery from President Benes of Czechoslovakia. Benes believed the information to be true but it appears to have been fabricated by German counter-intelligence and then leaked to Benes. In May 1937 Tukhachevsky was downgraded to commander of the Volga military district. In June 1937 he was arrested and executed for high treason and conspiring with the military leaders of foreign powers (the leaked material was never mentioned in the Soviet press). This was a coup for German counter-intelligence and Tukhachevsky's execution led to the mass slaughter of the top ranks of the Soviet military. The Soviet Union paid a heavy price for this during the first year of the war against Germany. He was rehabilitated under GORBACHEV.

Tupolev, Andrei Nikolaevich (1888–1972), one of the most brilliant aeronautical engineers in the Soviet Union,

and indeed the world, who played a key role in the development of both military and civilian aircraft. He was born into a Russian family, his father was a lawyer, in present-day Tver oblast, and graduated from the Moscow Higher Technical School, where one of his teachers was Nikolai Zhukovsky. Tupolev was one of the founders of the Aerodynamic Aircraft Design Bureau, 1916, which after the October Revolution became the Central Aerodynamics and Hydrodynamics Institute. He helped to develop heavy bombers during the early 1930s but was arrested in 1937 and falsely charged with selling aircraft designs to Germany. He was put into a special prison design bureau and told to earn his remission. He was released from the bureau in 1943 after the TU-2 bomber (named after him) proved itself. After 1945 he contributed to the development of many other military and civil aircraft (all aircraft in the Soviet Union were dual purpose, military and civil). Among these were the passenger aircraft TU-104 and the Soviet version of the Concorde, the TU-144, which was a commercial failure. The name of the supersonic aircraft indicated it was the 144th aircraft to be principally designed by Tupolev. After his death, his son, Andrei Andreevich continued the family tradition and helped to develop other military and civil aircraft. Tupolev was elected to the USSR Academy of Sciences, 1953, but never joined the Communist Party.

Turishcheva, Lyudmila Ivanovna (b. 1952), an outstandingly successful gymnast, she won all the major competitions she entered. She was born in Grozny, Chechnya, graduated from the Rostov Pedagogical Institute, 1974, and moved to Kiev Dinamo, 1978, when she was already a world champion. She was a member of the Communist Party from 1978 to 1991. She first participated in the Olympic Games in Mexico, 1968, at the age of sixteen, winning a team gold medal. She won her first solo Olympic title in 1972 and won further team gold medals in 1972 and 1976. She was USSR champion, 1970–5, world champion, 1970 and 1974, European champion, 1971 and 1973 and world cup winner, 1975–6. Altogether she won twenty-four gold medals in competition. She married Valery BORZOV, the first Soviet athlete to win the 100 metres gold in the Olympics.

Tvardovsky, Aleksandr Trofimovich (1910–71), a fine Russian poet and the greatest literary editor at a seminal period in Soviet culture. He was born into a Russian family near Smolensk and his family was classified as kulak and dispossessed. He graduated from the Moscow Institute of Philosophy and Literature, 1939, and joined the Communist Party, 1940. During the 1930s his poetry lauded collectivisation and he became the most popular poet in the country while a war correspondent from 1939 onwards. This experience provided the material for his long narrative poem on the life and travails of the simple soldier, *Vasily (Vasya) Terkin*. As editor of *Novy Mir*, 1950–4, and 1958–70, he transformed it into the leading literary journal and made it hugely influential. He obtained KHRUSHCHEV's permission to publish Aleksandr SOLZHENITSYN's *One Day in the Life of Ivan Denisovich*, 1962. This created a sensation as it broke the taboo about telling the truth about the camps. In 1961 he was elected a candidate member of the Central Committee but lost this in 1966, partly due to his closeness to Solzhenitsyn. He wrote a sequel to *Vasily Terkin*, which is bitter and morose. The late 1960s were uncongenial and he became despondent and took to the bottle. He was replaced as editor in 1970, died soon after and was buried in Novodeviche Cemetery. In 1988 GORBACHEV decided to donate the royalties from his works to a foundation to erect a memorial to Vasily Terkin.

U

Unshlikht, Iosif Stanislavovich (1879–1918), one of the original hard men of the Cheka, his execution in August 1918 led to the rapid expansion of the Red Terror against opponents of the Bolshevik regime. He was of Polish Jewish origin and soon converted to social democracy, joining the Social Democratic Party of the Kingdom of Poland and Lithuania, gaining rapid promotion. After spending years in imperial jails and exile, he returned to Petrograd and as a member of TROTSKY's Mezhraionka and joined the Bolshevik Party in August 1917 when the two groups merged. Unshlikht was elected a member of the Central Committee. He participated in the October Revolution and became a top Cheka officer when the organisation was formally set up in December 1917. One of his tasks was to help suppress the Constituent Assembly in January 1918. He was ruthless in eliminating perceived counter-revolutionaries but he fell to an assassin's bullet in August 1918.

Usmankhodzhaev, Inamzhon Buzrukovich (*b.* 1930), the main casualty of the great Uzbek cotton scandal which involved fabricating output data and then paying bribes to every official necessary to conceal the falsehoods. He was born into an Uzbek family, graduated from the Central Asian Polytechnic Institute, Tashkent, 1955, and joined the Communist Party, 1958. He worked as an engineer on the Fergana irrigation project and entered the Uzbek Party apparatus, before moving to Moscow as an instructor of the CPSU Central Committee, 1969–72. He was first secretary, Andizhan obkom,

1974–8, when he was elected to the Central Committee, Communist Party of Uzbekistan. In the same year he became chair of the Presidium, Uzbek Supreme Soviet (head of state), and he became *ex officio* a deputy chair of the Presidium, USSR Supreme Soviet. He was elected to the CPSU Central Committee in 1981. In 1983 he became first secretary, Communist Party of Uzbekistan, and remained in office until he was dismissed in January 1988 as investigations into the cotton scandal pointed to his guilt. He was tried and sentenced to twelve years in jail, December 1989. Corruption in Moscow's eyes was something different to the Uzbeks. They regarded it as part and parcel of reclaiming their republic from the Russians. The CPSU agonised about putting a top Party official on trial as it could confirm the belief of many ordinary citizens that the Party nomenklatura all feathered their own nests.

Ustinov, Marshal Dmitry Fedorovich (1908–84), a very influential administrator of the Soviet defence sector, winning for it during the BREZHNEV years an unprecedented proportion of the Soviet state budget. He was born into a Russian family in Samara, joined the Communist Party, 1927, and then graduated as an engineer from the Bauman Higher Technical School, Moscow, and the Leningrad Military Technical Institute, 1934. He worked in the armaments industry and was director of the Bolshevik arms enterprise, Leningrad. He became People's Commissar for the Arms Industry shortly after the German invasion of June 1941 at the exceptionally young age of thirty-two. His skills were put to the test by the German advance and he successfully supervised the transfer of much industry to the rear. In 1946 he became USSR Minister for Armaments. One of his major concerns after 1945 was debriefing captured German scientists and this contributed to Soviet rocket development. On STALIN's death he was appointed USSR Minister for the Defence Industry and as such promoted space research. In 1957–63, he was deputy chair, USSR Council of Ministers, and 1963–5 first deputy chair, with his main responsibility being the defence sector. Elected to the Central Committee, 1952, he moved into the Party apparatus in 1965, probably at BREZHNEV's instigation, as Central Committee secretary for the defence industry. He was also made a candidate member of the Politburo, becoming a full member in 1976. When Marshal GRECHKO died in 1976 he was chosen to succeed him as USSR Minister of Defence. Ustinov, a civilian, broke the tradition that a military man should be Defence Minister. He was promoted marshal a few months afterwards because, according to some sources, the top military would not talk to a mere nonprofessional military general. Ustinov remained in office until he died. In his memoirs GORBACHEV relates that discussion of the military budget and the burden to the country was taboo at Politburo meetings. He later estimated defence spending at 40 per cent of the state budget. This burden gradually denuded other sectors, especially health and education, of funds, as military expenditure rose faster than GDP. During the late Brezhnev era the military enjoyed an unprecedented influence over defence and foreign policy.

V

Vasilevsky, Marshal Aleksandr Mikhailovich (1895–1977), he played a key role in the success of the Red Army during the Great Fatherland War. He was Chief of Staff for most of the war, participated in all major planning meetings, and was co-ordinator of many fronts and strategic flanks. He was an officer during the First World War, joined the Red Army and participated in the Civil War. He graduated from the Academy of the General Staff in 1937. During the 1930s he held various posts in the Commissariat of Defence. He was deputy chief of Operations Control, then Chief of the General Staff, 1941–2, and deputy Commissar for Defence, 1942. His reputation rests on his co-ordination of three different fronts which took part in the Stalingrad Offensive, November 1942, together with VORONOV and ZHUKOV. In July 1943, Vasilevsky and Zhukov personally oversaw preparations and the construction of defensive fortifications at the Kursk salient. He vetoed the proposal of VATUTIN and KHRUSHCHEV that the Red Army should attack first, arguing that the Wehrmacht should be enticed into an offensive, thereby weakening it by attrition. The Red Army, however, learnt the exact time of the German offensive and launched a bombardment of the German positions, thereby restricting the impact of the offensive. In 1944, Vasilevsky was put in charge of co-ordinating operations of the 2nd and 3rd Fronts in East Prussia and Belorussia and masterminded the final offensive from Warsaw to Berlin, 1944–5. He maintained constant contact with STALIN throughout this period and when CHERNYA-KHOVSKY was killed in action, Vasilevsky took over from him and led the East Prussian campaign himself. Vasilevsky deputised for Stalin in Moscow when the latter was attending the Yalta Conference, February 1945. In June 1945 he was posted to the Far East Front as commander-in-chief against the Japanese. After the war he again became Chief of the General Staff and deputy USSR Minister of Defence, 1946. He was Minister of the Armed Forces, 1949–53 and deputy USSR Minister of Defence, 1953–7. He was a member of the Central Committee of the Communist Party from 1952 to 1961 and was one of the most decorated military officers, receiving seven Orders of Lenin.

Vatutin, General Nikolai Fedorovich (1887–1943), one of the most successful Red Army commanders during the Great Fatherland War. He joined the Red Army in 1920 and participated in the Civil War. He graduated from the Frunze Military Academy in 1929 and the Academy of the General Staff, 1937. In 1941 he was head of General Staff Operations. He assumed command of the Voronezh Front in 1942, his first important command post. In November 1942 he commanded the South-west Front during its offensive at Stalingrad and together with SOKO-SSOVSKY and EREMENKO intercepted and trapped Paulus's 6th Army. During the Kursk campaign of July 1943 Vatutin halted the advance of von Manstein's forces and went on to liberate Kharkov. His forces then moved towards Kiev and the offensive launched in December 1943 took the Ukrainian capital in January

1944. In March 1944 he and his troops, heading for Rovno, were ambushed by anti-communist Ukrainian partisans. He was fatally wounded and consequently became the most senior Red Army officer to be killed by Ukrainian anti-communists.

Vavilov, Nikolai Ivanovich (1887–1943), the leading Soviet geneticist of his generation, he fell victim to the machinations of his political and scientific competitors. He was born into a Russian family and graduated from the Moscow Agricultural Institute (now the Timiryazev Academy) and studied plant immunity in England, coming into contact with William Bateson, one of the founders of genetics. He was director of the Botanical Institute, 1921–4, and director when it was renamed the All-Union Institute of Plant Breeding, 1924–40. He travelled the world during the 1920s and 1930s and built up a remarkable collection of cultivated plants to use in breeding. In 1929 he was elected to the RSFSR Central Executive Committee (subsequently the USSR Supreme Soviet), the USSR Academy of Sciences, and he founded and was the first director of the Lenin All-Union Academy of Agricultural Sciences, Moscow. In 1930 he became director of the USSR Academy of Sciences genetics laboratory, and he upgraded this to the Institute of Genetics, heading it from 1933 to 1940. He was elected a Fellow of the Royal Society and to many other foreign bodies. In 1929 he promoted the career of T. D. LYSENKO but Lysenko attacked genetics in 1935 as a bourgeois pseudo-science and eventually took over as director of the Lenin All-Union Academy. He and his supporters hounded Vavilov (who was not adept at resisting political attacks) and his supporters, and Vavilov broke with Lysenko in 1939. Vavilov was arrested in August 1940, while collecting plants in western Ukraine (just taken from Poland by the Soviet Union), and was accused of being a British spy and of

sabotaging Soviet agriculture. He was found guilty, sentenced to death but this was commuted and he died of malnutrition in Saratov Jail in January 1943. He was later rehabilitated and his old institute now bears his name. There was also a Vavilov gold medal for outstanding achievement in the development of Soviet agriculture. Mark Popovsky: *The Vavilov Affair*, Hamden, Conn., 1984.

Velikhov, Evgeny Pavlovich (*b.* 1935), one of the leading nuclear physicists in the Soviet Union, he became well known after the Chernobyl disaster, 1986, when he visited the site to study the origins and consequences of the explosion. He was born into a Russian family in Moscow and graduated from Moscow State University, where he became a professor in 1973. He successfully presented his candidate (PhD) and his doctoral (Dsc) dissertations in physics and mathematics, 1964, at the Kurchatov Institute. He joined the Kurchatov Institute of Atomic Energy, 1961, becoming a director of a branch of the institute from 1971 until 1984. He was elected a corresponding member of the USSR Academy of Sciences in 1968 and joined the Communist Party in 1971. In 1975 he was appointed head of the Soviet thermonuclear programme, was vice-president, USSR Academy of Sciences, 1978–90, and was elected director of the Kurchatov Institute, 1988. He was chair of the Committee of Soviet Scientists for the Defence of Peace and Against Nuclear War, 1983–8. He was a scientific adviser to GORBACHEV before he became leader and as such visited Great Britain with him in December 1984, helped by his fluent English. He was a candidate member of the Central Committee, 1986–9, and a full member, 1989–90. In 1991 Gorbachev made him a member of his Presidential Council. He was elected to the USSR Congress of People's Deputies in 1989. Rarely has an outstanding scientist played such a political and social role in the Soviet Union, and this was an indication of the new openness that the Gorbachev era had made possible.

Vilyams, Vasily Robertovich (1863–1939), a leading agronomist and soil scientist, his theories of grassland management were imposed on Soviet agriculture during the 1930s. He graduated from the Petrov Academy, 1887, and became head of the department of agronomy and soil science, Moscow Agricultural (now Timiryazev) Academy, 1894, and remained there until he died. He joined the Communist Party, 1928, and was quickly a favourite of the planners who wanted to increase agricultural productivity rapidly. He favoured organic fertilizers and fallow land but this fell out of favour during KHRUSHCHEV's drive to boost agricultural output more rapidly, including cutting back on fallow and using chemical fertilizers.

Vishnevskaya, Galina Pavlovna (b. 1926), a famous Russian soprano, married to Mstislav ROSTROPOVICH, who like him resisted the staid conservative cultural bureaucrats of the BREZHNEV era. She was born into a Russian family in Leningrad (now St Petersburg). She began her career in 1944 in operetta and in 1952 became a soloist at the Bolshoi, becoming well known for her interpretation of such roles as Tatyana (*Evgeny Onegin*), Liza (*The Queen of Spades*) and Violetta (*La Traviata*). She developed a repertory which included Mussorgsky, Tchaikovsky and Shostakovich. In 1974 she left the Soviet Union with her husband, continued giving concerts, made records and taught masterclasses. In 1978 the USSR Supreme Soviet deprived her and her husband of their Soviet citizenship but it was restored to both in 1990. The soprano part in Benjamin Britten's *War Requiem* was written for her, although she was not given permission by Moscow to attend the première in Coventry Cathedral. Britten's song cycle, *The Poet's Echo*, and Shostakovich's *Seven Romances*, op. 127, are dedicated to her. Her memoirs are a no-holds-barred account of Soviet culture. Galina Vishnevskaya: *Galina*, London, 1984.

Vlasov, Aleksandr Vladimirovich (b. 1932), a leading official under GORBACHEV who had to contend with the rising tide of nationalism as USSR Minister of Internal Affairs. He was born into a Russian family in the Buryat Autonomous Republic and graduated from the Irkutsk Mining Metallurgical Institute, 1954. He joined the Communist Party in 1956. He was appointed second secretary, Yakut Party obkom in 1965 and in 1972 he was called to Moscow to work in the Central Committee apparatus, especially with respect to alleged corruption in the Chechen-Ingush Autonomous Republic. In 1975 he became first Party secretary in the republic and remained there until 1984 when he transferred to Rostov as first secretary of the obkom. Gorbachev appointed him USSR Minister of Internal Affairs, 1986, and in October 1988 he was made chair, RSFSR Council of Ministers and a candidate member of the Politburo. In 1990 he was replaced as head of the Russian government by Ivan SILAEV.

Vlasov, General Andrei Andreevich (1900–46), the highest-ranking Red Army defector to the Germans during the Great Fatherland War. He joined the Red Army in 1919 and participated in the Civil War. He was a military adviser to Chiang Kai-shek in China, 1938–9. In August 1941 he showed great bravery in the defence of Kiev when completely surrounded by the Germans. STALIN permitted him to withdraw and made him commander of the 2nd Assault Army defending Moscow. He was promoted lieutenant general after the Battle of Moscow, January 1942. He was then made second in command of the Northwest Front, whose task was to break the

Leningrad siege. He was captured by the Germans outside Sevastopol, Crimea, May 1942. He had become disillusioned with the Red Army high command and refused to attempt to escape from Sevastopol. He soon began making propaganda broadcasts against Stalin and proposed to the Germans the formation of a People's Army to fight against Stalin but Hitler was very sceptical. In June 1943 Hitler personally ordered him to desist from all activities except propaganda and in October ordered the transfer of all Russian and other national units with the Wehrmacht to the Western Front. Hitler's orders were partly ignored by some German commanders. In November 1944 Himmler gave him permission to form the Committee for the Liberation of the Peoples of Russia which was to seek recruits in German prisoner-of-war camps and among Russian civilians who had been transported to Germany for forced labour. In Prague Vlasov published the Prague Manifesto attacking Stalin for his annexation of foreign territory and his maltreatment of nationalities. Vlasov became commander-in-chief of the Russian Liberation Army (ROA) and in February 1945 its first division was formed. However, Hitler preferred to use the army mainly for propagandistic purposes since he was not convinced of its loyalty. Their first taste of action was in April 1945 against the Red Army on the Oder Front but they made little impact and moved to Czechoslovakia. In May 1945 one division helped the Czechs during the Prague uprising, defeated the German SS and thereby ensured its success. Vlasov wanted to hand over Czechoslovakia to the Americans but this offer was declined. Many of Vlasov's men surrendered to the Americans but before being handed over to the Russians between 1945 and 1947 (according to the Yalta Agreement) they committed suicide rather than return to certain death in the Soviet Union. Vlasov was captured by the Red Army in

May 1945 and *Pravda* announced in August 1946 that he and several of his officers had been tried for espionage and treason against the Soviet Union, found guilty and hanged. Vlasov is a tragic figure who had to choose between the devil he knew and the devil he did not know. He chose Hitler who never trusted him. Under glasnost there was renewed interest in him, several articles were published and a film made about him. C. Andreyev: *Vlasov and the Russian Liberation Movement*, Cambridge, 1987; N. Bethell: *The Last Secret*, London, 1976; Nikolai Tolstoy: *Victims of Yalta*, London, 1987.

Voinovich, Vladimir Nikolaevich (*b.* 1932), a critical writer who became well known for his satire of Soviet army life and later emigrated. He was born in Dushanbe, Tajikistan, and was a shepherd, mechanic, and served four years in the Red Army. His first stories were published in *Novy Mir*, 1961–7, describing the life of ordinary workers and peasants. His fame rests on the *Life and Unusual Adventures of Private Ivan Chonkin*. It circulated in samizdat within the Soviet Union and the first part was published abroad without his knowledge, 1969, with later parts appearing in 1975 and 1979. He was expelled from the USSR Writers' Union, 1974, and his *Ivankiad*, 1976, satirises the Writers' Union. Other books appeared before he emigrated to West Germany in 1980. He was deprived of his Soviet citizenship, July 1981, but it was restored in 1990. Voinovich has been a professor at Princeton University and was elected a member of the Bavarian Academy of Fine Arts. Under glasnost, almost all of his works were published in the Soviet Union.

Volkogonov, Dmitry Antonovich (1928–95), a political general who, during GORBACHEV's glasnost, suddenly flowered into the leading contemporary historian who was fearless in revealing the unsavoury crimes of the STALIN era. Later he demolished LENIN's and TROTSKY's reputations in Russia. His father, an agrarian specialist, was arrested in 1937 for possessing a pamphlet by Nikolai BUKHARIN. Volkogonov had the mortifying experience of finding confirmation that his father had been shot while researching his biography of Stalin. He graduated from the Orlov Tank College and held posts in various military districts. He became a member of the Communist Party in 1951. His intellectual potential was recognised and he studied at the V. I. Lenin Military-Political Academy, 1963–6. In 1966 he successfully presented his candidate dissertation on the moral development of the Soviet soldier (PhD) and in 1971 successfully presented his doctoral dissertation in philosophy on the problems of military-ethical theory (DLitt), becoming a professor at the academy. He was in the main political administration of the army and navy, 1969–88, and was promoted colonel general, 1984. He was deputy head of the main administration, 1984–8 (1984–5 deputy to Aleksei EPISHEV). In 1988 he became head of the Institute of Military History of the USSR Ministry of Defence. In 1990 he successfully presented his doctoral dissertation in history (DLitt). As a senior political officer he visited pro-Moscow countries such as Vietnam, Yemen, Syria, Ethiopia and Afghanistan. He saw at first hand the brutalities of the dictatorships supported by Moscow. His official position gave him privileged access to Soviet archives and he created a sensation in the Soviet Union with his multi-volume demolition of Stalin, published in 1988. When he had originally presented it for publication, in 1984, he was blandly told that one person could not write on Stalin, such a task would require a whole institute. He then moved back in time to Lenin, a most difficult subject for a former Communist. 'This fortress was the last to fall in my heart,' he observed. He blamed Lenin for stealing his idealism and Stalin his youth. The biography of Lenin, published in 1994, caused a predictable storm of protest. His biography of Trotsky, whom he regards as the architect of state terror in the Soviet Union, appeared in 1996. An iconoclast, his first volume of a study of the Great Fatherland War (1941–5) placed Soviet orthodoxy on its head. He analysed Stalin's destruction of the officer corps, the defeats of 1941 and the arrest of returning prisoners-of-war in 1945. Much of this came as a shock to the average Soviet citizen. In March 1991, as a result, he was denounced as a traitor by Marshal Dmitry YAZOV, USSR Minister of Defence, and a host of generals. He resigned as director of the Institute of Military History and became a military adviser to President YELTSIN. He was also politically active, being elected as a deputy to the RSFSR Supreme Soviet in 1985 and was a delegate to the XXVIIth and XXVIIIth Party Congresses. He was elected as a deputy for Orenburg to the RSFSR Congress of People's Deputies and the RSFSR Supreme Soviet in 1990, defeating Viktor CHERNOMYRDIN, who became Russian Prime Minister in December 1992. He was elected to the State Duma in December 1993. He was a great populariser and set foot where professional historians were unwilling to tread. The latter are critical of his use of sources and desire to pass moral judgements. He is survived by his wife, Galina, and two daughters.

Volsky, Arkady Ivanovich (*b.* 1932), a highly successful and adaptable industrial official under GORBACHEV who became quite influential as the voice of the industrial lobby under YELTSIN for a time but then faded away. He was born into a Russian family in Gomel oblast and graduated from the Moscow Steel and Alloy Institute, 1955. He then began on the shop floor in the Likhachev car plant, Moscow, and became head of the

Party organisation there. He moved into the department for machine building, Central Committee Secretariat, 1969, progressing to become first deputy head of department, 1981–3. He was an assistant to Yury ANDROPOV and Konstantin CHERNENKO when they were Party General Secretaries. Volsky then returned to the department of machine building as head, 1985–8. He was then appointed the Party and USSR Supreme Soviet representative in Nagorno-Karabakh, and 1989–90 he was chair of the special administration which ruled the war-torn oblast. He returned to Moscow and was made head of the committee for the management of the USSR economy in 1991. In 1992 Volsky was elected president of the Russian Union of Industrialists and Entrepreneurs and one of the leaders of the political movement Civic Union. The movement did poorly in the December 1993 elections to the Duma and Volsky faded from view. He was elected to the USSR Congress of People's Deputies, 1989, was a member of the Communist Party, 1958–91, and a member of the Central Committee, 1986–91.

Voronov, Marshal Nikolai Nikolaevich (1899–1968), the leading artillery specialist in the Red Army, he was mainly responsible for the massive artillery build-up from the 1930s to the 1950s. He joined the Red Army in 1918 and participated in the Civil War. He graduated from the Frunze Military Academy in 1930 and became director of the 1st Leningrad Artillery School in 1934. He was a military adviser to the republicans during the Spanish Civil War, 1936–7. He was then appointed head of artillery of the armed forces, until 1950. During the Soviet–Finnish War he was able to deploy artillery to breach the Mannerheim Line, 1939. He was a Marshal of Artillery and a member of Stavka during the Great Fatherland War. He commanded artillery on the Leningrad Front, 1941 and was deputy Commissar for Defence, July

1941–March 1943. His greatest achievement may have been the Stalingrad Offensive which he planned with VASILEVSKY and ZHUKOV. The offensive began with 2,000 of Voronov's guns pounding the German lines. He then moved on to Kursk where he planned the deployment of artillery and anti-aircraft guns, July 1943. He was director of the Artillery Academy, 1950–8, and among his many decorations were six Orders of Lenin.

Vorontsov, Yuly Mikhailovich (*b.* 1929), a leading Soviet diplomat who played an important role in Soviet–American relations under GORBACHEV. He was born into a Russian family in Leningrad (St Petersburg) and graduated from the Moscow State Institute of International Relations, 1952. He joined the USSR Ministry of Foreign Affairs (MID) and worked in the second European department until 1954 when he was posted to the Soviet mission to the United Nations, New York. In 1958 he returned to MID but then moved back to New York as a counsellor to the permanent Soviet representative, 1963–5. In 1966 he became a counsellor envoy in the Soviet embassy in Washington, until in 1977 he was appointed Soviet Ambassador to India. In 1983 he became Soviet Ambassador to France and in 1986–90 he was first deputy USSR Minister of Foreign Affairs, and simultaneously was given the difficult task of being Soviet Ambassador to Afghanistan, 1988–9. In 1990 he became permanent Soviet representative to the United Nations with the rank of a deputy USSR Minister of Foreign Affairs, until the collapse of the Soviet Union in 1991. A skilful diplomat he forged good relations with the US administration at a time when there was increasing co-operation between the superpowers, for example, on the Gulf War. Vorontsov was head of the Soviet delegation during the negotiations on nuclear and space weapons in Geneva and was the personal envoy of President Gorbachev in Ethiopia. In January 1992 he became the Russian permanent representative at the United Nations and in August 1992 President YELTSIN's personal adviser on foreign policy. Vorontsov joined the Communist Party in 1956 and was a member of the Central Committee, 1981–90.

Voroshilov, Marshal Klimenty Efremovich (1881–1969), close to STALIN from the Civil War, he proved a great survivor until KHRUSHCHEV decided he no longer had any need for him. He joined the Bolshevik Party, 1903, and was chair of the Lugansk Soviet in Ukraine during the 1905 revolution. He was arrested, exiled, escaped and worked underground for the Party, 1908–17. He again became chair of Lugansk Soviet after the October Revolution. He played a leading role in the formation of the Red Army in the south and commanded Red forces against WRANGEL at Tsaritsyn (Stalingrad/Volgograd). He and the future Marshal BUDENNY organised the 1st Cavalry Army. He worked closely with Stalin at this time and participated in the crushing of the Kronstadt revolt, 1921. He was commander of the Moscow military district, 1924–34, and sided with Stalin against TROTSKY. Voroshilov succeeded FRUNZE as People's Commissar for War and Navy, 1925. He was People's Commissar for Defence, 1934–40, and a close ally of Stalin during the latter's purging of the armed forces. Voroshilov became responsible for the mechanisation of the Red Army and was promoted marshal in 1935. He met the Anglo-French military mission, 1939, in Moscow, to discuss the defence of Poland if attacked by Germany. The talks were inconclusive as Stalin had decided on an agreement with Hitler. Voroshilov gave way to the more able TIMOSHENKO, May 1940, as part of the reorganisation of the Red Army. He then became a deputy chair of Sovnarkom and chair of the

Defence Committee. When Stalin set up the State Defence Committee (GKO), July 1941, its members were Stalin, Voroshilov, MOLOTOV and BERIA. GKO was responsible for the overall running of the war and the mobilisation of domestic Soviet resources. Voroshilov was put in command of the armies of the Northwest Front but could do little to stem the German advance on Leningrad partly due to his lack of military expertise but also because his troops were not well equipped. He and ZHDANOV set up a Military Soviet for the Defence of Leningrad without consulting Stalin. For this piece of insubordination (untypical for him), Voroshilov was dismissed (together with Zhdanov) when it became clear that they had failed. He was commander-in-chief of the partisan movement (under the NKVD) for three months in 1942 and was involved with staff work for the rest of the war. As a member of Stavka he was involved in talks with the Allies on the possibility of an allied air force in Transcaucasia, August 1942 and he attended the Tehran Conference in November 1943. He signed the armistice with Hungary for the Allies and later headed the Allied (Soviet) Control Commission in Hungary, 1946–7. He was deputy USSR Prime Minister, 1946–53, and then became chair of the Presidium of the USSR Supreme Soviet (which made him head of state) until 1960. He was a member of the Anti-Party Group against Khrushchev in July 1957, but because of his willingness to engage in self-criticism and his long-term association with Khrushchev, he kept his position. He was a member of the Central Committee of the Communist Party, 1921–61, and a member of the Politburo, 1926–60. In 1970, Lugansk, which had borne his name from 1935–58, was again called Voroshilovgrad, but reverted to its original name again in 1989.

Vorotnikov, Vitaly Ivanovich (b. 1926), like many other politicians who achieved high office under GORBACHEV, he came to question the direction the General Secretary was taking. He was born into a Russian family in Voronezh, joined the Communist Party, 1947, and progressed through various supervisory jobs in a Samara aviation enterprise, becoming head of the Party organisation there, 1955. He transferred to Party work in the Samara obkom, 1960, and he became second secretary, 1965. Then in 1967 he became chair of the Samara oblast soviet executive committee (it was quite common at that time for a Party official to switch to local government functions and then to return to Party work). In 1971 he returned to Voronezh to become first secretary of the obkom. He was also elected a member of the Central Committee. In 1975 he was called to Moscow to become first deputy chair, RSFSR Council of Ministers, but he fell out with the group around BREZHNEV and in 1979 he was sent abroad as Soviet Ambassador to Cuba. When ANDROPOV entered the Central Committee Secretariat in 1982 he recalled Vorotnikov and made him first secretary, Krasnodar kraikom. He made further progress under Andropov in 1983 when he was appointed chair, RSFSR Council of Ministers. The same year he was appointed a candidate, then a full member of the Politburo. He did not take to Gorbachev and his radical concepts and in 1988 he ceased to be Russian Prime Minister and became chair, Presidium of the RSFSR Supreme Soviet (head of state) but at that time the post was more honorific than real. When the new RSFSR Congress of People's Deputies and Supreme Soviet was established in 1990 YELTSIN quickly took over as chair (speaker) and later as President of Russia. Vorotnikov's career was over.

Voznesensky, Aleksandr Alekseevich (1900–50), a brother of Nikolai VOZNESENSKY, a leading economist and deputy USSR Prime Minister, who also fell victim to foul play after the death of Andrei

ZHDANOV in August 1948. Aleksandr rose to become RSFSR Minister of Education and rector of the Kirov Leningrad State University. He was one of the many victims of the Leningrad Affair (which was probably masterminded by MALENKOV for political gain) and was found guilty of conspiring to separate the RSFSR from the USSR and proclaim Leningrad the Russian capital (it had been the Russian capital from 1703 to 1914 as St Petersburg and from 1914 to 1918 as Petrograd). His sister, Mariya, a Party official, was also executed. The Leningrad Affair underlined the continuing tension between the 'old' capital and the new (Moscow).

Voznesensky, Andrei Andreevich (b. 1933), an immensely popular poet in the early 1960s when stadia were filled to hear him declaim his verse. He was born into a Russian family in Moscow and graduated from the Moscow Architectural Institute, 1957. He began publishing in the late 1950s and was a member of a group of promising young poets which also included Evgeny EVTUSHENKO and Bella AKHMADULINA. After the appearance of *Parabola*, 1960, he was criticised for formalism but it did not harm his career. Other works, such as *The Three-cornered Pear*, 1962, contributed to his reputation. He adapted one of his poems into a rock musical and it was successful in the Soviet Union and the United States. After 1985 he was recognised in the Soviet Union as one of the leading poets of his generation.

Voznesensky, Nikolai Alekseevich (1903–50), a leading Soviet economist who fell victim to political infighting after the death of his patron, Andrei ZHDANOV. He graduated from the Sverdlov Communist University, Moscow, 1921, then studied and taught at the Institute of Red Professors, 1928–31. He was made chair of Gosplan, 1938, and also elected to the Central Committee of the Communist

Party in the same year. He became first deputy chair of Sovnarkom, 1941, and as such the top state economist. He played a key role in managing the wartime economy and wrote an account of it, *Wartime Economy of the USSR in the Period of the Patriotic War*, 1945. Voznesensky was a member of the Special Committee on the Atom Bomb, set up in August 1945, and headed by BERIA. There was considerable tension between the politicians and the scientists on the committee and Petr KAPITSA went so far as to write to STALIN in October 1945 complaining about Beria's behaviour. In November 1945 he again wrote to Stalin claiming that Beria, MALENKOV and Voznesensky conducted themselves in the Special Committee 'as if they were supermen'. In late 1944 the Committee for the Rehabilitation of the Economy of Liberated Areas was formed. A goal of the committee was to deprive the Soviet Occupation Zone of (east) Germany of its economic and military potential by dismantling industry there. Some members of the Soviet leadership, including Andrei Zhdanov and Anastas MIKOYAN, People's Commissar for Foreign Trade, favoured allowing east Germany to recover to pay reparations through output. They wanted Voznesensky to take control of the east German economy and to work closely with Mikoyan's commissariat. The death of Zhdanov in August 1948 deprived Voznesensky of his political protector. Beria was jealous of his influence in the USSR Council of Ministers (successor to Sovnarkom) and MOLOTOV later claimed that Beria persuaded Stalin to remove Voznesensky. Another source states that the police had originally charged him with losing secret documents but Voznesensky managed to escape this snare. He was arrested again in late 1949, tried and executed with the other defendants in the Leningrad Affair in late 1950. Among the accusations levelled at him and the others was that they had conspired to separate the Russian Federation

from the USSR and make Leningrad its capital. His brother, ALEKSANDR ALEKSEEVICH, was also executed.

Vyalyas, Vaino Iosipovich (Väljas, Vaino in Estonian) (*b.* 1931), an Estonian who was brought back from the Soviet embassy in Nicaragua in 1988 to take over as first secretary, Communist Party of Estonia (CPE), but who in 1990 went over to the pro-independence Communist Party of Estonia. He was head of the Komsomol at Tartu University when studying history there in the early 1950s and successfully defended his candidate dissertation (PhD) there. He was first secretary, Estonian Komsomol, 1955–61, and then moved into the Party apparatus, becoming first secretary, Tallinn gorkom, 1961–71. He then transferred to the CPE Central Committee as secretary for ideology, 1971–80, before becoming Soviet Ambassador to Venezuela, 1980–6, and Soviet Ambassador to Nicaragua, 1986–8. GORBACHEV needed someone who would be loyal to Moscow and who was not involved in local cliques to take over the CPE in June 1988. However, Vyalyas soon came to the conclusion that there was no future for a Moscow-loyal Communist Party in Estonia and in 1990 went over to the pro-independence Communist Party. He was elected to the USSR Congress of People's Deputies, 1989, and the Estonian Supreme Council, 1990.

Vynnychenko, Volodymyr Kyrylovich (1880–1951), a prolific left of centre Ukrainian writer who played a key role in Ukraine before it fell to the Bolsheviks. He studied at Kiev University but spent most of the period 1903–17 in western Europe. When he returned to Ukraine in 1917 he was elected vice-president of the Central Rada. He drafted the various Universals on a range of policy themes, issued by the Central Rada. He opposed Hetman SKOROPADSKY's rule and became a member of the Directorate which took over from Skoropadsky. He resigned in 1919 over policy but in 1920 negotiated with the Bolsheviks over the future direction of Ukraine. Since Moscow's goal was the incorporation of Ukraine, the talks failed. Vynnychenko moved to France and died in Paris.

Vyshinsky, Andrei Yanuarevich (1883–1954), a merciless, venomous state prosecutor who gained world-wide notoriety for his courtroom behaviour during the great show trials in the 1930s during which he humiliated some former communist leaders. His violent language and behaviour may have been geared to prove to STALIN that he was absolutely loyal to him. It was necessary to renew his credentials since he had become a Menshevik when joining the RSDRP in 1903. He qualified as a lawyer in 1913 and joined the Communist Party in 1920. While teaching at Moscow State University he honed his skills as a prosecutor in trials of alleged saboteurs and counter-revolutionaries. His style suited the period and he became prosecutor of the Russian Federation in 1931, deputy prosecutor, 1933, and then, in 1935, prosecutor of the Soviet Union. He became well known abroad during the Metro–Vickers trial, 1933, when several British engineers were accused of attempting to wreck the construction of Soviet hydroelectric stations. He starred during the three great show trials (1936–8), featuring, among many others, ZINOVIEV, KAMENEV, BUKHARIN and RYKOV. His approach to character assassination can be neatly illustrated by quoting from his closing speech during the first great show trial: 'I demand that these mad dogs be shot, every last one of them!' They were. However, the executioner was not Vyshinsky but his master, Stalin. One of his rewards was election to the Central Committee of the Communist Party, 1939. He exhibited great skill in keeping his head at a time when many of his high-profile contemporaries were losing theirs. In 1940,

as deputy Commissar for Foreign Affairs, he supervised the incorporation of Latvia into the USSR and supervised the advent to power of the communists in Romania, 1945. He was deputy chair of Sovnarkom, 1939–44, and when he was Foreign Commissar MOLOTOV's spokesman on Poland he declared during the Warsaw uprising that allied planes, seeking to aid the insurgents, would not be permitted to land at Russian air bases. Vyshinsky was Soviet representative on the Allied Mediterranean Commission and attended the Yalta Conference, 1945. Even though he was Molotov's deputy, he is believed to have reported over Molotov's head directly to Stalin. In 1949 he became USSR Minister of Foreign Affairs and the permanent Soviet representative at the United Nations where he turned his venom on the United States, especially during the Korean War, 1950–3. Like Molotov, Vyshinsky was not an assertive Foreign Minister. US Ambassador Walter Kirk observed after a meeting with Stalin in August 1949, 'He [Stalin] certainly dominated the situation here – and Vyshinsky was hopping around like a pea on a hot griddle to do his slightest wish.' After Stalin's death, Molotov took over again as Foreign Minister and Vyshinsky dropped to being his first deputy. However, he remained at the United Nations and he died of a heart attack in New York. Had he lived he would most probably have been targeted by KHRUSHCHEV for his debasement of Soviet law under Stalin. He died unloved in the west and Leonard Schapiro once described him, memorably, as the nearest thing to a human rat he had ever seen!

Vysotsky, Vladimir Semenovich (1938–80), the greatest pop star and balladeer of his generation, he was born into a Russian family in Moscow (his father was a military officer and Vysotsky spent some time in the GDR when his father was posted there) and graduated from the Moscow Construction Engineering

Institute and also the Moscow Arts Theatre as an actor. In 1964 he joined the newly founded Taganka Theatre, directed by Yury Lyubimov, and remained with the theatre for the rest of his life. He acted in many major productions and films and in the early 1960s began writing lyrics which he sang, accompanying himself on the guitar. His songs circulated on tape throughout the Soviet Union although a few official records of his music were published. He enjoyed immense popularity towards the end of his life and his fans included Yury ANDROPOV and many KGB officers. He died prematurely from alcoholism and drug abuse and was mourned throughout the country. After his death his records and poems became widely available and he was regarded as the voice of protest during the grey BREZHNEV era.

W

Witte, Sergei Yulevich (1849–1915), the most gifted minister to serve NICHOLAS II, he might have saved the monarchy had it trusted him. He graduated in mathematics from the University of Odessa and worked in railways, demonstrating a firm grasp of economics and management. He became Minister of Finance in 1893 and promoted the building of the Chinese Eastern Railway. Russian finances were strong enough for the country to join the gold standard in 1897. He was the driving force behind Russia's first industrial revolution in the 1890s. In the Far East and elsewhere Witte opposed the imperialist ambitions of many ministers, arguing that economic penetration was a much more effective way of promoting Russian influence. He was dismissed in August 1903 and became chair of the committee of ministers, a post without any policy impact. He was partly to blame for his demotion because, as he did not suffer fools gladly, he had been abrasive and undiplomatic to too many. Intellectually, Witte towered over the Tsar and his colleagues and this rankled. Fabricated evidence was passed to Nicholas II about Witte's alleged participation in a Masonic–Jewish conspiracy against Russia, and the Tsar was predisposed to believe it. Nicholas II turned to him in June 1905 to negotiate the peace with Japan at Portsmouth (New Hampshire) and he acquitted himself brilliantly. Thereupon the Tsar made him a count. Witte drafted the October Manifesto of 1905 and became chair of the Council of Ministers. He was not a success as head of government and when the monarchy was safe,

in April 1906, Witte was allowed to go. Again the Tsar had lost confidence in him. He took to retirement very badly and it was a tragedy for Russia that his dynamism and abilities were denied the country at an important juncture in its development.

Wrangel, General Petr Nikolaevich (1878–1928), probably the best White commander during the Civil War in Russia, Wrangel came from a Baltic noble family of Swedish origin. He fought in the Russo-Japanese War and graduated from the Academy of the General Staff in 1910. He was commander of a cavalry corps during the First World War. He narrowly escaped being executed by the Bolsheviks in Crimea and joined the Whites in August 1918, becoming prominent in 1919 when his army was successful in the north Caucasus, capturing Tsaritsyn (now Volgograd) in July (STALIN was the political commissar there with VOROSHILOV as the Red commander). He never developed good relations with General DENIKIN and after quarrelling with him was dismissed and sent to Constantinople but in April 1920 he became Denikin's successor in Crimea. By then the White cause was lost. However, he initiated land reform, passing land to the peasants, and proposed an alliance with Poland which Pilsudski rejected. He supervised the evacuation of over 150,000 Whites to Turkey after defeat by the Reds in November 1920. In exile in Europe, he organised the Russian Social Union, an association of White veterans. He died in Brussels but is buried in Belgrade.

Y

Yagoda, Genrikh Grigorevich (né Yehuda, Heinrich) (1891–1938), one of STALIN's bloodiest police chiefs who himself fell victim to the executioner's bullet. He was born into a Jewish family and joined the Bolshevik Party, 1907, being exiled for revolutionary activities, 1911–13. He served in the Russian Army from 1915. He worked in the People's Commissariat for Foreign Trade, 1919–22, and joined the Cheka, 1920. He advanced to deputy head of the GPU (KGB), 1924. He was referred to by some as Mephistopheles from the (Jewish) Pale. Stalin made him head of the NKVD (KGB), 1934–July 1936, and he was the implementer of the early purges. Stalin dismissed him and replaced him with EZHOV. Just to keep him dangling before he decided to strike, Stalin made him People's Commissar for Posts and Telegraph, 1936–7, but then had him arrested. (He treated Ezhov in the same way later.) Yagoda was one of the main defendants at the trial of the Anti-Soviet Bloc of Rightists and Trotskyites (perhaps Stalin was being ironical here, since Yagoda had spent his time disposing of Rightists and Trotskyites, among others). He was shot in the Lubyanka. When the defendants were rehabilitated by a Party commission, 1988, Yagoda's name was missing.

Yakir, Iona Emmanuilovich (1896–1937), a high-ranking Red Army commander who was executed in the purge of the military. He joined the Communist Party, 1917, and the Red Army, 1918, and fought in the Civil War in Ukraine, mainly as a political officer. Afterwards he continued to serve in Ukraine and was elected a candidate member of the CPSU Central Committee, 1930, and then a full member, 1934. He was a member of the USSR Revolutionary Military Council, 1930–4. He was arrested when commander of the Leningrad military district and executed.

Yakir, Petr Ionovich (1923–82), a leading human rights activist who broke under KGB pressure and was thereafter ostracised by the dissident community. He was born in Kiev, the son of an executed Red Army officer, Iona YAKIR, and was arrested and imprisoned in 1937 for being the son of an enemy of the people. In 1972, his memoirs, *Detstvo v Tyurme* (*A Prison Childhood*), were published in London. He was released in 1954 and studied at the Moscow State Historical Archive Institute. He became a dissident in the mid-1960s in response to the partial rehabilitation of STALIN and became one of the founders of the human rights movement in Moscow and Leningrad (St Petersburg). He collected a great deal of material about arrests, imprisonments and the abuse of psychiatry for political ends. He was arrested in 1972 and broke under KGB interrogation, was released in 1974, but lived afterwards in isolation, dying in Moscow.

Yakovlev, Aleksandr Nikolaevich (*b.* 1923), the father of glasnost, he was a committed reformer who eventually came to realise that Marxism–Leninism was a brake on Soviet society and the country should move forward to social democracy. He was born into a Russian peasant family in Yaroslavl and his father later became a kolkhoz chairman. He joined the Red Army in 1941 and was severely wounded at the front, 1943. He was invalided out, joined the Communist Party, 1944, and graduated from the Yaroslavl Pedagogical Institute, 1946. He joined the Party apparatus in Yaroslavl obkom, 1946, and worked on a local newspaper, 1948–50, after which he returned to the obkom apparatus. In 1953 he moved to Moscow to work in the Central Committee apparatus but spent the years 1956–60 studying at the Academy of Social Sciences of the Central Committee. He was one of the first exchange students at Columbia University, 1959. He was first deputy head, then acting head, department of propaganda, Central Committee, 1965–73, but an article he wrote in 1972 attacking nationalisms and chauvinisms of all hues raised eyebrows and angered conservative Russians. Yakovlev was packed off as Soviet Ambassador to Canada, 1973–83. He accompanied Mikhail GORBACHEV on an agricultural tour of Canada and made quite an impression on the future Soviet leader. ANDROPOV brought Yakovlev back from Canada and made him director of the Institute of World Economy and International Relations. In July 1985 Gorbachev made him head of the Central Committee propaganda department, a key centre from which to promote perestroika. In February 1986 Yakovlev was elected a full member of the Central Committee, in March 1986 a Central Committee secretary, in January 1987 a candidate member of the Politburo, and in June 1987 a full member of the Politburo. Yakovlev, the radical, countered Egor LIGACHEV, the moderate reformer, in the Central Committee, and when Ligachev's influence declined in the wake of the XIXth Party Conference, June 1988, Yakovlev took over as supervisor of the USSR's international policy in the Central Committee apparatus, as chair of the commission on international policy. He was a founder member of the

Presidential Council, March 1990, and stepped down from the Central Committee at the XXVIIIth Party Congress, July 1990, and thus forfeited his seat on the Politburo and his secretaryship of the Central Committee. By 1991 he was Gorbachev's senior adviser. Yakovlev developed a reputation as an anti-American before the Gorbachev era but this was softened in the light of the new political thinking and he fully supported arms control and reduction. In Canada he had studied the impact of television on politics and was able to help Gorbachev to develop his media personality. Yakovlev was pushed aside in the last days of the Soviet Union but after the failed coup of August 1991 he remained loyal to Gorbachev. In 1992 he became vice-president of the Gorbachev Foundation.

Yakovlev, Aleksandr Sergeevich (1906–89), a brilliant Soviet aircraft designer after whom many aircraft were named, he was born into a Russian family in Moscow and joined the Red Army in 1924. He graduated from the Zhukovsky Air Force Academy, 1931, became a design engineer, 1935, and was deputy People's Commissar for the Aviation Industry, 1940–6. He designed a wide range of military aircraft, including the Yak-1, Yak-15 (one of the first Soviet jets), and civil aircraft (Yak-40 and Yak-42). He also designed helicopters (Yak-24) and vertical take-off aircraft (Yak-38). He joined the Communist Party, 1938, won many honours, and was elected to the USSR Academy of Sciences in 1976.

Yakovlev, Egor Vladimirovich (b. 1930), he became famous under glasnost as the editor-in-chief of *Moskovskie Novosti* (*Moscow News*) which was transformed under his guidance into a major influence for reform during the GORBACHEV era. He was born into a Russian family in Moscow and his father rose to be head of the Cheka (KGB) in Odessa and later deputy head of the Cheka in Ukraine. His natural death in 1937 may have saved him from an unnatural one during those violent days. Yakovlev graduated from the Moscow State Historical Archive Institute, 1954, the year he joined the Communist Party, and thereafter worked on many Soviet newspapers, including *Komsomolskaya Pravda* and *Sovetskaya Rossiya*. He usually fell out with his editors and when he left involuntarily as editor-in-chief of *Zhurnalist*, the official publication of the USSR Union of Journalists, 1972, he moved to Prague to work on *World Marxist Review*. He returned to Moscow, 1975, to work on *Izvestiya*, but headed back to Prague, as *Izvestiya* correspondent there, 1984–5. Valentin FALIN, head of the Novosti Press Agency, invited Yakovlev to become editor-in-chief of *Moskovskie Novosti*, August 1986, with an invitation to publish material that no other paper or magazine would touch. Yakovlev transformed the paper, previously a propaganda publication which appeared in many foreign languages, into a highly provocative and successful outlet for glasnost. Its circulation rose to over 1 million, most of these abroad. He was elected to the USSR Congress of People's Deputies in 1989. After the failure of the August 1991 coup Yakovlev was appointed head of USSR Gosteleradio (state TV and radio). He was a member of Gorbachev's Presidential Council, September–December 1991. From December 1991 to November 1992 he was head of Ostankino, the Russian state television and radio company. He has written over twenty books, was awarded the Milan Prize, 1990, for European journalism and Pope John Paul II has presented him with an official medal.

Yakubovsky, Marshal Ivan Ignatevich (1908–76), commander of the Warsaw Pact forces during the invasion of Czechoslovakia in August 1968, he was born into a Belorussian family, joined the Red Army, 1932, and served in the Soviet–Finnish War, 1939–40, as a tank commander. He had a distinguished record during the Great Fatherland War, taking part in the Battle of Moscow and the Battle for Berlin. He was first deputy commander-in-chief, Soviet Armed Forces in (East) Germany, 1957–60 and 1961–2. Marshal KONEV took over during the Berlin crisis of 1961 which led to the building of the Berlin Wall. Yakubovsky succeeded Konev as commander-in-chief, 1962–5. Yakubovsky was elected a member of the Central Committee in 1961. He was commander-in-chief of the Kiev military district from 1965 to 1967, when he was appointed commander-in-chief of the Warsaw Pact forces and first deputy USSR Minister for Defence.

Yakunin, Father Gleb Pavlovich (b. 1934), a politically influential Russian Orthodox priest who proved a thorn in the flesh of the Orthodox hierarchy. He was born into a Russian family and his father played the clarinet in a military band but died of hunger, 1943. Yakunin graduated from the Irkutsk Agricultural Institute and entered the Moscow Theological Seminary, 1958, but was expelled. He was ordained as a priest in 1962. He served in parishes in Moscow oblast but in 1966 he was banned from officiating as a priest for sending an open letter to Patriarch Aleksi protesting against the passive nature of the Orthodox hierarchy towards the communist authorities. In 1975 he wrote to the World Council of Churches providing details of the harassment of believers. He was a marked man but continued to provide information on the difficult life of believers and founded the Christian Committee for the Protection of Believers' Rights in the USSR in 1979. He was arrested the same year and sentenced to five years' strict regime and five years' exile. He was freed from exile, March 1987, and took charge of Shchelkovo parish near Moscow. He was rehabilitated by the Russian Supreme

Soviet in October 1991. Yakunin was elected to the Russian Congress of People's Deputies, 1990, for Shchelkovo, and also the Russian Supreme Soviet. He was a founder member of the Democratic Russia 90 electoral bloc.

Yanaev, Gennady Ivanovich (*b.* 1937), he became notorious when he took over from Mikhail GORBACHEV during the August 1991 attempted coup but was found wanting. His nervousness at the first press conference, announcing Gorbachev's retirement for 'health reasons', was evident when the drumming of his fingers on the table attracted attention. He was born into a Russian peasant family in Gorky (now Nizhny Novgorod) oblast and graduated from the Gorky Agricultural Institute. Later he graduated as an external student from the All-Union Law Institute and successfully presented his candidate dissertation (PhD) in history. He rose to become head of the Komsomol, Gorky oblast, 1963–8, chair of USSR youth organisations, and deputy chair of the presidium of the Union of Soviet Societies of Friendship and Cultural Relations with Foreign Countries, 1968–86. He was secretary of the All-Union Council of Soviet Trade Unions, 1986–9, then deputy chair, and chair of the trade union movement, April–July 1990. In December 1990 Gorbachev took the fateful step of choosing him as his vice-president but he was not accepted during the first round of voting. Yanaev was a member of the USSR Security Council, March–August 1991. He was declared President by the Emergency Committee, 19 August, but only lasted until 21 August when the attempted coup failed. He was arrested but later amnestied by the Russian Duma. Yanaev was a member of the Communist Party, 1962–91, a member of the Central Committee, July 1990–August 1991, a Central Committee secretary and a member of the Politburo, July 1990–January 1991. He was elected to the USSR Congress of People's Deputies, 1989. As Gorbachev concedes in his memoirs, choosing Yanaev as his vice-president was one of the most fateful mistakes of his years in office.

Yashin, Lev Ivanovich (1929–90), one of the most famous goalkeepers of all time, he became a legend in his own lifetime and was welcome wherever football was played. He was also a talented ice hockey player but eventually chose football with Moscow Dinamo. He joined the Communist Party, 1957, and graduated from the Moscow Higher Party School of the Central Committee. Among his many achievements were an Olympic gold medal playing for the Soviet national team, 1956, a European Championship winners' medal, 1960, and a bronze medal in the 1966 World Cup. He was named as Europe's player of the year, 1963, and was also awarded the Golden Ball for achievement. During his 408 games for Dinamo, he recorded the formidable achievement of keeping a clean sheet 207 times, a record which is never likely to be approached, let alone equalled. He retired in 1971 and coached and administered afterwards. In October 1984 his right leg was amputated.

Yavlinsky, Grigory Alekseevich (*b.* 1952), one of the leading economists who rose to prominence under GORBACHEV but proved too radical for the Soviet leader. He was born in Lvov where his father was a military officer and he is partly Jewish. He left school after completing nine years and worked as a fitter, studying at night school. He graduated from the Plekhanov Institute of the National Economy, 1973, and successfully presented his candidate dissertation on labour in the chemical industry (PhD (Econ)), under the supervision of Academician Leonid ABALKIN, 1978. He then specialised in labour economics in the coal industry, then in industry, and was employed in the state committee for labour and social questions, 1984–9. Yavlinsky put his career at risk in 1982 when he published the book *Problems in Perfecting the Economic Mechanism in the USSR*, which reached the conclusion that the Soviet economic mechanism could not be perfected. The book was taken from the printers, the printed copies destroyed and the manuscript seized. Yavlinsky was obliged to undergo treatment in a closed hospital, 1984–5. In 1987 he took part in drafting the USSR law on state enterprises but his draft was rejected by the commission, headed by Geidat ALIEV. After Leonid Abalkin was appointed deputy chair, USSR Council of Ministers, June 1989, Yavlinsky was head of department, state commission on economic reform of the USSR Council of Ministers. In early 1990 he and other radical economists began drafting a programme for the stabilisation and reform of the Soviet economy and when Boris YELTSIN heard of this Yavlinsky was made deputy chair of the Russian Federation government, July 1990. Academician SHATALIN and Yavlinsky headed the team which drafted what became known as the 500-day programme for the Soviet economy, envisaging the transition to a market economy in 500 days, something which was highly improbable. Gorbachev presented the programme to the USSR Supreme Soviet in September 1990 but Prime Minister Nikolai RYZHKOV opposed it and it was eventually watered down. Yavlinsky resigned as deputy chair, RSFSR Council of Ministers, October 1990, and declined Gorbachev's invitation to continue working on draft USSR economic legislation. He was a member of the USSR Presidential Council, 1991. Also in 1991 he became chair of the Council of the Centre for Economic and Political Research (Epitsentr). In April 1991 he was invited by the US Department of State to participate in a meeting of the council of the Group of 7 (G7). His speech aroused great interest and at Harvard University he and a

group of American economists drafted a programme for the transition of the Soviet economy to the market. In late August 1991 he was appointed by President Mikhail Gorbachev head of the committee on the operational management of the Soviet economy and in September 1991 he drafted a treaty on the economic union of the Soviet republics, but Yavlinsky's programme, based on the retention of a single Soviet economic space, became inoperative after the collapse of the USSR. In late 1991 Epitsentr signed an agreement with Nizhny Novgorod oblast on the transition to a market economy and Yavlinsky became an adviser to the governor, Boris NEMTSOV. Yavlinsky became active politically in postcommunist Russia and in the December 1993 elections to the lower house, the Duma, his party, Yabloko, did reasonably well, regarding as its constituency the rising middle-class professionals.

Yazov, Marshal Dmitry Timofeevich (*b.* 1923), one of the ringleaders of the attempted coup in August 1991, something which he came to regret bitterly. He was born into a Russian family in Omsk oblast and joined the Red Army, 1941, graduated from the Frunze Military Academy, 1956, and the Academy of the General Staff, 1967. He was engaged in the personnel department, USSR Ministry of Defence, 1974–6, after which he became first deputy commander, Far East military district. In 1979 he was appointed commander of the Central Group of Armies in Czechoslovakia and in 1980 he became commander of the Central Asian military district. In 1981 he was elected a candidate member of the Central Committee. In 1984 he returned to the Soviet Far East military district as commander. He impressed GORBACHEV who made him USSR Minister of Defence in 1987. His promotion was swift as he was viewed as an officer of a new type committed to perestroika in the armed forces. He was elected a full member of the Central Committee, June 1987, was a candidate member of the Politburo, September 1989–July 1990, a member of the Presidential Council, March 1990, and became a Marshal of the Soviet Union, April 1990. His illustrious career came to an ignominious end in August 1991 when he was a member of the Emergency Committee. He was arrested, charged with treason, but was amnestied by the State Duma later.

Yeltsin, Boris Nikolaevich (*b.* 1931), the first democratically elected President of Russia, leader of the opposition to the attempted coup against President Mikhail GORBACHEV, August 1991, his star began to wane in the mid-1990s when he was dubbed Tsar Boris, adrift in his Kremlin court. Yeltsin, a Russian, was born near Sverdlovsk (Ekaterinburg) and had an unprivileged childhood, growing up in workers' huts on construction sites. This background always made him ill at ease with luxury living later in his career. Another thing he retained from his youth was a love of vodka. He was very keen on sport, especially volleyball and boxing but later lost part of his left thumb in a shooting accident. He graduated from the Urals Polytechnic Institute, 1955, as a construction engineer, and his project was the building of a TV transmission tower. He then worked in the construction industry, joined the Communist Party, 1961, in 1963 became chief engineer, then head of the Sverdlovsk home construction combine, and in 1968 moved into Party work in the Sverdlovsk oblast Party committee (obkom). He was elected secretary for industry, 1975, and first secretary, 1976, of Sverdlovsk obkom. Under his direction, during the night of 17–18 September 1977, the house of the merchant Ipatev, a fine example of nineteenth-century Russian architecture, in which Tsar NICHOLAS II and his family had been murdered in July 1918, and which was under the protection of the state, was razed to the ground

(he came to regret this act of vandalism later). One of his particular concerns as first secretary was to build housing for workers and this made him very popular. Yeltsin was elected a member of the Party Central Committee in 1981. He was also a member of the Presidium of the USSR Supreme Soviet, 1984–8. As an obkom first secretary he knew Gorbachev and when the latter became General Secretary of the Party in March 1985 Yeltsin was one of the first to be summoned to Moscow, together with such upwardly mobile politicians as Egor LIGACHEV. A major advantage was that they were untainted with corruption. Yeltsin became head of the construction department of the Central Committee Secretariat, June 1985, and when Gorbachev wanted his own man to take over the Moscow Party apparatus (gorkom), he chose Yeltsin. The new first secretary began to clear out the corrupt officials and liked to travel to work by underground. Muscovites hailed him as the people's champion. Gorbachev made him a candidate member of the Politburo in March 1986. Yeltsin, an outsider, was no match for the Moscow nomenklatura, and they orchestrated a vicious campaign against him. During the summer of 1987 Yeltsin sent Gorbachev a letter intimating that he wished to resign but this did not please the General Secretary. Gorbachev asked Yeltsin to curb his tongue and bide his time but this was beyond the emotional Yeltsin. In October 1987 Gorbachev threw him to the wolves. Ligachev launched into a violent tirade against Yeltsin, especially the damage Yeltsin's campaign against Party privilege was doing. Yeltsin had broken one of the golden rules of Politburo life: never reveal to the public the splits which existed in the top Party body. Yeltsin suffered a heart attack on 9 November 1987. Still ill, he was called to account by the Moscow gorkom and given another dressing down. He was not banished from Moscow or political life but was given a post in construction which afforded him the rank of minister. In February 1988, at Gorbachev's suggestion, he lost his seat as a candidate member of the Politburo. This episode led to an unbridgeable gap between Gorbachev and Yeltsin and henceforth the country was too small for both of them, one of them had to destroy the other. Barred from expressing his criticisms of the slowness of perestroika in the official Soviet media, Yeltsin resorted to giving revealing interviews to foreign correspondents in Moscow. His views met with a mixed reception in the west, which was almost totally enamoured of Gorbachev. Most readers would have preferred Yeltsin to have praised the fine work that Gorbachev was doing. Yeltsin was elected a delegate, from Karelia, to the XIXth Party Conference, June 1988, despite attempts by the leadership to prevent it. During President Reagan's summit visit to Moscow, also in June 1988, Yeltsin gave a TV interview to the foreign press criticising the pace of perestroika and Ligachev personally. The XIXth Party Conference was carried live on TV and, on the last day, Yeltsin asked for the floor and delivered a detailed apologia of his position, requesting that the Party rehabilitate him now, not posthumously. This was a fine piece of cheek by Yeltsin and made him the most popular politician in the country. Besides emasculating the Party Secretariat by withdrawing its role as the co-ordinator of state and economy, the conference also agreed to the first multi-candidate elections since the early years of the revolution, to the USSR Congress of People's Deputies. Yeltsin won a stunning victory, 89.6 per cent of the vote, in his Moscow constituency but there was little likelihood that the overwhelmingly communist Congress would elect Yeltsin to the USSR Supreme Soviet. The careful plans of Gorbachev and his aides were undone when a deputy from Omsk (later to become Russian Procurator General) stood down and

opened the way for Yeltsin to enter the Supreme Soviet. He and other democrats, such as Academician Andrei SAKHAROV, now had a national platform from which to pillory the shortcomings of perestroika and the Party. Yeltsin became active in the Party's Democratic Platform, an opposition group within the parliament. When Yeltsin visited the United States in September 1989 the Soviet press reprinted an article from an Italian newspaper which commented on his drinking habits and his wont to regard America as one long bar. There was a storm of protest and the Soviet press backtracked. In March 1990 Yeltsin was elected to the RSFSR Congress of People's Deputies and became chair (speaker) of the RSFSR Supreme Soviet, May 1990, despite many manoeuvres by the Kremlin. Yeltsin was a skilled speaker, presenting himself as a reasonable man but always championing Russia at the expense of the Soviet Union. He engaged in the 'war of laws' enthusiastically (when a Russian law infringed USSR sovereignty it was annulled by the USSR Supreme Soviet; this in turn was annulled by the Russian Supreme Soviet, and so on). He also supported the aspirations of the Baltic republics for independence. When Gorbachev backed away from the 500-day programme – moving from the planned to a market economy in 500 days – he had it adopted for the Russian Federation, October 1990. This meant very little since USSR Gosplan managed the economy and Russia was subordinate to it. It was good politics but poor economics. President Gorbachev held a referendum on 17 March 1991, seeking support for a new Union of Sovereign States. Republics added their own questions and Yeltsin asked Russian voters if they were in favour of a directly elected Russian President, which they were. Yeltsin became President of Russia in June 1991. His hour of glory came in August 1991 when he became the people's champion by leading the opposition to victory over the Emergency Committee. He drove home the point that the episode was aimed at Russia and reducing its sovereignty. Skilfully he had demanded that President Gorbachev be restored to power, but when he did return to Moscow Yeltsin was the victor. He banned the activities of the Communist Party, with Gorbachev protesting in vain, and the Party itself in November 1991. When Gorbachev stepped down in December 1991, Yeltsin and Russia were there to take over from him and the Soviet Union. John Morrison: *Boris Yeltsin: From Bolshevik to Democrat*, London, 1991; Boris Yeltsin: *Against the Grain*, London, 1990; *The View from the Kremlin*, London, 1994.

Yudenich, General Nikolai Nikolaevich (1862–1933), a White commander who appeared to be on the verge of capturing Petrograd in 1919. He participated in the Russo-Japanese War and became Chief of Staff of the Caucasian military district in 1912. He was commander-in-chief of the Caucasian Army in 1915 and had several successes against the Turks. He was dismissed by the provisional government in April 1917 and after the October Revolution went underground in Petrograd. He managed to get to Finland in November 1918 and then to Estonia. He became commander of the White forces in the Baltic in September 1919 and in October advanced on Petrograd. He was forced back to Estonia where he was interned but later emigrated to France. He failed to unite the disparate anti-Bolshevik forces in the Baltic and did not mobilise Finnish and Estonian opposition to LENIN.

Z

Zagladin, Vadim Valentinovich (*b.* 1927), a prominent foreign policy adviser during the BREZHNEV era whose influence declined with the onset of the new political thinking of GORBACHEV. He was born into a Russian family in Moscow, graduated from the Moscow State Institute of International Relations and then joined the staff, 1952–4. He successfully presented his candidate dissertation in history (PhD) and his doctoral dissertation in philosophy (Marxism–Leninism) (DLitt). He joined the Communist Party in 1955. He worked on *World Marxist Review*, in Prague, 1960–4, and then moved into the international department, Central Committee apparatus, becoming deputy head, 1967–75, and head, 1975–88. He was appointed adviser to the chair of the Presidium, USSR Supreme Soviet, 1988–90, and then an adviser to the USSR President on international relations. He was elected a member of the Central Committee, 1981, but was not re-elected in 1990. He was also involved in various committees concerned with security and European civilisation and was a prolific author. Although he held high appointments under Gorbachev he was never influential in the new climate of international relations.

Zaikov, Lev Nikolaevich (*b.* 1923), a prominent politician during the GORBACHEV era, he was on the moderate rather than the radical reform wing of perestroika. He was born into a Russian family in Tula and worked in the metal industry in Leningrad, becoming an enterprise manager, 1961, and head of a scientific production association in the defence sector, 1974–6. He graduated from the Leningrad Engineering Economics Institute in 1963. In 1976 he was elected chair of the Leningrad city soviet executive committee (Lensovet) and then in 1983 he became first secretary, Leningrad Party obkom. He joined the Communist Party, 1957, and was elected a member of the Central Committee, 1981. Under Gorbachev his promotion was rapid and he became a secretary of the Central Committee, July 1985, and a member of the Politburo, March 1986. His rise paralleled the fall of Grigory ROMANOV as Zaikov took over responsibility for the defence industry in the Central Committee. When Boris YELTSIN was dismissed as first secretary of Moscow gorkom, November 1987, Gorbachev chose Zaikov to take over. He held this post until November 1989 when Yury Prokofev succeeded him. Zaikov was not among the members of the Presidential Council in March 1990 and he was not re-elected to the Central Committee at the XXVIIIth Party Congress, July 1990, and hence forfeited his place on the Politburo and his secretaryship of the Central Committee. He was elected to the USSR Congress of People's Deputies, 1989, as one of the nominees of the Communist Party.

Zalygin, Sergei Pavlovich (*b.* 1913), as editor-in-chief of *Novy Mir* he managed to publish Aleksandr SOLZHENITSYN's previously banned works and became a leading literary figure under glasnost. He was born into a Russian family in present-day Bashkortostan but spent most of his youth in Siberia, graduating from the Omsk Agricultural Institute, 1939, and worked as an engineer and hydrologist in the Siberian branch of the USSR Academy of Sciences. Along with others he campaigned successfully for an end to the project to divert Siberian rivers south to irrigate Central Asia, 1986. When he was appointed editor-in-chief of *Novy Mir*, 1987, he was the first non-Party person to occupy the post. His own writing is in the village prose tradition but he has covered many themes, notably NEP in *Posle Buri* (*After the Storm*), 1980–5. As well as Solzhenitsyn he published PASTERNAK's *Doctor Zhivago*. He was elected to the USSR Congress of People's Deputies and the USSR Supreme Soviet in 1989.

Zamyatin, Evgeny Ivanovich (1884–1937), sympathetic to Bolshevism before the October Revolution, he became disillusioned with the great experiment and penned the anti-Utopian novel, *My* (*We*), 1920, which afterwards isolated him from mainstream revolutionary culture (the novel was published in the Soviet Union in 1988). He was born into a Russian family near Lipetsk and studied shipbuilding at the St Petersburg Technological Institute. Zamyatin became widely known for his satire of Russian provincial life, *Uezdnoe* (*A Province*), 1913. He was sent to England in 1916 to supervise the construction of icebreakers for Russia, and he returned to Russia in September 1917. His experiences provided material for his anti-British novel, *Ostrovityane* (*The Islanders*), 1918. *My* appears to have helped George Orwell to create *1984* as in both novels there is harsh humour and a strictly regimented society. Zamyatin wrote to STALIN in 1931 and requested permission to move abroad and this wish was granted, 1932, when he settled in France.

Zamyatin, Leonid Mitrofanovich (*b.* 1922), as Soviet Ambassador to the Court of St James during the GOR-BACHEV era, he never gave the impression of being really enthusiastic about perestroika. He was regarded as having sided with the conspirators during the attempted coup of August 1991 and this hastened the demise of his career. He was born into a Russian family in Voronezh oblast and graduated from the Moscow Ordzhonikidze Aviation Institute, 1944, and also joined the Communist Party the same year. He entered the USSR Ministry of Foreign Affairs, 1946, served in the Soviet delegation to the United Nations, New York, and was head of the American department, USSR Ministry of Foreign Affairs, 1962. He was then head of the ministry's press department, 1962–70 before becoming head of Tass, and in 1978 he headed the international information department, Central Committee. In 1986 he was appointed Soviet Ambassador to Great Britain. During his time in London he was noted for his diplomatic feel. On one occasion when Eduard SHEVARDNADZE misplaced a stress in Russian (Georgian was his native language), Zamyatin immediately copied the incorrect stress.

Zaslavskaya, Tatyana Ivanovna (*b.* 1927), she became a leading sociologist under perestroika and highlighted the problems posed by Party control of the economy. She was born into a Russian family in Kiev, her father being a professor of physics, graduated in economics from the Moscow State University, 1950, and presented successfully her candidate dissertation in economics (PhD (Econ)), and her doctoral dissertation (DSc (Econ)). In 1950 she joined the USSR Academy of Sciences and in 1963 she moved to the Institute of Economics and the Organisation of Industrial Production, USSR Academy of Sciences, Novosibirsk, headed by Abel AGANBEGYAN. She was elected a corresponding member of the USSR Academy of Sciences, 1968, and an academician, 1980, in economics. In Novosibirsk she concentrated on sociological questions from 1967. She specialised in agriculture and published books on Soviet and US agricultural labour productivity, 1960, the migration of the rural population, 1970, the social development of the village, 1978, and others. She came into contact with GORBACHEV as she was one of the experts he consulted when Central Committee secretary for agriculture. She shot to prominence in 1983 when a paper she had read to a closed seminar in Novosibirsk was leaked and published abroad. It presented a bleak picture of the Soviet economy and she received a Party reprimand for her pains. In 1986 she was elected president of the Soviet Sociological Association and in 1988 moved to Moscow to head the All-Union Centre for the Study of Public Opinion. The latter organisation took up where Soviet sociology had left off at the end of the 1920s and produced some stimulating results. She joined the Communist Party, 1957, and was elected to the USSR Congress of People's Deputies, 1989. Tatyana Zaslavskaya: *The Second Socialist Revolution*, London, 1990.

Zhdanov, Andrei Aleksandrovich (1896–1948), the guardian of Stalinist cultural orthodoxy, from socialist realism to the xenophobia of the late 1940s, known as the Zhdanovshchina. He joined the Bolshevik Party, 1915, and engaged in Bolshevik propaganda in reserve regiments in the rear during the First World War. During the Civil War he was a political commissar. He then became Party secretary in Tver and Nizhny Novgorod oblasts. He was elected a secretary of the Central Committee at the XVIIth Party Congress, 1934, and also a member of the Organisational Bureau (Orgburo). When Sergei KIROV was murdered in December 1934, STALIN chose Zhdanov to succeed him as Party leader in Leningrad. He was elected to the Politburo at the XVIIIth Party Congress, 1939. At the Ist Congress of the Union of Soviet Writers, 1934, Zhdanov, speaking for Stalin, laid down the new cultural rules, known as socialist realism. Culture was to be a weapon in the struggle for socialism and was to be didactic and optimistic. He led the defence of Leningrad during the siege, 1941–4. He had formidable political enemies in MALENKOV and BERIA. Stalin played one off against the other. The period from 1946 to August 1948, when Zhdanov expired, is known as the Zhdanovshchina. It is a period of gross cultural intolerance and anti-Semitism. Stalin set the tone in February 1946, soon followed by Zhdanov. The latter referred to Mikhail ZOSHCHENKO, the satirist, as the 'scum of the literary world'. He had written a story about a monkey escaping from the zoo which, after sampling Soviet life, gratefully returned to its cage where it could breathe more freely. Anna AKHMATOVA, the poetess, was treated very coarsely. 'It would be difficult to say if she is a nun or a whore; better perhaps to say she is a little of both, her lusts and her prayers intertwine.' Zhdanov's brief extended to the world communist movement and he presided at the founding congress of the Communist Information Bureau (Cominform), in Poland in 1947. His death was sudden and caught everyone by surprise. One of his bitterest enemies, Malenkov (together with Beria), grasped the opportunity to settle scores with the Zhdanovites and the notorious Leningrad Affair followed. This resulted in several executions and many hundreds of officials being dismissed. The Doctors' Plot, fabricated by the Ministry of State Security, was launched in January 1953, and allegedly involved a group of doctors whose aim had been to cut short the lives of Soviet leaders. One of their victims had been Zhdanov.

Zhirinovsky, Vladimir Volfovich (b. 1946), known as 'Mad Vlad', the 'Russian Hitler', and some other unflattering sobriquets, he has made a dazzling career as an extreme Russian nationalist, appearing at times to be anti-Semitic, xenophobic and imperialist. He was born in Alma Ata (Almaty), Kazakhstan, and quips that his father was a lawyer but his mother was Russian. Many observers accept that he is part-Jewish but he denies this. He has led a remarkable life and has demonstrated considerable intelligence and great skill in promoting himself. He graduated with distinction from the Institute of the Countries of Asia and Africa, Moscow State University, 1970, and was later a postgraduate student in Turkey. He was thrown out of Turkey which has led many to believe that he was working for the KGB but again this is something he denies. From 1984 to 1991 he was head of the legal department at Mir publishing house. He was politically active from 1967 but never joined the Communist Party. His political career took off in 1988 when he was one of the founders of the Liberal Democratic Party of the USSR. The party split several ways and a part of it was registered by Zhirinovsky. A group, calling itself the Liberal Democratic Party of Russia split from Zhirinovsky, accusing him of imperialism and behaving in a dictatorial manner. The Liberal Democratic Party of the USSR nominated him for President of the RSFSR in June 1991. During the election campaign he promised to restore order to the country and to remove the nationality question from the political agenda. He threatened the Baltic states and Moldova with military force. He polled 6.2 million votes and came third to Boris YELTSIN and Nikolai RYZHKOV. It was a remarkable performance for an almost unknown candidate and henceforth he personified Russian nationalism, or rather the extreme face of it. His party, now the Liberal Democratic Party of Russia (the usual comment was that it was neither liberal nor democratic) came second in the December 1993 elections to the State Duma, the lower house, causing consternation among President Yeltsin's

supporters and foreign observers. Long feared as a threat to the security of the post-Soviet states and indeed the world at large (he once referred to Russian soldiers bathing their feet in the Indian Ocean) he was, in reality, the Russian voice of protest at the pain, suffering and disorientation of the late GORBACHEV and the early Yeltsin eras.

Zhukov, Marshal Georgy Konstantinovich (1896–1974), the most prominent and successful Red Army commander during the Great Fatherland War. He joined the Red Army, 1918, and fought in the Civil War. He graduated from the higher military courses for Red Army commanders, 1930, and came to international notice as commander of Red Army forces at Khalkin Gol, Mongolia, 1939, against the Japanese. This was one of the two decisive battles which led to the Japanese deciding not to press on with their attack into the Soviet Union. Zhukov was made Chief of the General Staff and deputy Commissar for Defence, January–July 1941. He rapidly came to the fore after the German invasion after it became clear that STALIN's trusted cronies from the Civil War, BUDENNY, VOROSHILOV and TIMOSHENKO, could not cope with modern mechanised warfare. In October 1941 he replaced Voroshilov as commander of the northern sector, and was personally responsible for the defence of Leningrad. He was then moved to Moscow and made commander-in-chief of the entire Western Front, successfully repelling two German offensives against the capital. He counter-attacked in December 1941, drove the Wehrmacht back, and reached a standstill by February 1942. He then became deputy Commissar for Defence. He was responsible for the defence of Stalingrad and took part in the planning of the offensive in November 1942 which broke through the German lines and eventually encircled Paulus's 6th Army. He participated in the Battle of Kursk,

July 1943, the greatest tank battle the world had witnessed. He was in overall command in Ukraine, became commander of the 1st Ukrainian Front, March 1944; afterwards commander of the 1st Belorussian Front, November 1944. The 1st Ukrainian Front advanced at the rate of almost 100 kilometres per day in February and March 1944. Zhukov then took command of the fronts in June 1944 which drove through the German Army Group Centre and eventually halted outside Warsaw in August 1944. The offensive was resumed in January 1945 and by April his troops crossed the River Oder and launched the final assault on Berlin. He was the Soviet representative at the signing of the surrender of the German armed forces. He then became the first commander of the Soviet Occupation Forces in Germany. Zhukov emerged as a brilliant and decisive commander, very cautious in the beginning but very daring at the end of the war. He was enormously popular with his troops and struck up a close relationship with General Eisenhower, the US commander-in-chief. He could be rude, abrasive and ruthless. If there were minefields ahead he would sometimes order his infantry to march straight through them, irrespective of the casualties. Stalin learnt to respect his expertise but never trusted him. Zhukov was deputy commander-in-chief of the Red Army for most of the war. A case against him was being prepared by BERIA in the summer of 1945 and Stalin denounced him in late 1945 at a large Kremlin gathering for ascribing all war victories to himself. There was no love lost between Zhukov and the security forces (for instance, Beria had not informed Zhukov that Hitler's body had been found and that autopsies were being carried out to establish identity and cause of death). In April 1946, after a clash with Viktor ABAKUMOV, head of Smersh, who had come to Berlin to arrest Soviet officers, Zhukov was summoned to Moscow. At a meeting of the Stavka

he was accused by Stalin, Beria and KAGANOVICH of conspiratorial tendencies. Apparently Stalin had planned to arrest Zhukov but, sensing the strong solidarity of the military, he desisted and demoted him to commander of the Odessa military district and removed him from the Central Committee of the Party. Zhukov spent the years commanding military districts well away from the capital until Stalin's death, after which he again became deputy USSR Minister of Defence, 1953. He was part of the conspiracy against Beria and was involved in his arrest. Zhukov was most valuable to KHRUSHCHEV during the struggle for power in June–July 1957. He ensured that Khrushchev's supporters in the Central Committee got to town to take part in the crucial Central Committee meeting which saved Khrushchev. In the Politburo discussions (Zhukov was a candidate member of the Politburo), he caused quite a stir by stating that the army was loyal to him and would not move unless he (Zhukov) gave the order. Khrushchev rewarded Zhukov by making him USSR Minister of Defence. Zhukov, unwittingly, had sown the seeds of his own demise and while he was away in Albania in October 1957 the decision was taken to remove him as Minister of Defence and from the Politburo. Things which had irked Khrushchev included the revelations that Zhukov had introduced military reforms without consulting the Party and that he treated political officers in the military with contempt. Khrushchev labelled Zhukov a 'Bonapartist' (a soldier with political ambitions). His memoirs, published in 1974, disappointed many. They praised Stalin as supreme commander and the Stalinist style of leadership. Zhukov received many Soviet and foreign decorations.

Zinoviev, Grigory Evseevich (né Radomyslsky) (1883–1936), in TROTSKY's memorable phrase, Zinoviev was either in seventh heaven or in the depths of despair. A volatile politician, a passionate orator, he proved no match for the master game player, STALIN. His Jewish family owned a dairy farm. He joined the RSDRP in 1901 and moved abroad, meeting LENIN and PLEKHANOV in 1903, and after the Party split he sided with Lenin, remaining close to him in exile until 1917. He was in St Petersburg during the 1905 revolution and was elected to the Central Committee of the RSDRP in 1907. He became editor of Lenin's publications in exile and passed the war in Switzerland, returning with him and others to Petrograd in April 1917. He went into hiding with Lenin in Finland after the July Days but, together with KAMENEV, he opposed the Bolshevik armed uprising in October. They published an article to this effect in *Novaya Zhizn*, and this threatened to derail the uprising. Fortunately for the Bolsheviks, KERENSKY laughed it off by saying that had the Bolsheviks been planning an insurrection they would hardly announce it beforehand in the press. After the October Revolution Zinoviev favoured the formation of a broad socialist coalition government and opposed Lenin's insistence on a Bolshevik government. He and four others resigned from the Central Committee in protest but were quickly readmitted. He was elected chair of the executive committee of the Communist International (Comintern) at its first congress in 1919. During the Kronstadt uprising Trotsky found him in a panic and he was saved by Trotsky and TUKHACHEVSKY. Stalin drew him and Kamenev into a tactical alliance against Trotsky after Lenin's death but after Trotsky's defeat Stalin turned on his erstwhile allies. In 1926 Zinoviev lost his place on the Politburo and his Comintern post, and was expelled from the Party in November 1927 after going on to the streets, with Trotsky and others, to protest vainly against Stalin's policies. He was readmitted to the Party in 1928 after recanting his views and praising Stalin to

the skies. He was expelled again in 1932. He (and Kamenev) were tried in secret in January 1935 and he was sentenced to ten years' imprisonment. In April 1936 he was the main accused in the first show trial. He cut a pathetic figure but abject submission did not save him from the executioner's bullet. As an Old Bolshevik (those who had joined the Party before 1917) he was a marked man as far as Stalin was concerned. He was rehabilitated under GORBACHEV.

Zoshchenko, Mikhail Mikhailovich (1895–1958), an immensely popular writer during the 1920s and 1930s, his humorous depiction of the trials and tribulations of the little man confronted with the new communist reality and desperately trying to adjust struck a very responsive chord. He was born in St Petersburg into a Ukrainian family and studied law at St Petersburg University. He served in the First World War, suffered poison gas and retired from the army in 1917. He served in the Red Army, 1918–20. He belonged to the literary group the Serapion Brothers and became well known in 1922 with *Rasskazy Nazara Ilicha (Tales of Nazar Ilich)*. He wrote in a more socialist realist vein during the 1930s but the criticism became vicious in 1946 when AKHMATOVA and he were attacked by Andrei ZHDANOV during the campaign against modernism. They were expelled from the USSR Writers' Union. Zoshchenko was readmitted after STALIN's death in 1953 and his works were published again in 1956.

Zyuganov, Gennady Andreevich (*b.* 1944), one of the leading figures of the Russian Communist Party under GORBACHEV who emerged as its leader under YELTSIN. He was born into a Russian family in Orlov oblast and graduated from the Orlov State Pedagogical Institute and the Academy of Social Sciences of the Party Central Committee. He successfully presented his candidate dissertation in philosophy (Marxism–Leninism) (PhD). He began his career in 1961 as a teacher in a village secondary school in Orlov oblast and in 1967 moved into trade union, Komsomol and Party work. Among his posts were second secretary, Orlov Party gorkom, and head of the department of agitation and propaganda, Orlov Party obkom, until 1983. Then he moved into the department of propaganda, Central Committee apparatus in Moscow, 1983 until 1989, when he was made deputy head of the ideology department, Central Committee, until 1990. When the Communist Party of the Russian Federation was established in July 1990 he was elected a secretary of its Central Committee and its Politburo. Gorbachev was very disappointed with the leadership of the Russian Communist Party, seeing them as the enemies of perestroika. Zyuganov became a Russian nationalist after 1991 and he was elected chair of the Co-ordinating Council of the National Patriotic Forces of Russia, 1992, and also co-speaker of the Duma of the Russian National Assembly, as well as co-chair of the political council of the Front of National Salvation of Russia. Later he emerged as the leader of the Russian Communist Party and stood for President, June 1996, coming second to Yeltsin in the second round, on 3 July.

Glossary

Agitprop Department of agitation and propaganda, CC Secretariat. Originally written and oral propaganda, the task of the official was to mobilise the population to achieve the economic goals set by the state by raising Party awareness. It was believed the more dedicated a communist was, the better he or she worked.

All-Union Ministries could be either all-Union, that is, responsible for the whole of the country, or republican, responsible for their own republic, but subordinate to Moscow. Hence there was a USSR Ministry of Agriculture and sixteen republican Ministries of Agriculture.

Alma Ata Meeting See **CIS**

Anti-Party Group Those in the Presidium (Politburo) in 1957, almost all representing government ministries, who opposed the transfer of responsibility for the implementation of economic plans from the government to the Party. Khrushchev was almost defeated but after victory he removed all his opponents from the Presidium. None of his defeated opponents ever made a political comeback. The Party dominated economic decision making until 1988 when Gorbachev, at the XIXth Party Conference, removed the Party from economic management.

ASSR Autonomous Soviet Socialist Republic. A territory (e.g. Komi ASSR) within a Soviet republic inhabited by non-Russians, indeed non-Slavs (i.e. not Russians, Belorussians or Ukrainians), which had its own government. The Communist Party organisation in an ASSR was equivalent to an obkom. In reality an ASSR was totally subordinate to the capital of the republic in which it was situated. Hence autonomous did not mean independent. Most ASSRs were in the Russian Federation.

August Coup The attempted coup of 19–21 August 1991. An eight-man Emergency Committee, lead by Kryuchkov (KGB), Pugo (MVD), Lukyanov and Yanaev, declared Gorbachev deposed as Soviet President on 19 August (due to ill health), placed him under arrest at Foros, his dacha in Crimea, declared a state of emergency and put troops on the streets. They demanded that all administrative organs throughout the country implement their instructions. The timing of the attempted coup was linked to the proposed signing of an agreement to establish a Union of Sovereign States which would have devolved much of the centre's powers to the republics, thus establishing a genuine federal state. The putsch collapsed and achieved the opposite of what the plotters had intended. Reform was given a powerful boost, the Communist Party was fatally weakened and Russia dominated the political scene with an agenda which favoured an independent Russian state.

Belovezh Agreement See **Minsk Agreement** and the **CIS**

Black Earth Zone or Chernozem One of the most fertile soils in the world, it runs as a triangle with its apex in west Siberia and then crossing southern Russia and northern Ukraine.

Bolsheviks When the Russian Social Democratic Labour Party (RSDRP) split in 1903, those in the majority, known as Bolsheviks. In October 1917 the Bolsheviks or Communist Party took power.

Cadres Personnel. Party cadres were Party officials. Stalin coined the expression, 'Cadres decide everything!'

Candidate Dissertation Soviet postgraduates prepared a dissertation for the candidate degree (*kandidat nauk*). This is slightly lower than a British or US PhD but in this book has been ranked similar. A doctoral dissertation is above a British or US doctor's degree and is translated as a DSc, DLitt or LLD in this book. Thus Soviet universities followed the German academic practice with the doctoral dissertation being equivalent to the *Habilitationsshrift*.

Candidate Member a) Before a person could become a full member of the Communist Party he or she had to serve a probationary period during which he or she was referred to as a candidate member; b) candidate members of the Party Central Committee and Politburo could attend, speak but not vote.

Cheka The All-Russian Extraordinary Commission for Combating Counter-revolution and Sabotage. Founded in 1917 it was the first Bolshevik secret police force whose task was to ensure the Bolsheviks stayed in power. It changed its name several times and under Gorbachev was known as the KGB.

Central Committee Central Committee of the Communist Party; this body acted in the name of the Party Congress when the latter was not in session. It contained all the most important Party officials, governmental ministers, leading army and navy personnel, top ambassadors, academics, and so on. It was elected at each Party Congress. The first meeting after election was known as a plenum or full meeting of candidate and full members. According to the Party statutes there were to be at least two plenums per year. The first meeting was the 1st plenum, the next, the 2nd plenum, until the next Party Congress, then the first meeting after that became again the 1st plenum, and so on.

CIS Commonwealth of Independent States. Established on 8 December 1991 by Russia, Ukraine and Belorussia (now known as Belarus) in Belovezh Forest, near Minsk, Belorussia. They reasoned they had the right to dissolve the Soviet Union because they had been the original signatories setting up the USSR in 1922. At a meeting in Alma Ata (now known as Almaty), Kazakhstan, on 21 December, other states were admitted: Armenia, Azerbaijan, Kazakhstan, Kyrgyzstan, Moldova, Tajikistan, Turkmenistan and Uzbekistan. Eventually Georgia also joined and this left Estonia, Latvia and Lithuania outside. Gorbachev fought hard to keep the former Soviet Union together and felt betrayed by Yeltsin whose goal was to destroy the Union.

Classes There were two classes in the Soviet Union: the working class and the collective farm peasantry (*kolkhozniks*), and a stratum, the intelligentsia.

CMEA See **Comecon**

Collectivisation Began in 1917 but had made little progress by 1929 when peasants (there were about 25 million peasant households) were not given a choice about joining a kolkhoz or collective farm. On land not previously farmed, sovkhozes or state farms were set up. Collectivisation was completed in 1937. In practice, several villages were lumped together and declared a kolkhoz. Peasant opposition was dealt with brutally, by using military force, deportation or expulsion. Initially almost everything was collectivised but in March 1930 the private plot around a peasant's cottage was legalised. As of May 1932, he could legally sell any surplus (after paying taxes) in an urban kolkhoz market where demand and supply determined prices. The more efficient farmers, kulaks, were not permitted to join the kolkhozes as they were viewed as class enemies. Hence Stalin deliberately eliminated the most successful farmers from agriculture. The Soviet state never developed socialist agriculture to the point that the demand of the population for food was met. By the 1980s about one-third of marketed produce came from the private plots, occupying less than 5 per cent of arable land. Gorbachev devoted considerable attention to agricultural production in Stavropol krai and then from 1978 he became responsible for Soviet agriculture. He failed in his mission to satisfy Soviet consumers.

Comecon Council for Mutual Economic Assistance. Set up in 1949 by Stalin it came alive after his death to assume the function of a socialist Common Market. Its membership eventually included Cuba, Mongolia and Vietnam but by the mid-1980s it was becoming a liability for the Soviet Union. Yugoslavia became an associate member in 1964. It was dissolved in June 1991.

Communist A member of the Communist Party. By 1990 there were about 18 million members.

Communist Party of Russia, also Communist Party of the Russian Federation Russia was never permitted to have its own communist party since Lenin believed this would allow Russians to dominate the young Soviet state too easily. There was a Russian Bureau under Khrushchev but it was dissolved in 1965. The RCP was founded in 1990 and elected Ivan Polozkov its first secretary, much to the disappointment of Gorbachev who regarded the Russian party as a bastion of conservatism.

Conference Differed from a Party Congress in that not all Party organisations were represented (an exception was the XIXth Party Conference, 1988). In the early years after the revolution logistics made it difficult to convene a Congress rapidly to deal with urgent business. A Conference did not have the right to elect members to the Central Committee and the Politburo.

Congress Most important meeting of the Party, soviet, trade union or other organisation. At a Congress, which had to meet once during a five-year period, the Communist Party reviewed its record over the period since the previous Congress and laid down goals for the future. A new Central Committee was elected and it, in turn, elected a new Politburo and Secretariat. The last Party Congress before it was banned by Yeltsin was the XXVIIIth in July 1990.

CPSU Communist Party of the Soviet Union. The party was founded in 1898 as the Russian Social Democratic Labour Party (RSDRP; until 1917 all social democratic parties were Marxist) but split, at its IInd Congress, 1903, into Bolshevik (majoritarians) and Menshevik (minoritarians) factions. It assumed the name of Russian Communist Party (Bolsheviks) in 1918, and adopted the name CPSU in 1952. Throughout this book this party is referred to as the Communist Party. In 1987 there were about 19 million Party members but on 1 July 1991, this had dropped to 15 million.

CPSU Programme The agenda of the Communist Party. The 1961 Party Programme, envisaging the foothills of communism being reached in 1980, was still valid when

Gorbachev became General Secretary. It was urgently in need of revision but this became a battleground between radicals and conservatives.

Democratic Platform A radical group within the Communist Party whose pro-gramme, published in *Pravda* in March 1990, demanded, among other things, the renunciation of a single state ideology and that the Party should reject communism as its goal. Its leading members were expelled while others resigned and some founded other parties, such as the Republican Party of the Russian Federation.

DemRossiya The Democratic Russia movement came into being in 1990 in order to support democratically minded candidates during the elections to the RSFSR Con-gress of People's Deputies, especially those associated with Yeltsin. It was an um-brella organisation which contained a wide range of parties and movements of views and failed to develop into a viable political party. One of the issues on which it could not agree in 1991 was whether Russia would be better off if the Soviet Union were destroyed. Their views were close to those of the Inter-Regional Group and Me-morial. They became the largest opposition group to the Communists in 1990, hav-ing, before their splits, over 4,000 members. Among leading members were Boris Yeltsin, Yury Afanasev, Anatoly Sobchak, Gavriil Popov, Nikolai Travkin and Sergei Stankevich. Yeltsin's victory in the presidential election of June 1991 owed much to the support of this movement. By 1996, it had shrunk to a small group.

District See **Raion**

Duma or State Duma The lower house of the Federal Assembly, the Russian parlia-ment, according to the December 1993 Russian Constitution. The Russian parlia-ment, 1905–17, was also called the Duma.

Federal Assembly The Russian parliament established by the new 1993 Russian Con-stitution. Consists of two houses, the Duma, the lower house, and the Council of the Federation, the upper house.

Five Year Plan The first Five Year Plan spanned the period October 1928–December 1932, the second, 1933–7, and so on. Plans were drafted by Gosplan and had the force of law. Non-fulfilment of the plan was, therefore, a criminal offence. Extremely detailed norms were laid down and these reached ludicrous proportions, for example, the amount of fat in milk in Estonia was laid down by Moscow!

G7 Group of advanced industrial states, consisting of the United States, Japan, Great Britain, France, Italy, Germany and Canada. The Soviet Union wished to join and transform it into G8. Gorbachev attended the G7 meeting in London during the summer of 1991.

GDR German Democratic Republic. In 1945 the eastern part of Germany was occu-pied by the Red Army and was called the Soviet Occupied Zone of Germany. In 1949 this territory was renamed the GDR in response to the establishment of the Federal Republic of Germany. It was also known as East Germany and its capital was East Berlin. The ruling communist party was called the Socialist Unity Party of Germany (SED) and there were other parties, such as the Christian Democratic Union of Germany, which were subordinate to the SED. The GDR merged with the Federal Republic in October 1990.

Glasnost A key element of Gorbachev's reforms which involved openness in eco-nomic and political decision making and the open discussion of all questions and freedom of information. This latter aspect led to vigorous debate about the Soviet past, including the crimes of the Stalin era. Glasnost was a key theme at the XIXth Party Conference and was confirmed in the conference resolutions.

Gorkom City Party committee, headed by a first secretary.

Gosagroprom State Agro-Industrial Committee (1985–9).

Gosplan State Planning Committee of the USSR Council of Ministers responsible for drafting economic plans and checking on their implementation. Founded in 1921, it continued to 1991. It produced Five Year Plans, annual plans, quarterly plans, and so on. Each Soviet republic had its own Gosplan whose task was to provide inputs for USSR Gosplan in order to draft the next plan and check on plan implementation. After 1985 Gosplan lost influence as the Soviet economy gradually fragmented. In 1990, when Gorbachev replaced the USSR Council of Ministers with a Cabinet of Ministers, Gosplan became the Ministry for Economics and Forecasting.

Gosstroi State Committee for Construction.

Gosteleradio State television and radio: the Soviet equivalent of the BBC before it lost its broadcasting monopoly.

Ideologists Those Party officials and academics who were concerned with propagating and developing Marxism–Leninism. Every university student was required to pass an examination in Marxism–Leninism before graduating. Gorbachev complained with justification that the great majority of these Communists merely justified the present and did not attempt to develop creatively the ideology. However, under Brezhnev the concept of developed, mature or ripe socialism was coined, and Gorbachev began his time in office with developing socialism. The negative western term for these officials is ideologues.

IMF The International Monetary Fund, based in Washington, which is concerned with macroeconomic issues. It was founded in 1945 as a result of the Bretton Woods agreement.

INF Intermediate-range nuclear forces.

INF Agreement Agreement signed on 8 December 1987 by the United States and the Soviet Union to eliminate a whole category of nuclear weapons, land-based nuclear intermediate-range weapons with a range between 500 and 5,500 kilometres.

Inter-Regional Group Deputies in the USSR Congress of People's Deputies and the USSR Supreme Soviet who formed the group in the summer of 1989 and who defended human rights, the introduction of private property, a multi-party system and a democratic rule of law state. Its members included Boris Yeltsin, Andrei Sakharov, Yury Afanasev and Gavriil Popov.

KGB Committee of State Security. Established as the Cheka in 1917 by Lenin to ensure that the Bolsheviks stayed in power; under Stalin its task became to keep him in power. There was a USSR KGB and each Soviet republic had its own KGB, subordinate to the KGB whose headquarters were in the Lubyanka, Moscow. The KGB was responsible for domestic and foreign intelligence. In the military, the GRU was responsible for intelligence gathering but the KGB checked on the political loyalty of the armed forces.

Kolkhoz Literally, collective economy; members farmed the land as a co-operative but, in reality, had little say in what was produced as this was laid down in the annual state plan. Before 1966 there was no guaranteed wage; if the farm made a profit wages were paid, if not, no wages were paid. Most peasants preferred to concentrate on their private plots.

Kolkhoznik A member of a kolkhoz.

Komsomol Lenin Young Communist League. For those between fourteen and twenty-eight years, except for the organisation's leadership. Most young people belonged to it and almost everyone who joined the Communist Party had previously belonged to the Komsomol. There was a USSR Komsomol and one in each Soviet republic. Like the Communist Party its leadership consisted of full-time officials. In the early 1980s the Komsomol had over 40 million members.

Kosygin Reforms Launched by Aleksei Kosygin, chairman of the USSR Council of Ministers, 1964–80, to give enterprise more control over what they produced and marketed. One problem which arose was what to do with surplus labour in an enterprise as it was not possible just to sack them. Kosygin was a technocrat and his reforms promised much but were interrupted by the invasion of Czechoslovakia in August 1968. Afterwards reform was a term which fell out of use as centralisation was reimposed. Kosygin lacked the willpower to fight for power and from being seen as the Soviet leader from 1964 to 1968 was gradually pushed aside by Brezhnev who was clearly *primus inter pares* by the early 1970s. The reining in of Kosygin's reforms was one of the reasons for the terminal decline of the Soviet economy.

Krai Administrative sub-division of a Soviet republic containing within it a territory inhabited by another (non-Slav) nationality, called an autonomous oblast. Can also be translated as territory.

Kraikom Krai Party committee, headed by a first secretary.

Kulak Peasants were divided into poor, middle and rich by Lenin and the Bolsheviks. The poor peasant did not have enough land to live off, the middle peasant did and the rich produced a surplus for the market. In west European terms the kulak would have been a moderately well-off farmer.

Lysenkoism Trofim Denisovich Lysenko was an agro-biologist who made a glittering career under Stalin undermining the existing scientific thinking in agricultural science and genetics. He very skilfully propagated the 'theory' of the inheritance of acquired characteristics which promised higher yields. He was a vigorous opponent of genetics, arguing that it was bourgeois pseudo-science. He reached the pinnacle of his influence in 1948. Khrushchev would not listen to those scientists who condemned him as a charlatan and it was only in 1966, under Brezhnev, that genetics was rehabilitated fully and Lysenko dispatched to the rubbish bin of science. His pseudo-science cost Soviet agriculture dearly.

Memorial Society Formed to remember the victims of Stalin's oppression. Politically it became active in early 1989 and concentrated on making public the Russian and Soviet past and laying bare the crimes of the Stalin period. It later became part of DemRossiya.

Minsk Agreement This agreement between Russia (Boris Yeltsin), Belorussia (Stanislav Shushkevich) and Ukraine (Leonid Kravchuk) was the death blow to the further existence of the Soviet Union under Gorbachev. The agreement states that the Soviet Union as a subject in international law has ceased to exist.

MVD Ministry of Internal Affairs responsible for law and order. There was a USSR MVD and each Soviet republic had its own MVD, subordinate to Moscow.

NATO North Atlantic Treaty Organisation, founded in 1949.

NEP New Economic Policy. Introduced in 1921 by Lenin as a compromise after War Communism (1918–21) had failed and the country was facing economic ruin and the fear that the peasants would not deliver food to the cities. It was not well received by Communists who saw it as a defeat and a retreat from socialism. Under NEP the commanding heights of the economy (energy, communications, heavy industry, and so on) stayed in state hands while light industry and agriculture reverted to private ownership. Trade was again legal. Soviet Russia recovered and by the mid-1920s the country was again achieving the Gross Domestic Product of 1913. For the peasant it was the golden era of Soviet rule. NEP was brought to an end by the victory of Stalin in the struggle to succeed Lenin when he launched the first Five Year Plan (October 1928–32). There was great interest during the Gorbachev era in NEP and it was seen as an option for the Soviet Union as it had been a mixed market economy under socialism. Stalin's Five Year Plan eliminated the market. In reality NEP was not an option for Gorbachev as Stalin had destroyed private farming and few farm workers in the 1980s wanted to farm on their own. Also during NEP there was a developed system of producers' and consumers' co-operatives, and a vibrant tradition of cottage industries, but all this was destroyed deliberately by Stalin who forced peasants to join collective (kolkhoz) and state (sovkhoz) farms, mainly to ensure that the state could feed workers during the industrialisation drive. Detailed plans for farms were laid down by Gosplan and it was the responsibility of the Party secretary to ensure implementation.

Nomenklatura Nomenclatura or nomenclature: consisted of a list of positions which the Party regarded as important and required Party assent to be filled and a list of persons capable of filling these positions. There were Party nomenklatura and the state nomenklatura. Each Party body, from the obkom upwards, had a list of nomenklatura appointments it could fill. The longer a first Party secretary remained in an oblast, for example, the greater the number of posts he could influence. In this way nepotism and corruption crept into the Party apparatus. For example, important Soviet ambassadors – to Washington, Bonn, and so on – were on the nomenklatura list of the Politburo. Nomenklatura officials were full time.

Non-Black Earth Zone or Non-Chernozem Zone Not very fertile but the Russian heartland, it extends from Moscow to southern Russia where the Black Earth Zone begins and eastwards to Siberia. Under Brezhnev considerable attention and investment was devoted to this region since if the depopulation continued there was a risk that vast tracks of the Russian heartland would return to wilderness.

Novo-Ogarevo Gorbachev's dacha near Moscow at which republican leaders (including Yeltsin) debated the formation of a genuinely federal state to succeed the Soviet Union with President Gorbachev during the spring and summer of 1991. The outcome was the draft Union of Sovereign States. These talks were also referred to as the 9 + 1, nine republican leaders and Gorbachev. The Baltic republics never participated in these deliberations, having demanded their independence.

Obkom Oblast Party committee, headed by a first secretary.

Oblast Administrative sub-division of a Soviet republic; oblasts were sub-divided into raions, as were cities. Can also be translated as territory, province.

Organ Agency.

Orgotdel Organisational bureau, CC Secretariat. Its tasks included Party organisation, cadres, and so on.

Orgpartotdel Department of Party organs, CC Secretariat, responsible for cadres, among other things.

Perestroika Restructuring, renaissance, reformation, the word goes back to the eighteenth century and was also used by Stalin often in the sense of changing Party structures. Under Gorbachev the word came to mean an all-embracing modernisation of the Party and state. It was to touch and transform all aspects of life, from the cradle to the grave. In 1985 the term *uskorenie* (acceleration) was used but in mid-1986 perestroika became the in word.

Politburo Political Bureau of the CC. It was the key decision-making body of the Communist Party; set up formally at the VIIIth Party Congress, 1919. It was called the Presidium between 1952 and 1966. In 1987 there were fourteen full and six candidate members, with Russians predominating.

Presidium Inner council or cabinet, hence supreme body. The Politburo of the Communist Party was known as the Presidium, 1952–66. The USSR Supreme Soviet Presidium contained all the worthies in the state and Party. The chairman of the Presidium of the USSR Supreme Soviet was the head of state, hence he was sometimes referred to as President. The term President officially entered the Soviet Constitution in 1989 when Gorbachev was elected Soviet President. The USSR Council of Ministers (Soviet government) also had a Presidium, consisting of key ministers – hence it was similar to a cabinet. At CC plenums and other meetings, important persons would sit on a podium facing the delegates; this was also known as a presidium.

Procurator General The top law official in the Soviet Union, he headed the USSR Procuracy. Each Soviet republic had its own procuracy, as did each raion, oblast and krai.

Prosecutor General See **Procurator General**

Raikom Raion Party committee, headed by a first secretary.

Raion Administrative sub-division of an oblast, krai and city. Can be translated as district.

RCP Russian Communist Party, founded 1990, dissolved 1991. Between 1918 and 1925 the Communist Party was known as the Russian Communist Party (Bolsheviks), becoming the CPSU in 1952. The Russian Federation was the only Soviet republic which did not have its own communist party: in Ukraine there was the Communist Party of Ukraine, in Estonia, the Communist Party of Estonia, and so on. All these parties were subordinate to the CPSU in Moscow. Despite the form of organisation it was a strictly centralised party. One of Gorbachev's proposals, in the late 1980s, was that the republican communist parties should become autonomous parties, running their own affairs but still under the umbrella of the CPSU. Hence he was proposing a federal Communist Party. The RCP was a disappointment to Gorbachev since it was dominated by conservatives, reluctant to implement perestroika.

Referendum On 17 March 1991 Gorbachev launched a referendum in order to gauge support for a successor state to the Soviet Union, the Union of Sovereign States. There was a majority in favour of keeping the Union but other republics added questions to the Union referendum, for example, Yeltsin asked Russian voters if they were in favour of a directly elected Russian President; they were. He was elected President of Russia in June 1991. This was one of the unforeseen consequences of the referendum.

Rootless Cosmopolitanism A term which became synonymous with anti-Semitism in the late 1940s in connection with the turn towards Russian nationalism and xenophobia.

RSDRP The Russian Social Democratic Labour (or Workers') Party was founded in Minsk in 1898 but it split in 1903 into Bolsheviks and Mensheviks. It was modelled on the German SPD and until 1917 all social democratic parties were Marxist.

RSFSR Russian Soviet Federated Socialist Republic or the Russian Federation or, simply, Russia. It was the largest of the fifteen Soviet republics and its capital was also Moscow.

RSFSR Congress of People's Deputies First convened in March 1990 with Yeltsin as speaker. It was a super-parliament and it elected from among its members an RSFSR Supreme Soviet with a rotating membership which exchanged some members at each new Congress. Russia was the only Soviet republic with a Congress as all the others declined to elect one and proceeded directly to the election of a Supreme Soviet which then enjoyed popular legitimacy. It was dissolved by a presidential decree in September 1991.

Rukh The Ukrainian Popular Front.

SALT Strategic Arms Limitation Talks. Discussions on the limitation of nuclear weapons which got under way in 1969 between the USA and the USSR. In 1972 the SALT I treaty was signed and in 1979 the SALT II treaty emerged. Due to the Soviet invasion of Afghanistan the Americans did not ratify SALT II.

Science The Russian word *nauka* is the same as the German *Wissenschaft* and is much wider than the English term *science*. All intellectual activity can be called *nauka* in Russian and the person involved a scientist.

SDI Strategic Defence Initiative. Conceived in 1983 by President Reagan as a space system to prevent incoming nuclear missiles penetrating the United States. It was more psychological than military but it was a useful bargaining chip for the Americans since the Soviets could never write if off, even though their top scientists did not give it much credence.

Secret Police They went under various names during the Soviet period. They began as the Cheka in 1917, then became OGPU in 1922, later GPU, then NKVD (People's Commissariat for Internal Affairs), then, in 1941, the NKGB (People's Commissariat for State Security), then in 1954 they were renamed the KGB (Committee of State Security); this was formally dissolved in 1991 but many of its officers moved into Russian security.

Secretariat The administrative centre of the Communist Party. It was set up by the

VIIIth Party Congress, 1919, and Stalin was elected the first General Secretary but at that time the post was not regarded as conferring much power on the incumbent. Its key officials were called CC secretaries and the leading one General Secretary. Between 1953 and 1966 the top man was called the First Secretary. The Secretariat had various departments, each headed by an official, and the handful of CC secretaries each supervised a group of departments. After 1957 the Secretariat assumed responsibility for the economy and a CC secretary was senior to a USSR Minister. It was responsible for ensuring that CC decisions were implemented. In 1987 there were eleven secretaries, including Gorbachev. When Gorbachev became General Secretary in 1985, Ligachev was elected to chair the secretaries' meetings and he became known unofficially as second secretary.

SED Socialist Unity Party of Germany. The ruling communist party in the GDR, it was founded in April 1946 and dissolved in 1990. Under Gorbachev, its General Secretary was Erich Honecker, until 1989, then Egon Krenz.

Shock Worker Sometimes called a Stakhanovite. A worker who leads by example and sets the norms for his fellow-workers.

Short Course The official Stalinist version of Bolshevik history, published in 1938 as *The History of the Communist Party (Bolsheviks) Short Course*. It continued to come out in new editions, until 1983.

Soviet a) Council; b) citizen of the USSR; c) name of the country. Soviets first emerged during the 1905 revolution and then blossomed after the February Revolution of 1917. It was all the rage, there were soviets of workers' deputies, soviets of peasants' deputies, soviets of soldiers' deputies, soviets of long-distance train travellers, and so on. The most influential was the Petrograd Soviet of Workers' and Soldiers' Deputies which spawned the October Revolution. The October Revolution was called a Soviet revolution, the government was called the Soviet of People's Commissars, and so on. The term became synonymous with worker power. Lenin changed his mind about the future role of the soviets and in his April (1917) Theses he stated that Russia would be a republic of soviets. Lenin and the Bolsheviks handed power to the IInd Congress of Soviets in October 1917, but power soon slipped way from them as they opposed Lenin's prescriptions for revolution. They had ceded primacy to the government by mid-1918 and it in turn to the Politburo of the Party by 1921. Soviets ran the countryside and towns and performed the function of local government but never had the power to tax independently of the centre or to keep local state taxation. Their finances were determined in Moscow. They had to implement Gosplan directives. Gorbachev attempted to reinvigorate them in 1988 but by then the Party boss ruled the localities. He hoped they would take over from the Party at local level and implement perestroika but they lacked the skill and personnel to do this.

Soviet-German Non-Aggression Pact or Stalin–Hitler Pact Signed by Molotov and Ribbentrop on 23 August 1939 (Stalin and Hitler never met). It envisaged that the Soviet Union and Germany would not attack one another and that if war did ensue elsewhere both states would remain neutral. The key part of the agreement was the secret protocol which the Soviets denied existed until the late 1980s. It divides Europe into zones of influence with the Soviet Union taking eastern Poland, Latvia, Estonia, Finland, Lithuania (as the result of an amendment) and Bessarabia. Germany bagged the rest of Europe. The original agreement turned up in the private papers of von Schulenburg, the German ambassador to Moscow at the time, after his death.

Soviet Republic There were fifteen, of which the Russian Federation was the largest and Estonia, Latvia and Lithuania had been the last to join in 1940. Each republic had its own government, many ministries and its own communist party which was, of course, part of the CPSU. The local communist party had its own Central Committee and a Bureau which played the same role as the central Politburo (Ukraine was the exception and had a Politburo). The communist parties split in many republics into pro-nationalist communist parties and pro-Moscow communist parties. This occurred in all three Baltic republics. The pro-nationalist communist parties then supported the bid for independence. Violent clashes occurred between the various groups, and twelve people lost their lives during the storming of the TV tower in Vilnius, Lithuania, on 12–13 January 1991. The attack was launched by the authorities with the support of the local pro-Moscow Communists. Gorbachev stated that he was unaware of what was being planned. Under glasnost, many informal associations (so called because they were not officially registered) sprang up and these included popular fronts, especially in the Baltic republics.

Sovkhoz Literally state economy. Set up on land not previously cultivated, it was run like a factory with a guaranteed minimum wage, higher than those of the average kolkhoznik. Operatives were classified as workers and enjoyed their social benefits.

Sovnarkhoz Council of the National Economy. Adopted by Khrushchev in 1957 and initially there were 105 which covered the whole country and were responsible for all economic activity on their territory (except military, security and other vital tasks which remained centralised). Khrushchev thought that by devolving decision making to the local level, economic efficiency would result. In fact the sovnarkhozes attempted to become mini-states in their own right. They were abolished in 1965, after Khrushchev's removal as Soviet leader.

Sovnarkom The Council of People's Commissars, the government of the country, from 1917 until 1946, when it was renamed the USSR Council of Ministers. Commissars then became ministers. There was a Union Sovnarkom, and each Soviet republic and autonomous republic also had its own Sovnarkom. The government resigned formally at the end of each legislature period. In reality the Union government ruled. The Soviet Union, according to the 1977 Constitution, was a federal state but Gorbachev admitted that it was, in reality, a unitary state. Federalism was a sham.

Soyuz Union. People's deputies at all levels were members. Established in December 1990 to defend the integrity of the Soviet Union, it argued that a state of emergency was the only way to restore order and ensure the survival of the Soviet Union. Among its leading members were Yury Blokhin, Viktor Alksnis, Evgeny Kogan and Sergei Baburin. Among the membership were representatives of the military-industrial complex, the KGB, the MVD and the Party apparatus. In the USSR Congress of People's Deputies and the USSR Supreme Soviet Soyuz was the largest anti-reform faction but did not command a majority.

Staraya Ploshchad Old Square, the headquarters of the Party CC until August 1991. It is very near Red Square.

START Strategic Arms Reduction Talks. Negotiations on the reduction of strategic weapon systems between the United States and the Soviet Union, then Russia, which resulted in the START I agreement in 1991 and the START II agreement, 1993.

State Procurements Output bought by the state and laid down by the plan in advance. In industry this applied to most of an enterprise's output but in agriculture it could vary. Kolkhozes and sovkhozes had to meet state procurement plans first before they disposed of any of their produce. Naturally they attempted to keep back as much for themselves as possible, sometimes stating that they did not have enough to meet the plan. The person responsible for ensuring that farms met their state obligations was the first Party secretary.

Strategic Nuclear Weapons Those nuclear weapons which can be fired from one continent to another.

Supreme Soviet See also **USSR Supreme Soviet**. Each Soviet republic and autonomous republic had its own Supreme Soviet which was unicameral. All important state legislation was passed by the USSR Supreme Soviet during its occasional and brief meetings.

Tactical Nuclear Weapons Short- and medium-range nuclear weapons for the theatre of war.

Territory See **Krai**

Union of Sovereign States Gorbachev intended it to be the successor state to the USSR but the attempted August coup was timed to prevent its signature. Afterwards it was too late and the dissolution of the USSR and the establishment of the CIS consigned it to the dustbin of history.

USSR Union of Soviet Socialist Republics; also known as the Soviet Union.

USSR Congress of People's Deputies Convened during the early years after the revolution, it was resurrected in March 1989 as the supreme agency of state power. Its 2,250 deputies were elected for five years and there was to be a Congress every year. Of the 2,250 deputies, two-thirds were directly elected, there were to be multi-candidate elections, with open campaigning beforehand. The other 750 deputies were elected indirectly, according to lists proposed by political and social organisations. For instance, the Communist Party received 100 seats. Gorbachev chaired it. It was a super-parliament and from its membership it elected a USSR Supreme Soviet, or standing parliament, with a rotating membership which exchanged some members at the next Congress. According to the amendments of the Soviet Constitution, the Congress could amend the Constitution, if a two-thirds majority approved. The Congress elected Gorbachev President of the Soviet Union. The initial proceedings were carried live on television and this led to many very tired workers because of the Soviet habit of debating until the early hours. The Congress, on 5 September 1991, voluntarily dissolved itself and conceded power to the RSFSR Congress of People's Deputies but there were deputies who were members of both.

USSR Council of Ministers The Soviet government, headed by a chairman or Prime Minister. The USSR Council of Ministers was dissolved in 1990 and replaced by a Cabinet of Ministers, headed by a Prime Minister.

USSR Council of the President or Presidential Council It was established in March 1990 and functioned until December 1990 with all members being nominated by Gorbachev. It was dominated by the power ministries (security, internal affairs, defence) but its precise functions were unclear. It was replaced in early 1991 by the newly constituted USSR Security Council which lasted until the attempted coup.

USSR Soviet (Council) of the Federation Established under Gorbachev as a supra-government for the Soviet Union, consisting of the President, Vice-President, and senior representatives from each of the fifteen Soviet republics. It ceased to exist in August 1991 and should not be confused with the Council of the Federation, the upper house of the Russian parliament, established in December 1993.

USSR State Council The successor to the USSR Soviet of the Federation with many of the same representatives but it only functioned for a short time after the attempted coup of August 1991.

USSR Supreme Soviet Founded in 1936, it was the supreme agency of state power in the Soviet Union, according to the Constitution. It was bicameral, the Soviet of the Union and the Soviet of Nationalities and in 1985 had 1,500 members. It was elected for four years and had to meet twice a year, amounting to about a week altogether. It elected a Presidium (thirty-nine members since 1977) from among its members and the chairman was the head of the Soviet state. Until Podgorny became chairman of the Presidium in 1964, the position had never been politically significant. Brezhnev made himself head of state in May 1977 and Podgorny was sent packing. Andropov and Chernenko also made themselves head of state but Gorbachev, in July 1985, suggested Gromyko for the post and he remained there until 1988 when Gorbachev himself took over. The USSR Supreme Soviet was superseded by the USSR Congress of People's Deputies in March 1989. Confusingly, the Congress then proceeded to elect its own USSR Supreme Soviet (which had a rotating membership) but the latter was subordinate to the former.

VLKSM All-Union Leninist Communist League of Youth or Komsomol.

VTsIK All-Union Central Executive Committee of the soviets. It became the USSR Supreme Soviet in 1936.

VTsSPS All-Union Central Council of Trade Unions, the central trade union body.

Warsaw Pact Organisation The Pact was founded in 1955 as a response to the Paris Treaties of October 1954 which had admitted the Federal Republic of Germany to NATO. The original members were the Soviet Union, Poland, Czechoslovakia, Hungary, the GDR, Bulgaria, Romania and Albania. Albania left in 1961. The Pact also had a Political Consultative Committee which was attended by foreign ministers. The Pact never permitted the East German Volksarmee to set up its own General Staff, for instance. All advanced military technology was manufactured in the Soviet Union and the Soviet Army was the best equipped. The Pact was dissolved on 1 July 1991.

White House The seat of the Russian parliament in Moscow.

XIXth Party Conference A rare event, the first Conference since 1941, and convened by Gorbachev between Party Congresses, and more significant than a CC plenum, to push through radical policies. The Party was withdrawn from economic management and it also lost its right to nominate candidates for state and soviet posts. Glasnost was also promoted through conference resolutions.

XXth Party Congress Convened in February 1956, it is famous for the Secret Speech (it was held behind closed doors) of Khrushchev laying bare Stalin's crimes since 1934. He did not use the expression Stalinism to describe what he was analysing but referred to it as the cult of the personality. The speech ended the claims to infallibility of the Communist Party. It became a focal point of interest under glasnost.

Maps

Map 1 The Russian Empire, 1914
Source: Martin McCauley, *Octobrists to Bolsheviks: Imperial Russia,*
1905–1917, Edward Arnold, London, 1984

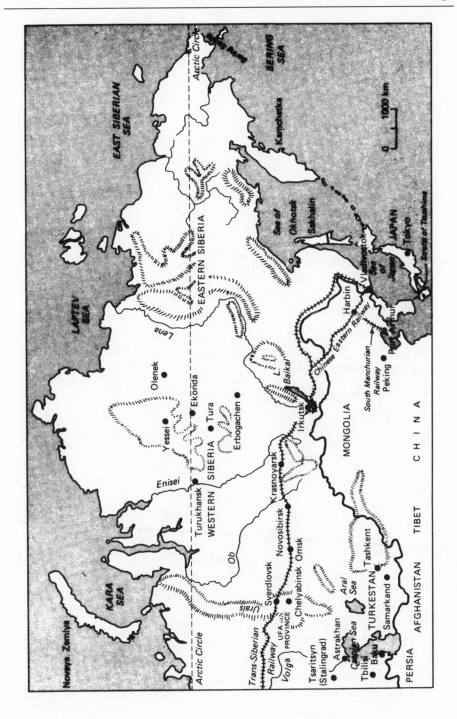

Map 2 Eastern Europe: territorial changes, 1939–47
Source: Martin McCauley (ed.), *Communist Power in Europe 1944–1949*,
Macmillan, London, 1977

Map 3 Europe, 1945–8
Source: Martin McCauley (ed.), *Communist Power in Europe 1944–1949*, Macmillan, London, 1977

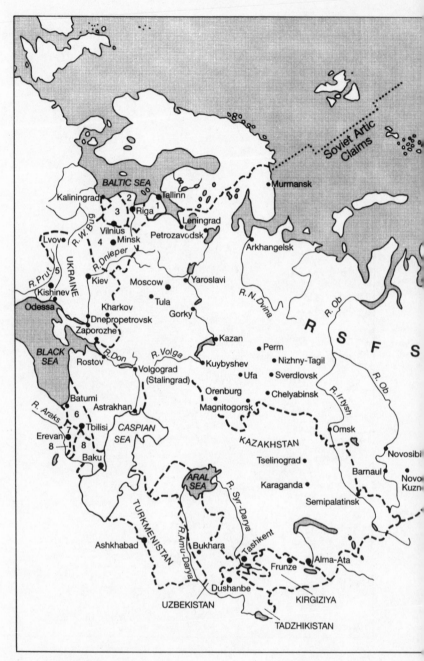

Map 4 The USSR, circa 1960
Source: Martin McCauley, *The Khrushchev Era 1953–1964*, 2nd edn, Longma
London, 1995

ARCTIC OCEAN

R. Kolyma

Magadan

Petropavlovsk

Yakutsk

SEA OF OKHOTSK

R. Lena

Kurile
Islands

Aleksandrovsk

R. Amur

Yuzhno-Sakhalinsk

R. Amur

asnoyarsk

Khabarovsk

R. Ussuri

Chita

Irkutsk

R. Argun

Ulan-Ude

Vladivostok

0   1000 miles

1. ESTONIA   5. MOLDAVIA   ●   Union Republic capitals

2. LATVIA   6. GEORGIA

3. LITHUANIA   7. ARMENIA   ---- Union Republic boundaries

4. BELORUSSIA   8. AZERBAIDZHAN

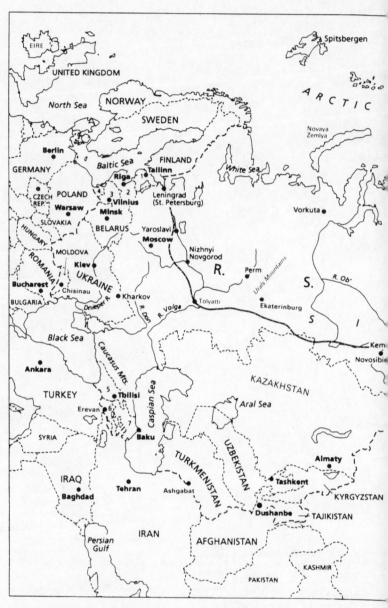

Map 5 The USSR, 1991
Source: John Keep, *The Last of the Empires: A History of the Soviet Union 1945–1991*, Oxford University Press, Oxford, 1995

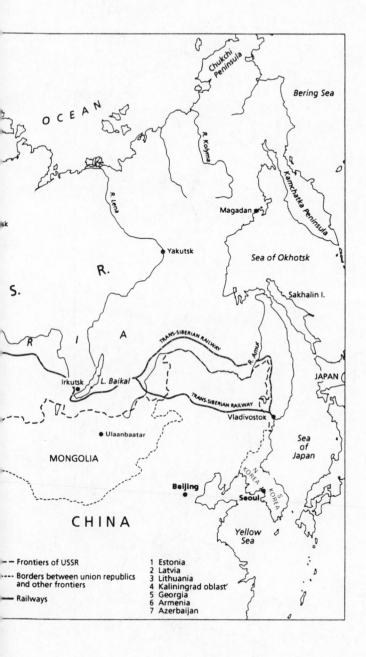

OCEAN

Chukchi Peninsula

Bering Sea

R. Kolyma

Kamchatka Peninsula

R. Lena

Magadan

Yakutsk

Sea of Okhotsk

S.

R.

S.

Sakhalin I.

R   I   A

TRANS-SIBERIAN RAILWAY

R. Amur

JAPAN

Irkutsk   L. Baikal

TRANS-SIBERIAN RAILWAY

Vladivostok

Sea
of
Japan

Ulaanbaatar

MONGOLIA

N. KOREA

S. KOREA

Beijing

Seoul

CHINA

Yellow
Sea

-- Frontiers of USSR

---- Borders between union republics
and other frontiers

— Railways

1 Estonia
2 Latvia
3 Lithuania
4 Kaliningrad oblast'
5 Georgia
6 Armenia
7 Azerbaijan

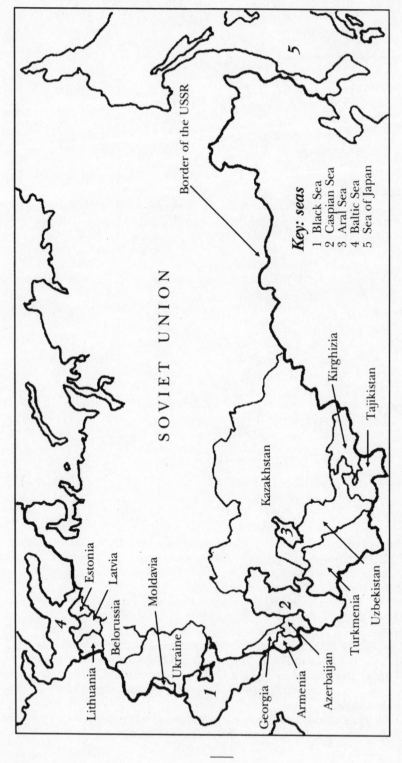

Map 6 The Soviet Republics in the USSR after 1924
Source: New Perspective, vol. I, no. 2, December 1995

Bibliography

IMPORTANT SOURCES

Archie Brown (ed.): *The Soviet Union: A Biographical Dictionary*, Weidenfeld and Nicolson, London, 1991

Jeanne Vronskaya and Vladimir Chuguev: *The Biographical Dictionary of the Former Soviet Union: Prominent People in all Fields from 1917 to the Present*, Bowker-Saur, London, 1992

John Keegan (ed.): *Who's Who in World War II*, Routledge, London, 1995

Kto est Kto v Rossii I v Blizhnem Zarubezhe, Novoe Vremya, Moscow, 1993

Harold Shukman (ed.): *The Blackwell Encyclopedia of the Russian Revolution*, rev. edn, Blackwell, Oxford, 1994

Hans-Joachim Torke (ed.): *Historisches Lexikon der Sowjetunion 1917/22 bis 1991*, C. H. Beck, Munich, 1993

MORE BIOGRAPHIES AND DETAIL

Martin McCauley (ed.): *Directory of Russian MPs: People's Deputies of the Supreme Soviet of Russia-Russian Federation*, Longman, London, 1992

Martin McCauley (ed.): *Longman Biographical Directory of Decision-Makers in Russia and the Successor States*, Longman, London, 1993

OTHER WORKS

Robert Auty and Dmitri Obolensky (eds): *Companion to Russian Studies, vol. 1: An Introduction to Russian History*, Cambridge University Press, Cambridge, 1976; vol. 2: *An Introduction to Russian Language and Literature*, Cambridge University Press, Cambridge, 1977; vol. 3: *An Introduction to Russian Art and Architecture*, Cambridge University Press, Cambridge, 1980

Archie Brown: *The Gorbachev Factor*, Oxford University Press, Oxford, 1996

The Cambridge Encyclopedia of Russia and the Soviet Union, 2nd rev. edn, Cambridge University Press, 1992

John Erickson: *The Road to Stalingrad*, Weidenfeld and Nicolson, London, 1975

John Erickson: *The Road to Berlin*, Weidenfeld and Nicolson, London, 1983

Donald Filtzer: *Soviet Workers and the Collapse of Perestroika: The Soviet Labour Process and Gorbachev's Reforms, 1985–1991*, Cambridge University Press, Cambridge, 1994

Graeme Gill: *The Collapse of a Single-party System: The Disintegration of the CPSU*, Cambridge University Press, Cambridge, 1994

Andrei S. Grachev: *The Inside Story of the Collapse of the Soviet Union*, Westview Press, Boulder, Co., 1995

Max Hayward (ed. Patricia Blake): *Writers in Russia 1917–1978*, Harvill Press, London, 1983

David Holloway: *Stalin and the Bomb: The Soviet Union and Atomic Energy 1939–1956*, Yale University Press, New Haven and London, 1994

Jerry F. Hough and Merle Fainsod: *How the Soviet Union is Governed*, Harvard University Press, Cambridge, Mass., 1979

Robert J. Kaiser: *The Geography of Nationalism in Russia and the USSR*, Princeton University Press, Princeton, NJ, 1994

Janos Kornai: *The Socialist System: The Political Economy of Communism*, Clarendon Press, Oxford, 1992

Gail W. Lapidus: *Women in Soviet Society: Equality, Development and Social Change*, University of California Press, Berkeley and London, 1978

Martin McCauley: *The Soviet Union 1917–1991*, 2nd edn, Longman, London, 1993

Roy Medvedev: *Let History Judge: The Origins and Consequences of Stalinism*, rev. edn, Oxford University Press, Oxford, 1989

Alec Nove: *Economic History of the USSR*, rev. edn, Penguin, London, 1992

Alec Nove: *Glasnost in Action: Cultural Renaissance in Russia*, Unwin Hyman, London, 1989

T. H. Rigby: *Lenin's Government: Sovnarkom 1917–1922*, Cambridge University Press, Cambridge, 1979

Leonard Schapiro: *The Communist Party of the Soviet Union*, Methuen, London, 1966

Robert Service: *Lenin: A Political Life*, vol. 2: *Worlds in Collision*, Macmillan, London, 1991; vol. 3: *The Iron Ring*, Macmillan, London, 1995

Vitaly Shentalinsky: *The KGB's Literary Archive*, The Harvill Press, London, 1995

Alexander Vucunich: *Empire of Knowledge: The Academy of Sciences of the USSR (1917–1970)*, University of California Press, Berkeley, 1984

HOUSTON PUBLIC LIBRARY

R01075 73588

SSCRA S R
920
.047
M122

MCCAULEY, MARTIN
    WHO'S WHO IN RUSSIA
SINCE 1900   PAPER

4-24-98